C. S. LEWIS
LIGHTBEARER IN THE SHADOWLANDS

C. S. LEWIS

LIGHTBEARER
IN THE
SHADOWLANDS

*The Evangelistic Vision
of C. S. Lewis*

Edited by Angus J. L. Menuge

CROSSWAY BOOKS • WHEATON, ILLINOIS
A DIVISION OF GOOD NEWS PUBLISHERS

C. S. Lewis: Lightbearer in the Shadowlands

Published by Crossway Books
        a division of Good News Publishers
        1300 Crescent Street
        Wheaton, Illinois 60187

Cover photo: From the collection of the Marion E. Wade Center, Wheaton College, Wheaton, IL.

Cover design: Cindy Kiple

First printing, 1997

Printed in the United States of America

ISBN 0-89107-961-0

"[Y]ou will do well to pay attention to it, as to a light shining in a dark place, until the day dawns and the morning star rises in your hearts." 2 PETER 1:19

To my wife Vicki, my sons Aidan and Corin,
my parents and brothers, and all who seek enlightenment

CONTENTS

PREFACE

The longevity of C. S. Lewis's influence continues to amaze people. Back in the early 1980s my wife and I were having tea with Mr. Lewis's solicitor, friend, and fellow Inkling, Mr. Owen Barfield. This generous and mild-mannered man who always measured his words and their nuances with utmost precision expressed astonishment at the reading public's continuing fascination with the writings of C. S. Lewis. There was not a hint of jealousy in Barfield's attitude. On the contrary, he obviously admired his long-time friend, but he told us that Lewis viewed his meteoric rise to prominence in a most casual manner. Indeed, Lewis confided in Barfield his certainty that his fame would pass quickly and that no one would read his books five years after his death.

Lewis was not alone in wearing his popularity like a loose garment. J. R. R. Tolkien, another friend and Inkling, rather insensitively chided Lewis for his literary efforts in theology. Perhaps Lewis's original contributions to literary history and criticism would live on, but Lewis was neither ordained nor trained in theology. Therefore, in Tolkien's rigid view of religion, Lewis had no expertise and therefore no business writing on matters of Christian faith and doctrine in any genre.

If Lewis's contemporaries misjudged the enduring quality of his writing, observers and commentators in more recent decades have been equally incapable of predicting his popularity. During the years I served as director of Wheaton College's Marion E. Wade Center, an endless throng of editors, critics, and scholars came through the doors

Preface

predicting the end of Lewis's ability to speak to a new generation. In the same vein I heard more than one pronouncement that with the possible exception of Lewis's poetry, we needed no new books on Lewis because there is nothing more to say.

Some people have predicted a last gasp—a sort of supernova of books on Lewis during the centennial celebration of his birth. But most of these prognosticators said this burst of energy would be inspired by the money-hungry publishers inasmuch as there is nothing new to say about C. S. Lewis.

Long ago I determined to ignore the would-be undertakers who have stepped forward to bury Lewis. The truth is, he is more alive than ever. Not only does his soul live on in the land of "unimpeded obedience" (his phrase for heaven), but his books sell more than ever as we are entering a new era with serious interest in supernaturalism. Furthermore, the nature of Lewis's writing is varied and rich enough that it still attracts the interests of serious scholars. In brief, the field of Lewis studies is alive, well, and thriving.

One piece of evidence to support my thesis is this important book edited by Angus J. L. Menuge. There are first-rate original essays here by well-known Lewis scholars Corbin Scott Carnell, Wayne Martindale, George Musacchio, Jerry Root, and Gene Edward Veith, proving that those who have contributed to Lewis studies for several years still find some worthwhile things to say. What I find particularly refreshing in this book is the work of a generation of younger scholars who are asking questions of Lewis and finding profound answers. Angus J. L. Menuge, one of this breed of new scholars, has made a valuable contribution by pulling together a group of authors who speak with a fresh voice. Lewis studies are richer for the work of Jon Balsbaugh, Patrick T. Ferry, Joel Heck, Douglas T. Hyatt, Reed Jolley, Christopher W. Mitchell, Steven P. Mueller, Francis C. Rossow, Philip Ryken, and Michael Ward. I have profited from these essays, and I eagerly await more work from these gifted people.

Lyle W. Dorsett
Professor of Educational Ministries and Evangelism
Wheaton College and Graduate School

Acknowledgments

The chapter "Old Wine in New Wineskins" originally appeared as "Giving Christian Doctrine a New Translation: Selected Essays from the Novels of C. S. Lewis" in *Concordia Journal*, July 1995, 281-297, and is reproduced here by kind permission of the author and the editors of *Concordia Journal*. Permission from Kathryn Lindskoog to quote from Clifford Morris's "C. S. Lewis Was My Friend" (*His*, Vol. 39, No. 1, 1978) is gratefully acknowledged. Sheldon Vanauken, whom we mourn, graciously permitted quotation from his *Encounter with Light* (Wheaton, IL: Marion E. Wade Center).

We are very grateful for the assistance of Elizabeth Stevens and Curtis Brown Ltd. of London. Acknowledgments include: Extracts from C. S. Lewis's previously unpublished letters—to Corbin Carnell in 1953 and to Stella Aldwinckle on 12th June 1950, copyright © C. S. Lewis Pte. Ltd. 1997, reproduced by permission of Curtis Brown, London. Extract from C. S. Lewis's letter to Dom Bede Griffiths of 27th June 1949, copyright © C. S. Lewis Pte. Ltd. 1997, reproduced by permission of Curtis Brown, London. Extracts from C. S. Lewis's letter to Dom Bede Griffiths of 22nd April 1954, copyright © C. S. Lewis Pte. Ltd. 1997, reproduced by permission of Curtis Brown, London. Extracts from C. S. Lewis's previously unpublished letters to Ruth Pitter, copyright © C. S. Lewis Pte. Ltd. 1997, reproduced by permission of Curtis Brown, London.

Many thanks also to Dr. Judith Priestman of the Bodleian Library,

Acknowledgments

University of Oxford. The Bodleian kindly granted permission to quote from C. S. Lewis's letter to Sister Penelope of May 15, 1941 (shelfmark MS. Eng. lett. c. 220/1, fol. 16). The Bodleian also gave permission to quote Lewis's letters to Ruth Pitter, including his letter of May 25th, 1947 (shelfmark MS. Eng. lett. c. 220/3, fol. 47) and his letter of May 12th, 1953 (shelfmark MS. Eng. lett. c. 220/3, fol. 115).

The Marion E. Wade Center kindly extended permission to use an unpublished letter to Corbin Scott Carnell of April 4, 1953 and an unpublished letter to Dom Bede Griffiths of April 22, 1954. In addition, permission was granted for quotation from Oral History Interviews with Stella Aldwinckle, Harry Blamires, Elizabeth Catherwood, A. G. Dickens, Stephen Olford, George Sayer, and Rachel Trickett.

INTRODUCTION

ANGUS J. L. MENUGE

In the year preceding the centenary celebration of C. S. Lewis's birth, the year of the writing of this book, it might seem that the more new books on Lewis the merrier and that this volume requires no justification. However, as Adam Schwartz laments, "Despite a steady stream of articles and monographs, satisfactory in-depth studies of Lewis's ideas remain rare," which is unfortunate because "thought as complex and rich as his demands careful analysis before its pragmatic implications can be worked out in detail."[1] The current volume represents a sustained effort to redress the balance, consisting, in large part, of focused, in-depth studies of various aspects of Lewis's approach to evangelism. I have no doubt that it too leaves many important questions unanswered, but my hope is that it lays the foundation for several avenues of the more substantial research that Schwartz and other serious scholars are calling for.

For those familiar with Lewis's works, it should hardly need arguing that evangelism is a theme of central significance. Indeed, Lewis himself said that "[m]ost of my books are evangelistic, addressed to *tous exo* [those outside]."[2] Yet the true significance of Lewis's contributions to evangelism has seldom been studied with the seriousness it deserves. In particular, four main areas, which correspond to the four parts of this book, have not been sufficiently pursued.

Introduction

The Motivation:
The Influence and Potential of Lewis's Evangelism

Although it is widely held that the testimony of Lewis's life has had, and will continue to have, a powerful evangelistic effect, the claim has rarely been documented. For example, although it undoubtedly caused a major resurgence of interest in Lewis, just how significant was the Attenborough movie *Shadowlands* in prompting serious Christian reflection, restoration of a dying faith, or even conversion? And while it may sometimes have had salutatory effects, how accurate was the movie's portrayal of Lewis? Were there any potentially harmful effects of viewing the movie in isolation from a serious study of the literature? These and related questions are thoroughly addressed by Dr. Wayne Martindale in the opening chapter, "Shadowlands: Inadvertent Evangelism." The chapter starts the book because it also functions as an accessible entryway to Lewis scholarship for any readers who have themselves become intrigued by Lewis mainly by viewing *Shadowlands*. It is hoped that any such reader will then be prompted to move "further up and further in"[3] the realm of Lewis studies.

It is often said that "countless" people have been brought to Christian faith by reading Lewis, but the evidence typically used to justify the claim is meager and largely anecdotal. In the end, of course, only God knows for certain who has a saving faith, but even from a human standpoint better evidence is available, as Dr. Philip G. Ryken convincingly shows in the second chapter, "Winsome Evangelist: The Influence of C. S. Lewis." Dr. Ryken gathers his data from both Great Britain and the United States and from a wide variety of sources, a significant number of which have not previously been published. We are all in his debt for the thoroughness of his research.

Ryken's excellent study is mainly historical, and convincing as it is, one might wonder if Lewis was too much of a "dinosaur" for his ideas to remain potent in the postmodern era. Yet it seems that both in his works and in his life, Lewis has a timeless appeal and in fact is particularly attractive to "Generation X-ers," who tend to be suspicious of insincerity in authority figures and wary of "signing on."

Lewis does not dodge the hard questions but talks to unbelieving skeptics exactly where they are (having been there himself), and his authenticity is unmistakable. One of Lewis's comments on evangelism is also a beautiful description of his own approach: "What we practice, not (save at rare intervals) what we preach, is usually our great contribution to the conversion of others."[4] These and related issues are skillfully addressed by Reed Jolley in the third chapter, "Apostle to Generation X: C. S. Lewis and the Future of Evangelism."

THE EXPLANATION:
WHY WAS LEWIS SUCH AN EFFECTIVE EVANGELIST?

Having established the potency of Lewis's evangelism, there follows an analysis of the source of this power insofar as it is humanly ascertainable. This task naturally divides into two. First, we need to understand Lewis the man. What sort of influences affected Lewis's own journey of faith? What was it about that journey that equipped him so well to be an evangelist in an age of rampant unbelief? The first question is beautifully and concisely answered by Professor Corbin Scott Carnell in the fourth chapter, "Longing, Reason, and the Moral Law in C. S. Lewis's Search." I address the second question in the following chapter by way of an extended comparison between Lewis and Saint Paul, "God's Chosen Instrument: The Temper of an Apostle."

Second, we need to understand the appeal of Lewis's thought to those outside the fold. Part of this appeal lies in Lewis's deep understanding of the incarnational use of language. Lewis realized that spiritual and emotional truths are only feebly conveyed in the explicitly spiritual and emotional language common in theological and devotional writings. A more effective approach is finding concrete "objective correlates" as vessels of those truths. For example, if a writer wants to convey a character's spiritual condition as good or bad, he should not say the condition is good or bad but rather should describe their behavior or circumstances in a way that projects and conveys that realization. Lewis also knew that the direct approach to evangelism was often less successful than indirect methods. Instead of inviting

Introduction

people to "Come to Jesus," Lewis preferred to subtly reveal ways in which He has already come to us. Instead of directly and explicitly calling for repentance, he portrayed the conversion of others using concrete symbols in a way that invites deep reader identification. This profoundly important matter is admirably pursued by Michael Ward in the sixth chapter, "Escape to Wallaby Wood: Lewis's Depictions of Conversion."

Another facet of Lewis's appeal is his studious avoidance, at least in public, of divisive denominational issues. There seems to be no end to the enthusiasm for Lewis's idea of "mere" Christianity; yet there is also a great deal of misunderstanding. For example, some think the idea amounts to no more than a bland ecumenism, or worse still, as simply yet another denomination to confuse the unchurched. In fact, Lewis was following the great church tradition of formulating by no means insipid credal statements (as in the Nicene creed) that, while they do exclude certain heresies, also succeed in uniting the vast majority of Christians on core doctrines. Lewis did not believe in diluting Christian doctrine for the sake of avoiding all disagreement, but he did wish to find a common ground in order to overcome the endless divisions that are a stumbling block to those outside the faith.

Lewis's motivation was his clear perception of the urgency of evangelism in a world of eternal beings and eternal consequences, and of the need to fight the perennial tendency of the "inner sanctum" to become an "inner ring," which does not merely exclude (as any definite statement inevitably does) but that derives its whole purpose from doing so. Dr. Patrick T. Ferry, a church historian, develops these themes in the seventh chapter, "Mere Christianity Because There Are No Mere Mortals: Reaching Beyond the Inner Ring."

Lewis was also very perceptive about the nature of his audience. He did not succumb to the convenient falsehood that unbelievers are a homogeneous group and that there was therefore only one approach to evangelism appropriate for all of them. A common enough claim is that contemporary society is basically pagan. Lewis, by contrast, lamented that it was not pagan enough, on the grounds that pagans are at least amenable to spiritual reality. In fact, most "modern" people, Lewis felt, were correctly described as "Post-Christians," those whose official views, at least, leave no room for anything supernatural. With the failures of modernism, so-called postmodern society has seen an increase in New Age religions that are basically pagan, though there are still a large number in the "Post-Christian" camp. Part of Lewis's greatness was that his corpus includes works addressed to the concerns of both groups, as is carefully substantiated by Jon Balsbaugh in the eighth chapter, "The Pagan and the Post-Christian: Lewis's Understanding of Diversity Outside the Faith."

THE TECHNIQUE:
MAKING CHRISTIANITY PLAUSIBLE

Lewis's greatest strength was as a "translator"[5] of theology, one who could take abstract doctrines, creeds, and confessions and convey them effectively through the potent medium of concrete imagery. The third part of the book focuses on three questions about this method of translating theology. First, why did he employ it? More specifically, what was it about the character of his audience that made him think a direct presentation of the Gospel, which had been effective in past ages, would no longer serve? To answer these questions adequately we need a careful analysis of the modernist worldview that held Lewis's audience in its enchanting embrace. The task is superbly accomplished by George Musacchio in the ninth chapter, "Exorcising the *Zeitgeist*: Lewis as Evangelist to the Modernists." Musacchio explores such modernist influences as Enlightenment reason, the empirical scientific method, scientism, logical positivism, and life-force philosophy.

Secondly, how did Lewis think his theological translation contributed to evangelism? Although, as we noted, Lewis claimed that most of his works were evangelistic, he retained a humble opinion of his own role in the conversion of others. For one thing, he was perfectly aware that it is ultimately the Holy Spirit, and not man, who creates faith. For another, he did not see his real talent as that of a preacher of the Word. His own role was more like that of John the Baptist, one who prepared the way for the Word to have its effect,

Introduction

making "straight in the wilderness a highway for our God" (Isaiah 40:3) and convicting his audience of sin. This was partly an honest reflection of Lewis on the nature of his own gifts, but partly also a recognition that in recent times this sort of preparation for the Gospel is essential: "It would have been inept to preach forgiveness and a Saviour to those who did not know they were in need of either."[6] These issues are pursued in a meticulous study by Joel Heck in the tenth chapter, "*Praeparatio Evangelica.*"

Thirdly, what methods did Lewis use to translate theology, and to which doctrines did he apply them? These questions are explored systematically by Dr. Francis C. Rossow in the eleventh chapter, "Old Wine in New Wineskins," which originally appeared in *Concordia Journal*. A study more narrowly focused on Lewis's presentation of Christ throughout his writings is thoughtfully pursued by Steven P. Mueller in the twelfth chapter, "Translated Theology: Christology in the Writings of C. S. Lewis."

THE ARGUMENT:
DEFENDING THE FAITH

Aslan, the Narnia Chronicles frequently remind us, is not a tame lion; he could be gentle and playful at times, but he also wore a stern and warlike countenance when necessary. Those who would categorize Lewis as a mild-mannered evangelist sensitive to the feelings of his audience have grasped only part of the reality. There was another Lewis, equally admirable but far more redoubtable. Reflecting on the occasion of his first hearing of C. S. Lewis, James Como found himself asking, "Could it be? Could a man who so unashamedly expressed his Christian beliefs not be laughed at as a fool, scorned as a zealot, or patronized as an eccentric? Could he not only be taken seriously but also, without apology, put the enemy to flight from the very center of his own strength, the university?"[7] The answer is a resounding yes. Lewis undertook a militant defense of Christianity against the anti-Christian influences of his time and anticipated many aspects of postmodern skepticism.

One of Lewis's most intriguing apologetic devices was what may be called his "Argument from Desire," the argument that human beings have in themselves an incompleteness, a thirst for something that no earthly object can satisfy and that thereby points us beyond this world to another. The origins of this argument in Lewis's own reflections on his conversion, and his subtle development of the approach in various works, are explored by Dr. Douglas T. Hyatt in the thirteenth chapter, "Joy, the Call of God in Man: A Critical Appraisal of Lewis's Argument from Desire." Dr. Hyatt notes certain limitations in Lewis's argument, yet also substantiates the overwhelming plausibility of the general line of reasoning.

We would get the wrong impression of Lewis, however, if we thought he merely wrote powerful apologetics in private. Lewis also took his ideas into the public lion's den of the Socratic Club, an Oxford debating society that he chaired for many years, dedicated to the discussion of the issues dividing Christians and non-Christians. This neglected area of Lewis's Christian activity is the focus of the fourteenth chapter by Christopher W. Mitchell, "University Battles: C. S. Lewis and the Oxford University Socratic Club."

Lewis knew too that a fundamental obstacle to Christian belief was the perennial tendency, exacerbated by relativism, to evade a confrontation with one's own evil. Indeed so complete is this evasion, and so sure are many of their own worth, that they put God on trial: mankind is the judge, and God is in the dock! In the fifteenth chapter, "C. S. Lewis and the Problem of Evil," Jerry Root examines this difficulty and explores Lewis's response to evil with an emphasis on its importance for evangelism.

Even more disturbing is the postmodern malaise that not only tries to evade evil, but that will even deny truth and the demands of logical consistency in order to maintain the absolute sovereignty of individual rights. Could Lewis, whose audience was primarily modernist, really speak to this condition? In the last chapter of this book, "A Vision, Within a Dream, Within the Truth: C. S. Lewis as Evangelist to the Postmodernists," Gene Edward Veith shows that indeed he could. It is very clear in such works as *The Abolition of Man* that Lewis was aware of those ideological influences now termed "postmodern." While Lewis does offer a striking logical critique of these ideas, he is also aware that direct argument will be of little avail to one who rejects truth and believes only in persuasion and the exertion of power. Lewis came to see that for many people, apologetics were less effective than a kind of symbolic narrative that brings certain ideas to life. As Veith argues, this method, as employed by Lewis in his imaginative fiction, actually relies on what are now regarded as postmodern approaches—for example, "magical realism," "artistic defamiliarization," and "levels of fictionality."

UNIFYING THEMES

Although the book has four parts, the reader may notice that there are certain unifying themes, aside from the common focus on Lewis's evangelism. One main theme is *diversity*. Lewis appealed, and continues to appeal, to an extraordinarily diverse audience, and this was because he communicated at various levels (from child to academic scholar) and in many different idioms and genres. If I may borrow a metaphor from Dr. Rossow (itself a variation on a biblical parable), few writers have succeeded in putting the old wine of the Gospel into such a wide variety of new and attractive wineskins.

A second main theme is *integrity*. Lewis's Christian thinking affected all his post-conversion writings (whether for scholars or a popular audience) and permeated and conditioned all his dealings with people, including personal correspondence and conversation. This integrity involved tremendous honesty and humility about his own contribution to the evangelistic task. Lewis liked to compare himself to Balaam's donkey[8] (Numbers 22:21-41) and to emphasize that God was fond of working his will through the most unlikely of mediums.

A third theme is *prophecy*. Still underestimated as an intellectual, owing to the very intellectual snobbery that Lewis both attacked and eschewed in his own writing, Lewis was a remarkably prescient thinker, foreseeing obstacles for Christianity that materialized or intensified only after his death, especially the varieties of contemporary relativism.

A fourth theme is *timelessness*. Many of those who use Lewis's *Mere Christianity* in their classes continue to be amazed that this book, containing material originally broadcast during the Second World War, makes a powerful and direct appeal to students born at least a decade after Lewis's death in 1963. Like many of the truly great writers he had veritably devoured, Lewis focused on themes of enduring relevance to the human condition, and his ideas continue to repay scrutiny.

In Gratitude

I first thank God for stirring up as unlikely a vessel as myself to be the editor of this book. If any human committee had selected an editor, they certainly would not have selected me, since I am neither internationally nor even nationally known in Lewis studies. But as Luther reminds us, "God carves the rotten wood, God rides the lame horse," and I can say that from the beginning, editing this book has been a lesson in the reality of grace. Despite my lack of name and reputation, excellent Lewis scholars and contacts from around the world have showered me with all sorts of unmerited assistance, so that the book that emerges is, I believe, a very fine book!

My thanks go to all of the contributors for their hard work, commitment, and scholarship. I am particularly indebted to Dr. Wayne Martindale for entering the inner sanctum of Crossway Books without veil and securing the book deal. He, Jerry Root, and Chris Mitchell, director of the Wade Center Collection, all at Wheaton College, have been invaluable in helping me make the right connections. The staff of the Wade Center Collection, including Marie Benware and Marjorie Mead, were very helpful and graciously overlooked my obvious inexperience in many matters. At this end of the line, I am very grateful to Dr. Gene Edward Veith and Dr. Joel Heck for their encouragement and willingness to share their experience and expertise in writing for publication. Many thanks to Dr. Philip G. Ryken for stepping in and defending the book where the "line" was "thinnest"[9] by documenting Lewis's influence in both Great Britain and the United States. Michael Ward is to be applauded for giving sup-

Introduction

port from the Oxford side of the operation and for his generous detours to Concordia and Wheaton en route to California. While on the subject of Oxford, I would like to express my thanks and appreciation for the delightful tours provided by Peter Cousin (the "Lewis taxi driver" and treasurer of the Oxford C. S. Lewis Society) and by Father Tom Honey, the vicar at Lewis's church in Headington Quarry.

Thanks too, to Bruce Edwards, J. Norris Beam, Douglas Gresham, and Walter Hooper for their encouragement. It is itself a significant testimony to the positive influence of Lewis that anyone such as myself who attempts a serious study of his life and work is surrounded by a cloud of witnesses, each one quite literally a Christopher.

Special thanks go to my wife for her sharp reading and typing skills and for enduring the birth pains of this book. Thanks also to the students of my C. S. Lewis class and to the many colleagues, friends, and relatives who have kept me going. Finally, I thank Concordia University Wisconsin for supporting and encouraging this venture.

BIBLIOGRAPHY

Como, James T., ed. *C. S. Lewis at the Breakfast Table and Other Reminiscences.* Second Edition. New York: Harcourt Brace & Company, 1992.

Lewis, C. S. *The Last Battle.* London: Bodley Head, 1956.

_____. *Mere Christianity.* Revised Edition. New York: Macmillan, 1952.

_____."Rejoinder to Dr Pittenger." In *God in the Dock.* Ed. Walter Hooper. Grand Rapids, MI: Eerdmans, 1970, 177-183.

Lewis, Warren and Hooper, Walter, eds. *Letters of C. S. Lewis: Revised and Enlarged Edition.* New York: Harcourt Brace and Company, 1988.

Rossow, Francis. "Giving Christian Doctrine a New Translation: Selected Examples from the Novels of C. S. Lewis." *Concordia Journal*, July 1995, 281-97.

Schwartz, Adam. Book review for *The Lamp-Post*, Vol. 20, No. 3, Autumn 1996, 31-35.

NOTES

1. Schwartz, *The Lamp-Post*, 34.

2. Lewis, "Rejoinder to Dr Pittenger," 181.

3. Lewis buffs will note that this is a reference to the title of the fifteenth chapter of *The Last Battle* and a frequent refrain of the last chapter of that book.

4. Letter to Mrs. Ashton of 2 February 1955, *Letters of C. S. Lewis*, 446.

5. Lewis, "Rejoinder to Dr Pittenger," 183.

6. Ibid., 181.

7. Como, "Introduction: Within the Realm of Plenitude," xxii.

8. See, for example, Lewis's letter to Sister Penelope of May 15, 1941, in *Letters of C. S. Lewis*, 359-60.

9. Lewis, Preface to *Mere Christianity*, 6.

The
Contributors

Jon P. Balsbaugh has recently completed his graduate studies at the University of St. Thomas in Saint Paul, Minnesota. His studies emphasized theological aesthetics and criticism. He has recently undertaken an in-depth examination of C. S. Lewis's *Till We Have Faces* as an example of Lewis's pagan transcendence thesis (the thesis that pagan myths contain elements that point to Christ as their fulfillment).

Corbin Scott Carnell is professor of English at the University of Florida in Gainesville. He is author of the book *Bright Shadow: C. S. Lewis and the Feeling Intellect* and many articles on Lewis and English literature. He was also in personal correspondence with Lewis during his lifetime. Professor Carnell currently serves as a contributing editor for the literary review *The Lamp-Post*, published by the Southern California C. S. Lewis Society.

Patrick T. Ferry, an ordained minister with a Ph.D. in history, served as professor of history and now serves as president at Concordia University Wisconsin. He has focused his research on church history, especially the preaching styles of the Reformation, and has presented and written numerous articles on the subject. He is a gifted preacher in his own right and often serves as a visiting minister.

Joel D. Heck is an ordained minister, a theologian, an expert in evangelism, and a long-time student of Lewis. Currently he serves as a professor of theology and assistant dean at Concordia University

The Contributors

Wisconsin. He has authored several books, including *The Art of Sharing Your Faith* and *New Member Assimilation: Practical Prevention of Backdoor Loss Through Frontdoor Care*. Dr. Heck is founding editor of the journal *Evangelism*, has written many articles on religion and evangelism, has served the church on a national level, and has taught on evangelism in general and on C. S. Lewis in particular. Perhaps to emphasize the fact that he still is not perfect, Joel is also an ardent L.A. Dodgers fan.

Douglas T. Hyatt is a theologian and mission worker. His doctoral dissertation, written at the University of Basel under Professor Jan Milic Lochman, was *C. S. Lewis: A Theological Assessment of His Propagation of the Faith*. He has been a busy missionary to Eastern Europe from 1973 to the present. Dr. Hyatt is the director of the Institute for Biblical and Theological Studies, a ministry of Campus Crusade for Christ in Eastern Europe. He currently resides in Hungary.

Reed Jolley is an ordained minister and an accomplished evangelist. He has read and applied Lewis's works for many years and has taught on Lewis's life and works at churches, family camps, and retreats in Oregon, California, and Croatia. He has tremendous practical experience in the application of evangelistic strategies. Reed is currently pastor at Santa Barbara Community Church in California.

Wayne Martindale is professor of English at Wheaton College. He is editor of *Journey to the Celestial City: Glimpses of Heaven from Great Literary Classics* and co-editor, with Jerry Root, of *The Quotable Lewis*. Dr. Martindale was a contributor to the critical discussion of the Attenborough *Shadowlands* movie in the journal *VII*. He recently presented a talk on Christianity in China for Concordia University's Christianity and Culture lecture series.

Angus J. L. Menuge is a professor of science and philosophy at Concordia University Wisconsin. He has written and presented articles about Lewis and his ideas, has taught courses on the life and works of C. S. Lewis, and is the instigator and editor of this book. He recently organized the lecture series "Christianity and Culture" at Concordia University Wisconsin.

Christopher W. Mitchell is the director of the Wade Center

Collection of seven Christian authors (including Lewis) at Wheaton College. Dr. Mitchell is a lecturer in theological studies, a frequent speaker, and an expert resource on the life and work of C. S. Lewis. He is also the Reviews Editor for the journal *VII*.

Steven P. Mueller is a professor of religion at Concordia Irvine, California. He is completing his doctoral dissertation on the christology of C. S. Lewis through Durham University. His research focuses on how Lewis translates aspects of Christ's human and divine natures into various literary idioms. Professor Mueller's background includes both teaching and pastoral ministry.

George Musacchio is professor of English and the Frank W. Mayborn Chair of Arts and Sciences at the University of Mary Hardin-Baylor. He is author of *C. S. Lewis: Man and Writer: Essays and Reviews* and *Milton's Adam and Eve: Fallible Perfection*. He was formerly editor of the Southern California C. S. Lewis Society literary review, *The Lamp-Post*, for which he is still a contributing editor, and has written numerous articles on Lewis. In addition to all this, Dr. Musacchio periodically leads discussions of Lewis's books at his local church.

Jerry Root has recently joined the Christian education faculty of Wheaton College. He is coauthor with Claudia Root of *Friendship Evangelism* and co-editor with Wayne Martindale of *The Quotable Lewis*. He is an accomplished evangelist and minister and has frequently taught on evangelism and Lewis. He is currently completing a doctoral dissertation on C. S. Lewis and the problem of evil through Oxford University. So far as I can tell, there are two classes of Lewis students: those who know Jerry Root, and those who will come to know him.

Francis C. Rossow is professor of practical theology at Concordia Seminary, Saint Louis. He is author of the book *Preaching the Creative Gospel Creatively* and co-editor of *Lectionary Preaching Resources*. He is remembered by his former students as an excellent teacher of C. S. Lewis's works.

Philip G. Ryken is Associate Minister for Preaching at Tenth Presbyterian Church in Philadelphia. He holds a D.Phil. in historical

The Contributors

theology from the University of Oxford, England. While in Oxford, he taught history and theology at the Centre for Medieval and Renaissance Studies and was an enthusiastic participant in and officer of the Oxford C. S. Lewis Society.

Gene Edward Veith is professor of humanities and dean of arts and sciences at Concordia University Wisconsin. He has written widely on Christianity, culture, and the arts. He is the author of seven books, including *Postmodern Times*, *Modern Fascism*, *Reading Between the Lines*, *State of the Arts*, and *Loving God with All Your Mind*. He has written a vast number of articles and has taught on the life and works of C. S. Lewis.

Michael Ward is a tutor at Oxford, England and is centenary secretary of Oxford's C. S. Lewis Society. He has written numerous papers and given many presentations on the life and works of C. S. Lewis. He recently assisted Walter Hooper in the preparation of *C. S. Lewis: A Companion and Guide* and is currently head resident in Lewis's former house, The Kilns, recently restored by the C. S. Lewis Foundation of Redlands, California.

PART ONE

The Motivation:
The Influence and Potential of
Lewis's Evangelism

SHADOWLANDS:

Inadvertent Evangelism

WAYNE MARTINDALE

For good or ill, movies matter. Shortly after *Shadowlands* hit the national scene in 1994 and before I had seen the movie myself, I got a letter from a former colleague in Southern California. I had given her a copy of *Mere Christianity* some sixteen years before. In the meantime, she had married and her husband had died of cancer. Her faith was shaken. Then she saw *Shadowlands*. She wrote to tell me she had seen her own feelings and struggle in the film and was now reading her way back to faith through Lewis's books. You can imagine the anticipation with which I hurriedly went to the movie.

As was the case with each of the first four times I saw the movie, I mopped my eyes along the way. Yet, at the end of that first showing, I was angry, too. I had not seen the real Lewis, and he hadn't lost his faith as the movie suggests. Yet my friend had been moved to reconsider the faith. Here is a fine kettle of fish, indeed. What ought we make of a "good" movie that distorts historical truth beyond recognition, yet has a desirable effect? The effort to sort out the good and bad effects of the movie, along with the true and false, is the purpose of this chapter.

THE THREE *Shadowlands*

Shadowlands is the name of three distinct productions, each telling the amazing story of the meeting and marriage of C. S. "Jack" Lewis, the

Inadvertent Evangelism

confirmed bachelor and brilliant Oxford don, to Helen Joy Davidman Gresham, along with the death of Joy and Jack's reaction. The first was a film conceived by Norman Stone, an evangelical Christian, who envisioned a series of TV films for Thames Television on famous Christians of each century, from St. Columba in the sixth to Lewis in the twentieth. Only the Lewis project made it onto film. When BBC (British) TV got interested, William Nicholson, an experienced documentary writer, was retained to rewrite the script initially penned by Brian Sibley.

The made-for-TV film first aired in 1985, with Joss Ackland playing Jack Lewis and Claire Bloom playing Joy Gresham. With Stone as director, the faith element was strong, both in the couple's relationship and Lewis's response to Joy's death. This version makes clear Lewis's meaning of "Shadowlands": this present world is temporary, "only shadows"; real life, our eternity in heaven, "has not begun."[1] Jack and Joy discuss this image early in their meeting and again at crucial moments as her death nears. In this first film, the shadowlands imagery is reinforced by references to diving as a symbol of faith.[2] "I learned how to dive the same summer I learned I was a Christian," says Lewis. "All you have to do is stop doing something; you have to learn to stop trying to preserve yourself." At the end of the film, after Joy has died, Lewis tells Douglas, "I'll teach you how to dive." With these words, faith is reasserted, not only for Lewis, but in the confidence that he can help his stepson to faith as well.

This version does, however, have its problems. For example, the character and personality of Joy as a tough, no-nonsense woman of towering intellect does not come through. But many historical elements and the crucial fact of their faith in Christ before, during, and after their time together do come through.

The next incarnation of *Shadowlands* was a stage play, opening at the Theatre Royal in Plymouth, October 5, 1989, and moving to the Queen's Theatre, London later the same month. After a year's run in the West End and good notices, the play opened on Broadway at the Brooks Atkinson Theatre in November 1990 and ran until April 1991. *Shadowlands* was one of the big success stories of the season on both sides of the Atlantic. By most accounts, the stage play was also the most powerful of the three versions. The imagery of mortal life as "Shadowlands" still serves as a unifying device in the play,[3] though the number of references is noticeably reduced, and the element of Christian faith is still unmistakable. The stars were Nigel Hawthorne (in both England and the U.S.), Jane Lapotaire (England), and Jane Alexander (who came to England to prepare and carried the role in the U.S.). Bill Nicholson was again the writer. In England, the play got Olivier nominations for Best Play, Best Actor, and Best Actress. It earned the Evening Standard Award for Play of the Year for 1990 and the Variety Club Award for Best Actress of 1990 (Lapotaire). In the U.S., Nigel Hawthorne won the Tony Award for Best Actor in 1991, and the New York Critics Circle gave it Best Play 1991. It has now been staged in at least a dozen countries.

With these successes, Brian Eastman decided to make a feature film. This brings us to the third production called *Shadowlands*—the film from Savoy, directed by Sir Richard Attenborough and starring Anthony Hopkins and Debra Winger—the film that is the main concern of this chapter. Eastman secured Nicholson to do yet another rewrite of the script. In the first version, Norman Stone insured that the Christian element was prominent; in the Attenborough film, Nicholson, an ex-atheist now agnostic, had a freer hand. Stone comments on the situation: "My motivation [was] to be true to the man. The Attenborough film didn't have the same aim at all. When I first saw it Bill [Nicholson] said to me, 'What do you think, Norm?' And I said, 'Well, I think probably, Bill, it's the film you always wanted to make anyway.' . . . Bill's aim was not to follow the band of faith in [the original] way."[4] As we shall see, the film has serious problems as a depiction of Lewis's life. But to my own amazement, the film has done an astonishing amount of good.

THE GOOD NEWS

If movies matter, then movies that capture and hold national and international attention, movies like *Shadowlands*, matter a great deal. The good news about this film is that many people have been motivated to

Inadvertent Evangelism

get beyond the film to the life and works of the historical people behind the movingly told story, especially C. S. Lewis. Anything that spurs a large number of people to read Lewis must have something positive going for it. Here are some illustrations.

A woman writes, "I'm waking up before my alarm clock almost every day to read Lewis because part of his life story—*Shadowlands*—captivated my mind."[5]

A man already acquainted with Lewis's work has a similar response: "The 1993 film *Shadowlands*, a fictionalized account of Lewis's love relationship with Joy Davidman, continues to inspire curiosity about Lewis and interest in his work. Though I had read a little of Lewis as a campus minister at Stanford in the 1970s and considered him a valued friend of the kind of Christianity I was espousing, it wasn't until after seeing *Shadowlands* that I immersed myself in his writings last year, acquiring and devouring virtually everything by and about him that I could find. My 'Lewis plunge' ultimately changed my life more than any other single factor ever has."[6]

An obviously knowledgeable person with a serious interest in Lewis for twenty-five years says: "I've also come to appreciate Lewis more as a human being—partly through the various versions of *Shadowlands* (despite their inaccuracies)."[7]

A grad student working on an M.A. in English writes: "My only brush with C. S. Lewis was reading *The Screwtape Letters* and watching *Shadowlands*. I'm interested in learning more about the man and his literature."[8]

An aerospace engineer and expatriate Englishman writes that he had read the Narnia Chronicles as a child and had a set for his own kids. In addition, he reports: "I had an old copy of *Mere Christianity* lying around the house which I had never read; after seeing *Shadowlands* recently I was moved to read it—quite a remarkable book, and I also read *Out of the Silent Planet* which I found in the library. I am thrilled to have stumbled across the whole body of Lewis's work and to have the future studying of it in store."[9]

My favorite has an appropriately international flavor. Its author is an executive in an organization that works with international students:

I sat talking with a Japanese American psychology professor at a conference where I was keynoting in Kuala Lumpur, Malaysia. This particular man has been exposed to the gospel, but had some bad experiences with Christians that resulted in his turning away from the message they had shared. Now, several years later as a professor in a Japanese university, he is still doing some searching for the answers to his spiritual quest. He approached me and asked if I were one of those "evangelical Christians," and when I told him that I certainly could be categorized as such he proceeded to ask me if I really believed at an intellectual level as well as a spiritual level the things we profess to believe. When I assured him that I did, his series of questions continued to probe, and obviously we came to the point of discussing C. S. Lewis. He is now reading *Mere Christianity*. It was interesting that just two weeks before our conversation he had seen the film *Shadowlands* and sensed that there was something going on there that was deeper than just a person dealing with the events of life apart from an awareness of God. This helped to spark his hunger and raised the questions he asked sitting by the hotel pool in Kuala Lumpur.[10]

Anyone with even a modicum of Lewis's evangelistic zeal has to be enthused by stories like these. But anecdotes are easy to get; when it comes to hard facts on which to ground generalizations about influence, the task is not easy. As we consider those facts, however, three things will emerge as true: 1) *Shadowlands* has had a significant influence; 2) its influence is largely positive; and 3) it leaves viewers with significant false impressions that need correcting.

Without question, the movie has captured the popular imagination. Here's an illustration of influence on the more ephemeral side, especially helpful because it says something about British interest. Just months after *Shadowlands* was released in England, Oxford's Randolph Hotel, where the scene of Jack and Joy's meeting was filmed, offered a "Shadowlands Weekend"—two nights and three days. It included the play version at a nearby theater and tea with Lewis scholar Walter Hooper. The price tag: about $600 per couple.

Inadvertent Evangelism

All this in spite of the fact that Jack and Joy did not meet at the Randolph; they met at the Eastgate Hotel.[11]

There are a few sources of information that serve to verify as broadly true what the above anecdotes exemplify. In the wake of the movie, about a dozen reporters and over 200 individual inquirers called the Wade Center at Wheaton College, which has a special collection on Lewis and his circle, to find out more information. Some callers even wanted the Gospel explained to them. For the most part, the callers' only clue was a bare mention of the Wade Center in the credits. Carla Wheeler, observing the flurry of post-*Shadowlands* activity at the C. S. Lewis Foundation in Redlands, California, reports that "The release of 'Shadowlands' has spawned a feeding frenzy for C. S. Lewis facts and philosophies, and the four-member staff answers the calls." She further notes that a Japanese film company called for permission to film the inside of The Kilns.[12]

I wrote to Douglas Gresham (Joy's son and Lewis's stepson), asking his opinion on the movie's influence. His response was resoundingly positive. "I continually encounter stories about people who not knowing Jack, or anything about him, have seen the film, and thereafter have noticed his name on a book, purchased the book, read it, become fascinated and begun the journey which leads to the Throne. *Shadowlands* has brought a huge number of people into an awareness of Jack, and thence, a lot of them into a relationship with Christ."[13] Later in the summer, I had the opportunity to ask him about the movie in person. He was as enthusiastic about the positive effects of the movie as ever. When I asked how he knew the movie had beneficial effects, he cited his own correspondence and the fact that "all of the protagonists in the movies [actors and actresses] have thousands of letters in their desks from people that have been helped." I asked if the "thousands" were intended as literal fact or overstatement for effect. He assured me that it was literal. I asked if he knew of any negative effects, anyone whose faith had been shaken. He said he did not. It has struck me as significant from the early days following the movie's release until now that among its strongest supporter has been the one living person closest to the events portrayed.[14] Douglas is not completely uncritical of the movie, however, as will be shown later.

Another indicator of influence is book sales. It's no secret that movies sell books. Sales of books by and about Lewis soared after *Shadowlands*. For example, James Como mentions that his book of reminiscences went into an extra printing, as did my book with Jerry Root, *The Quotable Lewis*. Many books on Lewis went into extra printings, and others that had gone out of print, like Leanne Payne's *Real Presence* on "the Christian worldview of C. S. Lewis," were picked up by other publishers and reissued. Evidence of new and renewed interest was only as far away as the bookstore. The local Barnes and Noble had prominent displays of books by and about Lewis and sponsored special lectures and new reading groups on Lewis. Leonard Goss, former Editorial VP for Crossway Books, reports that their biography of Joy by Lyle Dorsett, *And God Came In*, sold under 1,000 copies in 1993 but jumped to over 8,000 in 1994, the year the movie hit neighborhood theaters.[15] Dorsett reports that "because of the movie, HarperCollins in London brought out a new paperback edition of *And God Came In*–7000 [copies]. It sold over the first three months (March-June 1994)."[16] Crossway also published a paperback biography of Lewis by George Sayer called *Jack: A Life of C. S. Lewis* in 1994, which sold 17,000 copies; it was reprinted twice in 1994 and was picked up by a book club.[17]

An afternoon with back issues of *Publishers Weekly* yielded a broader sense of *Shadowlands'* influence on book sales. Unfortunately, the magazine's Religion Bestsellers List started as *Shadowlands* was just making its first appearance. However, there were no Lewis books on the first list, January 1994 (the film premiered on Christmas Day 1993). But by February, Lewis was on the list with *Mere Christianity*, which has remained on the list up to the present. He had two on the top ten list for February; sales of his books peaked in March with four of the top five Religion Bestsellers by Lewis, *A Grief Observed*, his journal of responses to Joy's death, besting his others. He continued to have four books on the lists for April, May, and June. One or two of his books have continued to show up on every list down to this writing. *Mere*

Inadvertent Evangelism

Christianity is the clear favorite, with *The Screwtape Letters* a clear second; the autobiographical books, *A Grief Observed* and *Surprised by Joy*, joined the list during the height of *Shadowlands'* popularity.

Writing for *Publishers Weekly*, Henry Carrigan reports, "It is the work of C. S. Lewis that has attracted the greatest attention of spiritual fiction readers. Perhaps it is Lewis's dramatic conversion from agnosticism to Christianity that draws readers; perhaps it is his exemplary narrative skill. The recent film *Shadowlands* certainly has contributed to the renewal of interest in Lewis."[18] Also for *Publishers Weekly*, Phyllis Tickle writes in the same vein: "Some three decades after his death, C. S. Lewis still maintains his position as the most loved, most read and best-selling Christian apologist of our time."[19] Of course, book sales do not automatically equate to conversions or to reaffirmations of Christianity. They do show a revival in spiritual searching, however, and as Jesus said, those who seek find. A reader of Lewis, even of the scholarly works, doesn't go far before confronting the claims of Christ.

Let's give *Shadowlands* its due in every way. It is a good movie. Syndicated movie critic (on TV and in newspapers) Roger Ebert gives it four stars. Were it not for the misfortune of coming out in the same season as *Schindler's List*, *Shadowlands* would probably have hauled in several Academy Awards. Good movies that affirm marriage and make us think about life and death and eternity are not so common that we can afford to be ungrateful for the few there are. I would also defend the movie's artistic integrity: it is not sentimental, even though it routinely moves viewers to tears. True sentiment, Lewis himself says, teaches us "to feel pleasure, liking, disgust, and hatred at those things which really are pleasant, likeable, disgusting, and hateful."[20] In fact, the emotional element of the film is precisely the part that Douglas Gresham says is "spot on." He assures us from his own lived experience with Jack and Joy that "the emotional content and transitions in *Shadowlands* are as absolutely accurate as it would be possible to make them."[21]

That's the good news; it outweighs the bad, I would argue. But the bad is significant and needs serious consideration. The issues involved are not unimportant.

The Bad News

The very success of *Shadowlands* makes the question well up within us: is this the real Jack and Joy Lewis? Many unsuspecting reviewers and moviegoers pick up on the moviemaker's bold-faced, up-front claim to be "a true story" (they hadn't even the decency to add the modest caveat "based on") and assume this is the real Jack and Joy Lewis, and this is their real story. It isn't. Bill Nicholson is honest enough to admit in interviews that "*Shadowlands* is based on events that occurred in the lives of two real people—C. S. Lewis and Joy Gresham—but it is not a documentary drama. I have used parts of their story, not used other parts, and imagined the rest."[22] Shouldn't he have said so in the film itself? The failure to indicate the film's vast quantity of pure fiction is perhaps the biggest problem of all.

Before addressing the other problems, it might be useful to say what can be safely credited. Joy converted from Jew to Communist to Christian, the last move largely from reading Lewis's books. She was bright, witty, feisty—even brash. She did initiate the contact with Jack, and she did win a Yale Younger Poets award. She was also running away from a bad marriage to an alcoholic, womanizing husband, and she did have cancer, a remission, and a recurrence that killed her. Jack was a confirmed bachelor, Oxford don, famous writer, caring and generous teacher, scorned by many colleagues for his public Christian witness, and slow to acknowledge his love for Joy. Jack and Joy were married in a civil ceremony to allow her and her *two* sons to stay in England. The religious ceremony followed, and the marriage, though brief, was happy. Then came the long, painful death and the deep, soul-shaking grief. Well, that's quite a lot, isn't it? Only shadows, really.

Let me start the critique by summarizing the story that this movie tells. This will allow me to highlight what is fictional, what fact. The movie tells the story of a man (I hesitate to call him "Lewis" at this point) who has the archetypal British reserve with a vengeance. Tortoise-like, he hides himself in a protective shell. He keeps company with inferior students and inferior friends and lectures to intellectually inferior audiences. To these audiences, he serves up platitudes about

Inadvertent Evangelism

pain. He dares not risk love. He is a confirmed and lifelong bachelor, living in a man's world, which early and mid-century Oxford surely was. Oh, he is clever, all right—even brilliant. And he is witty. But he is safe.

The plot thickens, however. Along comes his alter ego, a literary doppelganger. This American woman bursts onto the scene: loud, audacious, brash, sharp-tongued, fetching, persistent, risk-taking. As her own story of abuse, grief, and hardship unfolds, our hearts go out to her. The confirmed bachelor's heart goes out to her, too. "Kiss her, you fool," we find ourselves saying under our breaths. But ever safe, he demurs. It is not his romantic love that gets him off the dime to marry her, but his safer sense of Christian charity as he extends his name in a mere legal contract to keep her from deportation. Not until she is on her deathbed with cancer does our bachelor learn what we and she have seen all along: he loves her. He proposes—she insists upon it. They are married by a priest, and news of the marriage goes public by means of a newspaper announcement. Against all odds—almost, it seems, by the very strength of love itself—her cancer goes into remission. He takes her home from the hospital. She gently leads the shy little boy of a man into bed with her. Remember her words? "Like a little boy." They are supremely happy. The joy that had passed them by in youth, especially him, is now abundantly recompensed.

But the cancer returns, and Joy dies. Jack's grief nearly kills him. His faith is shaken, and he tells his stepson, Douglas, "When my mother died, I was your age. I thought that if I prayed for her to get better, and if I really believed she'd get better, then she wouldn't die. But she did." Douglas answers, "It doesn't work." Lewis responds, "No. It doesn't work." He no longer gives out platitudes about pain as "God's megaphone to rouse a deaf world" or God's "chisel" to carve our character. What he has learned by the end is that love is stronger than faith and that pain is the price he pays now for the love then.

That's the film's account, summarized to highlight its point of view. It is a great love story, told with artistic integrity. It is not, however, C. S. Lewis's and Joy Davidman Gresham's story. That is, except for the bare bones—and then not all of the bones. What the movie does not have is historical integrity. It is not, as it claims in the first frames, "a true story." No one expects a documentary from a Hollywood movie, but if it claims to be "true" and hasn't the humility to use even the respectable "based on," a film invites criticism.

The Real Lewis

George Sayer—Lewis's former pupil, friend for nearly thirty years, hiking companion, fellow teacher of literature, and the best biographer of Lewis to date—says quite bluntly that he never recognized in Hopkins's portrayal the Lewis he knew.[23] The real Lewis was not an insular inmate of the ivory tower but was hardy, loved a good laugh, and had wit, humor, good cheer, and most importantly of all, a robust faith. Hopkins's Lewis is guilt-ridden and morose. Lewis was guilt-free: "he had repented of his sins" and received forgiveness, Sayer reports.[24] "In the end, his faith was deeper. We spent hours talking about that after Joy died. For a time he was angry and he asked hard, honest questions about prayer and suffering. But I cannot think of a thing he said, or anything he did, that hinted that his faith was damaged, let alone destroyed."[25]

In addition, the real Lewis did not insulate himself from intellectual challengers. In fact, the opposite is true. One of the chief reasons he fell in love with Joy is that she was the first woman he had known who was his intellectual equal. This is Lewis's description of Joy's intellect in *A Grief Observed*:

Her mind was lithe and quick and muscular as a leopard. Passion, tenderness and pain were all equally unable to disarm it. It scented the first whiff of cant or slush; then sprang, and knocked you over before you knew what was happening. How many bubbles of mine she pricked! I soon learned not to talk rot to her unless I did it for the sheer pleasure—and there's another red-hot jab—of being exposed and laughed at. I was never less silly than as [Joy's] lover.[26]

Inadvertent Evangelism

Contrary to the film Lewis, the real Lewis loved debate and sought out persons of keen intellect. For years (from 1942 until he went to Cambridge in 1954), he presided over the most popular club in Oxford, the Socratic Club, which existed to foster debate among Christians and leading atheists in various fields. Oxford students wouldn't turn out in droves for "strawman" sideshows; they went to see the Who's Who among atheists confront Lewis. When he wasn't the formal respondent, Lewis was nonetheless the main attraction with his civility and good humor but ever-incisive logic. Why would he enter the lions' den of debate week after week if he feared confrontation by some of the best minds in England?

And what of his friends? They weren't the silly bunch of impertinent fools portrayed in the *Shadowlands* pub scene, supposedly reenacting a weekly meeting of the Inklings. They were men of towering intellect who, many of them, had important religious differences. One of the members, Owen Barfield, was a lifelong friend, but one with whom Lewis carried on, in conversation and letters, what they called "The Great War." Barfield concedes that he, like others, often "felt in his conversations with Lewis that he was wielding a pea-shooter against a howitzer."[27] Even so, no one speaks with fonder recollection of Lewis than Barfield. Understanding, as Lewis says, that friendship grows not so much out of agreement as an interest in the same subjects, Barfield dedicated *Poetic Diction* to "Clive Hamilton," Lewis's pseudonym, using a Blakean aphorism: "Opposition is true friendship."

Another example would be his lifelong friend from youth, Arthur Greeves. They were often at the opposite end of religious as well as other issues. And as an adolescent, Lewis thrived under the tutelage of W. T. Kirkpatrick or "The Great Knock" as the family affectionately called him. The Knock was an atheist, rationalist, and ruthless logician. Whereas many would have withered under his incessant logical challenges, Lewis blossomed.

Nevill Coghill, a fellow student of Lewis's when both had F. P. Wilson for a tutor in English literature and later an esteemed Oxford don, gives this general assessment of the man he knew so well and for so long: "Whoever thinks justly of him will find him impressive, and he was always impressive to meet; I prefer my first word, 'formidable.' But this was softened by joviality in youth and kindliness in maturity. Genius is formidable and so is goodness; he had both."[28]

In his Afterword to *A Grief Observed*, Chad Walsh, Lewis's first biographer, says: "To him an ideal conversation was an intellectual fencing match, and may the man with the best dialectic win. The few times I crossed swords with him, he won. I also noticed that he seemed singularly uninterested in introspection. He found so many things outside himself interesting that he had no time to study himself."[29]

Nor was Lewis a romantic shellfish who might never have married if some woman hadn't stormed the front gate with a battering ram. He very nearly married poet Ruth Pitter, both before and after he met Joy. Pitter was the first woman poet to receive the Queen's Medal for poetry, an award usually given to the Poet Laureate. The two three-ringed binders of unpublished letters from Lewis to Pitter show a growing warmth. In 1947 he writes to her, "If Sir Thingummy [Sir Ronald Storrs] doesn't agree to the first suggestion you make, come without him. We have not yet explored each other's minds so fully that we need a third to keep us going!"[30] And in 1953, the year following Lewis's first contact with Joy, he writes upon reading something new from Pitter:

> Bright Angel! I'm in a sea of glory! . . . I wonder have you yourself any notion how good some of these are? But, as you see, I'm drunk on them at this present. Glory be! Blessings on you! As sweet as sin and as innocent as milk. Thanks forever. Yours in great excitement.[31]

Does this sound like the shy, introverted character portrayed by Anthony Hopkins? Apparently, Joy saw enough or knew enough to perceive Ruth Pitter as a threat. Ruth wrote to Joy from time to time, but Joy never wrote back. With Lewis present, they even met at the Eastgate Hotel, site of Lewis's first meeting with Joy. It was not pleasant. Ruth wrote her impressions of Joy, with instructions that they not be opened for fifty years! Sayer says in his Afterword to the Crossway edition of his biography: "After Joy's death Jack 'came back to her'

Inadvertent Evangelism

(to quote Ruth's friend, Mary Thomas) and confided in her. If he had been in better health, they might still have married."[32]

Further, many who knew Jack and Joy during their courtship insist that he was the pursuer in the relationship. George Sayer, who at Lewis's invitation was present at the Oxford luncheon where Jack first met Joy face to face, says: "It was clear from the start that Jack was attracted to Joy, and she was very attracted to him. . . . He was quite taken with her humor, which was razor sharp, and with her deep and mystical Christian faith. . . . I can't stress too much that he considered her his equal—intellectually and spiritually."[33]

Their relationship deepened to the point that Jack asked God for permission to bear some of Joy's pain from the bone cancer. In fact, during her remission, doctors found that Lewis was developing osteoporosis. As her bones grew stronger, his weakened. Nor was Lewis sexually backward, as the *Shadowlands* bedroom scene makes him out to be. Joy did not have to talk him into bed; she says very frankly that he was a good lover. Lewis says the same of her in *A Grief Observed*.

More Bad News

There are other curious inaccuracies, of varying importance or unimportance: Lewis dressed carelessly, he never drove, Joy had two sons (not one), and the amount of time between the first contact and Joy's death was about a decade. It would surprise many moviegoers to learn that Douglas was eight when his mother first brought him to meet Lewis, but nearly fifteen when his mother died.

But by far the most important problem is the film's treatment of the faith element. Jack and Joy's faith was the thing that brought them together, sustained them in the darkest valley of human experience, and remained assuredly intact. The movie fails to show that Father Peter Bide prayed for Joy's healing in the hospital the day he married them. Jack, Joy, and their doctor were all convinced her healing was attributable to that prayer of faith and God's supernatural intervention. Viewers are not given the chance to decide for themselves. And for evidence that Jack retained a vigorous faith after Joy's death, one need only consult the written record Lewis left: correspondence, *A Grief Observed*, *Letters to Malcolm: Chiefly on Prayer*—not to mention written testimonials by those who knew him well. His theological convictions did not fail him in the severest test of his life. But this is what we get at the end of the movie (Lewis's voice): "I have no answers any more, only the life I have lived. Twice in that life I've been given the choice, as a boy and as a man. The boy chose safety; the man chooses suffering. The pain now is part of the happiness then. That's the deal."

Terry Mattingly's observation is confirmed in my own reading of well over a hundred reviews of the movies and numerous interviews: "I've had many conversations with Christians about this film. The more people knew about Lewis and Davidman, the more likely they were to be troubled by the film."[34]

Here is a sampling. Bruce Edwards agrees: "A movie about Jack and Joy that downplays or ignores the centrality of Christ to their lives is analogous to scripting the life of Michael Jordan with little reference to basketball."[35]

Syndicated columnist Joseph Sobran roundly condemns the movie for bleaching out the faith element:

> Lewis would have hated it. The movie treated his Christianity with condescension and became a banal story of an emotionally aloof man learning to get in touch with his feelings. The subtext was pure psychobabble.
>
> You could say that the film's creators, like many people in our age, were "in denial"—denying the need of every soul for God. Our public language is now shaped to avoid the most important subject in the world. Psychology has displaced theology and even tries to explain theology away. We look for happiness in our heads instead of in Heaven.[36]

Norman Stone, maker of the first film version, complains that the Lewis of the latest version comes off "being little more than a Zen Buddhist."[37]

Douglas Gresham asserts that the pain his mother experienced

Inadvertent Evangelism

was purifying, strengthening, and even essential to her faith. Regarding Jack's faith, Douglas reminds us that Lewis stood in the "front lines of the war against Satan, and in that war we must expect (as Paul makes quite plain) to suffer."[38] The experience tested Lewis's faith, but he never lost it. In his book *Lenten Lands*, Douglas illustrates the depth of Lewis's suffering at Joy's death and gives us some insight as to why he might be more forgiving of the film's other shortcomings for its faithfulness to the "emotional content":

> It has been said that Jack's years at Cambridge after Mother's death were happy. That is not true. Jack, when in company with his friends and colleagues, was (after a while) again the jovial, witty intellectual they had known for years, but only Warnie and I knew what effort that cost him, and Warnie knew less than I, for Jack was careful with him; I was more invisible. Jack's colleagues and friends never saw him as he turned from waving a cheery good-bye at the door of The Kilns and casting some pearls of a parting witticism to a departing guest; they never watched him suddenly slump, his whole body shrinking like a slowly deflating balloon, his face losing the light of laughter and becoming grey, until he became once more a tired, sick and grieving man, old beyond his years. Even Warnie did not know, but boys are sometimes hard to see, and many times I watched Jack, unseen by him, as he walked, his mind clear, through the pain of his own Gethsemane. On his way to Warnie's study, tray in hand, he would stop, take a deep breath, pull back his shoulders, raise his head and bring his facial expression under control, then, bold and cheerful of countenance, he would step into the study with a glad cry of "Tea, brother." . . . However, Jack saw no reason to inflict his agony on others and cause them to suffer as well. . . . He could not hide it from me, nor did he try, for I shared his grief.[39]

Lewis was genuinely overcome with a crushing grief at Joy's death, as anyone who loves deeply would be. But he was not blindsided. He understood the risk involved in loving. When he married Joy, he knew their days together were numbered. In many letters before and after the marriage, he speaks of having the "sword of Damocles" hanging over them. He wrote with penetrating insight about the probability of pain as an accompaniment to love. Joy's cancer came back in 1959. Lewis wrote the following in his book *The Four Loves*, published in 1960, the same year that Joy died:

> To love at all is to be vulnerable. Love anything, and your heart will certainly be wrung and possibly be broken. If you want to make sure of keeping it intact, you must give your heart to no one, not even to an animal. Wrap it carefully round with hobbies and little luxuries; avoid all entanglements; lock it up safe in the casket or coffin of your selfishness. But in that casket—safe, dark, motionless, airless—it will change. It will not be broken; it will become unbreakable, impenetrable, irredeemable. The alternative to tragedy, or at least to the risk of tragedy, is damnation. The only place outside Heaven where you can be perfectly safe from all the dangers and perturbations of love is Hell.[40]

This is one of my favorite quotes from Lewis. It has far more insight and truth than the sound-bite line from the movie: "The pain now is part of the happiness then. That's the deal." The line is not untrue in claiming that pain is an inevitable part of love. Apparently, Lewis never recovered from it. Doug Gresham asserts that "Jack's . . . life after Mother's death was merely an exercise in patience and obedience to the Lord's will."[41] But that is not the same as losing one's faith. In fact, Lewis was heroic in carrying on, in the teeth not only of his emotional pain, but also of his rapidly deteriorating health, from such ailments as osteoporosis and both kidney and heart disease. But *Shadowlands* gives us a Lewis who, as one of his colleagues observes, gives easy answers to hard questions; answers that won't stand up to the hard experience he is about to have.

How did this state of affairs come to be? From interviews, it is clear that three of the principal shapers of the movie cared little for the faith. Anthony Hopkins, for example, believes that "The script is the

Inadvertent Evangelism

essence. It contains all the information I need. Though I read a biography of Lewis before we started 'Shadowlands,' there is a limit to what I want to know. Acting is being yourself, really. . . . The director is the boss, it's his show. I just learn the lines and show up."[42] Here's part of the problem: Hopkins wasn't trying to act Lewis; he was being himself. He says, skeptically, that the film raised his consciousness, "making me realize how important it is to enjoy life while we've got it, because there may be nothing after. And if there is, all this is an illusion anyway."[43] What an ironic conclusion: for Hopkins, this world is not "shadowlands" but "illusionland."

As self-proclaimed agnostics and skeptics, Attenborough, Nicholson, and Hopkins have recast Lewis too much in their own image as a brooding doubter. I have no intrinsic objection to a film about a character losing his faith: it happens. But I do object to someone laying the ax to the root of faith that nourished the life, writing, and relationships of a man when it is an unmistakable matter of record. "It is no light offense," warns Victorian poet Christina Rossetti, "to traduce the dead, to blacken recklessly their memory."[44]

Debra Winger is a bright spot in all this. She did her homework. With a refreshing sense of responsibility, she read many books by both C. S. and Joy Lewis, spent time at the Wade Center, and interviewed Lyle Dorsett, Joy's biographer. She was as close to Joy's personality as the script allowed her to be. But Joy was a far more extraordinary woman than Nicholson's script suggests. Like Lewis, she had a photographic mind. Even as a girl, she could read a page of Shakespeare and recite it from memory[45] or look at a complicated piece of music once and play it from memory.[46] And her intelligence and editorial skills were such that she provided major contributions to Lewis's writing projects at a time when he was dry. She greatly influenced *The Four Loves*, and without her aid Lewis would never have written what he thought his best book, *Till We Have Faces*. One of Jack and Joy's favorite games was Scrabble, which they played allowing all known languages. Nicholson gives us a comparatively bland Joy with little of the intellectual and almost none of the spiritual depth.

The movie is finally untrue in its implication that romantic love in the earthly here and now is our whole concern. On the contrary, love is the engine that drives eternity, too. The one incapable of love and insulated from pain is out of rhythm with the cosmic dance. Lewis knew, too, that all earthly loves go bad if you put them first. But if we make the Author of all loves our first love, all earthly loves are freed to find their fulfillment in Him. Around the time of Joy's death, Lewis writes:

> For the dream of finding our end, the thing we were made for, in a Heaven of purely human love could not be true unless our whole Faith were wrong. We were made for God. Only by being in some respect like Him, only by being a manifestation of His beauty, loving kindness, wisdom or goodness, has any earthly Beloved excited our love. It is not that we have loved them too much, but that we did not quite understand what we were loving. It is not that we shall be asked to turn from them, so dearly familiar, to a Stranger. When we see the face of God we shall know that we have always known it. He has been a party to, has made, sustained and moved moment by moment within, all our earthly experiences of innocent love. All that was true love in them was, even on earth, far more His than ours and ours only because His. In Heaven there will be no anguish and no duty of turning away from our earthly Beloveds. First, because we shall have turned already; from the portraits to the Original, from the rivulets to the Fountain, from the creatures He made lovable to Love Himself. But secondly, because we shall find them all in Him. By loving Him more than them we shall love them more than we now do.[47]

THE BOTTOM LINE

So what is my bottom line on *Shadowlands*? I like it, I don't like it, it makes me happy, it makes me angry—all at the same time. But judging from the results, the situation is analogous to what confronted the apostle Paul: "It is true that some preach Christ out of envy and rivalry . . . out of selfish ambition, not sincerely, supposing that they can stir up trouble for me while I am in chains. But what does it matter? The impor-

Inadvertent Evangelism

tant thing is that in every way, whether from false motives or true, Christ is preached. And because of this I rejoice" (Philippians 1:15-18). But this isn't a justification; it's a consolation. God works in mysterious ways and has many means of bringing people into the kingdom. If God has set many on the path to himself even through such a flawed and unlikely vessel, there is precedence.

FURTHER READING

To learn more about C. S. and Joy Lewis, read the following:

- Lewis's own account of his reaction to Joy's death: *A Grief Observed*. Get the Bantam edition with Chad Walsh's Afterword, which is one of the best short biographies of Lewis available.

- Best biography of C. S. Lewis—George Sayer, *Jack: A Life of C. S. Lewis*, Crossway Books.

- Best biography of Joy—Lyle Dorsett, *And God Came In*, Crossway Books.

- See the autobiography by Douglas Gresham, Joy's son and Lewis's stepson, for an insider's perspective: *Lenten Lands*, Macmillan.

- For a book on Lewis's ideas about love: *The Four Loves*, Harcourt Brace, published the year Joy died.

BIBLIOGRAPHY

Barfield, Owen. Introduction to *Light on C. S. Lewis*. Ed. Jocelyn Gibb. New York: Harcourt, Brace & World, Inc., 1965.

Carrigan, Henry L. "Blending Faith and Fiction." *Publishers Weekly*, April 11, 1994, 28.

Coghill, Nevill. "The Approach to English," in *Light on C. S. Lewis*. Ed. Jocelyn Gibb. New York: Harcourt, Brace & World, Inc., 1965, 51-66.

Como, James. "*Shadowlands:* 'Even Though . . . '?" *Seven* (Vol. 11), 1994,: 31-33.

Davis, Donna. *Mere Lewis Digest*, Internet, merelewis@listserv.aol.com March 15, 1995.

Dorsett, Lyle. *And God Came In*. New York: Macmillan, 1983; Wheaton, IL: Crossway Books, 1991.

_____. Unpublished letter to Wayne Martindale. June 23, 1996.

Edwards, Bruce L. "*Shadowlands*: A Review." On *C. S. Lewis and the Inklings Web Site*, 1996.

Goss, Leonard. Phone interview, May 22, 1996.

Grant, Myrna. "Norman Stone, Interviewed by Myrna Grant, Summer 1994." *Seven 11*, 1994, 46-48.

Gresham, Douglas. E-mail letter to Wayne Martindale, May 20, 1996.

_____. "From the Inside." *Seven* (Vol. 11), 1994, 35-37.

_____. *Lenten Lands*. New York: Macmillan, 1988, 132-33.

Kachur, Robert M. "Abusing Christina." *Books & Culture*, July/August 1996, 17.

Lewis, C. S. *A Grief Observed*. New York: Bantam, 1976.

_____. *The Four Loves*. New York: Harcourt Brace Jovanovich, 1960.

_____. Unpublished letter to Ruth Pitter, Whitsunday, May 25, 1947, in Wade Center, Wheaton College, #025.

_____. Unpublished letter to Ruth Pitter, May 12, 1953, in Wade Center, Wheaton College, #061.

Lindskoog, Kathryn. "*Shadowlands* Revisited." Letter to Editor in *Cornerstone*, Vol. 23, No. 104, 1994, 4.

Matthews, Anthony. *Mere Lewis Digest*, Internet. March 15, 1995.

Mattingly, Terry. "Hollywood's *Shadowlands*." *Moody Monthly*, October 1994, 28.

_____. "*Shadowlands* Misses the Truth of Christian Writer's Deep Faith." From Pasadena, CA, newspaper in Wade Center file, title not given. Scripps Howard News Service article, January 29, 1994, A8.

Mead, Marjorie Lamp. "*Shadowlands* Observed." *Seven* (Vol. 11), 1994, 23-24.

Morrow, Molly. *Mere Lewis Digest*, Internet. April 22, 1996, quoting M. Taylor.

Pollack, Dave. *Mere Lewis Digest*, Internet. April 29, 1996.

Sayer, George. "The De-Christianisation of a Christian Love Story." *Seven* (Vol. 11), 1994, 29-31.

_____. *Jack: A Life of C. S. Lewis*. Second Edition. Wheaton, IL: Crossway Books, 1994.

Schakel, Peter. "The Importance of Shadows in *Shadowlands*." *Seven* (Vol. 11), 1994, 25-29.

Shadowlands Press Kit.

Sobran, Joseph. "Listening to God." *The Wanderer*, December 14, 1995, n.p.

Theophilus [pen name]. "Theophilus on C. S. Lewis," on John Visser's web site: *Into the Wardrobe: The C. S. Lewis WWW Page*, http://www.cache.net/~john/cslewis/, 1996.

Inadvertent Evangelism

Tickle, Phyllis. Religion Books section of Forecasts feature. *Publishers Weekly*, (Vol. 243, No. 7), February 12, 1996, 71.

Walsh, Chad. Afterword in C. S. Lewis, *A Grief Observed*. New York: Bantam, 1976.

Wheeler, Carla. "For the Love of Lewis." *The Sun*, San Diego, January 30, 1994, H5.

Wood, Ralph C. "The Tears of Things." *Christian Century*, February 23, 1994, 200-202.

Young, Bruce. *Mere Lewis Digest*, Internet. June 12, 1995.

NOTES

1. For a fuller discussion of "Shadowlands" imagery, see Schakel, "The Importance of Shadows in *Shadowlands*," 25-29.

2. In *Mere Christianity* (Book III, Chapter 11), Lewis uses the parallel metaphor of swimming in comparing religious faith to the natural faith a swimmer has that he or she won't drown when learning to swim. In both cases, the metaphor emphasizes risk and the paradoxical fact that a certain kind of acquiescence in the face of felt danger is ultimately safer than fighting, which may in fact drown a person (in unbelief).

3. Ibid., 26.

4. Myrna Grant, "Norman Stone, Interviewed," 46-48.

5. Molly Morrow, *Mere Lewis Digest*. It is not hard to find anecdotes of people who have been positively affected by the film. These anecdotes have all been taken from the Internet and are subject to public view and verification by anyone with computer access.

6. Theophilus [pen name], "Theophilus on C. S. Lewis," 1.

7. Young, *Mere Lewis Digest*.

8. Davis, *Mere Lewis Digest*.

9. Matthews, *Mere Lewis Digest* (some punctuation corrected).

10. Pollack, *Mere Lewis Digest* (spelling corrected in quote).

11. Mead, "*Shadowlands* Observed," 23.

12. Wheeler, "For the Love of Lewis," H5.

13. Gresham, E-mail, 1.

14. Gresham, interview.

15. Goss, interview.

16. Dorsett, letter. Note: Every version of *Shadowlands* has owed a great and unacknowledged debt to this biography.

17. Goss, interview. Both biographies were hardbacks with other publishers before they were paperbacks with Crossway.

18. Carrigan, "Blending Faith and Fiction," 28.

19. Tickle, 71.

20. Lewis quoted in Wood, "The Tears of Things," 200.

21. Gresham, "From the Inside," 35.

22. Lindskoog, "*Shadowlands* Revisited," 4.

23. Sayer, "The De-Christianisation of a Christian Love Story," 30.

24. Ibid.

25. Mattingly, "*Shadowlands* Misses the Truth of Christian Writer's Deep Faith," A8.

26. Lewis, *A Grief Observed*, 3.

27. Barfield, Introduction.

28. Coghill, "The Approach to English," 66.

29. Walsh, 97-98.

30. Lewis, letter to Ruth Pitter (Bodleian shelfmark MS. Eng. lett. c.220/3, fol. 47), 25.

31. Lewis, letter to Ruth Pitter (Bodleian shelfmark MS. Eng. lett. c.220/3, fol. 115), 61.

32. Sayer, *Jack: A Life of C. S. Lewis*, 423.

33. Mattingly, "*Shadowlands* Misses the Truth of Christian Writer's Deep Faith," A8.

34. Mattingly, "Hollywood's *Shadowlands*," 28.

35. Edwards, "*Shadowlands*: A Review."

36. Sobran, "Listening to God."

37. Grant, "Norman Stone, Interviewed," 47.

38. Gresham, "From the Inside," 36.

39. Gresham, *Lenten Lands*, 132-33.

40. Lewis, *The Four Loves*, 169.

41. Press Kit, 4.

42. Ibid., 26.

43. Ibid., 27.

44. Kachur, "Abusing Christina," 17.

45. Dorsett, *And God Came In*, 8.

46. Gresham, *Lenten Lands*, 32.

47. Lewis, *The Four Loves*, 190-92.

WINSOME EVANGELIST:

The Influence of C. S. Lewis

PHILIP G. RYKEN

In the autumn of 1996, on the occasion of its fortieth anniversary, *Christianity Today* attempted to identify the "books that have shaped American evangelicals in the last 40 years." The magazine concluded that "one author's books indisputably affected American evangelicals during this period more than . . . those of any of the other authors mentioned. . . . I mean, of course, C. S. Lewis."[1] Of course. Who else?

Not that the impact of Lewis has been limited to evangelicalism. C. S. Lewis holds sway among mere Christians everywhere. At the same time *Christianity Today* was celebrating its birthday, another publication (*Touchstone*) was rightly advertising Lewis as "an ally we all trust," Protestants, Catholics, and Orthodox alike.[2]

The marriage of British erudition to American consumerism has produced a marketing sensation. As one writer whimsically observed in *The Virginia Quarterly Review*:

> . . . [T]he Lewis devotee (and there are many, judging from the sales figures) could, upon rising, don his C. S. Lewis sweatshirt, ascertain the date from his C. S. Lewis calendar, make coffee wearing his C. S. Lewis apron and drink it from his C. S. Lewis mug, offer devotion to his Maker in the words of C. S. Lewis, and meditate on what C. S. had done on that date, before set-

The Influence of C. S. Lewis

ting off to work or school with his C. S. Lewis tote bag filled with C. S. Lewis books.[3]

Just how influential has C. S. Lewis been? One way to answer that question would be to quantify the sale of his books. The numbers are impressive. As many as 100 Lewis-related titles are in print at any given time.[4] Roughly two million copies of his works are sold every year in the United States and the United Kingdom.[5] According to one estimate, Lewis is the best-selling Christian author of all time, with some forty million copies in print.[6] He may also be the most frequently-quoted Christian author of all time.[7]

The trouble with statistics is that, although they can lie, they cannot tell stories. The important thing about C. S. Lewis is not how many people have read him, but the extent to which reading him has become a life-transforming experience. Popularity is not the same thing as influence; C. S. Lewis has had both.

C. S. Lewis is usually considered to have had a substantial influence on atheists, agnostics, and other unbelievers. In the first critical study of his thought, Chad Walsh identified him as the Apostle to the Skeptics.[8] One often sees references to the "numerous" or even "countless" people whom C. S. Lewis has brought to faith in Jesus Christ. To cite just one example, the evangelist Stephen F. Olford speaks of knowing "not just scores, but hundreds of intellectual people . . . [who] have come to Christ subsequent to reading [*Mere Christianity*]."[9]

Although the influence of C. S. Lewis is widely assumed, it has never been adequately documented. The purpose of this chapter is to describe the effectiveness of his work as an evangelist. Some questions one might like to answer—such as "How many souls did Lewis help save?"—are necessarily unanswerable. One reason his converts seem countless is that there is no good way to count them.

Among the questions that can be answered, there are one or two surprises. For one thing, C. S. Lewis was not very aggressive at personal evangelism.[10] For another, he seems to have been more gifted at internal evangelism (within the church) than at external evangelism (outside the church). In other words, he has been more successful at keeping people in the kingdom than ushering them in to begin with. Yet there are some valuable lessons to be learned from the evangelism of C. S. Lewis. His life is a portrait of the winsome evangelist: gifted in teaching, persuasive in writing, fervent in prayer, and thorough in discipling.

The Teaching Evangelist

C. S. Lewis was a man of firm evangelistic convictions. So strong was his fervor for the Christian Gospel that he became an object of ridicule to colleagues and a source of embarrassment to friends, even among the Inklings. For Lewis the salvation of human souls was "the real business of life."[11]

Yet the example of C. S. Lewis also challenges some evangelical stereotypes about how an evangelist ought to behave. He was not always winsome in the sense of being charming and engaging. He did not stand in the Oxford City Centre calling passersby to repentance. It was not his usual practice to ask students or colleagues if they had a "personal relationship with Jesus Christ." Nor did he go door-to-door in Headington Quarry passing out tracts and asking his neighbors, "If you were to die tonight . . ."

On occasion, Lewis seemed even reluctant to evangelize. His long-time driver, Clifford Morris, observed that he rarely used casual conversation as a context for evangelism. In Morris's words, C. S. Lewis "was no sort of Billy Graham type, at all." Perhaps this was because he was convinced that "[w]hat we practise, not what we preach, is usually our great contribution to the conversion of others."[12] It may also have been due to his awareness of "the risk of making a nuisance of ourselves by witnessing at improper times."[13]

C. S. Lewis was especially reticent to speak of his Christian faith to his students. When the noted ecclesiastical historian A. G. Dickens went to him for undergraduate tutorials, he observed that "Lewis never behaved as a Christian apologist. He wasn't a sort of heavyweight Christian."[14] Lewis's eventual biographer George Sayer was scarcely aware of his tutor's faith at all:

The Influence of C. S. Lewis

. . . [F]or the first two years when I was being tutored by him, I did not realize he was a Christian. He'd never brought Christianity up, and indeed I think he thought it would have been wrong and improper for him to have influenced his pupils in that sort of way. But when I remarked rather casually, I think in my third year, that I'd become a Roman Catholic, well he said, "Good. I'm glad you've become a Christian of some sort."[15]

The experience of Harry Blamires was much the same. It was not until nearly a decade after Blamires had been a student of Lewis that the two men discussed "religious matters."[16]

One place where C. S. Lewis's teaching did assume an evangelistic purpose was the Oxford University Socratic Club, which he served as president from 1941 to 1954. The Socratic Club was open to atheists, agnostics, and believers alike. From the beginning, its purpose was to encourage people to start "facing the question, is the Christian faith true, or not?" Meetings began with a talk on a religious subject by a prominent speaker, followed by vigorous open debate. Lewis always figured prominently in the disputations, and he always argued from the distinctively Christian point of view.

The founder of the Socratic Club, Stella Aldwinckle, also remembers Lewis attending a week-long house party during a vacation in 1943. The purpose of the party was to nurture students who were beginning to get serious about the Christian faith. Of the twelve agnostics in attendance, the full dozen returned to university professing faith in Jesus Christ.[17] The success of the holiday suggests how winsome Lewis could be as a personal evangelist.

C. S. Lewis's involvement with other student groups was less intimate. To some he came as the apostle Paul came to the Corinthians, "in weakness, and in fear, and in much trembling" (1 Corinthians 2:3, KJV). Lady Elizabeth Catherwood recalls Lewis's reluctance to be overtly associated with the Oxford Intercollegiate Christian Union (OICCU). On one of the rare occasions upon which he agreed to speak to the OICCU, his topic was "What is Christianity?" Catherwood describes the address as a "really splendid, perfect talk." Lewis presented four facts upon which Christianity depends: the fact of God, the fact of man, the fact of sin, and the fact of salvation.

After the address, a member of the audience stood up and asked, "You know, Dr. Lewis, in the light of all you've been saying, this is clearly of vital importance to us all. If everything you're saying is true, what do we do about it?" Lewis's reply was blunt: "God forbid, sir, that I should intervene in such a personal matter. Go and talk to your priest about that."[18] This was hardly winsome evangelism, yet the remark should not be misunderstood as petulance or indifference. C. S. Lewis viewed himself as an apologist rather than a preacher. He was an evangelist of a particular kind—a teaching evangelist—and he was always careful to observe the limitations of his gifts for evangelism.

Lewis's sense of his evangelistic limitations can be illustrated best from the approach he took in his talks to the Royal Air Force. Early in World War II, a mother who lost her pilot son in combat provided money for the YMCA to sponsor evangelistic work among pilots in training. The intent was for the RAF chaplaincy to wage war on "The Forgotten Front"—the spiritual front. C. S. Lewis was an obvious choice for a speaker. Though initially skeptical of his suitability for the task, Lewis accepted invitations to speak at RAF bases and camps throughout the summer of 1942.

Accounts of the effectiveness of the RAF talks vary. By Lewis's own account they started badly. Scarcely a handful of men attended his first addresses, and there was little response afterwards. As Lewis confessed to Sister Penelope, "I've given talks to the RAF at Abingdon already, and so far as I can judge, they were a complete failure."[19] The impression is sometimes given that the rest of the talks were equally ineffective as evangelism. George Sayer concluded that members of the RAF were "put off by his cool, rational approach, by the lack of emotional and obvious devotional content."[20] Canon H. A. Blair thought the talks featured C. S. Lewis "at his most characteristic, which is just clear 'I'm telling you clear sense.'" Yet Blair denied that they had an evangelistic thrust ("It wasn't evangelistic. It wasn't in the sense of being a conversion talk. It wasn't any kind of hot gospelling").[21]

The Influence of C. S. Lewis

These assessments seem unduly negative. Stuart Barton Babbage recounts a memorable meeting in Norfolk at which Lewis bared his soul to a chapel packed with bomber squadrons. He spoke winsomely about the personal cost of his own discipleship and about the greater cost of Christ's obedience.[22] Bishop A. W. Goodwin-Hudson, then an RAF chaplain, was enthusiastic about the response of his men to Lewis's presentation of the Gospel. After their first meeting, Goodwin-Hudson hurriedly telephoned his wife to say, "We've had a wonderful response tonight and some of the cream of English manhood have come forward to talk to us and to confess Christ as Saviour and Lord."

Lewis was both moved and humbled by this experience:

"Haddon [as Lewis affectionately called him, due to his confusion about Goodwin-Hudson's name when they first met on a railway platform], I wish I could do the heart stuff." He said, "I can't. I wish I could." He said, "I wish I could press home to these boys just how much they need Christ. . . . Haddon, you do the heart stuff and I'll do the head stuff."[23]

The two men agreed that Lewis would continue presenting a twenty-minute case for Christianity, after which Goodwin-Hudson would issue a passionate gospel appeal.

A similar strategy was employed when C. S. Lewis spoke at a "This Is Life" Crusade at Dr. Martyn Lloyd-Jones's Westminster Chapel in London. Lewis gave a convincing testimony of his own commitment to Christ. This was followed by a gospel invitation from Stephen F. Olford, to which there was a tremendous response.[24] Perhaps Lewis had these experiences in mind when he later wrote:

I am not sure that the ideal missionary team ought not to consist of one who argues and one who (in the fullest sense of the word) preaches. Put up your arguer first to undermine their intellectual prejudices; then let the evangelist proper launch his appeal. I have seen this done with great success.[25]

C. S. Lewis, of course, was the evangelistic set-up man, the arguer and underminer of intellectual prejudice.

Lewis's distinction between "the heart stuff" and "the head stuff" yields an important insight about evangelism. Although every Christian has a responsibility to evangelize, not all evangelists are created equal. "It was [Christ] who gave some to be apostles, some to be prophets, some to be evangelists, and some to be pastors and teachers" (Ephesians 4:11). Although his ministry had an apostolic flavor, C. S. Lewis was not, strictly speaking, an apostle. Nor was he a man of pastoral temper, as his reluctance to do "the heart stuff" indicates. Instead, C. S. Lewis was a teaching evangelist. His particular gift was to defend the reasonableness of the Christian faith with strong arguments expressed in simple terms.

The radio talks C. S. Lewis did for BBC radio during World War II played to his strengths as a teaching evangelist. Although he detested the radio, Lewis accepted the invitation to give the talks because he rightly expected them to reach people who would never read his books. The weekly fifteen-minute talks were given in three series between 1941 and 1944.[26] They were then published as booklets under the titles *Broadcast Talks* (1942), *Christian Behaviour* (1943), and *Beyond Personality* (1944). The booklets were later revised and published in a single volume as *Mere Christianity*, the book that remains Lewis's single most influential evangelistic book.

The BBC talks were a tremendous success. Lewis's vigor and no-nonsense style won him a wide hearing. Since the talks were given during the war, they reached people who were already pondering the ultimate questions of human existence (and non-existence). George Sayer recalls listening to one of the addresses with a pub full of soldiers who heeded the bartender's loud admonition to "listen to this bloke. He's really worth listening to."[27] Lewis was soon inundated with letters from listeners seeking spiritual help. A further measure of the evangelistic impact of the talks is that their published editions became immediate bestsellers.[28]

C. S. Lewis himself did not consider the broadcast talks to be evangelistic, in the strictest sense of the word:

The Influence of C. S. Lewis

> Mine are *praeparatio evangelica* rather than *evangelium*, an attempt to convince people that there is a moral law, that we disobey it, and that the existence of a Lawgiver is at least very probable and also (*unless* you add the Christian doctrine of the Atonement) that this imparts despair rather than comfort.[29]

C. S. Lewis notwithstanding, the talks were both pre-evangelism and evangelism. Once the atoning death of Jesus Christ had been introduced to the discussion, the talks became a presentation of the Gospel. If C. S. Lewis was not a radio preacher, he was at least a teaching evangelist.

THE WRITING EVANGELIST

C. S. Lewis was also a literary evangelist. Indeed, he has had a far greater evangelistic impact through his books and essays than through his tutorials and addresses combined. This is not surprising, since Lewis himself observed that most of his books were "evangelistic."[30] It is also unsurprising because of the natural intimacy between a writer and a reader. Lewis was most winsome in the pages of a book.

That Lewis was a writing evangelist is crucial to his lingering significance, for it enables his evangelistic work to transcend the limitations of time and space. As for time, "He being dead yet speaketh" (Hebrews 11:4, KJV). As for space, C. S. Lewis's ministry has extended far beyond the borders of Great Britain. His greatest influence by far has been upon the religious culture of the United States. This is despite the fact that Lewis never set foot upon American shores and treated the nation with some disdain. He once wryly observed to a pupil, "The so-called Renaissance produced three disasters: the invention of gunpowder, the invention of printing, and the discovery of America."[31]

One of Lewis's first American converts was Joy Davidman. Joy was a brilliant poet and writer raised in the Jewish community of New York City. Her path from atheism to Christianity passed through communism, as well as through a brief flirtation with Judaism.

Several spiritual experiences helped prepare the way for her conversion. One was her reading of the Old and New Testaments as a young girl. Another was her captivation by an ice storm that displayed a beauty that seemed to transcend the material world.[32] Still another was her occasional poetic writing on themes such as the crucifixion of Jesus Christ. In retrospect, it seemed as if her "inner personality" was "deeply interested in Christ and didn't know it."[33] Later Joy read *The Screwtape Letters* and *The Great Divorce* by C. S. Lewis. Although she still considered herself an atheist at the time, these books "stirred an unused part of [her] brain to momentary sluggish life."[34]

Joy's spiritual transformation was finally precipitated by the nervous breakdown of her first husband, William Lindsay Gresham.[35] Left alone and afraid by his collapse, Joy had a personal encounter with the presence of God. She described it like this: "All my defenses—the walls of arrogance and cocksureness and self-love behind which I had hid from God—went down momentarily—and God came in."[36]

Once God had come in, various Christian writers helped lead Joy to faith in Jesus Christ. Chief among these was C. S. Lewis:

> I snatched at books I had despised before. . . . I went back to C. S. Lewis and learned from him, slowly, how I had gone wrong. Without his works, I wonder if I and many others might not still be infants 'crying in the night.'[37]

Joy was so enamored by the writings of C. S. Lewis that she began to correspond with him. Their correspondence led to friendship, romance, and finally marriage.[38] Yet before C. S. Lewis became Joy's husband, he was her evangelist.

Lewis was equally influential in the conversion of Sheldon Vanauken. Vanauken was a sharp young agnostic from Virginia when he went to Oxford to study literature. Partly inspired by the soaring beauty of the University Church of St. Mary the Virgin, Vanauken determined to take a second look at Christianity. He did so as much to make sure that Christianity was not true as to discover if it was.

The first Christian books Vanauken read were the space trilogy of C. S. Lewis: *Out of the Silent Planet*, *Perelandra*, and *That Hideous Strength*. He went on to read many other Christian authors, includ-

The Influence of C. S. Lewis

ing G. K. Chesterton, Charles Williams, Graham Greene, Dorothy Sayers, and T. S. Eliot. But mostly he read everything he could find by C. S. Lewis.

Vanauken found himself on the precipice of the Christian faith but unsure how to take the next step. He wrote to C. S. Lewis for help, hoping that if Lewis could not make a leap of faith for him, he might at least "give a hint of how it's to be done."[39] A series of letters ensued, followed by a friendship. This serves as a reminder that winsome evangelism is always a form of friendship. In Vanauken's case the friendship was crucial, for he found living Christians to be among the strongest arguments for the truth of the Gospel. The two men were later drawn even closer by a shared grief: each lost the love of his life through illness.[40]

Lewis encouraged Vanauken's conversion through his letters and prayers. He soon perceived that his friend was on his way to becoming a Christian, writing, "I think you are already in the meshes of the net! The Holy Spirit is after you. I doubt if you'll get away!"[41] This terrified Vanauken, but Lewis was right. Vanauken had reached a point of no return. Not long afterwards he wrote to Lewis with news of his conversion: "I choose to believe in the Father, Son, and Holy Ghost— in Christ, my Lord and my God. . . . I confess my doubts and ask my Lord Christ to enter my life."[42] For his part, Lewis was elated:

> My prayers are answered. . . . Blessings on you and a hundred thousand welcomes. Make use of me in any way you please: and let us pray for each other always.[43]

The most famous of the American converts of C. S. Lewis remains Charles Colson, former Special Counsel to Richard M. Nixon. Often referred to as Nixon's "hatchet man," Colson was known for getting things done. As *Time* magazine put it, few men in the Nixon administration were "tougher, wilier, nastier or more tenaciously loyal to Richard Nixon." Colson was even said to have boasted that he "would walk over [his] grandmother if necessary" to get the President reelected.

As Colson was drawn into the maelstrom surrounding Watergate, he discovered that his life was empty. He was first confronted with his need for a personal relationship with Jesus Christ by Tom Phillips, president of the Raytheon Company. Phillips told Colson that "the first step" to facing God squarely was to read a book called *Mere Christianity*.

To help Colson get started, Phillips read aloud from a chapter entitled "The Great Sin." In that chapter C. S. Lewis exposes the evils of Pride. "Pride leads to every other vice: it is the complete anti-God state of mind. . . . Pride is spiritual cancer: it eats up the very possibility of love, or contentment, or even common sense."[44] These words exposed not only the evils of the Nixon administration, but the deepest sins of Colson's own heart. "Suddenly I felt naked and unclean, my bravado defenses gone. I was exposed, unprotected, for Lewis's words were describing me." Colson was not yet a Christian, but the transformation had begun. That night he begged God with many tears, "Take me, take me, take me."[45]

Colson left early the next day for a seaside vacation in Maine. He took his copy of *Mere Christianity* with him and wondered if knowing God was simply an emotional experience.

> *Perhaps*, I thought, *it is on this intuitive, emotional level that C. S. Lewis approaches God.* I opened *Mere Christianity* and found myself instead face-to-face with an intellect so disciplined, so lucid, so relentlessly logical that I could only be grateful I had never faced him in a court of law. Soon I had covered two pages of yellow paper with *pros* to my query, "Is there a God?"[46]

One by one the rest of Colson's questions began to be answered as well: "If God is good, why does He preside over such an evil world?" "If God is listening to my prayers, how can He hear those being uttered at the same time by many millions of others?"

The most important question was the one that still remained: "How does Jesus Christ figure into all this?" Here Colson was helped by Lewis's famous argument that Jesus Christ was either the Lord, a liar, or a lunatic.[47] As Colson put it, "For Christ to have talked as He talked, lived as He lived, died as He died, He was either God or a raving lunatic. . . . Lewis's question was the heart of the matter. The words—both exciting and disturbing—pounded at me: Jesus Christ—lunatic or God?"[48]

Colson was ready to make his commitment later that same evening.

> I knew the time had come for me: I could not sidestep the central question Lewis (or God) had placed squarely before me. Was I to accept without reservations Jesus Christ as Lord of my life? It was like a gate before me. There was no way to walk around it. I would step through, or I would remain outside.[49]

Charles Colson walked through the open gate to accept Jesus Christ. Indictment on charges related to Watergate, conviction, sentencing, and imprisonment were to follow, then release from prison and a national ministry to prison inmates. But the first step was to read *Mere Christianity* by C. S. Lewis.

The names of some of Lewis's other converts are also worthy of mention. Os Guinness, a gifted critic of church and culture, was converted by reading *Mere Christianity* as an Irish schoolboy.[50] C. E. M. Joad, professor of philosophy at the University of London, was an ardent defender of atheism before being converted by reading *The Problem of Pain*.[51] Chad Walsh is the writer and critic who first grasped the significance of C. S. Lewis for the American church. Walsh was "slowly thinking, feeling, and fumbling" his way toward the Christian faith, but his faith was "more of the mind than of the imagination and heart." When he read *Perelandra*, he finally "got the taste and smell of Christian truth. My senses as well as my soul were baptized."[52] Like Colson, Walsh was eventually helped to recognize the deity of Jesus Christ by pondering the "Lord or lunatic" dilemma posed in *Mere Christianity*.[53]

These brief conversion narratives remind us that evangelism is a team effort. Since the salvation of a soul rests upon a complex of experiences and relationships, each of these men and women was drawn to Christ by a web of influences. C. S. Lewis served merely as first among equals in the conversion process. Lewis himself was careful not to exaggerate the significance of his own involvement: "My feeling about people in whose conversion I have been allowed to play a part is always mixed with awe and even fear."[54]

There is another reason to avoid giving C. S. Lewis more credit than he deserves for these conversions. Coming to faith is never the work of a human being; it is always the work of the Holy Spirit (cf. John 3:8). A Christian testimony is a story about the grace of God, not a story about one's own spiritual development or the influence of friends and writers. What saved these converts was the death and resurrection of Jesus Christ. What convinced them to put their trust in Jesus Christ was the Spirit of Christ speaking through the Word of God. As C. S. Lewis once reminded his American readers, "We must remember that neither Paul nor Apollos gives the increase" (see 1 Corinthians 3:6).[55]

THE PRAYING EVANGELIST

It would be easy to miss the significance of what C. S. Lewis wrote to Sheldon Vanauken on the occasion of his conversion: "My prayers are answered." On the lips of some Christians this would be little more than a cliché. For C. S. Lewis, however, prayer was the foundation for effective evangelism. If conversion is a work of the Holy Spirit, and if the work of the Holy Spirit is often prompted by the prayers of believers, then prayer is indispensable to the evangelist.

In the summer of 1949 C. S. Lewis wrote a letter to Dom Bede Griffiths, a Benedictine monk and a former pupil in need of encouragement:

> I think a glance at my correspondence would cheer you up; letter after letter from recent converts, by ones and by twos, often (which is most hopeful) married couples with children . . . it amounts to nothing by the standards of world statistics. But are they the right standards? I sometimes have a feeling that the big mass conversions of the Dark Ages, often carried out by force, were all a false dawn, and that the whole work has to be done over again. . . . Oh, by the way, Barfield was baptised last Saturday: have him in your prayers.

The Influence of C. S. Lewis

> I have two lists of names in my prayers, those for whose
> conversion I pray and those for whose conversion I give thanks.
> The little trickle of *transferences* from List A to List B is a great
> comfort.[56]

This letter is significant for several reasons. First, it gives a hint of
the evangelistic influence of Lewis, with a steady stream of new converts always contacting him by mail. Second, it includes a helpful
caveat about the dangers of quantifying salvation. Most importantly,
it offers a glimpse of C. S. Lewis as a praying evangelist. He made it
his regular practice to pray for the unconverted by name, and to give
thanks to God when those prayers were answered. This practice also
extended to his books, for which he prayed that God would help him
"say things helpful to salvation."[57]

THE DISCIPLING EVANGELIST

In 1986 an unscientific survey was taken to determine the extent of
the influence of C. S. Lewis in the United States. The following adver-
tisement was placed in publications such as *Christian Century*,
Christianity Today, *Eternity*, and *The New York Times Book Review*:

> The Marion E. Wade Collection is seeking evidence of the impact
> of C. S. Lewis and his writing on people's lives. If you or others
> whom you know have been markedly influenced by Lewis, will
> you please write to us and share your reminiscences.[58]

Dozens of lengthy responses were received from America and around
the world.

Several respondents testified that C. S. Lewis had been influential
in their coming to Christ in the first instance. A theology student at
Berkeley explained that his "adult conversion to the faith [he] had
been raised in" was "guided by C. S. Lewis." A classicist chanced upon
a copy of *The Pilgrim's Regress* in a New York City bookshop, bought
it, started reading it that night, and discovered that he had become a

Christian by three o'clock the following morning. Lyle Dorsett wrote that during his days as a professor of history at Denver University, C. S. Lewis and G. K. Chesterton "were instrumental in moving me from agnosticism to faith in Jesus Christ." In each of these instances the writings of C. S. Lewis were decisive in an individual conversion to the Christian faith.

Other respondents used Lewis as a partner in their own evangelistic efforts. A minister from Pennsylvania wrote of "haunting the rows of shelves in used-book stores in a relentless search for used copies of *Mere Christianity*" to give away. An English professor at Arizona State University reported, "Several students in my university classes on Lewis have been converted, receiving Jesus Christ as their Savior, as a result of reading and discussing *Mere Christianity*." A Welsh mathematician remembered his father keeping copies of the same book in his glove compartment to give to hitchhikers. Thus one aspect of Lewis's influence has been to help other Christians become active evangelists. A questionnaire filled out by new Presbyterian missionaries during the 1950s revealed that C. S. Lewis had influenced more people to go to the mission field than all other names combined.[59]

The majority of those who responded to the Wade Center query did not write conversion narratives. Instead, men and women from all walks of life wanted to tell how C. S. Lewis had helped them stay on the pilgrim road. A lonely woman struggling with an unwanted pregnancy read and reread *A Grief Observed*. There "every feeling and thought I was having seemed to be written—anger, anguish, denial, hopelessness and the most burning one—who and where is God when we hurt." A professor of English wrote, "His apologetics helped settle and confirm my own faith." Another academic had allowed "high powered math and modern physics" to displace his faith almost entirely. When he read *The Screwtape Letters* his faith "came roaring back—adamant, larger than ever it had been." For a woman trapped in "dry, duty-bound orthodoxy," reading *Mere Christianity* was a "world-shaking event" that led to a "renewal or rebirth of spiritual vitality and fervor." For a student at a fundamentalist university, recently converted from Roman Catholicism, "it was C. S. Lewis who

The Influence of C. S. Lewis

provided a wonderful sense of Christian sanity in a warped, bitter environment." Lewis's apologetics arguments helped a woman from Stuyvesant "keep the faith," kept a student from Wheaton College "within orthodox Christianity," and enabled a bored Christian student in Akron to find "the Lord and God I had always longed for."

These testimonies conform to what one writer has called "an almost archetypal pattern in the lives of countless(!!) evangelical students of the past three decades":

> First in the traditional pattern of appreciating Lewis came a period of gnawing doubt about the whole Christian faith. . . . Into this dark night of the soul swept whatever happened to be the student's first Lewis book. That led inexorably to the others. And what he or she found there was not so much answers—though they were wonderful beyond all hope—but more, an irrefutable demonstration that at least one Christian mind actually existed.[60]

Such men and women were already Christians when they first encountered C. S. Lewis. He did not so much bring them to faith as keep them in the faith.[61] The value of this should not be underestimated. Part of the purpose of apologetics is to shore up the intellectual defenses of Christianity when they start to crumble. This apologetic work is as necessary inside as it is outside the church. Internal evangelism is as valuable as external evangelism. What is the use of rescuing lost sheep if the sheep already in the fold are wandering off, or worse, being pilfered by hungry wolves?

C. S. Lewis did not simply make and keep converts, he also discipled them. Nearly all those who responded to the 1986 survey explained that C. S. Lewis taught them how to live the Christian life. Some even spoke of him as a "mentor." A pastor from Maryland reckoned that, with the exception of the Bible, the writings of C. S. Lewis had done "more to shape [him] spiritually than any other influence." A Newbery medalist wrote that the characters in the Narnia Chronicles had shaped her understanding of patience as a virtue. Lewis's writings on English literature helped guide a doctoral student in her study of medieval literature. A student worker from West Germany spoke for all: "The impact of Lewis for me is that his words and thoughts have, to a certain extent, become my words and thoughts and have penetrated my lifestyle, my world-view, my values and attitudes."

A further attempt to solicit testimonies of the influence of C. S. Lewis was made via electronic mail in 1996. Visitors to one or another C. S. Lewis home page on the Internet were encouraged to tell their stories "about the influence of C. S. Lewis on [their] conversion to faith in Jesus Christ or on [their] subsequent Christian pilgrimage."[62]

Answers to this question followed a pattern similar to the one that emerged from the earlier survey. One or two respondents spoke of owing their salvation to C. S. Lewis. A former atheist, for example, wrote that Lewis helped him see "that if I was going to deny God's existence, I had better be prepared to explain why I sometimes wished so desperately that He did [exist]." Another young man was so convinced that Christianity was a hoax perpetuated by "hucksters and vain pompous types seeking fame and glory" that he was stunned when he was unable to rebut the arguments made in *Mere Christianity*.

Other respondents explained how C. S. Lewis kept them in the church. A man struggling with spiritual doubt identified Lewis's "logical arguments for the existence of God and the deity of Christ" as "the single most important factor in coming to complete and total belief in Christ." A seminarian testified that when he read *Mere Christianity*, "for the first time in my life I found solid reasons to bolster my belief." A lapsed Catholic explained how reading Lewis helped shepherd him back into the Roman church, especially because "the evangelical experience C. S. L. himself lived was so close in so many ways to the Catholic experience." Another Christian rejoiced that C. S. Lewis had inspired "a whole new commitment to my Lord and Saviour which grows fresher every day."

The Internet survey again revealed the importance of C. S. Lewis for Christian discipleship. In the words of one respondent, "Lewis has not been a solution for my sins, Christ has already taken care of that, but he has been a comfort in my daily struggle to be a better Christian." A Fortune 500 consultant allowed Lewis's thoughts about materialism and idolatry to shape his dealings with business clients. A Texas lawyer found in C. S. Lewis the authentic Christianity for which he had long yearned, free from the hypocrisy of outward appearances. Another man discovered the grace and joy to overcome his legalistic background by reading Lewis's preface to *Letters to Young Churches*, the J. B. Phillips translation of the New Testament epistles. A fourth grade teacher read the Narnia Chronicles to her students every year, hoping that the books would introduce them to the joy of life in Christ. Upon reading *The Abolition of Man*, a student at a midwestern Bible college devoted his life to presenting absolute truth to Generation X. C. S. Lewis has helped all kinds of Christians follow the Lord in all kinds of ways.

One striking feature of both the 1986 and 1996 surveys was the eagerness with which respondents wrote of their hope to meet C. S. Lewis in heaven. As they told the stories of their encounters with his writings, they spoke of him with an affection usually reserved for close friends. For C. S. Lewis and his readers, even literary evangelism can become a form of personal, winsome, friendship evangelism.

The foregoing testimonials suggest an important conclusion: the primary influence of C. S. Lewis has been in the area of Christian discipleship. That is to say, his primary impact has been to help people become disciples of the Lord Jesus Christ in heart, mind, and will. The unscientific nature of the evidence forces this conclusion to fall short of solid proof. Still, it seems stronger than a mere hypothesis. C. S. Lewis has been a disciple-maker as much as a soul-winner. However many people he has brought into the church, he has helped many more to think and act biblically once they arrived.

Much of the vast correspondence of C. S. Lewis also falls under the category of discipleship. Some of the letters Lewis received came from unbelievers who were curious about the Christian faith. A great many more came from Christians seeking pastoral counsel. These correspondents wrote to Lewis with doctrinal questions, spiritual burdens, and personal problems. To answer such letters was to become a discipling evangelist. One illuminating example comes from one of the Latin letters Lewis wrote to Don Giovanni Calabria, himself a venerable priest and the founder of an Italian orphanage:

You write much about your sins. Beware (permit me, my dearest Father, to say beware) lest humility should pass over into anxiety or sadness.[63]

Here Lewis was a pastor—counseling, confronting, and consoling.

The lives of Lewis's converts show that he has been most influential in the discipleship of the Christian mind, or perhaps the Christian imagination. Men and women such as Joy Davidman, Sheldon Vanauken, Charles Colson, and Os Guinness have gone on to make outstanding contributions to the imaginative and intellectual life of the church. Joy Davidman is something of a special case, of course, since Christian marriage is always a covenant of discipleship. Yet the others were also shaped by the mind of C. S. Lewis. His work reversed Charles Colson's view of politics, for example, by convincing him that the individual is more important than the state.[64]

One does not have to be a convert of C. S. Lewis to be discipled by him. Harry Blamires's valuable book *The Christian Mind* bears the unmistakable stamp of C. S. Lewis.[65] Clyde Kilby, a professor at Wheaton College, devoted much of his career to sharing his love for Lewis with colleagues, readers, and students. It is not surprising that many who responded to the 1986 and 1996 surveys work in fields that value the life of the mind: teaching, pastoral ministry, law, and the arts. A survey taken in 1984 identified C. S. Lewis as one of the leading half-dozen influences upon a generation of evangelical Bible scholars.[66] One sign that his intellectual influence is waxing rather than waning is the increasing amount of academic analysis his works are receiving.[67] Still another way Lewis continues to shape the Christian mind is through C. S. Lewis Societies in places like California, New York, Canada, Oxford, and Japan.

To emphasize the role of C. S. Lewis as a discipler of the Christian mind is not to diminish his stature as an evangelist. A good evangelist is a discipling evangelist. Fulfilling the Great Commission entails more than simply "going into all the world." It also includes "teaching them to observe all things whatsoever I have commanded you" (Matthew 28:20a, KJV). As a discipler of the mind and imagination, C. S. Lewis continues to be a winsome evangelist.

The Influence of C. S. Lewis

BIBLIOGRAPHY

Aldwinckle, Stella. Audio Interview, Oxford, England, July 26, 1985. Marion E. Wade Center, Wheaton College, Wheaton, IL.

Babbage, Stuart Barton. "C. S. Lewis Meets the R.A.F. (and Vice Versa)." *Eternity*, August 1971, 15, 26.

Blair, Canon H. A. Video Interview, Sherborne, England, July 28, 1984. Marion E. Wade Center, Wheaton College, Wheaton, IL.

Blamires, Harry. *The Christian Mind*. London: S.P.C.K., 1963.

_____. Video Interview, Wheaton, IL, October 23, 1983. Marion E. Wade Center, Wheaton College, Wheaton, IL.

Bradshaw, Norman. "Impressions of a Pupil," in *In Search of C. S. Lewis*. Ed. Stephen Schofield. South Plainfield, NJ: Bridge, 1983, 17-27.

"C. S. Lewis Testimonies," Marion E. Wade Center, Wheaton College, Wheaton, IL.

Catherwood, Lady Elizabeth. Audio Interview, Wheaton, IL, August 3, 1991. Marion E. Wade Center, Wheaton College, Wheaton, IL.

Colson, Charles W. *Born Again*. Old Tappan, NJ: Chosen, 1976.

Davidman, Joy. "The Longest Way Round," in *These Found the Way: Thirteen Converts to Protestant Christianity*. Ed. David Wesley Soper. Philadelphia: Westminster, 1951, 13-26.

Dickens, A. G. Audio Interview, London, England, April 17, 1989. Marion E. Wade Center, Wheaton College, Wheaton, IL.

Dorsett, Lyle W. *And God Came In*. Revised Edition. Wheaton, IL: Crossway, 1991.

_____. "Lewis, (C)live (S)taples (1898-1963)," in *Dictionary of Christianity in America*. Ed. Daniel G. Reid. Downers Grove, IL: InterVarsity, 1990, 644-45.

Edwards, Bruce L., ed. *The Taste of the Pineapple: Essays on C. S. Lewis as Reader, Critic, and Imaginative Writer*. Bowling Green, OH: Bowling Green State University Popular Press, 1988.

Goodwin-Hudson, A. W. Audio Interview, Forest Falls, CA. Marion E. Wade Center, Wheaton College, Wheaton, IL.

Gresham, William Lindsay. "From Communist to Christian," in *These Found the Way: Thirteen Converts to Protestant Christianity*. Ed. David Wesley Soper. Philadelphia: Westminster, 1951, 65-82.

Guinness, Os. "'Fools for Christ, Foolmakers for Christ'—The Recovery of Persuasive Christian Advocacy." *Journal of the Irish Christian Study Centre*, 1984 (Vol. 2), 1-11.

Lewis, Clive Staples. *The Abolition of Man*. London: Oxford, 1943.

_____. "Christian Apologetics," in *God in the Dock: Essays on Theology and Ethics*. Ed. Walter Hooper. Grand Rapids, MI: Eerdmans, 1970, 89-103.

_____. "Christianity and Culture," in *Christian Reflections*. Ed. Walter Hooper. Grand Rapids, MI: Eerdmans, 1967, 12-36.

_____. Correspondence to Dom Bede Griffiths, Camaldoleze Benedictine Monastery, India. Marion E. Wade Center, Wheaton College, Wheaton, IL.

_____. Correspondence to Sister Penelope, St. Mary the Virgin, Wantage, England. Marion E. Wade Center, Wheaton College, Wheaton, IL.

_____. "Cross-Examination," in *God in the Dock: Essays on Theology and Ethics*. Ed. Walter Hooper. Grand Rapids, MI: Eerdmans, 1970, 258-67.

_____. "I Was Decided Upon" (interview with Sherwood E. Wirt). *Decision*, September 1963 (Vol. 3, No. 3), 3.

_____. *Letters of C. S. Lewis*. Ed. W. H. Lewis. New York: Harcourt Brace Jovanovich, 1966.

_____. *Mere Christianity*. New York: Macmillan, 1952.

_____. *Perelandra*. London: John Lane, 1943.

_____. "A Rejoinder to Dr Pittenger," in *God in the Dock: Essays on Theology and Ethics*. Ed. Walter Hooper. Grand Rapids, MI: Eerdmans, 1970, 177-83.

_____. *The Screwtape Letters*. London: Geoffrey Bles, 1942.

Martindale, Wayne and Jerry Root, eds. *The Quotable Lewis*. Wheaton, IL: Tyndale, 1989.

Morris, Clifford. Video Interview, Oxford, England, May 27, 1986. Marion E. Wade Center, Wheaton College, Wheaton, IL.

Moynihan, Martin. *The Latin Letters of C. S. Lewis*. Wheaton, IL: Crossway Books, 1987.

Nelson, Michael. "C. S. Lewis and His Critics." *The Virginia Quarterly Review*, Winter 1988 (Vol. 64, No. 1), 1-19.

Noll, Mark A. *Between Faith and Criticism: Evangelicals, Scholarship, and the Bible*. Second Edition. Grand Rapids, MI: Baker, 1991.

Olford, Stephen F. Video Interview, Wheaton, IL, November 7, 1983. Marion E. Wade Center, Wheaton College, Wheaton, IL.

Person, James E., Jr. "The Legacy of C. S. Lewis." *Modern Age: The Republic of Arts and Letters*, Summer 1991 (No. 334), 409-11.

Phillips, J. B. *Letters to Young Churches*. London: Geoffrey Bles, 1947.

Ryken, Leland. *The Christian Imagination: Essays on Literature and the Arts*. Grand Rapids, MI: Baker, 1981.

Sayer, George. Audio Interview, Malvern, England, October 10, 12, 1989. Marion E. Wade Center, Wheaton College, Wheaton, IL.

Sayer, George. *Jack: A Life of C. S. Lewis*. Second Edition. Wheaton, IL: Crossway, 1994.

Schofield, Stephen. "Impact," in *In Search of C. S. Lewis*. Ed. Stephen Schofield. South Plainfield, NJ: Bridge, 1983, 131-44.

Stackhouse, John G., Jr. "By Their Books Ye Shall Know Them." *Christianity Today*, September 16, 1996, 58-59.

Vanauken, Sheldon. *Encounter with Light*. Wheaton, IL: Marion E. Wade Collection, Wheaton College, Wheaton, IL

————. *A Severe Mercy*. New York: Harper and Row, 1979.

Walsh, Chad. *C. S. Lewis: Apostle to the Skeptics*. New York: Macmillan, 1949.

————. "Impact on America," in *Light on C. S. Lewis*. Ed. Jocelyn Gibb. New York: Harcourt, Brace & World, 1966, 106-16.

————. "Several Roads Lead to Jerusalem," in *These Found the Way: Thirteen Converts to Protestant Christianity*. Ed. David Wesley Soper. Philadelphia: Westminster, 1951, 119-28.

Williams, Donald T. "A Closer Look at the 'Unorthodox Lewis'." *Christianity Today*, December 21, 1979, 24-27.

Wilson, John. "An Appraisal of C. S. Lewis and His Influence on Modern Evangelicalism." *Scottish Bulletin of Evangelical Theology*, Spring 1991 (Vol. 9, No. 1), 22-39.

NOTES

1. Stackhouse, *Christianity Today*, 59.
2. *Touchstone* is a "Journal of Ecumenical Orthodoxy."
3. Nelson, "C. S. Lewis and His Critics," 2.
4. Ibid., 1.
5. Person, "The Legacy of C. S. Lewis," 409.
6. Dorsett, "Lewis, (C)live (S)taples (1898-1963)," 645.
7. See Martindale and Root, *The Quotable Lewis*.
8. Walsh, *C. S. Lewis: Apostle to the Skeptics*.
9. Video Interview with Stephen F. Olford, 9.
10. For an explanation and even a defense of this aspect of Lewis's character, see Michael Ward's chapter in this volume.
11. Lewis, "Christianity and Culture," 14.
12. Lewis, *Letters of C. S. Lewis*, 261.
13. Lewis, "Cross-Examination," 262.
14. Audio Interview with A. G. Dickens, 8.
15. Audio Interview with George Sayer, 10.

16. Video Interview with Harry Blamires, 9, 15.

17. Audio Interview with Stella Aldwinckle, 22-23.

18. Audio Interview with Lady Elizabeth Catherwood.

19. Letter to Sister Penelope, May 15, 1941.

20. Sayer, *Jack*, 282.

21. Interview with Canon H. A. Blair, 15.

22. Cited in Babbage, "C. S. Lewis Meets the R.A.F.," 26.

23. Audio Interview with Bishop A. W. Goodwin-Hudson.

24. Video Interview with Stephen F. Olford, 6-7.

25. Lewis, "Christian Apologetics," 99.

26. Sayer, *Jack*, 277-79.

27. Ibid., 278.

28. Ibid., 279.

29. Letter to Sister Penelope, May 15, 1941 (Bodleian shelfmark MS. Eng. lett. c.220/1, fol. 16). The theme of *praeparatio evangelica* is explored in more detail by Joel Heck in this volume.

30. Lewis, "A Rejoinder to Dr. Pittenger," 181.

31. Norman Bradshaw, "Impressions of a Pupil," 22.

32. Dorsett, *And God Came In*, 1.

33. Ibid., 16.

34. Davidman, "The Longest Way Round," 22.

35. In a published account of his own spiritual pilgrimage ("From Communist to Christian," 77), Gresham stated that his story would be incomplete "without a tribute to C. S. Lewis," whose vision "illumined the Mystery which lay behind the appearances of daily life." Sadly, Gresham's later wanderings led some to doubt the reality of his conversion.

36. Davidman, "The Longest Way Round," 23.

37. Ibid., 24.

38. The best place to get the true story of this relationship is not in the various stage and screen productions of *Shadowlands*, but in Lyle Dorsett's delightful biography of Joy Davidman, *And God Came In*.

39. Vanauken, *Encounter with Light*, 12.

40. Vanauken tells the full story of his romance and conversion in *A Severe Mercy*.

41. Vanauken, *Encounter with Light*, 19.

42. Ibid., 23.

43. Ibid., 24-25.

44. Lewis, *Mere Christianity*, 108-14.

The Influence of C. S. Lewis

45. Colson, *Born Again*, 113.

46. Ibid., 121.

47. Lewis, *Mere Christianity*, 55-56.

48. Colson, *Born Again*, 125-26.

49. Ibid., 129.

50. Guinness, "Fools for Christ, Foolmakers for Christ," 1.

51. Video Interview with Stephen F. Olford, 5.

52. Walsh, "Impact on America," 107.

53. Walsh, "Several Roads Lead to Jerusalem," 127.

54. Vanauken, *A Severe Mercy*, 134.

55. Lewis, interview in Wirt, "I Was Decided Upon," 3.

56. Letter to Dom Bede Griffiths, June 27, 1949.

57. Letter to Don Giovanni Calabria, March 28, 1959, in Moynihan, *The Latin Letters of C. S. Lewis*, 42: "*Ora pro me ut Deus mihi concedat aut salutaria . . . dicere*" (60n).

58. The responses are kept in a file entitled "C. S. Lewis Testimonies" at the Marion E. Wade Center, Wheaton College, Wheaton, IL.

59. Dorsett, "C. S. Lewis and Evangelism," 6.

60. Donald T. Williams, "A Closer Look at the 'Unorthodox Lewis'," 24.

61. An informal survey taken in Scotland reached much the same conclusion; see Wilson, "An Appraisal of C. S. Lewis and his Influence on Modern Evangelicalism," 38.

62. See "C. S. Lewis Testimonies: Appendix A," at the Marion E. Wade Center, Wheaton College, Wheaton, IL.

63. Letter to Don Giovanni Calabria, December 26, 1951, in Moynihan, *The Latin Letters of C. S. Lewis*, 12 (cf. 37): "*. . . multum scribis de tuis peccatis. Cave (liceat mihi, dilectissime pater, dicere cave) ne humilitas in anxietatem aut tristitiam tanseat*" (55n).

64. Colson, *Born Again*, 128.

65. See also Ryken, *The Christian Imagination*.

66. Noll, *Between Faith and Criticism*, 221-25.

67. For one recent example see Edwards, *The Taste of the Pineapple*.

Apostle to Generation X:

C. S. Lewis and the Future of Evangelism

Reed Jolley

I began to wonder what exactly I had believed in up until now that had allowed me to reach my present emotional circumstance. This is not an easy thing to do. Precisely articulating one's beliefs is difficult. My own task had been made more difficult because I had been raised without religion by parents who had broken with their own pasts and moved to the West Coast—who had raised their children clean of any ideology in a cantilevered modern house overlooking the Pacific Ocean—at the end of history, or so they had wanted to believe.

—*Douglas Coupland*

The above comes from Douglas Coupland's third semi-autobiographical novel *Life After God*.[1] The author, a self-appointed spokesperson for Generation X, is uncomfortable in the world in which he was raised, for it is a world without God or creed.[2] At the end of his story the narrator confides to the reader:

My secret is that I need God—that I am sick and can no longer make it alone. I need God to help me give, because I no longer seem to be capable of giving; to help me be kind, as I no longer seem capable of kindness; to help me love, as I seem beyond able to love.[3]

C. S. Lewis and the Future of Evangelism

As we near the close of the twentieth century, western society finds itself in a fundamental paradigm transition. The old paradigm, which maintained there was a reality "out there" to which civilizations, governments, and individuals should conform, is breaking down. The new paradigm maintains that everything, or almost everything, is up for grabs. Reason and rationality are "western" and therefore suspect. Ethical judgments are culture-bound propositions that merely reflect the values of a given population group. Truth, in the new paradigm, has been jettisoned and replaced with the quest for power.[4] If the microcomputer chip has "crunched" time and space, making them practically irrelevant, thinkers such as Michel Foucault, Jacques Derrida, and Richard Rorty have "crunched reality." Indeed, Walter Truett Anderson rejoices over the death of the modern worldview, proclaiming in the title of his 1990 book, *Reality Isn't What It Used to Be.*[5]

"Postmodernism," of course, is the catch-all term of the moment used to describe this seismic shift in our thinking. Out of this rapidly changing landscape comes a vague but discernible cultural malaise. Those in their twenties and early thirties, called "Generation X," "Xers," "Gen-x-ers," "Thirteeners,"[6] etc., are probably the most analyzed segment of our society. Whatever we decide to call them, they are the first generation reared under a postmodernist paradigm. When Xers look at the world, they see a mall-culture that lacks any real community, a future peppered with "McJobs," and a general hopelessness about their place in society. Body-piercing and tattoos mark this generation in the same way the BMW equipped with a cellular telephone was emblematic of the Yuppie generation of the late 1980s. The Yippies of the 1960s were determined to save the world; Generation X struggles simply to get through another season of life.

Can it really be suggested that C. S. Lewis, the Oxford don in an academic gown, has something to teach us about evangelism in postmodern times? It was Karl Barth who advised pastors to prepare their sermons with their Bible in one hand and their newspaper in the other. But Lewis, who preached few sermons because the concomitant adulation stirred his pride,[7] boasted from time to time that he didn't even read newspapers![8] We can picture the Fellow of the Royal Society of

Literature with his Bible in one hand, but in the other hand our mind's eye sees something by Milton or perhaps Chaucer. Nevertheless, while to some Lewis appeared out of touch with his own times (he probably enjoyed this perception), the man was truly a contemporary of his own generation. His books and letters show a familiarity with, for example, James Joyce, Virginia Woolf, and D. H. Lawrence along with his expertise in the classics. He interacts with and sharply critiques the trendy and debunking New Testament theology of Rudolf Bultmann and the existential theology of Paul Tillich even as he pokes fun at Bishop John A. T. Robinson.[9]

The Fellow of Magdalen College taught medieval and Renaissance literature to earn his living, but the conversion of the lost was his deepest passion.[10] Indeed Lewis identified the "salvation of souls" as "the real business of life."[11] The scope of his evangelistic efforts was broad. Clearly Lewis was unwilling to confine himself to the narrow, and rather safe, halls of Magdalen College. He made time in his demanding schedule as a tutor to share the Gospel with the Royal Air Force Troops during World War II.[12] Lewis's steady stream of Christian works brought him both fame and, at times, biting criticism. T. V. Smith, for example, called *Miracles* a "modernistic apologetics for Christian fundamentalism," even as theologian Norman Pittenger criticized Lewis's christology for being thoroughly "Docetic, even Gnostic."[13] Lewis was stung by such vituperations, but ultimately he was undeterred, as the truth of the Gospel deserved to be heard in the modern world.[14] After the harsh reaction among his colleagues to *Miracles*, Lewis shifted his emphasis to storytelling, believing that ". . . any amount of theology can be smuggled into men's minds under the guise of romance without their knowing it."[15] The seven Chronicles and *Till We Have Faces* were forthcoming.

Consider the primary impact of Lewis on several North American figures. It was in reading Lewis that Elton Trueblood, philosopher and chaplain at both Stanford University and Earlham College, was transformed from a liberal thinker to a contender for an evangelical faith. Lewis "shocked" the Quaker out of his "unexamined liberalism."[16] Jesus was either who he said he was—God incarnate, or a megalo-

C. S. Lewis and the Future of Evangelism

maniacal impostor, or a lunatic who belonged in an asylum. One who was merely a "good teacher" would not make the claims Jesus made.

> In reading Lewis I could not escape the conclusion that the popular view of Christ as being a Teacher, and only a Teacher, has within it a self-contradiction that cannot be resolved. I saw, in short, that conventional liberalism cannot survive rigorous and rational analysis.[17]

Trueblood, impressed with *The Screwtape Letters* as an attack on the "irrationality of the opposition," found *The Case for Christianity* "unanswerable." The philosopher of religion was boxed in. He read the Gospels anew, finding a Jesus who called not for admiration but for commitment. Elton Trueblood began to preach with confidence, and his ministry was forever changed.

A. W. Tozer, author and pastor of Chicago Southside Alliance Church, leaned toward the mystical side of Christianity. But Lewis's writings undergirded the faith of this prolific writer.

> I would classify Mr. Lewis as an apologist rather than as a creative religious writer. He brings to the defense of historic Christianity a mind as clear as sunlight and an amazing ability to make the faith of our fathers appear reasonable.[18]

Reading *Mere Christianity* set the hook in Charles Colson when he was regarded as the infamous "hatchet man" of Richard Nixon's administration. At the height of the Watergate scandal Colson spent the evening with a friend who shared his own story of conversion to Christ. Then Tom Phillips read aloud Lewis's chapter on pride. "That was the night Jesus Christ came into my life," Colson stated in a preface to a special edition of *Mere Christianity*, calling it "the book God has used most powerfully in my life, apart from His own word."

> It was one of the most extraordinary moments of my life. The words from that book—*Mere Christianity*, written by the great English scholar C. S. Lewis—ripped through the protective armor in which I had unknowingly encased myself for forty-one years.[19]

What was the key to Lewis's effectiveness as an evangelist? Why does the effect of his evangelistic efforts redound to this day? Generation X is coming of age in the late 1990s. Does C. S. Lewis serve as an exemplar of an apostle to this generation? Since none of us shares the exact giftedness of Clive Staples Lewis, the more appropriate question is, what can we glean from Lewis's approach as we ponder our own strategy for the future of evangelism? The following pages of this chapter will survey five features of Lewis's evangelistic efforts that are worthy of the attention and emulation of those who would attempt to persuade Generation X, along with other postmoderns, to trust in Jesus as Lord.

Showing Up

First, C. S. Lewis was authentic. If, from his celestial mansion, he is aware of all the fuss being made over him in our era, he would certainly respond with a hearty laugh. Hollywood has lionized Lewis as an academic paramour who swept Joy Davidman off her feet. But in today's vernacular this Oxford professor was unquestionably a "nerd." He had the ability to make a new suit old on the second wearing, his hat became famous for its frumpiness, he never learned to drive, he couldn't type, and his home, The Kilns, was a large hovel characterized by uncommon filth and disrepair. Nevertheless, Xers who are disillusioned with phony television personalities, sound-bite politicians, immoral moralists, etc., are likely to be impressed with the man behind the books.

Lewis showed up. We have record of Lewis's bellowing laugh heard from his rooms in Magdalen College. His deep friendships, fomented over Tuesday lunches at the Eagle and Child, testify to a hunger for genuine human relationships. Of course, we have to be cautious lest we become guilty of recasting our professor into the mold of our own choosing. This don was anything but Oxford's version of a California therapist always wanting to talk about his feelings. No, this professor was not revealing. He would qualify for adjectives such as guarded, stuffy, shy, and introverted. Nevertheless, his persona bore the marks of an authentic man, a man transformed by the lordship of Christ.

To change the tense of an oft-used phrase, what one saw is what

C. S. Lewis and the Future of Evangelism

one got. Lewis was no pretender. He never rose to the occasion of his celebrity status. As Walter Hooper recalls, "Lewis struck me as the most thoroughly converted man I ever met."[20] Hooper's point is that the Oxonian allowed Christ to permeate his life while going beyond the prescribed role of an English tutor. Lewis violated the unwritten Oxford law that prohibited tutors from expressing their faith in public or in prose. This don broke ranks with Oxford protocol when he wrote *The Pilgrim's Regress*. But in spite of his colleagues' criticisms, he continued to churn out books on theology, ethics, and apologetics in the years to come.

Clifford Morris, who was Lewis's driver during the Cambridge years, writes fondly of Lewis as a genuine friend. In spite of his worldwide fame, Jack saw himself as a professor who happened to write a few books.[21] Morris recalls the stops they would make during the drives between the two university towns. Lewis would engage the lorry drivers in conversation at one particular pub they frequented. Once, outside of Lewis's presence, one of the men asked Morris, "Hey, mate, who's the guv'nor?" Hearing that this was a man of letters on his way home from Cambridge, the inquirer responded, "Blimey, he's a toff, he is! A real nice bloke!"[22]

As we ponder reaching Xers, authenticity in our own lives is sorely needed. Any evangelistic methodology we employ must be deeply undergirded by lives that are thoroughly committed to the Lord we preach. The publicized sex scandals of television evangelists during the late 1980s confirmed Xers' cynicism toward authority. This generation remains highly suspicious of "buying in" or "signing on" to another "ism." We read in one of Lewis's letters, "What we practise, not (save at rare intervals) what we preach, is usually our great contribution to the conversions of others. . . ."[23] Xers are fed up with the slick, programmatic, packaged society of advertising. They will not find their way inside our mega-churches that buttress a well-polished sermon with a video presentation or a dramatic production. Xers would rather sit down over coffee and converse. Richard Cunningham's observation is worthy of our attention, for in Lewis we find

. . . an apostle to humanity, a sinner, a saint—a man who finally lets through "what matters more than ideas—a whole Christian life in operation—better say, Christ Himself operating in a man's life." Perhaps in the case of this fellow Lewis, the atheist turned evangelist and apologist, we learn what really we have known all along—that the best argument ever invented for the truth of the Christian faith is the argument that walks in shoes.[24]

Evangelicals who would seek to win those in their twenties and thirties to Christ must, at the outset, be an argument walking in shoes. Xers, deeply scarred by the hypocrisy of their parents, their divorce rate, their materialism, their betrayal of the idealism of the sixties, long for the real thing. "Do as I say, not as I do" will fall on deaf ears. If we intend to have an impact we must have the credibility to say with Paul, "Follow my example, as I follow the example of Christ" (1 Corinthians 11:1).

DEMOLISHING ARGUMENTS

A second, and a significant, ingredient of evangelism to any generation is that of apologetics. The evangelist needs to keep his or her ear to the ground, listening to the questions of the moment. Then the hard work of thinking through an adequate response from the Christian perspective begins. The apostle Paul employed this strategy in his own evangelistic endeavors. Writing to the Corinthian church, Paul states that it was his goal to "destroy arguments and every proud obstacle raised up against the knowledge of God . . ."(2 Corinthians 10:5, NRSV). The Greek verb rendered by the NRSV as "destroy" means "to cast down" or "to demolish." Moffatt translates this verse, "I demolish theories and any rampart thrown up to resist the knowledge of God." The context of Paul's claim is significant. The apostle is speaking to the Corinthian church about spiritual warfare. Paul's weapons are "not merely human, but they have divine power to destroy strongholds (2 Corinthians 10:4, NRSV)." Commentators point out that Paul may have been alluding to rhetoric used by both Epictetus and Philo. In both writers a "stronghold" is the imagistic equivalent

C. S. Lewis and the Future of Evangelism

to what we might call a worldview.[25] Paul listened to the spirit of his age and responded with conviction.

In similar fashion C. S. Lewis serves as a contemporary model of one who took the time to apply his mind to the arduous task of Christian apologetics. Notice Lewis's own understanding of the radio talks that eventually became codified in *The Case for Christianity*. Writing to Sister Penelope he says:

> We ought to meet about BBC talks. . . . Mine are *praeparatio evangelica* rather than *evangelium*, an attempt to convince people that there is a moral law, that we disobey it, and that the existence of a Lawgiver is at least very probable and also (*unless* you add the Christian doctrine of the Atonement) imparts despair rather than comfort. You will come after to heal any wounds I may succeed in making.[26]

Opening wounds and healing those wounds with the Gospel was what motivated Lewis. This was perhaps the dominant component of his strategy. On several occasions he participated in evangelistic crusades with both William Sangster and Stephen Olford.[27] Lewis would speak first, working on the intellect, "demolishing arguments," "destroying strongholds." Then he would be followed by a true preacher who would address the heart. Lewis claimed in his reply to Dr. Pittenger that "Most of my books are evangelistic."[28] But even a cursory perusal of those books would reveal that he evangelized through the discipline of apologetics. Lewis was tough-minded. He tested his ideas in his letter writing, in debate, in lecture, and finally in print.

His efforts, of course, did not go unnoticed. *Time* magazine estimated that the broadcast talks had an average listening audience of 600,000.[29] Since the talks were published as *Mere Christianity*, millions of copies have been printed, sold, and read.

Elton Trueblood, who himself became an internationally known apologist for the veracity of the Christian faith, credits Lewis as the harbinger of a new posture in Christian apologetics.

C. S. Lewis reached me primarily because he turned the intellectual tables. I was wholly accustomed to a world in which the
sophisticates engaged in attack, while the Christians sought
bravely to be on the defense, but Lewis turned this around and
forced the unbeliever into a posture of defense. In the *Screwtape
Letters* dated July 5, 1941, at Magdalen College, Oxford, Lewis,
who up to that time had been an inconspicuous academician,
inaugurated a new Christian strategy.[30]

In his 1963 essay *The Christian Mind* Harry Blamires issued a
clarion call for Christians to think clearly about the times in which
they lived. Ours, he averred, is an era of sloppy thinking. Even scholars, forced to conform to the prevailing orthodoxy of their guilds, are
poor thinkers. The true thinker, according to Blamires,

> challenges current prejudices. He disturbs the complacent. He
> obstructs the busy pragmatist. He questions the very founda-
> tions of all about him, and in so doing throws doubt upon aims,
> motives, and purposes which those who are running affairs have
> neither time nor patience to investigate. The thinker is a nui-
> sance.[31]

Lewis had supreme confidence in the sovereignty of God with
regard to an individual's salvation.[32] His own conversion is presented
as a chess match that he, the convert, lost when he acknowledged that
God was God! But he worked with diligence to be a "nuisance" to the
nonbelieving mind. God's sovereignty never lets the Christian off the
hook of evangelistic apologetics. "Woe to you if you do not evangelize," he said in an address to theology students.[33]

In our own era Mark Noll, Os Guinness, Carl Henry, and others
have called for a renewal of the Christian mind. Noll's well-received
The Scandal of the Evangelical Mind laments the failure of Christians,
leaders and otherwise, to think.[34] The American church, far from being
a nuisance, has abdicated her mind to the dominant culture. The scandal of the evangelical mind is that there isn't one! Noll's essay is part
historical analysis, part polemic, and part summons. The professor of

C. S. Lewis and the Future of Evangelism

history invites evangelicals to "scandalize the scandal," that is, to renew the practice of thinking in a Christian way about the world of politics, culture, art, family, economics, philosophy, and so on. The dividends would be fruitful for both evangelism and society.

As Trueblood writes, "Though the Christian faith can use people of modest endowment, in the long run it cannot become a truly redemptive force in the total culture until it has, in its service, the best minds."[35] To paraphrase one of the Proverbs, "As a society thinks, so it will become."[36] The lofty currency of university doctrine will soon become the small change of society-at-large. Lewis understood this, saying, "If you make the adults of today Christian, the children of tomorrow will receive a Christian education."[37] The truth of such an assertion should concern us greatly, for as Douglas Coupland points out, Generation X has been raised "without religion."

Lewis anticipated Postmodernism in *That Hideous Strength* and *The Abolition of Man*. In these works he senses the end of the classic virtues and probes the nightmarish implications of the new world. Ours is not a world returning to paganism. Lewis lamented that we are "falling into a much worse state," for "'Post-Christian man' is not the same as 'pre-Christian man.' He is as far removed as virgin is from widow: there is nothing in common except want of a spouse: but there is a great difference between a spouse-to-come and a spouse lost."[38]

As evangelical Christians face the beginning of the third millennium, there is a desperate need to do our homework in the area of pre-evangelism: to understand our times, to know the questions posed by Generation X, and finally to "demolish theories and any rampart thrown up to resist the knowledge of God." Will we do this as well as Clive Staples Lewis? Probably not. Will God honor our attempts to take seriously the cry of postmodern men and women? Undoubtedly.

CLARITY OF THOUGHT

When Lewis was sixteen he met a man who would refine his ability to think. In September 1914 young Jack went to live in Great Bookham,

Surrey to be tutored by the "Great Knock," W. T. Kirkpatrick. When the two first met, the nervous adolescent, seeking to make conversation, commented that the "scenery" of Surrey was "wilder" than expected. Within three and a half minutes Kirkpatrick had thoroughly dissected Lewis's comment. The young lad was informed that since he had no real definition of "wildness" and no prior knowledge of the flora of Surrey, his comment was meaningless and he "had no right to have any opinion whatever on the subject"![39] Lewis recalled that the tone of this initial conversation continued without a break for the next two and a half years.

Kirkpatrick's legacy to his pupil was the gift of clarity in thought, in speech, and in writing. This legacy paid huge dividends with regard to the effectiveness of Lewis's evangelism. It is not insignificant that Kirkpatrick, recognizing Jack's powerful intellect, wrote to Albert Lewis in Belfast recommending that young Lewis train to be an "advocate or attorney in court." Lewis ended up, of course, in a much larger court than his atheist mentor could have imagined, serving as an advocate for the Christian faith.

We should not think of Lewis as a tremendously original thinker. Many of the most well-known sections of *Mere Christianity*, for example, are undoubtedly borrowed from G. K. Chesterton's *Orthodoxy*. But Lewis is tremendously clear. His books are accessible to the non-specialist. They are surprisingly easy to read. We find no intentional obfuscation in Lewis, no desire to impress the academy with his erudition. He tackles tough philosophical and theological issues in *Miracles* and *The Problem of Pain*. But he does so with utmost clarity. One cannot help but notice how his letters to children "sound" the same as his letters written to adults. Lewis mastered the art of perspicuity, and he brought this art to his evangelistic books. His great competence was that of translation. He had the desire and the ability to take great ideas and make them accessible through the parlance of the common man.

Lewis wanted to find a middle course between the emotionalism of revivalists and the "unintelligible language" of cultured clergymen.

C. S. Lewis and the Future of Evangelism

He realized that both approaches were hopelessly out of touch with the common concerns of the masses.

> My task was therefore simply that of a translator—one turning Christian doctrine, or what he believed to be such, into the vernacular, into language that unscholarly people would attend to and could understand.[40]

There will always be a need for those with intellectual capabilities to continue this work of translation without academic hubris. Shame on the academic elite if they spend all their time talking to themselves. Gen-x-ers, like every generation, deserve to hear the truth in language they can understand.

While Lewis was precise and clear in his writings, he was far from cold. Along with his rational-propositional works, he made every effort to "smuggle" theology into his reader's minds through the use of story. Chesterton says in *Orthodoxy*, "I had always felt life first as a story." Lewis would agree. He avoided travel, for he didn't need it. He lived out his life in stories others had written. Indeed, his attraction to the Christian faith two years after his conversion to theism was that he saw the gospel story as the Great Myth. In a letter to Arthur Greeves he writes:

> Now the story of Christ is simply a true myth: a myth working on us in the same way as the others, but with this tremendous difference that it really happened: and one must be content to accept it in the same way, remembering that it is God's myth where the others are men's myths: i.e., the Pagan stories are God expressing Himself through the minds of poets, using such images as He found there, while Christianity is God expressing Himself through what we call "real things."[41]

In the Christ story Lewis found a narrative that gave all the components of his life meaning and purpose and had the added feature of being true!

Xers are a generation raised on images. They watch, on average, almost ninety movies per year, and almost half of Xers watch MTV in a given week.[42] Rational argument and propositional apologetics will not be as effective in this era as they have been in the past. Leighton Ford, therefore, argues for "narrative evangelism" as a strategy for reaching individuals for Christ.[43] A good narrative draws the listener in, changing his outlook while expanding his vision of the world. The Gospel, like all great stories, contains what J. R. R. Tolkien called a eucatastrophe—a catastrophe with good consequences. In his essay "On Fairy-Stories" Tolkien writes,

> The Gospels contain a fairy-story, or a story of a larger kind which embraces all the essence of fairy-stories. They contain many marvels—peculiarly artistic, beautiful, and moving: 'mythical' in their perfect, self-contained significance; and at the same time powerfully symbolic and allegorical; and among the marvels is the greatest and most completely conceivable eucatastrophe. The Birth of Christ is the eucatastrophe of Man's history. The Resurrection is the eucatastrophe of the story of the Incarnation. This story begins and ends in joy. There is no tale ever told that men would rather find was true, and none which so many skeptical men have accepted as true on its own merits.[44]

We are increasingly exposed to what some are calling "metafictions," stories about stories where the boundaries between story, author, and audience are blurred.[45] Cynical Xers appear to be hungry for the real thing, for a story that is both meaningful and true. Lewis's imagination was "baptized" when he read MacDonald's *Phantastes*. Years later Chad Walsh read *Perelandra* and found that his non-Christian imagination was baptized as well: "In *Perelandra* I got the taste and the smell of Christian truth. My senses as well as my soul were baptized."[46] The cultivation of good storytelling by writers committed to Christ can and will be an effective strategy for evangelizing future generations. Postmoderns need to savor the

C. S. Lewis and the Future of Evangelism

"taste and smell" of Christian truth. Clarity of thought will only abet
this needed indulgence.

MERE CHRISTIANITY

Xers are suspicious of signing on. Rightly or wrongly, they feel let down
by their parents' generation. They have, therefore, difficulty aligning
themselves with corporations, institutions, or political parties. Kevin
Ford, a self-described Xer, speaks for his generation when he writes:

> Thirteeners are indifferent and distrustful toward structures
> that have let them down, betrayed them or exploited them: the
> business world, the political structure and organized religion.
> "What have these institutions ever done for me besides screw
> things up?" they ask. So they feel no connection, no loyalty, no
> responsibility toward the outside world, which they view as hos-
> tile and rejecting.[47]

Multiculturalism is one of the watchwords of the day. People
increasingly define themselves according to smaller and smaller groups.
The "balkanization" of races, social classes, and generations may be
one of the outcomes of the end of modernism and its utopian optimism.

> The only world my generation feels any allegiance to or affec-
> tion for is the closer, more intimate world of our friends. We
> desire friends who will be loyal to us. At the same time we're
> afraid of commitment. We're afraid of vulnerability. We want to
> communicate but don't know how. So we surround ourselves
> with other people just like us.
> And we're all lonely together.[48]

In light of the fragmentation of society, should evangelists seek a
particular strategy for every group? Should 1970s-style evangelism be
re-tailored to fit the needs of Generation X? Lewis seems to say both
yes and no. Yes, we should pay attention to the questions people are
asking. In *A Preface to Paradise Lost* he challenges the "Doctrine of

the Unchanging Human Heart," which maintains that the differences separating the ages are superficial. If one wishes to understand Malory, for example, one needs to think like a medieval knight; if we want to read Samuel Johnson, we need to put ourselves in eighteenth-century London. We can hear Lewis the evangelist add, "If we want to understand Xers and win them to Christ, we need to think like an Xer."

> For the truth is that when you have stripped off what the human heart actually was in this or that culture, you are left with a miserable abstraction totally unlike the life really lived by any human being.[49]

On the other hand, Lewis would say no to altering the essential content of the message proclaimed. The message delivered remains the same for every epoch and culture. As an evangelist Lewis appealed to the broad "middle," calling his brand of the Christian faith "merely Christian." "Ever since I became a Christian I have thought that the best, perhaps the only service I could do for my unbelieving neighbours was to explain and defend the belief that has been common to nearly all Christians at all times."[50] Accordingly, he avoided taking sides on pedantic, peripheral issues in theology. Lewis went to an Anglican church because it was near his home. While he was a member of the Church of England, he described his membership as "ordinary . . . not especially 'high,' nor especially 'low,' nor especially anything else."[51] As a matter of fact, Lewis understood "Sectarianism as one of the Devil's keenest weapons" against the Christian faith.[52]

The emphasis on "mere" Christianity is significant as a strategy for evangelism in our era. Xers who are reluctant to "join" will have to be drawn to a Christ without denominational trappings. But there is an admitted danger here. The emphasis on the merely Christian could lead to a creedless and churchless faith. As Lewis himself points out in the preface to *Mere Christianity*, his job as evangelist was to get one into the house of faith. But once inside that house the convert, standing in the hallway, is invited into a room where there are "fires

C. S. Lewis and the Future of Evangelism

and chairs and meals." "The hall is a place to wait in, a place from which to try the various doors, not a place to live in. For that purpose the worst of the rooms (whichever that may be) is, I think, preferable."[53] In the end, Xers and others who find their way into the kingdom of God are called not to isolation but to Christian community, the church.

THE DIGNITY OF THE INDIVIDUAL

The operative story of our origins maintains that every man and woman is an accident of purposeless evolution. Jacob Bronowski's statement in *The Identity of Man* puts man in his place: "In the latter half of the twentieth century it seems self-evident to say that man is a part of nature, in the same sense that a stone is, or a cactus, or a camel."[54] The view that humans were "cast from birth in a supernatural mold" is the outdated delusion of prescientific thinking. Lewis, of course, stood against seeing man as a part of nature. But he also probed the nightmarish implications of scientism's creed. With the rise of scientism the individual has been "de-dignified."

In *The Abolition of Man*, Lewis complains that the modern world has rejected the source of all statements of value. Lewis calls this source the *Tao*, that is, a universal sense of right and wrong stamped upon the soul of every man and woman, every religion, every society. Scientism has produced "men without chests," that is, men without a heart, without sentiment or emotion, without "Magnanimity."[55] "Values" have become simple statements about our own feelings that have no transcendent imprimatur. While some may celebrate this emancipation from objective standards of good and evil, Lewis saw both the end of personal dignity and the very destruction of society as the inevitable consequences of such subjectivism. *The Abolition of Man* was based on three lectures given at the University of Durham in February 1943. Hitler and Stalin were terrorizing their own people. This Oxford don was exploring the worldview that made such terrorism possible.

We make men without chests and expect of them virtue and enterprise. We laugh at honour and are shocked to find traitors in our midst. We castrate and bid the geldings be fruitful.[56]

It is one of the hallmarks of C. S. Lewis that he refused to give up the dignity of every individual. In June 1941 Lewis preached what was arguably his most memorable sermon in St. Mary the Virgin Church in Oxford. There he proclaimed that there are no "mere mortals." Lewis didn't argue for an abstract love for "humanity." It is our neighbor who bears the God-given marks of dignity.

There are no *ordinary* people. You have never talked to a mere mortal. Nations, cultures, arts, civilizations—these are mortal, and their life is to ours as the life of a gnat. But it is immortals whom we joke with, work with, marry, snub, and exploit. . . . Next to the Blessed Sacrament itself, your neighbor is the holiest object presented to your senses.[57]

Xers feel the heavy weight of living in a technological society. Though, in increasing numbers, they "surf the net," chat on their cellular phones, and send E-mail, they sense their depersonalization in our "accelerated culture." "Reach out and touch someone," Xers contend, should imply that that someone is in the same room. This generation is growing up, and the process is proving to be a disappointment. Coupland writes:

When I was younger I used to worry so much about being alone—of being unlovable or incapable of love. As the years went on, my worries changed. I worried that I had become incapable of having a relationship, of offering intimacy. I felt as though the world lived inside a warm house at night and I was outside, and I couldn't be seen—because I was out there in the night. But now I am inside that house and it feels just the same.[58]

If we desire to reach Generation X for Jesus, it will not be through a modem. E-mail will make few disciples of Jesus Christ. Only a more

C. S. Lewis and the Future of Evangelism

personal model will suffice. In spite of our busy lives, we have something to learn from the C. S. Lewis who didn't quite fit into the twentieth century, the Lewis who personally answered every letter he received, the Lewis who served Mrs. Moore from their first meeting in 1917 until her death in 1951, the Lewis who found time for evangelistic crusades and wartime preaching to the RAF. Xers who yearn for human relationships in the wake of their parents' divorce would appreciate Lewis's rhetorical question to Dom Bede Griffiths: "Is any pleasure on earth as great as a circle of Christian friends by a good fire?"[59] We can almost hear them asking, "Is there a place by that fire for me?"

BIBLIOGRAPHY

Aeschliman, Michael D. *The Restitution of Man: C. S. Lewis and the Case Against Scientism*. Grand Rapids, MI: Eerdmans, 1983.

Anderson, Walter Truett. *Reality Isn't What It Used to Be: Theatrical Politics, Ready-to-Wear Religion, Global Myths, Primitive Chic, and Other Wonders of the Postmodern World*. San Francisco: Harper & Row, 1990.

Blamires, Harry. *The Christian Mind: How Should a Christian Think?* Ann Arbor, MI: Servant Books, 1978.

Bronowski, Jacob. *The Identity of Man*. Garden City, NJ: The Natural History Press, 1965.

Coupland, Douglas. *Life After God*. New York: Pocket Books, 1994.

Cunningham, Richard. *C. S. Lewis: Defender of the Faith*. Philadelphia: Westminister Press, 1987.

Danker, Fredrick W. *Augsburg Commentary on the New Testament, II Corinthians*. Minneapolis: Augsburg, 1989.

Fish, Stanley. *There's No Such Thing as Free Speech and It's a Good Thing, Too*. New York: Oxford University Press, 1994.

Ford, Kevin. *Jesus for a New Generation: Putting the Gospel in the Language of Xers*. Downers Grove, IL: InterVarsity Press, 1995.

Ford, Leighton. *The Power of Story: Rediscovering the Oldest, Most Natural Way to Reach People for Christ*. Colorado Springs: NavPress, 1994.

Gresham, Douglas. *Lenten Lands*. London: Collins, 1989.

Lewis, C. S. *The Abolition of Man*. New York: Macmillan, 1978

_____. *Christian Reflections*. Ed. Walter Hooper. Grand Rapids, MI: Eerdmans, 1967.

_____. (editor) *Essays Presented to Charles Williams*. Grand Rapids, MI: Eerdmans, 1966.

_____. *God in the Dock: Essays on Theology and Ethics*. Ed. Walter Hooper. Grand Rapids, MI: Eerdmans, 1970.

_____. *Letters: A Study in Friendship*. Ann Arbor, MI: Servant Books, 1988.

_____. *Letters to an American Lady*. Grand Rapids, MI: Eerdmans, 1967.

_____. *Mere Christianity*. Westwood, NJ: The Christian Library, Barbour and Company, 1987.

_____. *A Preface to Paradise Lost*. London: Oxford University Press, 1942, 1961.

_____. *Reflections on the Psalms*. London: Geoffrey Bles, Ltd., 1940.

_____. *Surprised by Joy*. New York: Harcourt, Brace & World, Inc., 1955.

_____. *The Weight of Glory and Other Addresses*. Grand Rapids, MI: Eerdmans, 1949.

Lewis, Warren and Hooper, Walter, eds. *Letters of C. S. Lewis*. Revised and Enlarged Edition. New York: Harcourt, Brace and Company, 1988.

Morris, Clifford. "C. S. Lewis Was My Friend," *His* (Vol. 39, No. 1), 1978.

Noll, Mark. *The Scandal of the Evangelical Mind*. Grand Rapids, MI: Eerdmans, 1994.

Sangster, Paul. *Doctor Sangster*. London: The Epworth Press, 1962.

Strauss, William and Howe, Neil. *13th Gen: Abort, Retry, Ignore, Fail?* New York: Random House, 1993.

Tozer, A. W. *God Tells the Man Who Cares*. Harrisburg, PA: Christian Publishing, 1970.

Trueblood, Elton. *While It Is Day: An Autobiography*. New York: Harper & Row, 1974.

Veith, Gene Edward, Jr. *Postmodern Times*. Wheaton, IL: Crossway Books, 1994.

Walsh, Chad. *Light on C. S. Lewis*. London: Geoffrey Bles, 1965.

NOTES

1. Coupland, *Life After God*, 178.

2. Coupland's first novel is titled *Generation X: Tales for an Accelerated Culture* (New York: St. Martins Press, 1991). The name "Generation X" became popularized in the mainstream press and thus a part of our vocabulary. Generation X usually refers to those born from 1961-1981.

C. S. Lewis and the Future of Evangelism

3. Coupland, *Life After God*, 359.

4. Cf. Fish, *There's No Such Thing as Free Speech, and It's a Good Thing, Too.*

5. *Reality Isn't What It Used to Be: Theatrical Politics, Ready-to-Wear Religion, Global Myths, Primitive Chic, and Other Wonders of the Postmodern World*, 6.

6. "Thirteener" is yet another designation for Generation X. The term refers to the thirteenth generation since the signing of the U. S. Constitution.

7. Lewis confided to his friend Clifford Morris that when he preached, the inevitable praise would spark the thought, "What a jolly fine and clever fellow Jack Lewis was. . . ." Morris, "C. S. Lewis Was My Friend: A Personal Recollection," 12.

8. "I never read the papers. Why does anyone? They're nearly all lies, and one has to wade thru' such reams of verbiage and 'write up' to find out even what they are saying." Lewis, *Letters to an American Lady*, 45.

9. Rudolph Bultmann (1884-1976) was one of our century's most influential theologians. As a New Testament scholar, Bultmann employed the historico-critical method of biblical interpretation in order to "de-mythologize" the text and make it "relevant" to modern men and women. All references to the supernatural (miracles, the resurrection of Jesus, etc.) were to be understood existentially (personally) as opposed to literally. John A. T. Robinson, Anglican bishop of Woolwich, popularized the thinking of both Tillich and Bultmann with his notorious book *Honest to God* (London, 1963). When asked in an interview what he thought of Robinson's book, Lewis replied, "I prefer being honest to being 'honest to God'." cf. *God in the Dock: Essays on Theology and Ethics*, 260.

10. "But the Christian knows from the outset that the salvation of a single soul is more important than the production or preservation of all the epics and tragedies in the world. . . ." Lewis, "Christianity and Literature," *Christian Reflections*, 10.

11. Ibid., 14.

12. It is interesting to note Lewis's lack of confidence in these sermons. Following a reference to his upcoming BBC radio talks (*praeparatio evangelica*) Lewis writes, "I've given talks to the RAF at Abingdon already, and so far as I can judge they were a complete failure. . . . Yes—jobs one dare neither refuse or perform. One must take comfort in remembering that God used an ass to convert the prophet; perhaps if we do our poor best we shall be allowed a stall near it in the celestial stable. . . ." *Letters*, 359.

13. Cited by Chad Walsh in *Light on C. S. Lewis*, 114.

14. We know from a letter Lewis wrote to Don Giovanni Calabria that he felt his literary skills were spent. On January 14, 1949, the Oxford don wrote, "As for my own work, I would not wish to deceive you with vain hope. I am now in my fiftieth year. I feel my zeal for writing, and whatever talent I originally possessed, to be decreasing; nor (I believe) do I please my readers as I used to. I labour under many difficulties." *Letters: A Study in Friendship*, 51.

15. Ibid., 322.

16. Trueblood, *While It is Day: An Autobiography*, 99.

17. Ibid.

18. Tozer, *God Tells the Man Who Cares*, 99.

19. Lewis, *Mere Christianity*, v-vi.

20. From Hooper's preface to *God in the Dock: Essays on Theology and Ethics*, 12.

21. Cf. Morris, "C. S. Lewis Was My Friend," 8.

22. Ibid., 11.

23. C. S. Lewis, *Letters*, 446.

24. Cunningham, *C. S. Lewis: Defender of the Faith*, 205. The quotation is from *Reflections on the Psalms*, 114.

25. Cf. Danker, *Augsburg Commentary on the New Testament, II Corinthians*, 151-52.

26. Lewis, *Letters*, 359.

27. Cf. Sangster, *Doctor Sangster*, 147, 303. Speaking to a group of Anglican priests and youth workers Lewis said, "I am not sure that the ideal missionary team ought not to consist of one who argues and one who (in the fullest sense of the word) preaches. Put up your arguer first to undermine their intellectual prejudices; then let the evangelist proper launch his appeal. I have seen this done with great success" (C. S. Lewis, "Christian Apologetics," *God in the Dock*, 99).

28. Lewis, "Reply to Dr Pittenger," *God in the Dock*, 181.

29. "Don v. Devil," *Time*, September 8, 1947, 65.

30. Ibid., 65.

31. Blamires, *The Christian Mind*, 50. Blamires was one of Lewis's students at Oxford.

32. Lewis answered some theological questions Mrs. Sonia Graham had sent to him. He concluded his letter, "P.S. Of course God does not consider you hopeless. If He did He would not be moving you to seek Him (and He obviously is). What is going on in you at present is simply the beginning of the treatment. Continue seeking Him with seriousness. Unless He wanted you, you would not be wanting Him." *Letters*, 411-12.

33. Lewis, "Modern Theology and Biblical Criticism," *Christian Reflections*, 152.

34. Noll, *The Scandal of the Evangelical Mind*.

35. Trueblood, *While It Is Day*, 97.

36. Proverbs 23:7.

37. Lewis, "On the Transmission of Christianity," *God in the Dock*, 119.

38. Lewis, *Letters: A Study in Friendship*, 81.

39. Lewis, *Surprised by Joy*, 135.

C. S. Lewis and the Future of Evangelism

40. C. S. Lewis, "Rejoinder to Dr Pittenger," *God in the Dock*, 183.

41. Lewis, *Letters*, 288-89.

42. Cf. Strauss and Howe. *13th Gen: Abort, Retry, Ignore, Fail?*

43. Ford, *The Power of Story*.

44. Tolkien, "On Fairy-Stories," *Essays Presented to Charles Williams*, 83-84.

45. Cf. Veith, *Postmodern Times*, 121-40. See also Veith's applications of these ideas to Lewis's fiction in particular in this volume.

46. Walsh, *Light on C. S. Lewis*, 107.

47. Ford, *Jesus for a New Generation*, 49.

48. Ibid.

49. Lewis, *A Preface to Paradise Lost*, 64.

50. Lewis, *Mere Christianity*, 6.

51. Ibid.

52. Cf. Gresham, *Lenten Lands*, x. Writing to Don Giovanni Calabria, a Roman Catholic priest, Lewis says, "Be assured that for me too schism in the Body of Christ is both a source of grief and a matter for prayers, being a most serious stumbling block to those coming in and one which makes even the faithful weaker in repelling the common foe." *Letters: A Study in Friendship*, 31.

53. Lewis, *Mere Christianity*, 12.

54. Bronowski, *The Identity of Man*, 2.

55. Lewis, *The Abolition of Man*, 34. Lewis defines the *Tao* as ". . . The Doctrine of Objective Value, the belief that certain attitudes are really true, and others really false, to the kind of thing the universe is and the kinds of things we are," 29. Cf. Aeschliman, *The Restitution of Man*. Aeschliman quotes Jacques Maritain, *The Peasant of the Garonne* (New York: Holt, Rinehart, 1968), 14: ". . . when everyone starts scorning these things, obscurely perceived by the instinct of the spirit, such as good and evil, moral obligation, justice, law, or even extra-mental reality, truth, the distinction between substance and accident, the principle of identity—it means that everyone is beginning to lose his head."

56. Lewis, *The Abolition of Man*, 35.

57. Lewis, *The Weight of Glory and Other Addresses*, 15.

58. Coupland, *Life After God*, 142.

59. Lewis, *Letters*, 363.

PART TWO

The Explanation:
Why Was C. S. Lewis Such
an Effective Evangelist?

4

LONGING, REASON, AND THE MORAL LAW IN C. S. LEWIS'S SEARCH

CORBIN SCOTT CARNELL

I would like first to summarize Lewis's outer journey and then discuss the three concepts that are so important in his inner journey. He was born in Ireland in 1898. His mother died when he was nine, a very severe blow for him. First he prayed that God would heal her, and then when that prayer was not answered, he prayed that God would bring his mother back to life. When neither prayer was answered, Lewis gave up believing in God. His father sent him and his older brother Warren to various schools in England, usually not well chosen, and Lewis was terribly unhappy at these schools, partly because his thumbs would not bend, which meant that he was no good at any game that involved handling a ball.

Finally his father allowed him to go to study with his own old tutor, a man named Kirkpatrick, who honed Lewis's skills in logic and reasoning. A casual comment by Lewis that he found the countryside in Kirkpatrick's Surrey "wild" was subjected to relentless critical inquiry, an early experience that set the tone for Lewis's stay with Kirkpatrick. Kirkpatrick prepared Lewis so well for Oxford that he won a scholarship, but he had been at the university only a few weeks when he was drafted into the trenches of France during World War I. Wounded in the backside, he was at pains to explain to an aunt that it was because the shell had fallen behind the lines—he wasn't running from the enemy.

Recovering in a military hospital in England, Lewis read the

French Vitalist philosopher Bergson and G. K. Chesterton, both of whom made chinks in his staunch atheism. Returning to Oxford, Lewis saw himself as a monist materialist, believing that matter is all we can know about. But his atheism was subjected to doubts when he discovered that the writers who most appealed to him—Chaucer, Spenser, Shakespeare, Milton, Samuel Johnson—were all Christian believers!

Lewis received his B.A. from Oxford, earning a First in Classics and in English. He then got his M.A. in English and taught philosophy for a year at Oxford, joining the English faculty in 1925 and serving on it for the next thirty years.

Lewis made his reputation as a literary scholar with the books described below. *The Allegory of Love* (1936) was a study of courtly love tradition in medieval and Renaissance literature. In it Lewis elaborates romantic love theory and shows its relevance to Christianity. A second major work is *A Preface to Paradise Lost* (1942), a study that changed the course of Milton criticism. Since the Romantic period it had been fashionable to regard Satan as the hero of *Paradise Lost*, but Lewis showed that Christ is the true hero. His contribution to the *Oxford History of English Literature, English Literature in the 16th Century* (1954) is a monumental study of major and minor writers of the period. Lewis's *An Experiment in Criticism* (1961) and numerous essays helped establish Lewis as a major critic.

Lewis made a second reputation, that as a writer of interplanetary fiction, based on three novels. *Out of the Silent Planet* (1938) was set on the unfallen planet Malacandra (Mars). The second book in the trilogy is *Perelandra* (1943), which retells the Garden of Eden story, set on Perelandra (Venus); it is a sensuous prose poem in which the influence of Milton is strong. (Lewis was working on his Milton book at the time he was writing *Perelandra*.) The third book, *That Hideous Strength* (1945), concerns the struggle between Logres (Arthur's ideal kingdom) and Britain (the mundane England) in twentieth-century England. In it Lewis attacks secularism, social engineering, and relativism and champions nature and human community as countering evil.

In 1943 Lewis published *The Screwtape Letters*, the instructions of a senior tempter written for a junior tempter. In a witty, subversive format, Lewis says many true things about spirituality and moods, prayer, church, sex, humor, and many other subjects. This book got Lewis on the cover of *Time* magazine.

The Great Divorce (1945) was Lewis's next book. It is not exactly a novel but rather a dream fantasy telling of a trip to hell and to heaven. The narrator's guide is nineteenth-century Scottish clergyman-author George MacDonald, who was a major influence on Lewis's ethical and aesthetic beliefs.

In the early 1950s Lewis published his seven Chronicles of Narnia, written for children of all ages. The first published was *The Lion, the Witch and the Wardrobe*, and the seventh was *The Last Battle*. In all these stories various children get into the magic land of Narnia and meet a remarkable lion, Aslan, who represents Christ.

Perhaps Lewis's most rewarding novel is his *Till We Have Faces* (1956), which tells the Cupid-Psyche myth in a new way. It explores many themes, but especially interesting are the nature of the holy and the frighteningly ambiguous nature of love. It is not allegory but myth, into which, Lewis says, we put things that we do not yet know.

Lewis's theological works reflect his development from atheism to an idealism rooted in Greene-Bradley Hegelianism, hence to theism in 1929 (because idealism could not be lived), and then reluctantly to Christianity in 1931. Freud considered religion to be wish fulfillment, but Lewis's experience contradicts that premise. He didn't want Christianity to be true, because if it were, he would be accountable to Someone, and he wanted to be free and independent. He accepted the Christian faith only because reason led him inexorably to believe it to be true.

Reflections on the Psalms (1958) and *Letters to Malcolm: Chiefly on Prayer* (1964) were written late in Lewis's life. The first book drew the attention of the Archbishop of Canterbury (Geoffrey Fisher), who invited him, along with T. S. Eliot, to serve as a literary consultant for the new translation of the Psalms.

In his fifties Lewis met Joy Davidman Gresham and married her, at first in a marriage of convenience to enable her to become a British subject and remain in England. But it grew into a real love relationship, and Jack (as he called himself) and Joy were married by a priest while she was hospitalized for bone cancer. At the same time she received the laying on of hands for healing and enjoyed a three-year remission. During that time Jack and Joy knew great happiness, including a memorable wedding trip to Greece. (This was the only time Lewis traveled outside Great Britain except for his time in France during World War I.) Joy finally succumbed to cancer, dying in 1960. Lewis wrote a beautiful epitaph for her:

> *Here the whole world (stars, water, air,*
>   *And field, and forest, as they were*
> *Reflected in a single mind)*
>   *Like cast off clothes was left behind*
> *In ashes, yet with hope that she,*
>   *Re-born from holy poverty,*
> *In lenten lands, hereafter may*
>   *Resume them on her Easter Day.*

Lewis suffered greatly in his grief but produced a book that has been a comfort to many bereaved, *A Grief Observed* (1961), published pseudonymously in his lifetime. He died in late 1963, on the same day as John F. Kennedy. He had been suffering from heart disease and other problems.

Longing

Now to turn to the three ideas that are so important in understanding Lewis's inner journey. When he was preschool age, his brother brought into the playroom a toy garden, a terrarium that he had made with shells, moss, twigs, and bits of glass. When Lewis held it up to the sunlight, he was struck by a pang of inexpressible longing, a feeling that while painful was also filled with joy. He did not know what to make of it, but he said his idea of paradise would ever after have something of that toy garden in it. And as the reader will see, this experience was to become a pointer to heaven. He experienced the same longing when he looked at the Castlereagh Hills, visible from his Belfast home, when he read Greek and Norse mythology, when he heard Wagner's music or read Wordsworth's poetry. He was to call this experience *Sehnsucht*, the German word for longing or nostalgia.

In school in England, his atheism (launched at his mother's death) fed on his unhappiness. He was to sports, he says in the autobiographical *Surprised by Joy* (1955), as the ass is to the harp, and he was fond of quoting Lucretius: "Had God designed the world, it would not be a world so frail and faulty as we see." The argument from Un-Design haunted Lewis, and he tackles this argument in *The Problem of Pain* (1940) and here and there in other books.

Thus longing is the first of the three major ideas that were to influence Lewis's journey to faith.

REASON AND MYTH

The second major idea is the nature and role of reason. Lewis's philosophical training caused him to speculate on the origin of reason. It is inevitable that we use reason if we are to explore anything. This was brought home to me in 1953 in some correspondence with Lewis. As a graduate student at Columbia I began to question the validity of reason. Freud and Existentialist writers like Kierkegaard, Sartre, and Camus seemed to denigrate reason, and I wrote to Lewis about my misgivings. His reply was the shortest letter I received from him—two sentences: "Your letter finds me in the midst of exams and a complete reply is impossible now. If you are losing your faith in reason, why did you use all those reasons to tell me so?"

Lewis came to believe that for reason to be valid, it must not be simply the chance product of blind evolution. For it to be valid, there must be correspondences between what the mind thinks and what is really out there. Would that mean there must be a divine mind behind reason and the universe?

Linked with his interest in reason was Lewis's profound interest in the nature of myth. Once at an informal gathering of Oxford dons a hard-bitten, no-nonsense anthropologist said that the "rum thing" about all those stories about the dying and rising god was that it looked as if it had really happened once. Lewis says the conversation went on to other things, but he remained thunderstruck by the anthropologist's observation. Could it be, as he says in *Perelandra*, that what we see as myths on earth are scattered throughout the universe as realities? Could myth be related to the human being's amphibious nature—part spirit, part animal? Where do we get those spiritual intimations that we put into myth?

Lewis did not arrive at a completely rational understanding of myth. The subject is too mysterious for that, but he came to conclude that reason and myth arise out of our being created in the divine image. The language God uses to communicate with His creatures is inevitably mythic, partaking as it does of time and eternity. And mythic narratives are always rich in possibilities and meanings—for example, the Garden of Eden story, or the Jonah story, or the story of Jesus, wherein myth has become fact.

I had some interesting correspondence with Lewis on narratives like the Jonah story. It started with my reading a footnote in *Miracles* (1947).

> A consideration of the Old Testament miracles is beyond the scope of this book and would require many kinds of knowledge which I do not possess. My present view—which is tentative and liable to any amount of correction—would be that just as, on the factual side, a long preparation culminates in God's becoming incarnate as Man, so, on the documentary side, the truth first appears in mythical form and then by a long process of condensing or focussing finally becomes incarnate as History. This involves the belief that Myth in general is not merely misunderstood history (as Euhemerus thought) nor diabolical allusion (as some of the Fathers thought) nor priestly lying (as the philosophers of the Enlightenment thought), but, at its best, a real though unfocussed gleam of divine truth falling on human imagination. The Hebrews, like other peoples, had mythology;

but as they were the chosen people so their mythology was the chosen mythology—the mythology chosen by God to be the vehicle of the earliest sacred truths, the first step in that process which ends in the New Testament where truth has become completely historical. Whether we can ever say with certainty where, in this process of crystallisation, any particular Old Testament story falls, is another matter. I take it that the memoirs of David's court come at one end of the scale and are scarcely less historical than St. Mark or Acts; and that the Book of Jonah is at the opposite end. It should be noted that on this view (a) Just as God, in becoming Man, is 'emptied' of His glory, so the truth, when it comes down from the 'heaven' of myth to the 'earth' of history, undergoes a certain humiliation. Hence the New Testament is, and ought to be, more prosaic, in some ways less splendid, than the Old; just as the Old Testament is and ought to be less rich in many kinds of imaginative beauty than the Pagan mythologies. (b) Just as God is none the less God by being Man, so the Myth remains Myth even when it becomes Fact. The story of Christ demands from us, and repays, not only a religious and historical but also an imaginative response. It is directed to the child, the poet, and the savage in us as well as to the conscience and to the intellect. One of its functions is to break down dividing walls.[1]

A letter came from Magdalen College on April 4, 1953:

Dear Mr. Carnell,

I am myself a little uneasy about the question you raise; there seems to be almost equal objection to the position taken up in my footnote and to its alternative of attributing the same kind and degree of historicity to all the books of the Bible. You see, the question about Jonah and the great fish does not turn simply on intrinsic probability. The point is that the whole Book of Jonah has to me the air of being a moral romance, a quite different kind of thing from, say the account of King David or the New Testament narratives, not pegged, like them, into any historical situation.

In what sense does the Bible "present" the Jonah story "as historical"? Of course, it doesn't say "This is fiction", but then neither does our Lord say that the Unjust Judge, Good Samaritan, or Prodigal Son are fiction. (I would put Esther in the same category as Jonah for the same reason.) How does a denial, a doubt, of their historicity lead logically to a similar denial of New Testament miracles? Supposing (as I think is the case), that sound critical reading revealed different kinds of narrative in the Bible, surely it would be illogical to suppose that these different kinds should all be read in the same way?

This is not a "rationalistic approach" to miracles. Where I doubt the historicity of an Old Testament narrative I never do so on the ground that the miraculous as such is incredible. Nor does it deny a unique sort of inspiration: allegory, parable, romance, and lyric might be inspired as well as chronicle. I wish I could direct you to a good book on the subject, but I don't know one.

With all good wishes,
Yours sincerely,
C. S. Lewis.

Lewis's point is that Scripture can be taken seriously without taking it literally, that not all the books of the Bible should be assumed to be chronicle. He does say that if one cannot hold onto a story without thinking of it literally, to go ahead and be literal. But to ask someone whose literary training leads him to view Jonah as a moral romance to cast aside that training and approach the book as chronicle is to ask someone to believe too much. There are two kinds of heresy: believing too little and believing too much. The fundamentalist-literalist heresy asks that we believe more than we should.

In his inner journey Lewis reached several decision points. One involved a bus ride home to the Headington suburb of Oxford. As the bus went up a hill, Lewis was suddenly aware that he could open himself to further truth or he could shut the truth out. He consciously opened himself, and he says in *Surprised by Joy* that he felt like a snowman melting. And then in July 1929, at the age of thirty-one, he knelt in his study at Oxford and admitted that God was God and that human responsibility was real. His conversion was to theism, not yet to Christianity. But one sunny morning two years later, his brother Warren proposed that he and Jack travel on Warren's motorcycle to Whipsnade Zoo north of London. As Lewis records in *Surprised by Joy*, when he left Oxford he did not believe that Jesus was the Son of God and when he got to the zoo, he did believe. Such is the work of the Spirit; things have a way of falling into place when there has been ample preparation. Lewis began at once to attend services daily at Oxford and to be part of his parish church on Sunday. He was later to give some memorable sermons, several of which appear in *The Weight of Glory* (1949).

The Moral Law

Lewis now faced up to the third major idea in his inner journey: the moral law within. He took very seriously Christian discipleship, giving away the royalties from his books and providing a home for the mother of a wartime friend. This woman, who could be domineering and abrasive, took no interest in books, church, or spiritual things. Yet Lewis provided for her for thirty-two years. He also took into his home his brother Warren, retired from the military and an alcoholic. With Jack's loving support, Warren coped remarkably well with his drinking problem. During the war Lewis traveled around to various Royal Air Force bases lecturing on Christianity. He joked about his call to be a hot gospeler being an example of "the unscrupulousness of God." He also gave a series of talks on the BBC. These talks were later published as *Mere Christianity* (1952). And then, perhaps the most dramatic instance of listening to the moral law within, Lewis married an American divorcée to prevent her from being deported. Becoming a British subject, she could receive national health care benefits, which she needed, for she had cancer.

All during his years as a noted author, Lewis received thousands of letters from all over the world, and he must have written, sometimes with Warren's help, some 10,000 replies, rising at 6 A.M. or earlier to tackle the job—a most convincing instance of obeying the moral imperative.

Also, during most of his life at Oxford Lewis was part of a group called the Inklings, which included J. R. R. Tolkien, Charles Williams, Owen Barfield (from time to time—he had a law practice in London), Christopher Tolkien (J. R. R.'s son), Dr. Humphrey Havard (Lewis's physician), Warren Lewis, John Wain, and from time to time Nevill Coghill, Lord David Cecil, and others. The group met at the Eagle and Child pub at midday on Tuesdays and in Lewis's rooms at Oxford on Thursday evenings. The evening usually included reading aloud from works in progress. Lewis read *Perelandra*, Williams read *All Hallows' Eve*, and Tolkien read parts of *The Lord of the Rings*. The latter as well as Tolkien's *The Hobbit*, were published only with Lewis's constant prodding. Tolkien was a perfectionist, and it was only through Lewis's persistence that Tolkien's works ever saw print.

Visible theists when it was fashionable in academia to hide one's religious convictions, Romantics when Romanticism was out of fashion, the Inklings supported each other, and Lewis was at ease with being few against the world. The conversations and interests of this group were to help mold Lewis's thought and writings. No small part of the life of this group were the walking tours Lewis went on with Tolkien especially but with others from the group as well. They would go into Scotland or Wales and walk twenty-five miles a day. It was sometimes frustrating to walk with Tolkien who occasionally would stop to embrace a tree and listen to it. Tolkien was fascinated by the details of their terrain, just as he was interested in details in his fiction.

The three ideas that so haunted Lewis's intellectual and spiritual search—longing, reason, and the moral law—all came to be understood by Lewis as being the results of living in a world made by a gracious Creator who seeks to draw human beings to Himself.

A concluding word on Lewis as a citizen of academia: he had no interest in academic politics, and the idea of holding power did not appeal to him. One need only look at his essay on "The Inner Ring" to see how he viewed the search for power. And one of his fictional villains, Devine, is a big politico in his college. Lewis conducted his tutorials, lectured, and published scholarly works, but beyond an occasional committee he did not participate much in the governance of the university. With Tolkien, he did shape the content of the curriculum in English literature for many years, but except for that, Lewis was largely uninterested in governance.

Lewis wisely focused on the life of the mind and the spirit, and we are very much in his debt.

We are particularly indebted to him for modeling a style of evangelism that is effective for our age. This style involves not only a strong, systematic Christian apologetic but a sharing out of his own spiritual journey. And that sharing is exactly what this paper is about. In *Surprised by Joy* Lewis tells his story chronologically, but he alludes to his personal search for meaning throughout his writings. Even in the fiction there are many ideas that reflect his spiritual journey. For example, in *Till We Have Faces* there is Orual's demand for visible, palpable certainty. In *Perelandra* there is the idea that what is seen as myth on one planet may be factual reality on another. In *The Lion, the Witch and the Wardrobe* there is an echo of Christ's atoning death.

The nature of myth and his continuing struggle to understand myth was crucial in Lewis's conversion. And he drew on myth in much of his writing. Lewis believed that Christian theology can be implicit in fiction, drama, and poetry, and that the reader's guard against Christianity is down when he is reading literature, that the truth strikes home "past watchful dragons," to use his phrase.

Lewis worked in many literary forms: letters as in *The Screwtape Letters*, children's stories as in the Chronicles of Narnia, space fiction as in the trilogy beginning with *Out of the Silent Planet*, narrative poetry as in *Dymer*, allegory as in *The Pilgrim's Regress*, and others. His style is immensely varied, though he is always careful to do three things: 1) to not talk down to his readers, 2) to use vivid analogies and examples, as in the image of the red lizard of lust being changed into the glorious stallion of good desire in *The Great Divorce*, and 3) to address the whole person, especially through his use of the mythic, which Lewis says addresses us deeply, including the child and the savage in us.

Would that God would raise up a new apologist/evangelist with Lewis's literary gifts. The time is ripe.

Longing, Reason, and the Moral Law in C. S. Lewis's Search

BIBLIOGRAPHY

Lewis, C. S. *The Allegory of Love: A Study in Medieval Tradition*. Oxford: Clarendon Press, 1936.

_____. *English Literature in the Sixteenth Century, Excluding Drama*. Vol. 3 of the *Oxford History of English Literature*. Oxford: Clarendon Press, 1954.

_____. *An Experiment in Criticism*. Cambridge: Cambridge University Press, 1961.

_____. *The Great Divorce: A Dream*. London: Geoffrey Bles, 1945.

_____. [N. W. Clerk, pseud.] *A Grief Observed*. London: Faber and Faber, 1961.

_____. *The Last Battle*. London: Bodley Head, 1956.

_____. *Letters to Malcolm: Chiefly on Prayer*. London: Geoffrey Bles, 1964.

_____. *The Lion, the Witch and the Wardrobe*. London: Geoffrey Bles, 1950.

_____. *Mere Christianity*. London: Geoffrey Bles, 1952.

_____. *Miracles: a Preliminary Study*. New York: Macmillan, 1947.

_____. *Out of the Silent Planet*. London: John Lane, 1938.

_____. *Perelandra*. London: John Lane, 1943.

_____. *A Preface to Paradise Lost*. London: Oxford University Press, 1942.

_____. *The Problem of Pain*. London: Geoffrey Bles, 1940.

_____. *Reflections on the Psalms*. London: Geoffrey Bles, 1958.

_____. *The Screwtape Letters*. London: Geoffrey Bles, 1942.

_____. *Surprised by Joy: The Shape of My Early Life*. London: Geoffrey Bles, 1955.

_____. *That Hideous Strength: A Modern Fairy Tale for Grown Ups*. London: John Lane, 1945.

_____. *Till We Have Faces: A Myth Retold*. London: Geoffrey Bles, 1956.

_____. *The Weight of Glory and Other Addresses*. New York: Macmillan, 1949.

NOTES

1. Lewis, *Miracles*, 161.

5

GOD'S CHOSEN INSTRUMENT:

The Temper of an Apostle

ANGUS J. L. MENUGE

Yet take Thy way; for, sure, Thy way is best:
Stretch or contract me Thy poor debtor:
This is but tuning of my breast,
To make the music better.[1]

As a child, C. S. Lewis had a naive but sincere faith, but during adolescence he descended into apostasy.[2] By the time he was a young man, and although he carefully concealed it from his father (even agreeing to his confirmation and first communion in complete unbelief[3]), he was a committed atheist. In 1916, he wrote to his friend Arthur Greeves:

> [Y]ou know, I think, that I believe in no religion. There is absolutely no proof for any of them, and from a philosophical standpoint, Christianity is not even the best. All religions, that is, all mythologies to give them their proper name, are merely man's own invention.[4]

These are hardly the opinions one would expect from a man who would become perhaps the best-known Christian apologist of the twentieth century. Yet despite the seemingly impossible task of penetrating the carapace of his unbelief, God initiated a spiritual game of chess with Lewis that culminated in his mental and spiritual transfiguration. In his middle years, Lewis became an outstanding representative of Christianity, both in his personal life and in the staggering output of his books, articles, talks, and correspondence. The peculiar route of this pilgrim's "regress" to his lost faith is examined in this volume by Corbin Scott Carnell.[5] By contrast, the focus of the present chapter is not how Lewis rediscovered Christianity, but what it was about his life that made him such an effective evangelist when he did.

I will begin with an extended comparison of the spiritual lives of Lewis and Saint Paul, attempting to show that despite many differences, there are revealing similarities between the two figures that help explain why both were great evangelists. Although both were chosen by grace, each had qualities that, when transformed by faith, superbly equipped him for his appointed role. A further section explores how Lewis put his newfound Christian armor to the test, battling the seductive anti-Christian philosophies of the spirit of the age.

The Formation of an Apostle:
A Comparison of C. S. Lewis to Saint Paul[6]

> *"This man is my chosen instrument to carry my name before the Gentiles. . . . I will show him how much he must suffer for my name."*
>
> —*Acts 9:15-16*

Before I begin, a disclaimer is in order. There are, of course, many important differences between Paul and Lewis. For example, even as an inwardly firm atheist, Lewis was never a persecutor of the church; and though his career did suffer because of his faith, he was never flogged or imprisoned for it as Paul was. It should also go without saying that Paul was, and is, far more important to the Christian Church than C. S. Lewis. Yet, just as Christianity might have remained an elite and obscure sect without the missionary work of Paul, so it might have atrophied again in this century were it not for those like Lewis who translated Christian doctrine into contemporary idiom. Thus although Paul is far greater than Lewis, Lewis is following in the same footsteps as Paul, and this is all I am claiming in making a comparison between the two.

Preparation

> *I was advancing in Judaism beyond many Jews of my own age and was extremely zealous for the traditions of my fathers.*
> —*Galatians 1:14*

Saint Paul and C. S. Lewis were both schooled in many ways of non-Christian thought prior to an adult conversion to Christianity. Paul was born in Tarsus, a cultural intersection of Roman, Jewish, and Greek thought. Tarsus was in a Roman province, so Paul was eligible for Roman citizenship. Paul's parents were well-educated. It is generally thought that his mother was a devout Jew, concerned to send Paul to a school in Jerusalem that adhered to the strictest sect of the Pharisees. Paul's father may have been of a more liberal persuasion, sympathetic with Hellenistic Judaism. At any rate, Paul was also exposed to Greek philosophy and religion through the teachings of the Hellenistic Diaspora. Paul's intellectual development was combined with a tremendous zeal for the Lord. Before his conversion to Christianity, he was a highly energetic missionary to the Gentiles on behalf of Judaism. Thus Paul was raised with a broad-minded understanding of the leading non-Christian worldviews of the day and a great enthusiasm for evangelism, which eminently qualified him for his future role as a Christian missionary to Jews and Gentiles.

C. S. Lewis was born on the outskirts of Belfast. Like Paul, he was the son of highly educated parents (his father was a solicitor, his mother had a degree in mathematics and logic). Lewis, like Paul, developed a broad understanding of non-Christian thought, aided by his unsupervised and catholic reading from the vast array of books in his parents' house: "There were . . . books of all kinds reflecting every transient stage of my parents' interest, books readable and unreadable, books suitable for a child and books most emphatically not."[7] He was particularly fascinated by mythology, which sometimes provoked stabs of "joy," a spiritual thirsting that he could not as yet decipher, but that later enabled him to understand the pagan search for the tran-scendent,[8] personified by the character John in *The Pilgrim's Regress*, the first major work after his conversion.

Just as Paul was an outstanding Pharisee, expert in knowledge and zealous in observance of the Law, so Lewis was to become a highly trained intellectual atheist. He benefited greatly from exposure to the powerful atheistic mind of William T. Kirkpatrick, Lewis's personal tutor before he studied at Oxford. Kirkpatrick relentlessly eradicated ambiguity, vagueness, unthinking prejudice, and unguarded assertion from Lewis's thought and expression, replacing them with a steely yet fluid logical reasoning.[9] At the time, this only made Lewis a more redoubtable atheist, but reason, he would learn, was a two-edged sword, as apt to vanquish the secular *Zeitgeist* as to pose problems for Christianity.[10] In the end, as we shall see, it was through the maturity of his reason that Lewis demolished many of his own stumbling blocks and, after his conversion, advanced the Christian cause.

Unlike Paul, Lewis was not a missionary before his conversion. But as we shall see, the peculiar manner of his apostasy equipped Lewis to become a Christian evangelist by helping him understand the obstacles lying in the path of unbelievers. By a careful examination of each assault made on his faith, Lewis would learn how to shield others from similar attacks.

Unlikely Converts

> [A]nd last of all he appeared to me also, as to one abnormally born.
>
> —*1 Corinthians 15:8*

It is hard to imagine a more unlikely convert to Christianity than Paul. Before his conversion, he was the leading persecutor of "the way," so zealous that he even sought out Christian exiles in foreign cities for extradition (Acts 26:11). Furthermore, Paul believed there were unanswerable objections to Christianity. From the perspective of his devout Judaism, a "crucified Messiah was a contradiction in terms,"[11] because "anyone who is hung on a tree is under God's curse" (Deuteronomy 21:23). Only later did Paul see that Christ's being a curse for us was essential to his salvific role (Galatians 3:13). Likewise, Christianity seemed out of court because it contradicted the Jews' insistence on circumcision as the seal of divine election. After his conversion, it was Paul who argued that what mattered was not "outward and physical" circumcision but "circumcision of the heart" (Romans 2:28-29).

While he was no persecutor of Christianity, Lewis had a powerful antipathy towards it, owing to his pronounced dislike of being interfered with and his realization that, if He existed, the Christian God was the Great Interferer. Thus Lewis describes himself as a most unwilling convert:

> That which I had greatly feared had at last come upon me. In the Trinity Term of 1929 I gave in, and admitted that God was God, and knelt and prayed: perhaps, that night, the most dejected and reluctant convert in all England. . . . The Prodigal Son at least walked home on his own feet. But who can duly adore that Love which will open the high gates to a prodigal who is brought in kicking, struggling, resentful, and darting his eyes in every direction for a chance of escape?[12]

There were also the many conscious and unconscious objections to Christianity that provoked his apostasy. While at Cherbourg school, he had not yet identified joy as a thirst for the heavenly, and, unintentionally, the spiritually immature matron corrupted him with alternative, attractive, and above all, less demanding explanations such as those offered by Theosophy, Rosicrucianism, and Spiritualism.[13] This excited in Lewis a "spiritual lust" for alternative realities, replacing the demands of belief with those of feeling only,[14] prefiguring the dangerous contemporary phenomenon of feel-good religion. Above all, Lewis

The Temper of an Apostle

enjoyed the lack of responsibility afforded by a vague spiritualism. He was relieved to give up prayer, as his faulty understanding of Christian teaching had led him into an impossibly demanding prayer righteousness,[15] which he would later warn against for the benefit of others.[16] Instead of having faith that God hears our prayers, however incompetent, and even sends His Spirit to pray for us when we do not know how, Lewis believed true prayer involved a subjective experience of authenticity, a "realization." The problem, of course, was that one could never know if one had really reached that state, leading to frustration, guilt, and exhaustion.[17]

Further intellectual support for Lewis's apostasy came from the attitude taken to Christianity's pagan rivals: "all teachers and editors took it for granted from the outset that these religious ideas were sheer illusion."[18] This being so, Lewis could not see why Christianity should be any different: how could it be true, when all the similar mythologies and religions were false? It was only later and with the help of J. R. R. Tolkien and Hugo Dyson that Lewis was able to expose the fallacy of this line of thinking. He realized that pagan myths often did contain glimpses of truth, albeit in a distorted form, and his question now became, "Where has religion reached its true maturity? Where, if anywhere, have the hints of all Paganism been fulfilled?"[19] He came to see, and then helped others to see in *The Pilgrim's Regress* and elsewhere, that pagan ideas were not to be dismissed as simply false, but to be viewed as valuable pointers on the way to the truth.

Also stacked against Lewis's crumbling faith was an ingrained pessimism, a tendency to think that bad was inherently more likely than good. This was fueled by the early death of his mother, his manual clumsiness, which made it seem as if the world was at odds with him, his father's baseless threats of impending financial doom, and his sympathy with the spirit of Lucretius' argument from "undesign"[20]:

> *Had God designed the world, it would not be*
> *A world so frail and faulty as we see.*

Later Lewis was to see that faith in any person, including a Divine Person, inevitably involves commitment in the face of apparent evidence of a lack of love,[21] and he argued at length that evil is compatible with the existence of a loving God.[22]

Further inside experience of the spiritual obstacles to Christianity was Lewis's gradual slide into worldly snobbery. He became a social snob through emulation of the master he dubbed "Pogo," a sophisticated follower of fashion.[23] But he became an intellectual snob (or prig) by perceiving his intellectual superiority to the elite "Bloods" of Malvern College, delighting in Loki's riposte to Thor: "I pay respect to wisdom not to strength."[24] As Lewis said, "Loki was a projection of myself; he voiced that sense of priggish superiority whereby I was, unfortunately, beginning to compensate myself for my unhappiness."[25]

Lewis's social snobbery was demolished by the poverty in which he was forced to live after the First World War and before his election to a fellowship in 1925. On a meager scholarship and an allowance from his father, Lewis had to provide for himself and for both Mrs. Moore and her daughter Maureen (Lewis's friend Paddy Moore had died in the war, and Lewis had promised to look after his family if he did). From this, and the many needy people Mrs. Moore invited to stay, Lewis gained a real understanding of poverty[26] and later warned others about the dangers of worldliness.[27]

The dragon of Lewis's intellectual snobbery was slain by his many relations with those less well-educated than himself during and after the First World War. This is surely one of the reasons for the simple style and concrete workaday examples used by Lewis in his popular writings. (Sadly, it seems that not all critics of Lewis have overcome this snobbery themselves, apparently mistaking his simplicity and directness for a lack of intellect or study.) Later, when Lewis's public Christianity led him to be isolated from some parts of the intellectual establishment, he spoke out against self-righteous exclusivism[28] and the desire of an elite group to control the destinies of the rest of mankind.[29]

The Temper of an Apostle

Tempered by Suffering

> *I want to know Christ and the power of his resurrection and the fellowship of sharing in his sufferings.*
>   —*Philippians 3:10*

Both Paul and Lewis were strengthened by suffering. Before their conversion, they each suffered powerful inner tensions and craved a reconciliation that, though they did not know it, could only be found in Christ. For Paul, the tension was between a burning desire to evangelize the Gentiles and the strict separation from others that was the negative part of the Pharisaic understanding of holiness. Scholars believe that the word *Pharisee* almost certainly means "separated one,"[30] and if that is so, a Pharisee who seeks to evangelize the Gentiles is a practical contradiction in terms. Lewis too, was a walking oxymoron. Before he became an idealist, Lewis was officially committed to a materialism that excluded all spirituality from the universe; yet his powerful romantic longings could be meaningful only if a transcendent realm existed.

Both men needed a view of life that ended the divorce between their hearts and minds; both found their marriage in Christianity. In fact, this union had both an internal and an external dimension. Internally, Christianity reconciled Paul's concern for the Gentiles with his zeal for the Law since it offers a righteousness through faith that is available to all (Romans 3:21-22), and it reconciled Lewis's romantic longing with his logical scruples because he saw how a reasoned case could be made for the supernatural aspects of the universe.[31] Externally, Paul was partially successful in reconciling Pharisees and Gentiles with one another by showing that sin and a need for faith were common to both, and Lewis helped draw together the logically minded with those of a romantic persuasion.

Before his conversion, Lewis also suffered in ways that would later help him identify with the pain of others. He was sent to several highly disagreeable schools. His mother died when he was not quite ten years old. He saw men horribly killed in the First World War, which led not to nightmares, but to a single, recurring nightmare.[32]

After their conversion, both Paul and Lewis suffered for their faith. Paul faced many physical hardships and persecutions from non-Christians on account of his preaching of the Gospel (2 Corinthians 11:23ff.). He responded with still more energetic preaching, even using his trials as opportunities for evangelism.[33] Harder to bear was the naked rebellion of fellow Christians when Paul confronted the wayward church at Corinth.[34] Paul did his best, however, to offer the reconciliation that comes from God (2 Corinthians 5:11-21) and to defend his ministry (2 Corinthians 10).

When he made his Christianity public, Lewis felt the pain of intellectual isolation from some of his colleagues and was undoubtedly denied deserved promotions, never attaining the rank of Professor while he remained at Oxford University. As in Paul's case, it was especially hard for Lewis to bear the rejection of fellow Christians, who viewed faith as something to be kept private.[35] This exclusion encouraged Lewis to form strong, close-knit relations with his real friends, such as the Inklings; it helped him to be sympathetic with the many lost sheep who feel shut out of organized religion; and, just as in the case of Paul, it made him only the more determined to carry out his mission. When criticized by his peers for not writing the "serious" academic work of which he was capable, Lewis responded by an even greater output of unmistakably Christian apologetics and with children's stories and adult novels with a latent Christian message as well.[36] Finally, Lewis suffered the loss of his late-won wife to cancer; yet even this devastating event enabled him to help others work through similar trials by provoking his penetrating study of the grieving process.[37]

Both Lewis and Paul learned humility by encountering failure in their missionary work. For example, Paul met only ridicule when he attempted to evangelize Agrippa: "Do you think that in such a short time you can persuade me to be a Christian?" (Acts 26:28). Likewise Lewis, in his attempts to promote Christianity among the armed forces during the Second World War, "considered his first talks, which were

The Temper of an Apostle

at the RAF station near Abingdon, a complete failure."[38] One of the things we should learn to emulate is Paul's and Lewis's response to failure; they learned from their mistakes and tried again even harder.

Transfiguration

> *I am the least of the apostles and do not even deserve to be called an apostle, because I persecuted the church of God. But by the grace of God I am what I am, and his grace to me was not without effect.*
> —*1 Corinthians 15:9-10*

Despite their longing for reconciliation, the decisive change in Paul's and Lewis's lives came not from their own activity, but from God. Paul was not starting to reevaluate Christianity when he was stopped in his tracks on the road to Damascus; he was intent on capturing Christian prisoners (Acts 9:2). The roadblock he met, Jesus Christ, permanently altered his worldview. Lewis, by contrast, was engaged, rather fearfully, in removing some of the stumbling blocks to belief. But the decisive move in this protracted game of chess was God's, as is evidenced by the passive descriptions of the process Lewis himself gives. At one point he says, "I felt as if I were a man of snow at long last beginning to melt."[39] Later he tells us:

> When we set out I did not believe that Jesus Christ is the Son of God, and when we reached the zoo I did. Yet I had not exactly spent the journey in thought. Nor in great emotion. . . . It was more like when a man, after long sleep, still lying motionless in bed, becomes aware that he is now awake.[40]

Though none are chosen by God because of their merit, we know that Paul was chosen by God to bring the light of the Gospel to the Gentiles (Acts 9:15) and that, as we have seen, he was uniquely well-qualified to do so. Likewise, Lewis was surely appointed to bring Christianity to a world floundering in materialism and moral relativism, which, having lost the unity of mind and heart achieved by the medievals, was bifurcated in its reason and imagination. And as we have seen, even the most unfortunate things that happened to Lewis only equipped him the better to be an evangelist.

What happened to both Paul and Lewis is best described as a transfiguration, a complete change in their spiritual life and in their worldview. Yet at the same time, the skills, attitudes, and knowledge acquired in their pre-conversion life were not merely discarded. So far as these characteristics were bad, or badly used, they did in a sense have to die in order for the "new men"[41] to appear. But as Lewis argued, the bad that is in us dies only so it may be reborn and transformed into something good.[42] Here, of course, Lewis is echoing Paul's teaching that through union with Christ we can, as he did, die to sin and live a new life (Romans 6:4-7).

In response to the personal revelation of Christ on the road to Damascus, Paul was changed from indefatigable enemy of the Way to leading evangelist and church-builder: "With astonishing suddenness the persecutor of the church became the apostle of Jesus Christ."[43] Paul indeed is very clear about his own appointed role upon conversion: "God, who set me apart from birth and called me by his grace, was pleased to reveal his Son in me so that I might preach him among the Gentiles" (Galatians 1:15-16). Commenting on this verse, F. F. Bruce insightfully points out that there seems to have been no inertial gap between Paul's conversion and his mission work: "He speaks as if the call and commission were part of the one conversion experience."[44]

Lewis's response to Christ was no less striking. He had been a private man who resented interference and used the character John in *The Pilgrim's Regress* to express how he initially found the presence of God in his life a claustrophobic prospect:

[C]aught into slavery again, to walk warily and on sufferance all his days, never to be alone; never the master of his own soul, to have no privacy, no corner whereof you could say to the whole universe: This is my own, here I can do as I please.[45]

The Temper of an Apostle

By contrast, after Lewis's conversion, God permeated every aspect of his life, and in many ways Lewis became an intensely public man. He wrote many popular Christian books, gave radio talks despite hating the radio because he knew he would reach a wider audience, visited military bases, preached at a Tom Rees rally at Westminster Chapel in London with Stephen Olford, wrote reams of personal correspondence giving individualized Christian advice to the many people who had questions for him, and shared bonhomie with truck drivers whom he met in a transport cafe on the way to Cambridge with his driver, Clifford Morris.[46] Looking only at his written output, a careful study shows that all his post-conversion work revealed his Christian outlook; even in his most scholarly works (where the pressure to conform to the secular expectations prevailing in academia is greater) such as *A Preface to Paradise Lost*, Lewis emphasizes the contribution of Christian ideas.

For Lewis too, there was little delay between conversion and apostleship, except that humility led him to spend some time learning the idiom of a popular audience:

> He devoted himself to developing and strengthening his belief, and almost from the year of his conversion, he wanted to become an evangelist for the Christian faith. . . . But first of all, highbrow and intellectual as he was, he would have to learn to write simply.[47]

There is, in this willingness to speak the language of one's audience,[48] a significant echo of the divine humility that moved God to become man. In both cases there is a descent, a willingness to rub shoulders with ordinary people, even with outcasts and undesirables, a descent that invites scorn and ridicule from the elite and self-righteous, but that carries out God's plan for mankind.

Vision of an Inclusive Christianity

> *There is neither Jew nor Greek, slave nor free, male nor female, for you are all one in Christ.*
>
> *—Galatians 3:28*

The missions of Paul and Lewis were worldwide in their scope. This was intentional in Paul's case: he set up mission posts as centers for further growth throughout the Mediterranean world, his astonishing zeal and endurance fueled by his perception of the urgency of evangelism. "How, then, can they call on the one they have not believed in? And how can they believe in the one of whom they have not heard? And how can they hear without someone preaching to them?" (Romans 10:14). For Paul, his "sole task as apostle is to go on to complete God's action and to proclaim it to the ends of the earth."[49] And in this task, and despite great sufferings and sometimes failure, Paul was spectacularly successful: "he outstripped all others as a pioneer missionary and planter of churches."[50]

While Lewis certainly sought a wide audience in the English-speaking world, it is unlikely that he thought of himself as having a worldwide mission. God, however, seems to have had different ideas, and my guess is that Lewis would be astonished to see the number of languages into which his books have been translated and the high volume of sales that they continue to command. Lewis is one of the best-known Christian authors in the world, although not all those who know his works know they are Christian.

In an important sense, Christianity is an exclusive view; it says that those who continue to reject Christ will be excluded from salvation. However, both Paul and Lewis were keenly aware through their own life experience that there were many unnecessary obstacles to faith that could be removed without in any way diluting or changing the Gospel, in order to allow the inclusion of as many as possible.

Paul clearly states the duty of an evangelist: "We put no stumbling block in anyone's path, so that our ministry will not be discredited" (2 Corinthians 6:3). Among the obstacles to faith are the various divisions within the Church, which he himself, as one great preacher among many, might inadvertently cause. Paul is powerful in his attack on this dangerous cult of personalities other than Christ's:

> One of you says, "I follow Paul"; another, "I follow Apollos"; another, "I follow Cephas"; still another, "I follow Christ." Is

The Temper of an Apostle

> *Christ divided? Was Paul crucified for you? . . . What, after all,*
> *is Apollos? And what is Paul? Only servants, through whom*
> *you came to believe. . . . I planted the seed, Apollos watered it,*
> *but God made it grow.*
>   —*1 Corinthians 1:12-13; 3:5-6*

Paul was particularly concerned to heal the divisions between Jews and Gentiles, emphasizing the universality of the Gospel (Romans 1:16) and advising them to avoid offending each other through their different customs and eating habits: "So whether you eat or drink or whatever you do, do it all for the glory of God. Do not cause anyone to stumble, whether Jews, Greeks or the church of God" (1 Corinthians 10:31-32). Thus Paul chastised Peter, who had acculturated himself to the Gentiles, for hypocritically reverting to Jewish customs when he knew that Jewish Christians were visiting (Galatians 2:11-21).

In Paul's efforts to bind Christians together, he does not suggest they become the indistinguishable drones of a collective, but that each play their distinctive role in an organized body (1 Corinthians 12:12-27). This vision of Christian unity is one that Lewis, who had a horror of the collective, clearly endorsed, arguing that we shall reach our truest identity as "organs in the body of Christ."[51] Both would agree that each "organ" has a distinctive role, that each depends on the others, and that while the variety is essential to a well-functioning body and in that sense makes a difference, it does not make a difference to salvation (see Galatians 3:28, quoted above).

By contrast with Paul, Lewis's concern for Christian unity arose in the modern climate of denominationalism. His best-known contribution to Christian unity is his idea of "mere Christianity,"[52] a core of fundamental ideas common among the various denominations. Although he credits Richard Baxter with the term "mere Christianity,"[53] I suspect the philosophical idea derived from Lewis's reading of Chesterton, who said of his defense of Christianity, "When the word 'orthodoxy' is used here it means the Apostles' creed, as understood by everybody calling himself Christian."[54] It is not that Lewis thought the differences between denominations were unimportant; he sincerely felt they were matters that should only be discussed between Christians (and often only by experts) and never in the company of unbelievers who will naturally find them a stumbling block to belief.

> [T]he discussion of . . . disputed points has no tendency at all to bring an outsider into the Christian fold. . . . Our divisions should never be discussed except in the presence of those who have already come to believe that there is one God and that Jesus Christ is his only Son.[55]

That Lewis has been successful in his attempts to foster unity among diversity is clear. It is quite hard to find a major Christian denomination that does not claim Lewis as its representative. In this, Lewis has carried on the same basic mission so valiantly begun by Paul.

Sensitivity to Audience

> *I have become all things to all men so that by all possible means I might save some.*
>   —1 Corinthians 9:22

A popular saying has it that "It takes one to know one." Christ Himself, who knew all about us, chose to know us more personally by being one of us. Paul and Lewis understood their non-Christian audience so well because they had been such talented members of it, and this enabled them to speak in ways with which their hearers could identify.[56] Paul had the remarkable fortune to be a Pharisee, educated in Greek culture, and a Roman citizen, all characteristics that he at some time used to advantage in his preaching of the Gospel. Paul knew well that the Gospel was "a stumbling block to Jews and foolishness to Gentiles" (1 Corinthians 1:23).

For Jews, Paul knew that a major obstacle was the one he had encountered: a crucified Messiah was a blasphemous contradiction in terms. Against this Paul argued that "Christ redeemed us from the

The Temper of an Apostle

curse of the law by becoming a curse for us" (Galatians 3:13) and that righteousness was to be attained through faith, not works, as was clear from the Jews' own teaching about Abraham and David (Romans 4). To show that he knew what he was talking about, Paul reminded his Jewish audience that he was a Jew trained in the Law under Gamaliel, used Aramaic to show he was a Hebrew (Acts 22:1-3), and confessed to being a Pharisee (Acts 23:6), pointing out that Christianity agrees with the Pharisees' tradition of holding to the resurrection of the dead.

While the Jews were held back by a very narrow and exclusive tradition, the Greeks had the opposite problem—an incontinent proliferation of gods of all kinds, and yet, in that very fact, a strong indication that they were still searching and did not really know what to believe. Paul sensed the agnosticism that underlay their apparently religious lives and masterfully located Christ as someone already latent and sought after in their culture.

> *Men of Athens! I see that in every way you are very religious. For as I walked around and observed your objects of worship, I even found an altar with this inscription: TO AN UNKNOWN GOD. Now what you worship as something unknown I am going to proclaim to you.*
>
> —*Acts 17:22-23*

(Here there is a striking parallel to Lewis. One might say that joy was an altar to an unknown God, a God greater than any of the pagan candidates.) At the same time, however, Paul was careful not to attempt the sort of philosophical defense of Christianity that the Greeks expected, for that would obscure the real meaning of the Gospel. He sought "to preach the gospel—not with words of human wisdom, lest the cross of Christ be emptied of its power" (1 Corinthians 1:17). Paul wanted to convey the important fact that what Christ did, and not human rhetoric, must be the cornerstone of their faith. It was thus important for Paul to undermine the Greeks' confidence in human wisdom: "For the foolishness of God is wiser than man's wisdom" (1 Corinthians 1:25).

When preaching to the Romans, Paul was less certain of his audience, though he used his status as a Roman citizen to continue his mission work unhindered (Acts 22:22-29), and his letter to the Romans employs the style, familiar to Roman discourse, of the stoic "diatribe,"[57] a lengthy discussion including a statement of, and answer to, the anticipated questions of the audience. Paul's careful and honest consideration of the real objections and difficulties of his hearers is one of his strongest resemblances to C. S. Lewis. In reading Lewis's apologetic work, one often gets the impression that in defending a Christian claim, he harks back to the very objections he himself once had to it and with patience and understanding attempts to defuse them.

Lewis, like Paul, had a clear grasp of the obstacles, natural as well as intellectual, that his audience faced. For the thoroughly modern materialist, the supernatural claims of orthodox Christianity must seem incredible when compared to "real life," by which is meant the world of ordinary experience. To defuse this favoritism for the familiar, Lewis pointed out that the fundamental entities of modern physics, in which the materialist does believe, are invisible and intangible.[58] Lewis knew, too, that our enchantment with the ordinary is powerful because it is natural; what he feared was "that soft tidal return of your habitual outlook as you close the book and the familiar four walls about you and the familiar noises from the street re-assert themselves."[59] Against this, Lewis argues that such an outlook is irrational.

> The moment rational thought ceases, imagination, mental habit, temperament, and the "spirit of the age" take charge of you again.[60]

Lewis also knew there was tremendous diversity among his audience both in education and in the sort of difficulties that people had. To deal with this diversity, as many of the writers in this volume attest, Lewis employed an extraordinary variety of literary methods (poetry, science fiction, children's stories, allegory, apologetics, and scholarly articles) and directed his works to people at many different levels, ranging from children with limited education to trained academics.

The Temper of an Apostle

PUTTING ON THE FULL ARMOR OF GOD:
LEWIS IN DARKEST *Zeitgeistheim*[61]

> *Put on the full armor of God so that you can take your stand*
> *against the devil's schemes.*
>   —*Ephesians 6:11*

I will now examine a little more closely how Lewis used the skills
and abilities he had acquired as an atheist, once they were transformed
by his conversion.[62]

Logic: A Two-Edged Sword

> *We demolish arguments and every pretension that sets itself up*
> *against the knowledge of God, and we take captive every*
> *thought to make it obedient to Christ.*
>   —*2 Corinthians 10:4-5*

Logic, which had made Lewis a formidable atheist, eventually
helped him clear the path back to Christianity. His belief that
Christians were necessarily complacent, weak-minded fools was eliminated by his discovery of believers both during and after the First
World War who were among the ablest minds of their generation.[63]
His feeling of the modern's intellectual superiority over an ancient
myth was unmasked by Owen Barfield as mere chronological snobbery, "the uncritical acceptance of the intellectual climate common to
our own age and the assumption that whatever has gone out of date
is on that account discredited."[64] Logically, Lewis realized, the antiq-
uity of an idea has nothing to do with its truth or falsity; what he
needed to examine were arguments for or against it.

Around the same time, Lewis came to realize that none of the popular debunking philosophies provided a satisfactory account of the
nature and meaning of joy, but that Christianity did. This discovery
arose from no mere intellectual use of logic but from a consideration
of the logical consequences of his own life. Soon after his conversion,

Lewis expressed this through an Arthurian hermit speaking to the protagonist John:

> You have proved it for yourself: you have lived the proof. Has not every object which fancy and sense suggested for the desire, proved a failure, confessed itself, after trial, not to be what you wanted? Have you not found by elimination that this desire is the perilous siege in which only one can sit?[65]

How did Lewis unmask the unworthy pretenders for this holy seat? One idea was that joy was a disguised yearning for sexuality (represented by "brown girls" in *The Pilgrim's Regress*). Lewis found, however, that his desire for joy remained even when sexual desires were satisfied, that pursuing sex to satisfy joy was like taking Leah for Rachel. A second idea was that the thirst that is joy can be quenched through aesthetic experience, and temporarily this is effective,[66] but only as a fantasy.[67] After this draft, Lewis was always thirsty again; so this was not the water that ends all thirst (John 4:14).

Then there is the Freudian idea that joy is the product of wish-fulfillment and that any nobler image of joy's object was merely a pretense designed to obscure sexual lust.[68] This idea is backed by the generally reductionist *Zeitgeist*, which turns out to be a more difficult giant to slay.[69]

The Copy and the Original

> *For Christ did not enter a man-made sanctuary that was only a copy of the true one: he entered heaven itself, now to appear for us in God's presence.*
>
> —*Hebrews 9:24*

In *The Pilgrim's Regress*, John attempts to refute the Freudians by arguing that there is a clear difference between the noble and the ignoble, so that the former cannot be reduced to the latter. He is obstructed by the claim that an argument such as his is merely "the attempted rationalization of the arguer's desires."[70] Later he realizes that this stance is untenable, since it is an attempt to argue that arguments have no credibility: if so, no argument including the Freudian's is credible. On the other hand, if the Freudian argument is credible, then so may be others, so each argument will have to be examined on its merits.[71]

In his attempt to defend the noble ideas of morality and religion against the Freudians, Lewis finds a general argument that reveals a fundamental flaw in all the debunking philosophies arrayed against Christianity. Reason, portrayed by a mounted woman in armor, asks John, "By what rule do you tell a copy from the original?"[72] John then begins to see that the debunking views have the common assumption that all our noble ideas are merely copies of some ignoble original. Thus for Freudians the noble ideas of God and a moral law are copies of the infantile desire for security or the desire to obscure one's own lust, for Marxists they are masks for inequitable distribution of capital, and for Fascists they are a means of subverting the superman's will to power.[73]

But why should we believe that "if two things are similar, the fair one is always the copy of the foul one"?[74] This assumption is not obviously true, and as Lewis realized, it comes into conflict with the metaphysical insight of many great thinkers that an effect cannot be greater in its positive characteristics than its cause. Thus if one photocopies a document, then copies the copy, then copies that copy and so on, one finds that the copies degrade in quality the more remote they are from the original, that the positive characteristics distinct in the original are progressively blurred and finally obliterated. What could never happen using this process is that a distorted original would produce an excellent copy. Descartes put the point this way:

> [I]t is . . . clear by the light of nature that the complete efficient cause must contain at least as much as the effect of that cause. For where, pray, could the effect get its reality if not from the cause? . . . it follows . . . that what is more perfect, or contains in itself a greater amount of reality, cannot be made by what is, or has, less.[75]

Yet the debunkers suppose that the ignoble cause has more reality than its apparently noble effect. Starting from base and primitive desires, the debunker wants us to believe we can somehow produce the idea of a perfect, infinite being or a universal moral law, projects significantly less viable than making a silk purse out of a sow's ear.

The debunker's error might seem impossible for an intelligent person to make, but this is not so. In effect, Plato gave a brilliant diagnosis of the enchanting power of the debunker's delusion in his Simile of the Cave[76] (recapitulated in the prison of *The Pilgrim's Regress*[77]). Imagine, says Plato, that men are in a cave chained up with their backs to a fire and only able to see the far wall. On this wall they see shadows, cast by the fire, of passing people carrying goods, and the echoes of the sounds made by the people seem to emanate from the shadows. Since the shadows are all the men ever see, it is natural for them to think that the shadows are just as real as themselves.

Now what would happen, Plato asks, if one of the men were set free and shown the real things that cast the shadows? At first he would be unwilling to believe in the real things, arguing that they were delusions and that the shadows were the reality. Likewise, the Freudian who focuses all his attention on the "shadows" of our mental life will try to explain anything apparently greater as a delusion whose real source is the shadows. However, an honest and impartial person would eventually see that he is mistaken, because while the shadows are similar in form to the people, the people have many positive characteristics lacked by the shadows. Thus the shadows have to be the copies of the people and not vice versa.

The difficulty, though, is to draw people's attention away from the shadows to the light that casts them: "The light shines in the darkness, but the darkness has not understood it" (John 1:5). Lewis knew only too well how enchanting the shadowlands are. In *The Silver Chair*, when Jill, Eustace, and Puddleglum are in the dark Underworld attempting to free Prince Rilian, the Witch tries to persuade them that the world above is a delusion. When Puddleglum protests that there is a sun,[78] and the Prince supports this by saying it is like a lamp, only

The Temper of an Apostle

greater, the Witch tries to persuade them that all their ideas of the sun are illusions: "The lamp is the real thing; the sun is but a tale, a children's story."[79] The Witch is surprisingly successful, since the "real life" of their immediate surroundings is nothing but shadows, and it is hard to believe in the unfamiliar. The enchantment is broken by two doses of unmistakable reality: Puddleglum's pain as he plunges his foot in the fire and his invincible common sense:

> Suppose we have only dreamed, or made up, all those things. . . . Then all I can say is that, in that case, the made-up things seem a good deal more important than the real ones.[80]

Debunkers Debunked

> *These are a shadow of the things that were to come; the reality, however, is found in Christ.*
> —*Colossians* 2:17

Still, the debunker might say, our beliefs in higher realities are illusions, "fulfillments of the oldest, strongest and most urgent wishes of mankind."[81] Lewis argued repeatedly and persuasively that it was hopeless to use wish-fulfillment as a criterion for the truth or falsity of a view. If the wishes of a Christian that there is a God count against his belief, then the evident wishes of many atheists that there is no God, so they can live without interference or judgment, would equally count against their belief.[82] Indeed, it is easy to construct a Freudian account of the origins of atheism along these lines:

> If Freud is right about the Oedipus complex, the universal pressure of the wish that God should not exist must be enormous, and atheism must be an admirable gratification to one of our strongest suppressed impulses.[83]

Of course, the Freudian may cry foul and point out that the origin of a belief has nothing to do with its truth, but if that is allowed, the

Freudian account of the origin of religious ideas would not stop them from being true either, as in fact Freud concedes.[84]

Finally, even if wish-fulfillment is sometimes a factor in religious belief-formation, it clearly is not always so. Lewis himself became a Christian in spite of fearing very much that there might be a God. The Freudian may seek to explain Lewis's belief in terms of fear-fulfillment, but this is equally useless, since there are many atheists who because they are pessimists tend to disbelieve in God *because* they fear he does not exist. So we have the situation that one may believe either through wishing or fearing God exists and disbelieve either through wishing or fearing He does not exist. If so, what we wish or fear is completely useless in determining whether or not God exists,[85] as Lewis taught Sheldon Vanauken on his road to Christian faith.[86]

The most decisive reply to the debunking strategy is made by exposing the hidden assumption that it cannot be applied to itself. If a Freudian analysis of religious ideas shows them to be delusions, a Freudian analysis of Freudianism will show it to be delusive. If a Marxist analysis of our ideas of social justice shows it to be a mask obscuring a certain oppressive distribution of capital, the same can be said of Marxism itself. If the fascist rejects conventional morality as an attempt to exert power over him, his rejection can be analyzed as an attempt by him to exert power over others. One who intends to demolish the foundations of a building should make quite sure that he is not standing on those foundations or on foundations that will collapse if they do. As Lewis puts the point:

> If you see through everything, then everything is transparent. But a wholly transparent world is an invisible world. To 'see through' all things is the same as not to see.[87]

CONCLUSION

Lewis, like Paul, was a great evangelist because, when transformed by faith, the qualities he acquired before conversion enabled him to speak to the true condition of his audience after conversion. For both men there was an almost seamless connection between personal faith and zeal for missionary work. Lewis, like Paul, was a true champion of the Christian faith, slaying the dragons and clearing the stumbling blocks that lay, first on his own, then on his unbelieving neighbors' path.

BIBLIOGRAPHY

Bornkamm, Gunther. *Paul.* New York: Harper and Row, 1971.

Bruce, F. F. *Paul: Apostle of the Heart Set Free.* Exeter, England: The Paternoster Press, 1977.

Buttrick, George (general editor). *The Interpreter's Dictionary of the Bible*, Vol. 3. New York: Abingdon Press, 1962.

Chesterton, Gilbert Keith. *Orthodoxy.* Norwood, MA: John Lane Company, 1908.

Descartes, René. "Meditations on First Philosophy." In *Descartes: Philosophical Writings.* Trans., eds. Elizabeth Anscombe and Peter Geach. Sunbury on Thames: Nelson, 1970.

Freud, Sigmund. *The Future of an Illusion.* Trans. James Strachey. New York: Norton, 1961.

Herbert, George. *The Works of George Herbert in Prose and Verse.* New York: John Wurtele Lovell, 1881.

Lewis, C. S. *The Abolition of Man.* New York: Macmillan, 1955.

_____. *The Great Divorce: A Dream.* New York: Macmillan, 1946.

_____. *A Grief Observed.* New York: Bantam Press, 1961, 1976.

_____. "The Inner Ring," in *The Weight of Glory and Other Addresses.* Revised and Expanded Edition. New York: Macmillan, 1980.

_____. "Membership," in *The Weight of Glory and Other Addresses.* Revised and Expanded Edition. New York: Macmillan, 1980.

_____. *Miracles.* New York: Macmillan, 1947, 1978.

_____. "On Obstinacy in Belief," in *The World's Last Night and Other Essays.* New York: Harcourt Brace and Company, 1952, 1987.

_____. *The Pilgrim's Regress.* Originally published London: Geoffrey Bles, 1933. Deluxe illustrated edition Grand Rapids, MI: Eerdmans, 1992.

_____. *A Preface to Paradise Lost.* London: Oxford University Press, 1942.

_____. *The Problem of Pain.* London: Geoffrey Bles, Centenary Press, 1940.

_____. *The Screwtape Letters.* Revised Edition. New York: Macmillan, 1982.

_____. *The Silver Chair.* New York: Harper Trophy, 1953, 1994.

_____. *Surprised by Joy*. New York: Harcourt, Brace & Company, 1956, 1984.

_____. *That Hideous Strength*. New York: Scribner Press, 1996.

Lewis, Warren and Hooper, Walter, eds. *Letters of C. S. Lewis*. Revised and Enlarged Edition. New York: Harcourt, Brace & Company, 1988.

Morris, Clifford. "C. S. Lewis Was My Friend." *His* (Vol. 39, No. 1), 1978.

Plato. *The Republic*. New York: Penguin Books, 1955.

Sayer, George. *Jack: A Life of C. S. Lewis*. Second Edition. Wheaton, IL: Crossway Books, 1994.

Vanauken, Sheldon. *Encounter with Light*. Wheaton, IL: Marion E. Wade Center.

NOTES

1. Herbert, "The Temper," 138.

2. Lewis, *Surprised by Joy*, 58-70.

3. Ibid., 161.

4. Lewis and Hooper, *Letters of C. S. Lewis*, 52.

5. Carnell, "Longing, Reason, and the Moral Law in C. S. Lewis's Search" in this volume.

6. Much of the information about Saint Paul used in this section is derived from Bornkamm's *Paul*, F. F. Bruce's *Paul: Apostle of the Heart Set Free*, and *The Interpreter's Dictionary of the Bible*. All Scripture references are from the *New International Version*.

7. Lewis, *Surprised by Joy*, 10.

8. For more on this, see Jon Balsbaugh's "The Pagan and the Post-Christian: Lewis's Understanding of Diversity Outside the Faith" in this volume.

9. See *Surprised by Joy*, chapter IX.

10. Lewis, *The Pilgrim's Regress*, 50-53.

11. Bruce, *Paul: Apostle of the Heart Set Free*, 70-71.

12. Lewis, *Surprised by Joy*, 228-29.

13. Ibid., 59.

14. Ibid., 60.

15. Ibid., 61-62.

16. Lewis, *The Screwtape Letters*, IV.

17. Lewis, *Surprised by Joy*, 61-62.

18. Ibid., 62-63.

The Temper of an Apostle

19. Ibid., 235.

20. Ibid., 64-65.

21. Lewis, "On Obstinacy in Belief."

22. Lewis, *The Problem of Pain.*

23. Lewis, *Surprised by Joy*, 67-70.

24. Ibid., 115.

25. Ibid.

26. See Sayer, *Jack*, 184.

27. Lewis, *The Screwtape Letters*, X and XI.

28. Lewis, "The Inner Ring."

29. This is the main theme of *That Hideous Strength* and *The Abolition of Man.*

30. Bruce, *Paul: Apostle of the Heart Set Free*, 46.

31. This task is undertaken most thoroughly in Lewis's *Miracles.*

32. Sayer, *Jack*, 139.

33. For example, when tried by Felix in Acts 24.

34. Bruce, *Paul: Apostle of the Heart Set Free*, 274.

35. Ibid., 286.

36. For more on this theme, see Joel Heck's "*Praeparatio Evangelica*" in this volume.

37. Lewis, *A Grief Observed.*

38. Sayer, *Jack*, 282.

39. Lewis, *Surprised by Joy*, 225.

40. Ibid., 237.

41. Lewis, *Mere Christianity*, Book IV, chapters 10 and 11.

42. Lewis, *The Great Divorce*, 106.

43. Bruce, *Paul: Apostle of the Heart Set Free*, 74.

44. Ibid., 75.

45. Lewis, *The Pilgrim's Regress*, 142.

46. Morris, "C. S. Lewis Was My Friend," 11.

47. Sayer, *Jack*, 231.

48. This issue is taken up at greater length by Joel Heck's "*Praeparatio Evangelica*" in this volume.

49. Bornkamm, *Paul*, 57.

50. Bruce, *Paul: Apostle of the Heart Set Free*, 18.

51. Lewis, "Membership," 117.

52. For more on this see Patrick Ferry's "Mere Christianity Because There Are No Mere Mortals: Reaching Beyond the Inner Ring" in this volume.

53. Lewis, *Mere Christianity*, 6.

54. Chesterton, *Orthodoxy*, 20.

55. Lewis, *Mere Christianity*, 6.

56. For more on the idea of reader identification, see Michael Ward's "Escape to Wallaby Wood—Lewis's Depictions of Conversion" in this volume.

57. Buttrick, ed., *The Interpreter's Dictionary of the Bible*, Vol. 3, 688.

58. Lewis, *The Screwtape Letters*, 9-10.

59. Lewis, *Miracles*, 166.

60. Ibid.

61. For an analysis of the spirit of the age, see Musacchio's "Exorcising the *Zeitgeist*: Lewis as Evangelist to the Modernists" in this volume.

62. For an account of how Lewis used his skills in a university setting, see Christopher Mitchell's "University Battles: C. S. Lewis and the Oxford University Socratic Club" in this volume.

63. Lewis, *Surprised by Joy*, chapters XII and XIII.

64. Ibid., 207.

65. Lewis, *The Pilgrim's Regress*, 155.

66. Ibid., 28-30.

67. Ibid., 32-33.

68. Ibid., 46.

69. Ibid., 50.

70. Ibid., 49.

71. Ibid., 63.

72. Ibid., 52.

73. Ibid., 98-100.

74. Ibid., 59.

75. Descartes, "Meditations on First Philosophy," 81.

76. Plato, *The Republic*, 316-325.

77. Lewis, *The Pilgrim's Regress*, 47-50.

78. Lewis, *The Silver Chair*, 176-77.

79. Ibid., 178.

80. Ibid., 182. This is a beautiful echo of Joshua 24:15.

81. Freud, *The Future of an Illusion*, 30.

82. Lewis, *The Pilgrim's Regress*, 64.

83. Lewis, "On Obstinacy in Belief," 19.

84. Freud, *The Future of an Illusion*, 31-33.

85. Lewis, "On Obstinacy in Belief," 19-20.

86. Vanauken, *Encounter with Light*, 14.

87. Lewis, *The Abolition of Man*, 91.

6

ESCAPE TO WALLABY WOOD:

Lewis's Depictions of Conversion

MICHAEL WARD

C. S. Lewis never invited unbelievers to come to Jesus. He was a very successful evangelist.

In case those two sentences seem bewilderingly contradictory, it might be worth considering other pairs of statements. Such as: "Einstein failed his entrance exam to the Federal Polytechnic. He was a very successful physicist." Or again: "Gandhi never fought against the British. He successfully ejected them from India." Life is not as simple as we think.

Lewis explicitly rejects the "Come to Jesus" school as his own approach in at least three places. In "God in the Dock" he observes that he lacks the gift for making such a "simple, emotional appeal" and concludes that he had therefore better not attempt it.[1] In "Modern Man and His Categories of Thought" he makes the closely related point that the limitations of his own gifts have caused him always to avoid a "pneumatic" approach.[2] And in an interview with the Billy Graham Evangelistic Association he confesses that bringing about an encounter between his readers and Jesus Christ is "not my language," though it is the purpose he has in view.[3]

In the first two of these three disavowals, Lewis is referring primarily to his evangelistic technique in public meetings, but I think they are applicable to his written works too, an application that the third statement bears out. They are strange admissions from a man who described most of his own books as "evangelistic."[4] Is he embarrassed? Is he being precious about "my language"? If an encounter between his readers and Jesus Christ is the purpose he has in view, why does he not honestly say so? It is not like Lewis to be mealy-mouthed.

This chapter has three aims. First, to ask why Lewis wanted to attract people to Christ without using the words "Come to Jesus." Second, to see how he thought this could be done. Third, to look at where he put his theories into practice.

WHY

First, why. And we can start by giving three quick reasons that need not be elaborated upon: the spiritual, the psychological, and the theological. Lewis himself frankly admits that there was a spiritual reason for his reluctance to make a direct appeal to the heart: it is not his "gift." Presumably he knew this either by intuition or painful personal experience, and we must be prepared to take his word for it. Psychologically, we know, he disliked emotionalism.[5] And theologically, he was wary of "Jesus worship."[6]

There is also a practical reason. The hortatory style of evangelism is like water off a duck's back to people who do not recognize either a need or a desire to come to Jesus. Why should they come? They're quite comfortable as they are. As Lewis wrote to his friend and former pupil Alan Griffiths in 1939:

> The purpose of living seems to consist in coming to realize truths so ancient and simple that, if stated, they sound like barren platitudes. They cannot sound otherwise to those who have not had the relevant experience: that is why there is no real teaching of such truths possible and every generation starts from scratch.[7]

No doubt Lewis had in mind, when he spoke of ancient and simple truths, such truths as "All have sinned and fallen short of the glory of God," "He who loses his life for my sake will find it," "My yoke is easy and my burden light." To a Christian readership—that is, to a readership with the relevant experience—these truths are pregnant with meaning. But to a readership of unbelievers they are "barren platitudes." To exhort the non-Christian to come to Jesus on the basis of these platitudes is to add irritation to ignorance, to utter "abracadabra" over hocus-pocus. Somehow the evangelist must excite or reveal or remind his audience of the experiences that will transform "hocus-pocus" back into *hoc est corpus*.[8]

Which brings us to a linguistic reason: "No real teaching is possible." This might appear to be a counsel of despair to the would-be evangelist if he did not know how much teaching Lewis actually achieved. For, of course, Lewis also believed that the Word can speak through a teacher's words, or else why did Christ have a larynx? This puts all teachers under an obligation to use words so they can most easily become a channel of truth. And in Lewis's view, the simple, emotional language of the traditional altar call is not the best language for truth-bearing because it is always in danger of cutting its own throat. He gives his reasons in the final chapter of *Studies in Words*:

> In general, emotional words, to be effective, must not be solely emotional. What expresses or stimulates emotion directly, without the intervention of an image or concept, expresses or stimulates it feebly. . . . [A]s words become exclusively emotional they cease to be words and therefore of course cease to perform any strictly linguistic function. They operate as growls or barks or tears. "Exclusively" is an important adverb here. They die as words not because there is too much emotion in them but because there is too little—and finally nothing at all—of anything else.[9]

Hence, a sentence such as, "Jesus loves you; Jesus is lovely; come to Jesus for peace and joy" would be highly emotional, theologically unimpeachable, and evangelistically ineffective. Not evangelistically useless. If this is the best the speaker can manage or the right approach for the given situation, who can tell how useful it might be? Lewis readily concedes the effectiveness of Balaam's ass and of babes and sucklings in conveying God's truth.[10] But usually the intelligent adult evangelist will not be called upon to be asinine or childish. The message will remain folly to the world however wise the medium; but deliberate stupidity or immaturity will merely confirm worst opinion.

Lewis's linguistic strategy is dependent on his understanding of human nature. Note how he argues the ineffectiveness of emotional language not on grounds of its emotion, but on grounds of its exclusive emotion. Let language be as emotional as you like, Lewis maintains, but never let it become solely emotional. The biggest heart in the world will not be too big for all the emotion locked up in the Gospel story, but it will always be only a heartbeat away from (above) the head and (below) the belly, and it cannot say to its fellow members, "I have no need of you." In *The Abolition of Man* Lewis argues that "the head rules the belly through the chest," a view that required him, in his evangelism, to acknowledge the corporeality of man and to impart a rationale and a dynamo, in that logical order, by means of which it could be governed. Intellect on its own, as Aristotle said, never moved anyone. And emotions on their own never found direction. This is, if you like, the philosophical reason for Lewis's avoidance of the "Come to Jesus" school of evangelism.

Finally, there are three political reasons. First, the words "Come to Jesus," by suggesting that the speaker is with or alongside or is a spokesman for the Son of God, play into a skeptical readership's hands. Of course, Lewis believed that Christians were, in a sense, spokesmen for Christ, but he was also aware of the tendency of "moderns" to assume that Christianity is recommended not because it is true, but merely because the speaker happens to like it or perhaps has a financial interest (however indirect) in disseminating it. It is therefore wise to maintain some sort of objective distance between evangelist and evangel.

Second, the "Come to Jesus" mantra runs the risk of sounding like, "Reject Jesus and you reject me" (which is bad theology) or, alternatively, "Become a Christian, become my friend" (which is bad psychology). Such an approach makes a disinterested response more difficult. And so, rather than asking non-Christians to "Come to Jesus," Lewis preferred urging them (when he urged at all) to "Look for Christ."[11] He keeps his own Christian persona off-stage almost entirely; if he talks in the first person, it is his pre-Christian self that he brings forward. Never does he give the impression that he wants the reader to copy his practice of Christianity (unlike Saint Paul); but he quite often calls up his own "search" for Christ.

I put "search" in quotation marks, because Lewis was well aware that the real search was not his for God, but God's for him. And this is the third political reason for steering clear of a "Come to Jesus" formula (and even of a "Look for Christ" formula). If the unbeliever gets the impression that the evangelist is chiefly concerned about getting a response, he is likely to have a skewed understanding of the faith. Although Lewis is quite clear that a response to Christ is necessary, and although he has little time for developed Calvinism, he is keen to keep in mind the fact that man's response to God is not of central importance. In "The Weight of Glory" he reports how "I read in a periodical the other day that the fundamental thing is how we think of God. By God Himself it is not! How God thinks of us is not only more important, but infinitely more important. Indeed, how we think of Him is of no importance except in so far as it is related to how He thinks of us." Elsewhere he points out the comic elements of "the fly sitting deciding what it is going to make of the elephant."[12] And in the third Narnia Chronicle, Eustace asks Edmund, "Do you know Aslan?," to which Edmund replies, "Well—he knows me." The chief end of man is not to love God but to be loved by God.

So the mainspring of evangelism should not be the importunate cry of "Come to Jesus" but the generous, revelatory impulse of "Jesus has come to you." Therefore, it is politic generally to avoid the language of religious initiation, and still more the language of doctrinal formulations or creedal statements or theological abstractions. Christ's own incarnation, crucifixion, and resurrection comprise "a language more adequate" than any other.[13] That is the good news, the Gospel, the evangel. Evangelism is merely the process of retelling that story or translating that language. On the day of Pentecost, it was only after his hearers had been "cut to the heart" that Peter instructed them to "repent and be baptized." His evangelism consisted not in their response, but in his preceding sermon, which centers exclusively on the acts of a distinctly trinitarian God.

How

If the task of the evangelist is to retell the story of God in Christ and the sending of the Holy Spirit, to do so one must imitate that story's language. (This is our first *how*.) It is a story written in the language of descent and then of utter descent and then of ascent to a place higher than the starting-point. The beautiful passage about God's great dive into humanity in Chapter XIV of *Miracles* is Lewis's most explicit rewording of Christ's life, death, and new life; the architectonics of *The Silver Chair* perhaps his most implicit. Any talk about conversion must somehow be couched in terms that reflect this divine pattern, the missing chapter of the human story, the forgotten movement of the universal symphony, which makes sense of all the rest. Christ, the audible word of the inaudible God, has provided the syllables that echo in all second births. The pattern of His sacrifice is the template to which all accounts of conversion must be cut. Like the Israelites swooping down upon the Philistines in the wake of David's victory over Goliath, Christians reenact in their conversions Christ's own eternal victory over sin and death. "If we have died with Christ, we believe that we shall also live with him." There must be, at the barest minimum, this basic shape to all presentations of the Gospel: down, down further, up, up higher than before. It is no accident that the Spare Room where the Wardrobe stands in the first Narnia tale is reached by "three steps down and five steps up," nor that Jane can find Ransom's rooms in *That Hideous Strength* only "by descending to a landing and ascending again."

In the same way that Christ's descent and re-ascent only really mean something because they actually happened to a particular man at a particular time in a particular place, so the language used to describe it (and therefore to encourage or invite imitations) must deal in particularities and not in airy abstractions. (This is our second *how*.) As Lewis wrote to his brother in 1932:

"Religion and poetry are about the only languages . . . which . . . still have something to say. Compare 'Our Father which art in Heaven' with 'The supreme being transcends time and space.' The first goes to pieces if you begin to apply the literal meaning to it. How can anything but a sexual animal really be a father? How can it be in the sky? The second falls into no such traps. On the other hand, the first really means something, really represents a concrete experience in the minds of those who use it: the second is mere dexterous playing with counters. . . ."[14]

Lewis's advocacy of concrete, as opposed to abstract, language is not simply the result of a casual personal preference; it springs from a set of deeply held beliefs. The letter quoted above represents in compressed form the argument of Lewis's essay "Bluspels and Flalansferes," in which he defends a sacramental view of language (there encoded as "a kind of psycho-physical parallelism"). It also prefigures the thoughts he expressed in the last chapter of *Studies in Words*, where he writes: "Poetry most often communicates emotions, not directly, but by creating imaginatively the grounds for those emotions. It therefore communicates something more than emotion; only by means of that something more does it communicate the emotion at all."[15] There is a rich vein connecting Lewis's thought here in *Studies in Words* and the address "Transposition," which, as Owen Barfield has pointed out is, among other things, a theory of imagination.[16] We do not have time to mine it now, but it is worth noting how much importance Lewis attaches to the "something more than emotion." It is his belief in that "something more" that informs his view of the Incarnation, the resurrection of the body, the sacraments and that supplies the un-Manichaean cast of his whole theology. It is only when the theological skeleton of the Gospel is fleshed out (or incarnated) with an image or a symbol that the words of the message start to become living and active—thus making the message a fit vehicle for the Word of God. For "it is not the spiritual which is first but the physical, and then the spiritual."

Incidentally, it is the lack of "something more" that explains the weakness of the conversion account in *Robinson Crusoe*, one of the very few such accounts in popular English literature outside Lewis's own works.[17] Crusoe's conversion is disappointing because it is conveyed predominantly through direct description of his Bible reading and prayer, and there is little attempt made to let the non-Christian reader know imaginatively what sort of transition he is undergoing. From the evangelistic point of view, Defoe would have done better to leave out the explicit passages and to have infused their spiritual essence into Crusoe's discovery of the footprint in the sand and his friendship with Man Friday. For as Lewis early discovered, expressions must not merely state, they must suggest. That is what writing means.[18] Almost anyone can say *what* good writing is like. "It is the man who sees *how* to do something that matters."[19]

And we now come to our third *how*. Lewis attracts his readers to Christ by retelling the Great Story in concrete terms, and in comprehensible concrete terms. Not any old concrete terms. To tell a non-Christian that he must "be washed in the blood of the Lamb" is a concrete expression (and therefore better than its abstract equivalent—"be purified in the essential life-fluid of innocence"), but it will not mean much to him. One must find terms into which the Great Story may be translated so the non-Christian reader can get an inkling of what the evangelist means. Of course, much of the meaning will remain latent to the unbeliever (as indeed it will to the evangelist, who will often speak more wisely than he knows), but insofar as any elements of God's truth are conveyed and understood, the unbeliever will necessarily be moved and will return imaginatively to God as Christ returned bodily to the Father; it is then that the Holy Spirit descends.[20] This presupposes in the writer a wide knowledge of concrete terms and a lively appreciation of every aspect of life, which is just what we find in Lewis. He believed that whether a writer acknowledged it or not, composition was merely the process of "re-combining elements made by [God] and already containing *His* meanings."[21] Therefore, it behooves the Christian writer to get to know "things" as intimately as possible, the more effectively to mirror the story of Christ's life and death.

Or rather I should say "Christ's death and life," for it is His pass-

ing over from death to life that is the center of the story of "the wonderful works of God." The mysterious silence of Holy Saturday, the
hinge that somehow opens the Crucifixion into the Resurrection, is the
part of the story that most needs retelling. Lewis, in true Shakespearean
fashion, "nibbles" at this biscuit (or knot) from numerous angles, trying and trying again to find an insightful way of interpreting it.[22] Even
when he is writing nonfiction, his work abounds with similes,
metaphors, and analogies that create imaginatively the grounds for the
appropriate emotion. A brief survey of *Mere Christianity* supplies the
following list: becoming a Christian (passing over from death to life) is
like joining a campaign of sabotage, like falling at someone's feet or
putting yourself in someone's hands, like taking on board fuel or food,
like laying down your rebel arms and surrendering, saying sorry, laying
yourself open, turning full speed astern; it is like killing part of yourself,
like learning to walk or to write, like buying God a present with his own
money; it is like a drowning man clutching at a rescuer's hand, like a tin
soldier or a statue becoming alive, like waking after a long sleep, like getting close to someone or becoming infected, like dressing up or pre-
tending or playing; it is like emerging from the womb or hatching from
an egg; it is like a compass needle swinging to north, or a cottage being
made into a palace, or a field being plowed and resown, or a horse turning into a Pegasus, or a greenhouse roof becoming bright in the sunlight;
it is like coming around from anesthetic, like coming in out of the wind,
like going home.

Rather than saying, "Come to Jesus," Lewis is saying, "This is what
it is like to come to Jesus. If you're not attracted or interested or assisted
by this way of putting it, here are a dozen other ways of considering the
same thing." The man who wrote *A Preface to Paradise Lost* was ready
to write any number of prefaces to paradise regained. For Lewis was not
at all prescriptive when he talked about the spiritual life. (This is our final
how.) The fact of Christ's saving death and resurrection was far more
important for him than any theory about how it should be appropriated
by individuals. If, for instance, one is looking for a place where Lewis
explicitly uses the terms of the formula "salvation by grace through faith
alone," one will find it neither in his apologetics nor in his fiction, but

in the introduction to *English Literature in the Sixteenth Century*. Hard and fast theories of the Atonement were, to him, distracting and potentially divisive. And theories of conversion were pointless, because God brings people to Himself in a startling variety of ways, some of which Lewis particularly disliked. Hence his free use of imagery from all areas of human life and his impatience with those "high-minded" Christians, like Norman Pittenger, who objected to his indiscriminate and "vulgar" analogies. With Dickens, Lewis would have opined: "That every man who seeks heaven must be born again in the good thoughts of his Maker, I sincerely believe; that it is expedient for every hound to say so in a certain snuffling form of words, to which he attaches no good meaning, I do not believe."[23]

We have now reached the point where we can summarize Lewis's evangelistic method in his depictions of conversion. By encoding the Great Story in concrete terms comprehensible to the reader and containing no prescriptive theological "spin," Lewis aims to give the non-Christian an imaginative experience of the "ancient and simple truths" that are so relevant to spiritual life but that cannot be taught directly. The rest of the chapter will look at those books where this method seems most in evidence, and two of them will not be by Lewis.

WHERE

Lewis's method was not simply a tactic to attract unbelievers; it was the very means by which he interpreted Christianity to himself. He talks about his personal path to faith by means of analogies and pictures similar to those we find in *Mere Christianity*. Lewis's own "coming to Jesus" is described in *Surprised by Joy* using such pictures as a soldier unbuckling his protective armor, a snowman beginning to melt, a man being arrested or a fox being hounded, of check and then checkmate in a game of chess. And when the climactic moment comes, Lewis conveys it with customary skill.

> I know very well when, but hardly how, the final step was taken.
> I was driven to Whipsnade one sunny morning. When we set out

I did not believe that Jesus Christ is the Son of God, and when we reached the zoo I did. . . .

They have spoiled Whipsnade since then. Wallaby Wood, with the birds singing overhead and the bluebells underfoot and the Wallabies hopping all round one, was almost Eden come again.[24]

The expression of emotion (suitably concreted) comes in the second paragraph, after the conversion itself. Like rain that comes after thunder, like the mountaintop experience that came to Wordsworth after he had crossed the Alps, Lewis's feeling of spiritual fulfillment is described after the fact and is introduced with a distinctly downbeat sentence. Head and heart, but in that logical order. That the wallabies spoke deeply to Lewis of the beauty of salvation is clear from a letter he wrote a year after this life-changing trip, when he revisited both the wood and the experience. But who can fail to hear the gentle chuckle behind the whole account? After years of wrestling with Romanticism, Rationalism, Hegelianism, and what-not, all his defenses collapsed in the side-car of a motorbike on the way to a zoo where children go and finally evaporated in an absurdly named enclosure full of furry animals from Australia. It is gloriously pathetic. "The poor dragon that had been Eustace lifted up its voice and wept. A powerful dragon crying its eyes out under the moon in a deserted valley is a sight and sound hardly to be imagined."[25]

Many readers find *Surprised by Joy* a difficult book. It is true that it contains a lot of close argument, a lot of dense and intense reflection, and, apart from the instances of poetry mentioned above, comparatively few examples of "leavening." Lewis himself acknowledges that the book may well be "suffocatingly subjective."[26]

But there may be another reason *Surprised by Joy* is unsatisfactory. As Lewis himself admits elsewhere, "The story which gives us the experience most like the experiences of living is not necessarily the story whose events are most like those in a biography or a newspaper."[27] If we include autobiography under biography and assume that Lewis is talking as much of his own writings as of literature in general, this may well explain why *Surprised by Joy* is quite hard going and why the alle-

Lewis's Depictions of Conversion

gorization of his conversion story in *The Pilgrim's Regress* is so much
more enjoyable, for it gives much more effectively (because more concretely) the experience of living through a conversion.

We do not have time to examine the latter book in detail, but it
may be worth taking a brief glance at what I regard as the crucial part
of the story, when John finally glimpses the object of his desire.

> What the others saw I do not know: but John saw the Island.
> And the morning wind, blowing off-shore from it, brought the
> sweet smell of its orchards to them, but rarefied and made faint
> with the thinness and purity of early air, and mixed with a lit-
> tle sharpness of the sea. But for John, because so many thou-
> sands looked at it with him, the pain and the longing were
> changed and all unlike what they had been of old: for humility
> was mixed with their wildness, and the sweetness came not
> with pride and with the lonely dreams of poets nor with the
> glamour of a secret, but with the homespun truth of folk-tales,
> and with the sadness of graves and freshness as of earth in the
> morning. There was fear in it also, and hope: and it began to
> seem well to him that the Island should be different from his
> desires, and so different that, if he had known it, he would not
> have sought it.[28]

Note how Lewis is continually fluctuating between the bane and the
blessing, between condolence and congratulation, between Good
Friday and Easter Sunday.[29] He mentions the sharpness of the sea but
also the sweet smell of the orchards; he mentions the sadness of graves
but also the freshness as of earth in the mornings; without any medi-
ating image he brings in fear and hope; and then the poles of the experience seem almost to merge in the final crush-note: "If he had known
it, he would not have sought it." There is no question but that he has
been deceived. True. But thanks be to God for deception! For how
could John ever have desired such holiness in his natural state? The
apparent disaster is really a testimony to the spirit of incarnate grace
that is humble enough to woo John even under the mask of "the little
brown girls," the objects of the lust in which his pilgrimage originated,

the paltry tale in which snatches of the Great Story could unwittingly be heard. And not only does grace give John unmerited reward, it excites in him the capacity for enjoying it. In all of Lewis's works there is not another sentence that so perfectly encapsulates both the loss and the more than compensatory gain of regeneration. *The Pilgrim's Regress* is the first book he wrote following his conversion, when the poignancy of the transition was perhaps most keenly upon him, and he hit the jackpot the first time.

The Pilgrim's Regress, of course, is modeled to a certain extent upon John Bunyan's *Pilgrim's Progress*, a book that has "astonished the world," according to Lewis. It is interesting to note that Lewis did not think particularly highly of the conversion moment in that story, when the pilgrim, Christian, standing at the foot of a cross, loses the burden from his back, and it rolls downhill into the mouth of a sepulchre. He thought much more highly of the scene in the Valley of Humiliation, which he said "is the most beautiful thing in Bunyan and can be the most beautiful thing in life if a man takes it quite rightly."[30] As we read *Progress*, Lewis contends, we ought to be discovering that humility is like that green valley, not that the green valley "represents" humility. "That way, moving always into the book, not out of it, from the concept to the image, enriches the concept. And that is what allegory is for."[31]

It is typical of Lewis to value not the fictional moment when Christian comes to Jesus, but the moment in the book that he feels is most like the process of coming to Jesus, and he reworks it on the last page of *That Hideous Strength* when Jane walks through the warm garden, over the wet lawn, "descending the ladder of humility," down to the lodge where her husband waits. And in *Till We Have Faces* Orual travels through a "warm, green valley" beyond Essur to visit a hot spring, there encountering a priest in the woods who tells her all she ever did. Ironically, seven years before his own conversion, Lewis had made use of the unburdening episode in his poem *Joy*: "Like Christian when his burden dropt behind / I was set free."[32] Before he had acquired the relevant experience, he treated as important the "official" conversion moment in Bunyan, a moment that puts all the crucifixion side of the story in Christ's experience, and none of it in the pilgrim's.[33] After his own regeneration, Lewis sees that, from the literary point of view, the going down into a green valley is a much more efficient way of portraying salvation, because it gets in both the crucifixion and the resurrection elements, almost simultaneously. There is descent, but descent into greenness and fertility, which symbolize ascent. Like John's vision of the island, Christian's passage through the valley conveys powerfully "the old bittersweet of first falling in love."[34]

It is this "bittersweet" that, for Lewis, is the essence of the conversion experience. It is the "turn," the Tolkienian eucatastrophe, the moment in the fairy tale when Beauty kisses the Beast as if it were a man, and miraculously it turns into a man. It is that split second when emigration becomes immigration, when one crosses the border and for a brief moment stands with a foot in each camp—death and life, shadow and sunshine. Such a view of conversion springs from the realization that the Crucifixion, the judicial murder of God (in Dorothy L. Sayers's phrase), is both the most heinous act in the history of the world and the salvation of that world. The spearing of Christ's side, like the splitting of the rock in the desert, is at one and the same moment the shattering of perfection and the means by which perfection impregnates the imperfect. Like Sydney Carton's sacrifice in *A Tale of Two Cities*, it signifies "the best of times and the worst of times." Like Rilian's oath in *The Silver Chair*, it is what the three rescuers most want to hear and what they have sworn never to obey. The Lizard Man's face "shone with tears, but it may have been only the liquid love and brightness (one cannot distinguish them in that country) which flowed from him." The remaking of Jane's soul "went on amidst a kind of splendour or sorrow or both, whereof she could not tell whether it was in the moulding hands or in the kneaded lump."

As well as liking Bunyan's bittersweet valley, Lewis was a great admirer of the following passage in George MacDonald's *Lilith*, which conveys with appalling clarity the bitter side of the oxymoron. He quotes from it as an epigraph to the climactic Book Nine of *The Pilgrim's Regress*, and it is the last passage he selected for his anthology of MacDonald that he published in 1946. It is worth quoting in full:

"Lilith," said Mara, "you will not sleep, if you lie there a thousand years, until you have opened your hand and yielded that which is not yours to give or to withhold."

"I cannot," she answered, "I would if I could, for I am weary, and the shadows of death are gathering about me."

"They will gather and gather, but they cannot infold you while yet your hand remains unopened. You may think you are dead, but it will be only a dream; you may think you have come awake, but it will still be only a dream. Open your hand, and you will sleep indeed—then wake indeed."

"I am trying hard, but the fingers have grown together and into the palm."

"I pray you, put forth the strength of your will. For the love of life, draw together your forces and break its bonds!"

The princess turned her eyes upon Eve, beseechingly. "There was a sword I once saw in your husband's hands," she murmured. "I fled when I saw it. I heard him who bore it say it would divide whatever was not one and indivisible."

"I have the sword," said Adam. "The angel gave it me when he left the gate."

"Bring it, Adam," pleaded Lilith, "and cut me off this hand that I may sleep."

"I will," he answered.[35]

The thing Lilith most wants is only obtainable if she submits to the thing she wants least, the pain of losing her hand. And Adam's agreement to hurt her is said with the same solemnity—indeed, with the same words—as a marriage vow. It is an image that Lewis felt was terrible but true. As he wrote in his address "Membership": "some tendencies in each natural man may have to be simply rejected. Our Lord speaks of eyes being plucked out and hands lopped off—a frankly Procrustean method of adaptation."[36]

The undragoning of Eustace in *The Voyage of the "Dawn Treader"* is his most obvious reworking of MacDonald's passage. Eustace sheds his own skin three times but each time finds himself still trapped. Only when he lies back to be undressed by the Lion does he feel a claw go deep enough into his heart to rip off the thick, dark, knobbly hide. Orual's dream in which she falls through three versions of the Pillar Room has certain affinities with the Lilith passage too, but, as with most aspects of *Till We Have Faces*, is not easily susceptible of brief analysis or of parallel-drawing.

The killing of the lizard in *The Great Divorce* is yet another example of the Procrustean method of coming to Jesus. But the passage is interesting as much for its setting as for its own sake and is the first of three examples of larger-scale effects with which this investigation will close. Note how the passage comes just after the incident with Michael's mother, Pam. This woman is envious of heaven; she cannot understand why it should take possession of a son who belongs by rights to her. She argues bitterly with an angel, demanding that her love for Michael be respected, and is dumbfounded when she is told that no one can hurt or be hurt in that country. It is a strong and moving passage, and all the sadder if one supposes it to have been modeled on Mrs. Moore's own reaction to the loss of her son, Paddy, Lewis's war-time friend. Pam's maternal love is potentially a high love and therefore potentially a "fiercer devil" than the mere lust of the Lizard Man. She is both better and worse off than he. It is he, however, who is successfully redeemed, and in fact his is the only story we see through to its conclusion, his crucified lust metamorphosing from a lizard into a magnificent stallion. The interesting thing is that this redemption scene is really only an interruption of the story of Pam, for as soon as the regenerate Lizard Man has left the stage, Lewis returns our thoughts to the envious mother and asks, "If the risen body of appetite is as grand a horse as ye saw, what would the risen body of maternal love or friendship be?"

Thus Lewis invites his readers to exercise their own imaginations, having given them a model or template on which to work, a literary method that is at once directive and nondirective. It reflects his understanding of the Great Story itself as a kind of template and of Christ as the Pioneer. It may even be a commentary on that mysterious saying recorded by St. John, that "He who believes in me will also do the works that I do; and greater works than these will he do, because I go to the Father."

In *That Hideous Strength*, a slightly different technique of inter-weaving stories is used in the lead-up to Jane Studdock's conversion in Chapter 11, "Real Life Is Meeting." Ransom says to Jane, "You had better agree with your adversary quickly."

> "You mean I shall have to become a Christian?" said Jane.
>
> "It looks like it," said the Director.
>
> "But I still don't see what this has to do with . . . Mark," said Jane. . . . There was a sudden knock on the door and Grace Ironwood entered.
>
> "Ivy is back, Sir," she said. "I think you'd better see her. No; she's alone. She never saw her husband. The sentence is over but they haven't released him. He's been sent on to Belbury for reme-dial treatment. Under some new regulation. Apparently, it does not require a sentence from a court . . . but she's not very coher-ent. She is in great distress."[37]

So, on the one hand, we have Jane, who cares little for her husband Mark, facing an unwelcome encounter with Maledil (her "adver-sary"); on the other hand we have Ivy being prevented from seeing her husband, Mr. Maggs, and not only prevented, but burdened with the knowledge that he is about to undergo torture. It is with this as his set-ting that Lewis introduces Jane's conversion: "Then, at one particular corner of the gooseberry patch, the change came. . . . She had come into a world, or into a Person, or into the presence of a Person. Something expectant, patient, inexorable met her with no veil or pro-tection between."[38] Jane Studdock's stubborn and pretentiously intel-lectual path to faith is, in this chapter, brought into sharp focus by her own charwoman's domestic anguish. By means of the contrast with Ivy Maggs's personal tragedy, the tragedy of an uneducated but lov-ing woman, Lewis contrives to point out the etiolated and enfeebled state of Jane's marriage and Jane's soul.

Jane's contracepted relationship with Mark reflects her frigidity

Lewis's Depictions of Conversion

toward God. After masculine Mars in *Out of the Silent Planet* and feminine Venus in *Perelandra*, it is no accident that the first word of *That Hideous Strength* is "matrimony," nor that Jane's encounter with God occurs "with no veil or protection between." All the weight of the previous two books in the trilogy, and all the implicit imagery of Christ and His Bride, come bursting through the dam wall of Jane's rebellion once it is cracked by the news that a poor woman's husband is about to suffer. For we may suppose "there is no experience of the spirit so transcendent and supernatural, no vision of Deity Himself so close and so far beyond all images and emotions, that to it there cannot be an appropriate correspondence on the sensory level."[39] Ivy Maggs's distress is an objective correlative of Jane's marital and spiritual torment. And it is surely no coincidence that her transformation occurs at a corner of the gooseberry patch. "Gooseberry" sums up Jane's entire role in the household of St. Anne's until this moment.[40]

Lewis sets up his readers for the conversion of the Lizard Man by the immediately preceding example of a woman who is in a much worse (but potentially much better) state. He sets up Jane Studdock's conversion by contrast with a woman who is in a much better (and now, tragically, much worse) state. In the case of Edmund Pevensie there is no such preceding point of contrast and, indeed, Edmund's whole conversion is something of a nonevent. He goes off for a talk with Aslan, comes back to his brother and sisters, says sorry, they say, "That's all right," and it's over. Lewis makes no attempt to get inside Edmund's experience either from the point of view of authorial narration (as he does with Shasta) or by means of first-person recounting (as he does with Eustace). Edmund's betrayal and rescue are the mainsprings of the plot of *The Lion, the Witch and the Wardrobe*, but his own personal delivery is surprisingly sparsely treated.

I think there are three main reasons for this. The first is that the book already abounds with redemption motifs; to provide an in-depth account of Edmund's redemption might over-egg the pudding. Most obviously, of course, we have the death of Aslan and his return to life; before that there is the coming of summer after the long-lasting winter of the White Witch; there is the defeat of the Witch in the battle and the revivifying of the stone statues at her castle; finally, there is the coronation of the four children at Cair Paravel. Overarching all is the fact of the Pevensies' journey through the back of the wardrobe, which I believe is itself a very carefully conceived symbol of spiritual awakening.[41] To parade Edmund's individual salvation on top of all these varying types of redemption might be to risk "wearisomely explicit pietism."[42] Like a virtuoso violinist, Lewis knows when to "open up" and when to "cover" his top notes. Edmund's story is a case of *con brio ma non troppo.*

The second reason is that although technically speaking Edmund's betrayal and rescue are the two main events of the plot, yet it is the means of the rescue that is thematically of the greatest importance. Aslan's death and resurrection are, within the world of Narnia, the central story, to which all other stories must defer and from which all other stories gain their significance. Furthermore, although Aslan apparently dies only for Edmund, it is conceded in later books that he died for the whole of Narnia, for if Edmund had been lost, the prophecy about the four thrones could not have been fulfilled and the White Witch would have ruled forever. It is therefore the story of Aslan that must dominate. Edmund's salvation is commensurate with that of an Old Testament character: he was saved before the Christ of his world had died. Logically, the importance of Christ's death and resurrection is more easily understood this way. Edmund needed rescuing; therefore Aslan rescued him. Cause and effect. As Lewis knew from personal experience, it is hard for a non-Christian to see how "the life and death of Someone Else (whoever he was) 2000 years ago could help us here and now."[43] By making Edmund an inhabitant of "the old dispensation," Lewis avoids these difficulties.

The third reason for the absence of detailed analysis of Edmund's salvation may be that Lewis wanted a *carte blanche* on which his readers could write their own story. One of the mottoes of the Narnia Chronicles is, "No one is ever told any story but his own," a rewording of John 21:21-22, and by keeping Edmund's story "hollow," Lewis practices what he preaches. This is uncharacteristic! As we have seen,

Lewis's Depictions of Conversion

Lewis usually gives us details, sometimes intimate details, of his characters' destinies, whether for good or ill. Here, in his most famous book, he shows a rare reticence, so that what passes between Edmund and Aslan remains a secret. Susan and Lucy also display a fine sensitivity when discussing it.

> "Does he know," whispered Lucy to Susan, "what Aslan did for him? Does he know what the arrangement with the Witch really was?"
> "Hush! No. Of course not," said Susan.
> "Oughtn't he to be told?" said Lucy.
> "Oh, surely not," said Susan. "It would be too awful for him. Think how you'd feel if you were he."
> "All the same I think he ought to know," said Lucy. But at that moment they were interrupted.[44]

Of course, Susan has no idea what Edmund has actually been told, nor does Lucy; but between them they show the right mix of hesitation and resolution in deciding to let their brother know "what the arrangement really was." It provides a neat summary of Lewis's own approach to evangelism.

CONCLUSION

What are we to make of Lewis's evangelistic technique in his fiction and in the "poetic" passages of his other writings? I imagine that the methods outlined in this chapter will be thought suspect by certain Christians who, with the apostle Peter, will want to say, "We did not follow cleverly devised myths when we made known to you the power and coming of our Lord Jesus Christ" (2 Peter 1:16, RSV). Lewis's "Great Story in miniature" style of evangelism will seem to them to be so indirect and encrypted as to be almost useless. Other kinds of Christians (among whom I would number myself) would prefer to say that since all things were made for and through Christ and hold together in Him, it is fair to assume that all things speak of Him, including things like stories and the things that go into stories. As Lewis was fond of remarking, the highest does not stand without the lowest, and it is no good trying to be more spiritual than God. In the Old Testament, Christ is typified by a boat, a ladder, a goat, Jonah the disobedient fish-food, and David the murderous adulterer. In the New, Saint Paul preaches Christ by quoting pagan poets and by becoming all things to all men that he might "by all means save some." Lewis is an heir to this tradition. Indeed, in the passage detailing Emeth's salvation in *The Last Battle*, Lewis might as well be writing a commentary on Paul's sermon in the Areopagus. Emeth is a character who is very literally saved by "an unknown God."

With Saint Paul and Lewis (and Hopkins), I would want to say "The world is charged with the grandeur of God. / It will flame out like shining from shook foil."[45] All "Little Stories" have something in them of the "Great Story." Those who would forbid such a method would seem to circumscribe God's freedom of action and deny his name of "All in All," aligning themselves with Swinburne's "pale Galilean" whose breath makes the world grow grey.[46]

And yet—and yet—life is not as simple as we think. When all is said and done, stories are only stories. Lewis knew of this danger. Indeed, this is one of the messages he gets out of his favorite MacDonald passage. Lilith's dream that she has awakened only to find that she is still asleep "has a terrible meaning, specially for imaginative people. We read of spiritual efforts, and our imagination makes us believe that, because we enjoy the idea of doing them, we have done them. I am appalled to see how much of the change which I thought I had undergone lately was only imaginary. The real work seems still to be done. It is so fatally easy to confuse an aesthetic appreciation of the spiritual life with the life itself—to dream that you have waked, washed, and dressed, and then to find yourself still in bed."[47]

If this is a special danger for imaginative people, it is a huge risk for religious imaginative people, people who may have been brought up on C. S. Lewis. The imitation of Christ can so easily be corrupted into parrot learning that "any child, given a certain kind of religious education, will soon learn."[48] But to discover and know things about

Lewis's Depictions of Conversion

God in real living experience is to enter into a new realm. To know God, however dimly, and to be known by God—these things are far more important than reading evangelistic stories, more important even than reading Bible stories. What, after all, are stories? "Only words, words, to be led out to battle against other words." Since God himself is the Word, what other utterance could suffice?

Let us finish with Lewis's own essay "On Stories," written in honor of his friend, the Christian writer Charles Williams:

> If the author's plot is only a net, and usually an imperfect one, a net of time and event for catching what is not really a process at all, is life much more? . . . In life and art both, as it seems to me, we are always trying to catch in our net of successive moments something that is not successive. Whether in real life there is any doctor who can teach us how to do it, so that at last either the meshes will become fine enough to hold the bird, or we be so changed that we can throw our nets away and follow the bird to its own country, is not a question for this essay. But I think it is sometimes done—or very, very nearly done—in stories. I believe the effort to be well worth making.[49]

That is the conclusion. We can be almost certain that "the Great Story in miniature" evangelistic method is a good one. But not entirely certain, for, with Hooker, Lewis's sixteenth-century soul mate, we know that certainty resides only in heaven, the bird's own country. The bird, undoubtedly, is an albatross, a concrete symbol of Christ to Lewis no less than to Coleridge. For though he might remain shy of saying "Come to Jesus," that is what Lewis means in this passage (and throughout his works). And that is what James and John did once they had thrown away their nets.

BIBLIOGRAPHY

Barfield, Owen. *Owen Barfield on C. S. Lewis.* Ed. G. B. Tennyson. Hanover, NH: Wesleyan University Press, 1989.

Hopkins, G. M. *Gerard Manley Hopkins, Poems and Prose.* London: Penguin, 1988.

LIGHTBEARER IN THE SHADOWLANDS

Lewis, C. S. *Christian Reflections*. Ed. Walter Hooper. Glasgow: Fount, 1980.

————. *Christian Reunion*. Ed. Walter Hooper. Glasgow: Fount, 1990.

————. *Fern-seed and Elephants*. Ed. Walter Hooper. Glasgow: Fount, 1982.

————. *God in the Dock*. Ed. Walter Hooper. Glasgow: Fount, 1982.

————. *Letters*. Ed. Walter Hooper. London: Fount, 1988.

————. *Letters to Malcolm, Chiefly on Prayer*. Glasgow: Fount, 1983.

————. *The Lion, the Witch and the Wardrobe*. New York: HarperCollins, 1994.

————. *Mere Christianity*. Glasgow: Fount, 1990.

————. *Of This and Other Worlds*. Ed. Walter Hooper. London: Fount, 1984.

————. *The Pilgrim's Regress*. Glasgow: Fount, 1980.

————. *Poems*. Ed. Walter Hooper. London: Fount, 1994.

————. *Present Concerns*. Ed. Walter Hooper. London: Fount, 1986.

————. *Screwtape Proposes a Toast and Other Pieces*. Glasgow: Fount, 1981.

————. *Selected Literary Essays*. Ed. Walter Hooper. Cambridge: Cambridge University Press, 1980.

————. *Studies in Words*. Cambridge: Cambridge University Press, 1961.

————. *Surprised by Joy*. Glasgow: Fount, 1982.

————. *That Hideous Strength*. London: Pan, 1983.

————. *They Stand Together*. Ed. Walter Hooper. London: Collins, 1979.

————. *Timeless at Heart*. Ed. Walter Hooper. Glasgow: Fount, 1987.

————. *The Voyage of the "Dawn Treader."* Glasgow: Fontana Lions, 1981.

MacDonald, George. *George MacDonald: An Anthology*. Ed. C. S. Lewis. London: Fount, 1983

Pope, Norris. *Dickens and Charity*. London: Macmillan, 1978.

Swinburne, A. C. *Swinburne's Collected Poetical Works*. Vol. I. London: Heinemann, 1927.

Ward, Michael. *Through the Wardrobe: A Famous Image Explored*. Unpublished address to the Oxford University C. S. Lewis Society, 1995.

NOTES

1. Lewis, "God in the Dock," in *God in the Dock*, 101.

2. Lewis, "Modern Man and His Categories of Thought," *Present Concerns*, 66.

3. Lewis, "Cross Examination," *Christian Reunion*, 86.

Lewis's Depictions of Conversion

4. Lewis, "Rejoinder to Dr Pittenger," *Timeless at Heart*, 115.

5. Lewis, *Surprised by Joy*, 9.

6. Lewis, *Letters to Malcolm*, 86. Lewis considered "Jesus worship" to be "a religion which has its value; but not, in isolation, the religion Jesus taught."

7. Letter to Dom Bede Griffiths, 8 May 1939 in Lewis, *Letters*, 321.

8. "Hocus-pocus" possibly originated as a parody of the words of consecration in the Mass, *Hoc est corpus*.

9. *Studies in Words*, 225-26.

10. See, for example, the poem "Donkey's Delight," Lewis, *Poems*, 43.

11. Lewis, *Mere Christianity*, 189.

12. Lewis, "What Are We to Make of Jesus Christ?" in *God in the Dock*, 79.

13. Lewis, *They Stand Together*, 428.

14. Letter to his brother, 17 January 1932 in Lewis, *Letters*, 296.

15. C. S. Lewis, *Studies in Words*, 218.

16. Barfield, *Owen Barfield on C. S. Lewis*.

17. Though Lewis in various places refers to the concrete elements of *Robinson Crusoe* (the salvaging, the wood-chopping, the fence-building), he never, as far as I know, alludes to Crusoe's conversion. Indeed, he speaks slightly disparagingly of the book's "message" in "The Funeral of a Great Myth," *Christian Reflections*, 116.

18. Lewis, *Surprised by Joy*, 63-64.

19. Lewis, *They Stand Together*, 293.

20. This sentence should not be read in isolation from my conclusion.

21. Lewis, *Letters*, 371.

22. See Lewis, "Variation in Shakespeare and Others," *Selected Literary Essays*, 75.

23. Pope, *Dickens and Charity*, 22.

24. Lewis, *Surprised by Joy*, 189-90.

25. Lewis, *The Voyage of the "Dawn Treader,"* 74.

26. Lewis, *Surprised by Joy*, 7.

27. Lewis, "Hedonics," *Present Concerns*, 55.

28. Lewis, *The Pilgrim's Regress*, 218.

29. In a letter of 29 February 1952 Lewis sends to a recent convert both his condolences and congratulations. "For whatever people who have never undergone an adult conversion may say, it is a process not without its distresses. Indeed they are the very sign that it is a true initiation." See *Letters of C. S. Lewis*. Ed. W. H. Lewis (New York: Harcourt, Brace & World, Inc., 1966), 238.

30. Lewis, *Letters*, 415. It is with this statement in mind that I like to view the final scene of Richard Attenborough's film, *Shadowlands*.

31. Lewis, "The Vision of John Bunyan," *Selected Literary Essays*, 149.

32. Lewis, "Joy," *Poems*, 243.

33. Bunyan does not suggest that Christian experienced any pain in letting go of his burden. Compare Lewis's account in *The Pilgrim's Regress*, where we are told that John's clothes "were so stuck to him that they came away with pain and a little skin came with them" (214-15). John obviously undergoes some fraction of crucifixion in the moment of losing his sins.

34. Lewis, *They Stand Together*, 430.

35. Lewis, ed., *George MacDonald: An Anthology*, 148-49.

36. Lewis, "Membership," *Fern-seed and Elephants*, 23.

37. Lewis, *That Hideous Strength*, 316-17.

38. Ibid., 318.

39. Lewis, "Transposition," *Screwtape Proposes a Toast and Other Pieces*, 93.

40. In British English, a gooseberry, as well as being a fruit, is a third person in the company of a courting couple. The nearest American equivalent, I am told, is "a third wheel."

41. Ward, *Through the Wardrobe*.

42. Lewis, *Letters to Malcolm*, 34.

43. Lewis, *They Stand Together*, 427.

44. Lewis, *The Lion, the Witch and the Wardrobe*, 180-81.

45. Hopkins, "God's Grandeur," *Poems and Prose*, 27.

46. Swinburne, "Hymn to Proserpine," *Swinburne's Collected Poetical Works*, 69.

47. Lewis, *They Stand Together*, 361.

48. Lewis, *Mere Christianity*, 125.

49. Lewis, "On Stories," *Of This and Other Worlds*, 45.

7

MERE CHRISTIANITY
BECAUSE THERE ARE NO MERE MORTALS:
Reaching Beyond the Inner Ring

PATRICK T. FERRY

As far as C. S. Lewis was concerned, dissension among Christian believers clouded the light that is intended to illuminate the shadows. Experience and human nature, and certainly the pursuit of truth, may suggest that disagreements are difficult to avoid within the church militant, but disputes and divisions among the faithful may also create disconcerting detours for those who lack familiarity with the saving path that leads toward the church triumphant. This essay will evaluate the relationship between modern denominationalism and Christian outreach. It will be argued, in the spirit of Lewis, that the Church's confessions must be unequivocal and uncompromised; yet at the same time, many of the issues and traditions that have divided denominations should not be allowed to become insurmountable obstacles to effective evangelism. The Church's *raison d'être* is all too easily lost amid a crowd of secondary concerns. In *Mere Christianity* Lewis elaborated:

> It is so easy to think that the Church has a lot of different objects—education, building, missions, holding services . . . The Church exists for nothing else but to draw men into Christ, to make them little Christs. If they are not doing that, all the cathedrals, clergy, missions, sermons, even the Bible itself, are simply a waste of time. God became man for no other purpose. It is

Reaching Beyond the Inner Ring

even doubtful, you know, whether the whole universe was created for any other purpose.[1]

In much the same way, the purpose of doctrines and confessions must
be to bring brighter light to the shadows, rather than simply to produce added heat for the sake of argument or exclusion.

The motivations that drove Lewis toward a cogent summary of
Christian teaching are inseparable from his thoughts about eternity
and the urgent need to evangelize a world full of eternal beings. It is
necessary to underscore the importance that Lewis attached to the
lively hope of eternal life that he eagerly hoped his readers would
embrace. It will also be worthwhile to highlight the similarities
between Lewis and Saint Paul on this point. A respectful regard for the
glory of eternity finally must overcome factionalism for the benefit of
those who are still outside the faith. As Lewis suggests, "We must be
careful not to expect or demand that their salvation should conform
to some ready-made pattern of our own."[2] He resisted confining God's
ways and means to our ideas about how things ought to be done.
Indeed, Lewis stated that "there are many different ways for bringing
people into His Kingdom, even some ways that I specially dislike!"[3]
This attitude toward evangelism, however, does not come naturally,
and it does not come easily.

Here it will also be shown that one major impediment to outreach
is the natural human inclination to close ranks around what Lewis
calls the "inner ring." Although Lewis would not specifically connect
the issue of denominationalism to his critique of the esoteric inner ring,
the following will argue that unwavering insistence upon denominational loyalties may often have much to do with a corrupted need for
others to be designated out of bounds in order to uphold some tenu-
ous sense of what it means to be an insider. As this thesis unfolds it
will follow C. S. Lewis in affirming the necessity of unambiguous
Christian doctrine without allowing varying denominational pecu-
liarities to impinge upon Christian outreach. As long as there are people who are not numbered among those who comprise the
communion of saints, the *una sancta* remains in need of a "mere"

Christianity—because, as C. S. Lewis reminds us, there is no such thing as a "mere" mortal.

Evangelism and Ecumenism

The particular denominational affiliation of the author of *Mere Christianity* was never meant to be kept a secret. His approach to the popular book, and to the radio programs that preceded its publication, was emphatically ecumenical. Nevertheless, there was no mystery in the fact that C. S. Lewis regarded himself as a "very ordinary layman of the Church of England."[4] While his expressed interest was to serve his unbelieving neighbors by explaining and defending the core beliefs of Christians of all times and places, his decision to write *Mere Christianity* was not an attempt by Lewis "to conceal or evade responsibility" for his own beliefs.[5] Regarding those, he indicated plainly, "They are written in the Common-Prayer Book."[6] The quest of his work was not to convert anyone to this position. Lewis also stressed that *Mere Christianity* was not meant as yet another option to already existing creeds and communions. The reduction of Christianity to a simple skeleton was hardly the appearance that Lewis wanted to present to those who were outside the faith. Rather, with a heart for lost souls, he presented what he considered to be the inarguable heart and soul of Christian teaching. Lewis, however, explained that the full incarnational character of Christ's Church was manifested, not in the ideas of *Mere Christianity* but in and among flesh-and-blood Christians who lived and breathed their faith alongside their fellow believers within specific confessional churches.

Ironically, the same Common-Prayer Book to which Lewis acknowledged a personal affiliation had some peculiar ecumenical roots. The experience of Stephen Gardiner, Bishop of Winchester in the sixteenth century, illustrates the point. A key church leader under Henry VIII, Gardiner suddenly found himself having trouble coping with the religious innovations of the Edwardian Reformation. The Archbishop of Canterbury, Thomas Cranmer, was eager to introduce Protestant changes into the life of the English Church despite objec-

Reaching Beyond the Inner Ring

tions from conservatives such as Gardiner. When it became apparent that Cranmer intended to author a new prayer book in English, Gardiner and others braced for the worst. However, when presented with a copy of the initial edition in 1549, Gardiner announced that he was fully prepared to make use of the Book of Common Prayer. His consent was not coerced, but it was not a bow to Protestantism either. Neither threats and pressures, nor the force of argument caused the resolute Gardiner suddenly to become a willing compromiser. Instead, as the Reformation historian A. G. Dickens argues, the Book of Common Prayer was itself "a masterpiece of compromise"—it was a remarkable example of "studied ambiguity."[7]

As subsequent editions of the prayer book became increasingly Protestant in both ritual and theology, later English Catholics of Gardiner's bent surely found modifications decreasingly palatable. The search for a broad consensus based upon blurred doctrinal distinctions escalated once Queen Elizabeth ascended to the throne in 1559. Her religious policy of inclusion based on outward conformity produced a religious settlement that was completely uncharacteristic in an era of intense confessional rivalry. There were, of course, dissenters enough to be drawn from ardent English Catholics and zealous proto-Puritans alike, but theological ambiguity allowed the majority of English people at the turn of the seventeenth century to maintain at least superficial connections to the church that gathered around the Book of Common Prayer.

The Christian beliefs of C. S. Lewis may be found written in that same Book of Common Prayer, but he was no advocate of ambiguity, nor of superficiality. He supported ecclesiastical unity and found consolation in his observation that at the center, where the church's "truest children dwell," each Christian communion draws nearest to every other "in spirit, if not in doctrine."[8] Simple outward conformity for the purpose of creating ostensible unity, however, did not come near to the ultimate objective—perfunctory lip service could never be a substitute for a clear Christian confession. The ecumenical approach that Lewis follows in *Mere Christianity* was not an endorsement of bland ecumenism. Instead, his work more closely follows the spirit that was in evidence in the production of the ecumenical creeds and that pervaded the ecumenical councils of the early Christian Church. The Church Councils of Nicea and Constantinople in the fourth century, and of Ephesus and Chalcedon in the fifth century, for example, produced doctrinal formulations that were anything but ambiguous. They laid out with extraordinary precision the fundamental summaries of trinitarian and christological theology that have been observed within the Christian Church ever since.[9]

Indeed, throughout the history of the Christian Church, firm adherents have always sought to define the *sine qua non* articles of the faith, and the author of *Mere Christianity* follows in the same historical tradition. Lewis was aware that the attempt to distill Christian teaching to a generally accepted body of doctrines runs the risk of eviscerating, or at least of compromising, essential dimensions of the faith. Yet, the ecumenical creeds are themselves precedents for the idea that a "mere" Christianity is more than a reduction of the faith to the most common denominational denominators. Assertions about what encompasses clear and constitutive Christian truth, as Lewis noted, are the result of significant historical developments, and consensus has often been forged on the anvil of considerable theological strife. The all-inclusive character of the Christian Gospel is necessarily based upon certain exclusive claims about God and the divine plan of salvation for all people. Creeds, confessions, and other doctrinal formulas, while ecumenical, by necessity exclude those who reject their fundamental conclusions. Christian faith extends a universal invitation, but it is not universalistic.

Sometimes Lewis worried that Christians had the tendency to make too many compromises and concessions and give in too much to those who were outside the faith. He wrote that Christians must be willing to show their true colors. While the faithful run the risk of becoming a nuisance by witnessing at improper times (something Lewis discouraged), nevertheless, he stressed, "there comes a time when we must show that we disagree."[10]

Substantial statements of faith such as those produced at the early ecumenical councils reflect a specific salvific and unifying character. In other words, summaries of the key components of Christian doctrine have been drawn not only to exclude heretics and refute heresy, but also to hold forth with crystal clarity the saving gospel message and to unify Christian believers beneath that banner. The creeds and confessions of the early church were thus "mere Christianity" at its very best, and, although we may not place his work on a comparable level, Lewis's analysis of universally applicable Christian truths presents a thorough, ecumenical summary of Christian teaching. *Mere Christianity*, to put it directly, may not be equated with vague Christianity. Indeed, Lewis was convinced that the most satisfying expressions of the Christian faith were unavailable in generic brands. To the contrary, he fully appreciated the importance of drawing seekers further and deeper into the Christian communion that they were convinced taught what is true and modeled what is holy. *Mere Christianity*, therefore, was meant not as an end in itself, but as a means by which people are led toward a richer relationship with Christ and the Church.

Lewis compares his contribution to a vestibule that serves as a passageway into several rooms. In fact, the objective of *Mere Christianity* is to bring people into the vestibule by removing stumbling blocks that prevent initial entry. Lewis believed this could best be accomplished by demonstrating the plausibility of Christian doctrine, by answering the objections of detractors, and by encouraging thoughtful consideration of the essential tenets of the faith that have been held in common by believers of every time and place. Once the unbeliever becomes willing at least to survey the vestibule, the task of *Mere Christianity* is essentially completed. However, the spiritual journey is by no means over. Lewis indicates that the worst of the rooms (Christian denominations), whichever one it might be, is preferable to remaining in the vestibule. He writes, "the hall is a place to wait in, a place from which to try out the various doors, not a place to live in."[11] The vestibule could accommodate those who needed to pause, but it was not a place to camp or tarry for long. For outsiders to become insiders they had need only to enter further and make themselves at home. Not in the vestibule, but beyond the door and in a living room seekers were invited to find the "fires and chairs and meals," indeed all that was necessary to transform Christianity from general principles into a living, active faith.[12] The ending point of evangelism, therefore, must be more than the nondescript Christianity of the Elizabethan Settlement, or even the colorless vestibule that is occasionally trumpeted by modern ecumenists.

Beyond the vestibule and inside the door an outsider encounters a dwelling place. It should be noted that for Lewis the selection of rooms was not to be based upon what seemed most pleasant or enjoyable. In *The Screwtape Letters*, for instance, the tempter, Wormwood, is told that if a man cannot be "cured of churchgoing," then the next best thing is "to send him all over the neighborhood looking for a church that suits him until he becomes a taster or connoisseur of churches."[13] Lewis was no supporter of "church shopping," and he argued that membership in a church went far beyond one's tastes or comforts. He said that the question should not be, "Do I like that kind of service?" but instead "Are these doctrines true? Is holiness here?"[14] The methods of Lewis were certainly ecumenical, and his interests were clearly evangelistic, but boiling Christian teaching down to its essential center did not mean offering a watered-down version of the faith in order to make it easier to swallow. As Lewis writes in his apologetic for supernaturalism in *God in the Dock*, "Do not attempt to water Christianity down. There must be no pretense that you can have it with the Supernatural left out. . . . You must frankly argue for supernaturalism from the very outset."[15]

Indeed, *Mere Christianity* is a testament to the conviction of C. S. Lewis that Christian doctrine is crucial. With it also comes the recognition that full fellowship within the communion of saints means more than hanging around the fringes of a mere Christianity. Beyond the door and inside the room resides a community of saints that extends from time to eternity, an assembly with links from the here to the hereafter, a congregation that is rooted in history and pointed toward glory. The mission of the mere Christian evangelist is to break down barriers and to help outsiders begin to find the way inside.

Reaching Beyond the Inner Ring

The Weight of Glory

Few Christian writers have compelled us to think about heaven and hell more than C. S. Lewis. While he frequently stirs the imagination about what eternality entails, in books such as *The Great Divorce* Lewis gives readers cause to consider the eternal with regard to its implications for the temporal. He warns against simply anticipating the "retrospective vision" of celestial glory without pondering the meaning of heaven already for earthly existence. Lewis remarks that earth and its pleasures, if chosen above heaven, "will turn out to have been, all along, only a region in Hell." Meanwhile, if put second to heaven, the earthly life will be found "to have been from the beginning a part of Heaven itself."[16] In giving consideration to what Lewis describes as "the staggering nature" of the Gospel's eternal promises, he suggests that our human desires are typically aimed too low. Our problem is that we behave like the ignorant child "who wants to go on making mud pies in a slum because he cannot imagine what is meant by the offer of a holiday at the sea."[17] In his essay "The Weight of Glory," Lewis contends that people need to be awakened from "the evil enchantment of worldliness" that dupes them into concentrating upon the good that is to be found upon this earth rather than fixing their attention upon something as distant and remote as heaven. Against those who would divert the Christian away from the elusive eternal toward the tangible temporal, Lewis writes:

> When they want to convince you that earth is your home, notice how they set about it. They begin by trying to persuade you that earth can be made into heaven, thus giving a sop to your sense of exile in earth as it is. Next, they tell you that this fortunate event is still a good way off in the future, thus giving a sop to your knowledge that the fatherland is not here and now. Finally, lest your longing for the transtemporal should awake and spoil the whole affair, they use any rhetoric that comes to hand to keep out of your mind the recollection that even if all the happiness they promised could come to man on earth, yet still each generation would lose it by death. . . .[18]

To choose earth over heaven, Lewis argues in *The Great Divorce*, is to settle for a region of hell. It follows that the devilish guardians of hell would be most intent upon redirecting Christians away from a goal in the eternal elsewhere toward one in the more accessible temporal sphere. People are not left alone to meditate upon eternal issues all by themselves, and in *The Screwtape Letters* Lewis provides a reminder that heaven and hell are more than just matters of human interest. Powers and principalities not even of this world, to use the language of Saint Paul, are engaged in sinister and insidious work to divert believers away from the heavenly prize. One of their diabolical strategies, according to Lewis, is to modify the character of mere Christianity by updating it into "Christianity And."[19] The goal of "Christianity And" (whether it is "Christianity and the Crisis," "Christianity and the New Order," "Christianity and Faith Healing," "Christianity and Psychical Research," "Christianity and Vegetarianism," "Christianity and Spelling Reform," or Christianity and whatever else) is "to substitute for the faith itself some fashion with a Christian coloring."[20] The goal of Screwtape's "Father Below," to put it another way, is to turn mere Christianity's burden for things eternal into a religious obsession with the things of this world.

The weight of glory, however, is one that Christian believers cannot cast off lightly despite the deceptions of those who suggest that earthly burdens should take priority. "Do what they will," Lewis writes, "we remain conscious of a desire which no natural happiness will satisfy."[21] To Lewis, the fact that we are perpetually surprised at time ("How time flies, fancy John being grown up and married! I can hardly believe it!") is evidence of our inherent sense of the eternal. Surprised by time? "In heaven's name, why?" Lewis wonders, "Unless, indeed, there is something in us which is not temporal."[22] Of course, throughout our earthly pilgrimage Screwtape's sworn "Enemy" forgives sins, leads not into temptation, and delivers from evil. These truths provide immeasurable consolation for the Christian so often sidetracked by worldly worries and wants. In the end, Lewis declares, "that Face which is the delight or the terror of the universe must be turned upon each of us," and each will behold an expression that either confers "glory inexpressible" or inflicts "shame that can never be cured or disguised."[23] When compelled to stand before God and confronted with the final inspection, Lewis insists that our only recourse is the promise of glory. He writes, "The promise of glory is the promise, almost incredible and only possible by the work of Christ, that some of us, that any of us who really chooses, shall actually survive that examination, shall find approval, shall please God."[24] Here the real yearning of the believer, practically transcending imagination, is finally realized:

> To please God . . . to be a real ingredient in the divine happiness . . . to be loved by God, not merely pitied, but delighted in as an artist delights in his work or a father in a son—it seems impossible, a weight or burden of glory which our thoughts can hardly sustain. But so it is.[25]

C. S. Lewis develops his own emphasis upon eternity and the glorious, heavenly reward from his reading of Saint Paul. In "The Weight of Glory" Lewis certainly echoes many of the words and sentiments of the apostle. He follows the example of Paul who writes and urges the Colossians to "be eager for the things that are above, where Christ is sitting at the right hand of God." The apostle encourages his readers "to keep their minds on things above, not on earthly things." And he comforts them with the promise that "when Christ, your Life appears, then you too will appear with Him in glory."[26] Paul also offers comfort to the Christians residing in Corinth who struggle with the trials and troubles of this world. Do not be discouraged, even in the face of death, Paul preaches, for "the light trouble of this moment is preparing us for an everlasting weight of glory, greater than anything that we can imagine."[27]

Most important for this essay, Paul connects the promise of glory in heaven with Christian evangelism in the world. Compelled "by the love of Christ," convinced "that One died for all," Paul declares in 1 Corinthians that "from now on we do not think of anyone only as a human being." Mindful of "the terror of the Lord," Paul expresses his eagerness to win the confidence of people. He regards himself as an "ambassador for Christ," dispatched with the message of reconciliation between God and man: "for God made Him who did not know sin to be sin for us to make us God's righteousness in Him." With evangelistic fervor, Saint Paul exhorts, "Do not let God's love be wasted on you . . . now is the time when He welcomes us, now is the day of salvation."[28]

In the conclusion to "The Weight of Glory," Lewis revisits many of the same Pauline themes. Christians with eyes set upon heavenly things still endure troubles en route to glory. Lewis acknowledges that "the cross comes before the crown and tomorrow is a Monday morning. A cleft has opened in the pitiless walls of the world, and we are invited to follow our Captain inside."[29] But glory will come. For Lewis, as for Paul, the most practical benefit and use of meditation upon the glory hereafter is outreach to one's neighbor here and now. He writes:

> It may be possible for each to think too much of his own potential glory hereafter; it is hardly possible for him to think too often or too deeply about that of his neighbor. The load, or weight, or burden of my neighbor's glory should be laid daily on my back, a load so heavy that only humility can carry it, and the backs of the proud will be broken.[30]

Saint Paul told the Corinthians that he no longer thought of anyone as simply a human being. So also Lewis remarked that "it is a serious thing to live in a society of possible gods and goddesses." He speculated that the "dullest and most uninteresting person" that one encounters or shares a conversation with "may one day be a creature which, if you saw it now, you would be strongly tempted to worship." Or, the opposite might also be true—the same person might one day be "a horror and a corruption such as you now meet, if at all, only in a nightmare."[31] In *Mere Christianity* Lewis says concisely that "every individual human being is going to live forever."[32] If we were nothing more than biological entities, questions about life and death would have little meaning. But, Lewis says, our eternal identity means that "we shall live to remember the galaxies as an old tale."[33] His point for Christian evangelism is both sober and succinct: "it is immortals whom we joke with, work with, marry, snub, and exploit—immortal horrors or everlasting splendors." Lewis asserts that "all day long we are, in some degree, helping each other to one or the other of these destinations."[34]

Thoughts of glory and emphasis upon eternity provided the framework for the attitudes of Lewis toward evangelism. Nothing, in the final analysis, was of greater significance; even the lives of nations, cultures, arts, and civilizations were less enduring, and thus, of less consequence. Lewis said that "their life is to ours as the life of a gnat."[35] While evangelism is serious business, this does not imply that perpetual solemnity must replace play. Still, Lewis maintains that "awe and circumspection" should direct "all our dealings with one another, all friendships, all loves, all play, all politics."[36] Even merriment is to be of the sort that takes people seriously, Lewis insists, for "next to the Blessed Sacrament itself, your neighbor is the holiest object presented to your senses."[37] His thoughts about eternity define the significance of Christian evangelism, and Lewis states the point with force: "There are no ordinary people. You have never talked to a mere mortal."[38] And because there are no mere mortals, *Mere Christianity* becomes all the more essential.

Beyond the Inner Ring and into the Inner Sanctum

To C. S. Lewis the neighbor was a sacred object, and in a Christian neighbor the very glory of Christ was revealed.[39] Lewis wrote *Mere Christianity*, however, because not every neighbor shared in that glory. From the time that he became a Christian himself, Lewis thought the best service he could provide for his unbelieving neighbors was to explain and defend the beliefs that are common to all Christians.[40] He offered no help to the seeker who looked for direction in selecting a specific denomination. Indeed, he intentionally steered clear of such advice because he believed that discussion of disputed points between Christian groups "has no tendency to bring outsiders into the fold."[41]

Lewis maintained that by writing and talking about contentious issues he would more likely discourage outsiders from entering any Christian communion, and he insisted that doctrinal and denominational differences should never be discussed in their presence.[42] Dialogue and even debate over contended doctrinal issues have a place within the Christian Church, but for Lewis evangelistic efforts should avoid theological controversies.

In his writings Lewis alludes to another more subtle but equally poisonous problem related to groups within the Church that also has adverse consequences for evangelism. Outsiders are perhaps invited into the inner sanctum of the holy Christian Church, but what Lewis calls the inner ring might be even more difficult to get past. Lewis describes what he means by the inner ring in the Memorial Oration that he delivered for King's College at the University of London in 1944.[43] The inner ring does not need to be formally organized with specific rules. Indeed, it is typically indefinable. But there is no question that it exists. The objective is to be on the inside and, once in, to be very careful about allowing in another.[44] It is "the lust for the esoteric," "the longing to be inside," "the delicious sense of secret intimacy."[45]

The image of the inner ring is more concretely depicted in *That Hideous Strength*, the final volume in the famous space trilogy of Lewis. His character, Mark Studdock, embodies the sort of lust and longing that Lewis advised against. First, in his desire to work his way into the informal but powerful inner circle of colleagues at Bracton College, Studdock found "intense pleasure" when the pronoun "we" was used to include him. Only a short time before he had been an outsider, but once he suddenly found himself on the inside and "they" became "we," it certainly was "sweet in his mouth."[46] What began as "a giddy sensation of being whirled up from one plane of secrecy to another" eventually became more perilous.[47] Finally, Studdock's hunger to be included in the loop of the prestigious yet clandestine N.I.C.E. was insatiable, and in the end it very nearly consumed him. To gain entry, Studdock became willing to sacrifice nearly everything—family, career, even his soul. When acceptance into the diabolical circle was finally

Reaching Beyond the Inner Ring

obtained, "a glow of sheer pleasure passed over Mark's whole body." Lewis writes, "He was actually being waited for. He was wanted."[48]

In his King's College lecture Lewis warns that the inner ring is not worth the price of admission. The phenomenon of the inner ring is perhaps not itself an evil, according to Lewis, and in fact it may be as innocent as it is an unavoidable feature of life.[49] The problem is with the desire and the terror that it produces—desire to get inside the ring, and terror at the thought of being left out.[50] His lecture does not tie the notion of the inner ring to denominationalism or to subgroups within Christian denominations. Instead he confines his remarks to young men in college about to embark upon the rest of their lives and who are susceptible to the unfortunate yearnings that the inner ring produces. However, much the same theme applied to church life recurs repeatedly in other writings, and in particular *The Screwtape Letters*. When we place *The Screwtape Letters* alongside *That Hideous Strength* and the speech at King's College, it becomes clear that Lewis's caveat about the insidious inner ring pertains to Christian denominations and other church groups as well as to individuals.

In contrast to the inner ring, the inner sanctum exists to include rather than to exclude. Because the inner sanctum is a holy and mysterious place, however, the uninitiated might easily be daunted by the unknown and feel uncomfortable in its midst. The holy place is open to all, but those who fear that becoming too deeply entangled will intrude upon their own habitual ways of living might prefer to exclude themselves from the inner sanctum. For example, in *That Hideous Strength*, Mark Studdock's wife, Jane, is invited to join the (Christian) Belbury side that opposes N.I.C.E., but she hesitates. Her exchange with Miss Ironwood is illustrative of the sort of reluctance outsiders may feel toward the inner sanctum:

> "You keep on talking of We and Us. Are you some kind of company?"
> "Yes. You may call it a company."
> Jane had been standing for the last few minutes; and she had almost been believing what she heard. Then suddenly all her

repugnance came over her again—all her wounded vanity, her resentment of the seemingly meaningless complication in which she had been caught, and her general dislike of the mysterious and unfamiliar. At that moment, nothing seemed to matter but to get out of that room and away from the grave, patient voice of Miss Ironwood.[51]

The inner sanctum, open and accessible to all, is entered with reluctance. Meanwhile, the inner ring, closed to all but a select few, becomes the most urgent desire for many. From infancy to old age people are prone to the longing to be part of the inner ring.[52] Lewis regards this quest as "one of the great permanent mainsprings of human action."[53] Given that humans also act within the operation of the Church, it should come as no surprise that problems associated with the inner ring spill over into denominationalism. The act of drawing strict denominational lines may ostensibly be about preserving definitive doctrines or treasured traditions, but the underlying, and perhaps even the unconscious, motivation is often about maintaining an exclusive inner ring. Lines are crucial to the inner ring, but the boundaries would have no meaning unless they are drawn in such a way that most people end up on the wrong side. Lewis describes the issue concisely and penetratingly when he says, "Exclusion is no accident: it is the essence."[54]

Unless measures are taken to prevent it, the desire to be included within the inner ring and to exclude others will become one of the chief motives of a person's life.[55] Unless it is conscientiously kept in check, the same sort of unhelpful motivations could also be expanded and applied to Christian churches and Christian denominations. In *The Screwtape Letters* Lewis makes a number of observations about how this tendency infiltrates church life. To reiterate, the issue is not about legitimate doctrinal differences. Screwtape reminds Wormwood that "it is not the doctrines on which we chiefly depend for producing malice."[56] Nevertheless, Screwtape's strategy, if people cannot be kept out of the Church, is to find ways to get them "violently attached to some party within it."[57] Elsewhere Screwtape indicates that even when little groups originally come into existence "for the Enemy's own purposes," they may become

Reaching Beyond the Inner Ring

a defensive, self-righteous, secret society that shamelessly entertains a pride and hatred toward those outside the circle because they believe they are acting for the good of the "Cause."[58] Lewis deplored the fact that such uncritical confidences in churches or parties within the Church have been used to justify the most abominable actions and have contributed to the sum of human cruelty and treachery. Indeed, Lewis believed that many people worldwide will not even listen to the message of Christianity until Christians publicly disown much of their past.[59] This, of course, accounts for Screwtape's goal of creating factions, and he reminds his nephew that factionalism has "often produced admirable results, from the parties of Paul and Apollos at Corinth, down to the High and Low parties in the Church of England."[60]

Lewis, by way of distinction, believed that parochial organization was itself a good thing because it was "a unity of place and not of likings."[61] A place that united people of different classes and different psychology in such a God-pleasing manner had much to offer. On the other hand, the congregational principle makes each church into a kind of club, and perhaps even a coterie or faction.[62] The trouble here, in Lewis's view, is that the objective is to divide into cliques rather than to bring about a unity of disparate peoples under the Gospel. Can groups that draw rings within the Church to keep a distance from other believers open their circle in order to draw in unbelievers who are still on the outside?

It is necessary to mention that Lewis recognized a critical distinction between an "inner ring" and a natural association of people who shared common interests. Friendship, for instance, was a relationship between people that Lewis regarded very highly. A group of this sort might also exclude others simply because its interests and aims are not for everyone. The key difference, however, is that exclusion, while an inevitable by-product of friendship, is not the goal. "Friendship must exclude," writes Lewis, but he also warns that from "the innocent and necessary act of excluding to the spirit of exclusiveness is an easy step."[63]

In his critique of the inner ring Lewis is talking about more than simply avoiding a sanctimonious approach toward others outside the group. Screwtape tells Wormwood that it is not enough to make a person proud of being a Christian, though spiritual pride is one of the "strongest and most beautiful of the vices."[64] Still, he will not get far with his patient by encouraging a "holier than thou" attitude because there are ample warnings against pride and pietism. The tempter gains points, however, when his patient is led to self-congratulation for belonging to an inner ring. "The great thing," Screwtape declares, "is to make Christianity a mystery religion in which he feels himself one of the initiates."[65] The devils achieve their success when Christian women with clearly defined beliefs hold the "untroubled assumption that the outsiders who do not share this belief are really too stupid and ridiculous."[66] They succeed when, because the Christian man "is aware of a 'deeper,' 'spiritual' world within him" that others cannot understand, he feels a "continual undercurrent of self-satisfaction."[67] The temptation is to adopt an air of amusement at what the masses of unbelievers say and to pay serious attention only to the ideas of a select minority—some inner ring of trained theocrats.[68] Desires for the inner ring are never completely quenched unless entrance to that holiest of holies severely restricts unenlightened outsiders. The idea of welcoming them is never very seriously entertained.

Screwtape's schemes for keeping people out of heaven and delivering them to his "Father Below" have an unlikely source of support. He writes, "One of our great allies at present is the Church itself."[69] Not the Church spread out through time and rooted in eternity, but the Church as it is comprised of that odd selection of people who comprise the "Body of Christ." Ordinary neighbors may prove to be a disappointment, and the desire to exclude them may be great. They may "sing out of tune, or have boots that squeak, or double chins, or odd clothes."[70] Or, more disconcerting still, they may hold to different attitudes or opinions. Insofar as these neighbors are treated as objects of contempt, ridicule, or even indifference instead of as objects of holiness, the inner ring is exalted and the inner sanctum is obscured. The outsider's inclination to stay away or to flee, like Jane Studdock, could be reinforced by those who are inside. But where the Gospel of Christ is proclaimed, the temple curtain is torn in two, and access to all of the mysteries of the faith are unveiled.

Reaching Beyond the Inner Ring

His problem was not with the pursuit of doctrinal truth; indeed, C. S. Lewis was sorry that most Christians had a lukewarm attitude toward theology.[71] Nevertheless, C. S. Lewis was concerned that disputed points that caused divisions within Christianity created unhelpful impediments that prevent outsiders from being brought into the fold. Lewis believed that the more nonbelievers were exposed to divisive issues, the more likely they were to be deterred from investigating the meaning of Christianity or participating in any Christian communion.[72] He never supposed that conflicts of opinion were unnecessary, nor did he ever suggest that confessing Christians abandon confessional positions simply to avoid disagreement. Lewis, however, did regard most doctrinal discrepancies to be matters of subtle theological or historical development that may concern experts but not necessarily evangelists.[73] To his regret, Lewis felt that most talented Christian authors had concentrated their best efforts upon intra-Christian polemics rather than upon effective apologetics for "mere" Christianity. Lewis himself was occasionally the target of a share of criticism. His rejoinder to the sharp comments of Dr. Pittenger, quoted here at length, demonstrates the concern that Lewis felt about how theological energies were being expended:

When I began, Christianity came before the great mass of my unbelieving fellow-countrymen either in the highly emotional form offered by revivalists or in the unintelligible language of highly cultured clergymen. Most men were reached by neither. My task was therefore simply that of a *translator*—one turning Christian doctrine, or what he believed to be such, into the vernacular, into language that unscholarly people would attend to and could understand. For this purpose a style more guarded, more *nuancé*, finelier shaded, more rich in fruitful ambiguities— in fact, a style more like Dr. Pittenger's own—would have been worse than useless. It would not only have failed to enlighten the common reader's understanding; it would have aroused his suspicion. He would have thought, poor soul, that I was facing both ways, sitting on the fence, offering at one moment what I withdrew the next, and generally trying to trick him. I may have made theological errors. My manner may have been defective. Others may do better hereafter. I am ready, if I am young enough, to learn. Dr. Pittenger would be a more helpful critic if he advised a cure as well as asserting many diseases. How does he himself do such work? What methods, and with what success, does he employ when he is trying to convert the great mass of storekeepers, lawyers, realtors, morticians, policemen and artisans who surround him in his own city?

One thing at least is sure. If the real theologians had tackled this laborious work of translation about a hundred years ago, when they began to lose touch with the people (for whom Christ died), there would have been no place for me.[74]

Lewis, therefore, resolved very intentionally to pour the best of his own creative energies into the area of the Church's work that appeared most neglected. He wrote, "That part of the line where I thought I could serve best was also the part that seemed the thinnest. And to it I naturally went."[75] C. S. Lewis was effective as an evangelist because he saw the value of utilizing Christian doctrine as a tool for persuading unbelievers about the truth rather than as mainly an instrument for convincing other believers of their errors.

BIBLIOGRAPHY

Dickens, A. G. *The English Reformation*. New York: Schocken Books, 1964.

Lewis, C. S. *The Four Loves*. New York: Harcourt Brace Jovanovich, 1960.

————. *God in the Dock*. Ed. Walter Hooper. Grand Rapids, MI: Eerdmans, 1970.

————. *The Great Divorce*. New York: Macmillan, 1946.

————. "The Inner Ring," in *The Weight of Glory and Other Addresses*. New York: Macmillan, 1949, 55-66.

————. *Letters of C. S. Lewis*. Ed. W. H. Lewis. New York: Harcourt Brace Jovanovich, 1966.

————. "Membership," in *The Weight of Glory and Other Addresses*. New York: Macmillan, 1949, 30-42.

Reaching Beyond the Inner Ring

_____. *Mere Christianity*, Third Edition. New York: Macmillan, 1952.

_____. *The Screwtape Letters*. New York: Macmillan, 1961.

_____. *That Hideous Strength*. New York: Scribner Paperback Fiction, 1996.

_____. "The Weight of Glory." In *The Weight of Glory and Other Addresses*. New York: Macmillan, 1949, 1-15.

Sayer, George. *Jack: A Life of C. S. Lewis*. Second Edition. Wheaton, IL: Crossway Books, 1994.

Vanauken, Sheldon. *A Severe Mercy*. New York: Harper and Row, 1977.

NOTES

1. Lewis, *Mere Christianity*, 169-70.

2. Lewis, *Letters of C. S. Lewis*, 261.

3. Lewis, *God in the Dock*, 262.

4. Lewis, *Mere Christianity*, 6.

5. Ibid., 8.

6. Ibid.

7. Dickens, *The English Reformation*, 219.

8. Lewis, *Mere Christianity*, 9.

9. The Nicene Creed produced at Nicea in 325 and revised at Constantinople in 381 clarified trinitarian theology over and against the aberrations of Arianism, Monarchianism, and Macedonianism, while the conclusions of the Council of Ephesus in 435 and the formula drawn at the Council of Chalcedon in 455 defined the relationship between the divine and human natures in the person of Christ against the errors of Nestorius and Eutyches.

10. Lewis, *God in the Dock*, 262.

11. Lewis, *Mere Christianity*, 12.

12. Ibid.

13. Lewis, *The Screwtape Letters*, 72.

14. Lewis, *Mere Christianity*, 12.

15. Lewis, *God in the Dock*, 99.

16. Lewis, *The Great Divorce*, 7.

17. Lewis, "The Weight of Glory," 1-2.

18. Ibid., 5.

19. Lewis, *The Screwtape Letters*, 115.

20. Ibid., 115-16.

21. Lewis, "The Weight of Glory," 6.

22. Vanauken, *A Severe Mercy*, 93.

23. Lewis, "The Weight of Glory," 10.

24. Ibid.

25. Ibid.

26. Colossians 3:1-4.

27. 2 Corinthians 4:16-17.

28. 2 Corinthians 5:11—6:2.

29. Lewis, "The Weight of Glory," 14.

30. Ibid.

31. Ibid., 15.

32. Lewis, *Mere Christianity*, 73.

33. Lewis, "Membership," 40.

34. Lewis, "The Weight of Glory," 15.

35. Ibid.

36. Ibid.

37. Ibid.

38. Ibid.

39. Ibid.

40. Lewis, *Mere Christianity*, 6.

41. Ibid.

42. Ibid.

43. Lewis, "The Inner Ring," 55-66.

44. Ibid., 56-7.

45. Ibid., 61.

46. Lewis, *That Hideous Strength*, 17.

47. Ibid., 40.

48. Ibid., 128.

49. Lewis, "The Inner Ring," 60.

50. Ibid., 58.

51. Lewis, *That Hideous Strength*, 68.

52. Lewis, "The Inner Ring," 58.

53. Ibid., 61.

54. Ibid., 65.

Reaching Beyond the Inner Ring

55. Ibid., 62.

56. Lewis, *The Screwtape Letters*, 75.

57. Ibid.

58. Ibid., 34.

59. Lewis, *The Four Loves*, 49.

60. Lewis, *The Screwtape Letters*, 34.

61. Ibid., 73.

62. Ibid.

63. Lewis, *The Four Loves*, 122.

64. Lewis, *The Screwtape Letters*, 111.

65. Ibid., 113.

66. Ibid., 110.

67. Ibid., 48.

68. Ibid., 113.

69. Ibid., 12.

70. Ibid.

71. See, for example, Lewis, *The Screwtape Letters*, 75.

72. Lewis, *Mere Christianity*, 6.

73. Ibid.

74. Lewis, *God in the Dock*, 183.

75. Lewis, *Mere Christianity*, 6.

8

THE PAGAN AND THE POST-CHRISTIAN:
Lewis's Understanding of Diversity Outside the Faith

JON BALSBAUGH

Jews demand miraculous signs and Greeks look for wisdom, but we preach Christ crucified: a stumbling block to Jews and foolishness to Gentiles, but to those whom God has called, both Jews and Greeks, Christ the power of God and the wisdom of God.
—1 Corinthians 1:22-24

The *ideal end* of evangelism is the salvation of the unsaved—the transformation of a person from a state of immortal danger to a state of imminent glory. As C. S. Lewis writes in *The Great Divorce*, "There are only two kinds of people in the end: those who say to God, 'Thy will be done,' and those to whom God says, in the end, 'Thy will be done.'"[1] However, when we engage in the *practice* of evangelism we are forced to deal with people not as they *will be*, but as they *are*, and what they are cannot be reduced to simple categories. Not everyone who is outside Christianity is outside it to the same degree. There are those who have been turned off to the faith through personal experience with "religion" and those who have never *had* any personal experience. Some are familiar with the Scriptures, and some are not. Some worldviews are essentially compatible with Christianity, while others leave no room for the Gospel to be anything but nonsense. The need for the evangelist to recognize this diversity among non-Christians is what lingers behind the emphasis of this chapter—Lewis's repeated insistence upon maintaining the distinction between the pagan and the post-Christian.[2]

In "Is Theism Important?" Lewis makes this rather shocking statement: "When grave persons express their fear that England is relapsing into Paganism, I am tempted to reply, 'Would that she were.'"[3] According to Lewis, what these "grave persons" were actually observing and improperly labeling was a widespread "apostasy of the great part of Europe from the Christian faith"[4]—a divorce of culture from faith distinct from pre-Christian paganism. The confusion of these two worldviews is a symptom of failure on the part of Christians to recognize true diversity among our non-Christian peers. It betrays an "us vs. them" mind-set, in which anyone who is not a Christian must fall into some other homogeneous category (such as "pagan"). If the differences between paganism and post-Christianity mean nothing to us, then neither will the differences between our next-door neighbor who is steeped in spiritualism and our neighbor across the street who is a professing atheist.

The first two sections of this chapter are composite sketches of the pagan and the post-Christian as drawn from Lewis's nonfiction. Understanding the implications of these two radically different worldviews can be an important tool for evangelism, continually underscoring for us the need to be aware of what "sort" of non-Christian we are encountering in any given evangelistic situation.

Of course we must also allow the lines between these two categories to remain somewhat blurred. Each individual is unique and therefore poses a unique challenge to our task of evangelism. People inevitably resist strict categorization. Lewis's own pre-conversion story is a perfect example of this. In many ways he was the model of an intellectual post-Christian, yet his conversion narratives (both *Surprised by Joy* and *The Pilgrim's Regress*) are shot through with descriptions of an often secret and always powerful longing that he later came to call "joy," a spiritual state more attuned to the pagan worldview. Do not, therefore, mistake the sketches in this chapter (which are useful and justifiable generalizations) for absolute statements of who your neighbor is or what he believes. If you want to know that, you must (and should) go and ask him yourself.

These initial sketches of the pagan and the post-Christian, though they do reveal a good deal of Lewis's insight into human nature, fail to capture his real giftedness as an evangelist. For that, we must look at his fiction as well. Here the mere categories come to life. The pagan and the post-Christian take on flesh and bone and dwell in our imaginations. To know of post-Christian skepticism and denial in the abstract is one thing; but to experience the consequences of it as the Dwarves reject New Narnia in *The Last Battle* or to struggle through it with Mark and Jane Studdock in *That Hideous Strength* is to rise to another level of understanding altogether. The third section of the chapter is therefore dedicated to an exploration of the pagan and the post-Christian in *Till We Have Faces*, a novel in which Lewis fleshes out, more beautifully than in any of his other fiction, these two worldviews as we might meet them in human form.

The Post-Christian: Under the "Dark Wing" of This Present Age

Lewis was not entirely given over to pessimism concerning modern times, but he did believe that the world in which he lived was significantly in the grip of a post-Christian apostasy. As Ransom tells Merlin in *That Hideous Strength*, "The shadow of one dark wing is over all Tellus [Earth]."[5] While the present intellectual climate is somewhat different from the modernism against which Lewis struggled, we of the West must still consider ourselves to be living in an apostate society inhabited predominantly by post-Christians. The post-Christian worldview is likely present somewhere in the man who helps us do our taxes, who lifts the hood of our car to check the spark plugs, who writes articles for our local newspaper. We probably meet it daily in the woman who teaches history to our children, who sits on our city council, who rides in our car pool. Because of his own conversion experience, Lewis possessed a unique depth of insight into the mind of the post-Christian that helped him reach out effectively to this group of people. C. N. Manlove writes, "Because he himself had been an atheist [a position very much dependent upon the post-Christian worldview], he believed he understood the forces arrayed against his late-won faith and felt particularly equipped to take them on."[6]

It is impossible to disentangle Lewis's conception of the post-Christian from his understanding of modern history. So the first question we ought to address is, "Where did this post-Christian come from?" Lewis's best explanation is found in *"De Descriptione Temporum."* In this, his first address as the head of Cambridge's new Chair in Medieval and Renaissance Literature, he describes the "unchristening" of Europe—a cultural change he believed to have taken place "somewhere between us and the Waverley novels."[7] Lewis writes, ". . . roughly speaking we may say that whereas all history was for our ancestors divided into two periods, the pre-Christian and the Christian, and two only, for us it falls into three—the pre-Christian, the Christian and what may reasonably be called the Post-Christian."[8] He did not mean the "post-Christian" label to be a judgment on the "amount of Christian (that is, of penitent and regenerate) life"[9] in our age; but the cultural change did radically alter the relationship between Christianity and the western world. With this historical transformation, one set of cultural obstacles to the spread of Christianity was exchanged for another—and so was born the post-Christian. "A century ago," writes Lewis, "our task was to edify those who had been brought up in the Faith: our present task is chiefly to convert and instruct infidels."[10]

Various insights into the mind of the post-Christian are strewn throughout Lewis's nonfiction (a good sampling of which can be found in "Christian Apologetics"), but of first importance is the root of his separation from the Gospel. Unlike the pagan, it is not ignorance or the worship of false gods. The foundation of the post-Christian's worldview is his rejection of holiness. Here we run into a term that (like many theological words) seems to have lost its true meaning in our culture. True holiness has even been removed from our language. The average person's understanding of this term has something to do with proper behavior or moral goodness, but the real meaning of "holy" is "set apart." This is what the post-Christian rejects. It is unacceptable to him that there exists anything (let alone a personal being) that is other than, independent from, and superior to the order of which he himself is a part.

Lewis's best treatment of this negative philosophy is found in his apologetic work *Miracles* as a discussion of the difference between naturalism (which rejects holiness) and supernaturalism (which makes room for the Holy). He opens the book by saying, "In all my life I have met only one person who claims to have seen a ghost. And the interesting thing about the story is that that person disbelieved in the immortal soul before she saw the ghost and still disbelieves after seeing it. She says what she saw must have been an illusion or a trick of the nerves."[11] Here we see how deeply the post-Christian bias against holiness runs. Lewis goes on to explain the woman's perspective: "If anything extraordinary seems to have happened, we can always say that we have been victims of an illusion. If we hold a philosophy which excludes the supernatural, this is what we shall always say. What we learn from experience depends on the kind of philosophy we bring to the experience."[12] The philosophy that the naturalist brings to his experience is a conviction that ". . . the ultimate Fact, the thing which you can't go behind, is a vast process in space and time which is going on of its own accord."[13] The battle with the post-Christian is not over facts or experiences, but over a presupposition for or against holiness.

Of course, not every post-Christian will espouse such an extreme philosophic materialism. The real tragedy of post-Christianity is not the explicit belief in naturalism, but the implicit practice of it. Even the modern who does not claim to embrace the philosophy often operates as if he did. For every phenomenon he has a "perfectly natural" explanation; and science has placed its stamp of approval on an inexhaustible source of explanations from which he might draw. For example, Lewis writes:

> If the end of the world appeared in all the literal trappings of the Apocalypse, if the modern materialist saw with his own eyes the heavens rolled up and the great white throne appearing, if he had the sensation of being himself hurled into the Lake of Fire, he would continue forever, in that lake itself, to regard his expe-

rience as an illusion and find the explanation of it in psycho-analysis, or cerebral pathology.[14]

The post-Christian's rejection of holiness in the form of naturalism (whether conscious or not) secures him against any potential invasion of the divine. He is closed off to transcendence. In fact, there is nothing to transcend—no Platonic gap between the real and ideal, no ontological gap between God and man, no fundamental difference between himself and the dust to which he will return.

The practical implications of this are overwhelming. Right, Wrong, Beauty, Truth, Goodness—none of these concepts are available to the post-Christian worldview as transcendent ideals. If the post-Christian holds onto these concepts at all, he does so admitting that they are nothing but the pragmatic constructions of himself or his community. But the most shattering implication of all is the post-Christian's rejection of the full reality of Christ. He may believe that a man named Jesus lived, died, and left a good example for us to follow. He will not be "taken in" by any of the shocking dimensions of who Christ is and what He has accomplished. His attitude toward Christ is the same as Lewis's own pre-conversion view, expressed here in a letter to Arthur Greeves: "My puzzle was the whole doctrine of Redemption: in what sense the life and death of Christ 'saved' or 'opened salvation to' the world. . . . What I couldn't see was how the life and death of Someone Else (whoever he was) 2000 years ago could help us here and now—except in so far as his example helped us."[15] The post-Christian cannot believe in the fundamentals of Christianity because he will not believe in holiness. Lewis therefore advises, "You must frankly argue for supernaturalism from the very outset."[16]

But for all these negative characteristics of the post-Christian, we can take encouragement from one honest truth about him: he is almost never consistent. "My idea," Lewis writes, "is that sometimes they do forget. That is their glory. Holding a philosophy which excludes humanity, they yet remain human."[17] He may be moved by the beauty of an autumn landscape bathed in the light of an evening sun. He may shed tears of joy at birth and of sorrow at death. He may recoil from the manifestations of evil in the world. In fact, there may be many truths that nature (in its true, created sense) has whispered to him, truths that he is tempted very strongly to believe and that would lead in the direction of God if he were to give in to them. Paul tells us in the first chapter of Romans, "For since the creation of the world God's invisible qualities—his eternal power and divine nature—have been clearly seen, being understood from what has been made, so that men are without excuse" (Romans 1:20). The post-Christian—whether or not he has yet come to acknowledge it—does participate with us in a world that, as the poet writes, "is charged with the grandeur of God."[18]

THE PAGAN: POSSESSOR OF A DARK HOLINESS

Lewis writes of paganism, "[It] is not likely to be a live issue for most of my readers."[19] This is probably still true today, though things are changing. Small but genuine revivals in pagan practice and belief are taking place around the world. The rising emphasis on multicultural diversity has led to renewed interest in spiritual roots that predate Christian influence. And the "shrinking of the world" inevitably brings those of us in the West into contact more frequently with people outside our European tradition. Even if we never meet a "genuine Pagan," it is more likely today than it has been for centuries that elements of the pagan worldview will be present in the mind of the modern. What Lewis used in his day chiefly as a counterpoint to the post-Christian worldview—something to set it up against—is becoming a serious contender again even in the West. This being the case, even those of us who are not headed to an overseas mission field ought to be prepared for an encounter with the pagan.

Part of the preparation for such an encounter is coming to understand how much we as Christians really do have in common with the pagan. Lewis writes, ". . . a Pagan, as history shows, is a man imminently convertible to Christianity. He is essentially the pre-Christian or sub-Christian, religious man."[20] There is something about the pagan's worldview that inherently prepares him for the Gospel, and knowing what that is can be a starting point for evangelism.

Lewis's Understanding of Diversity Outside the Faith

Compared to the post-Christian apostasy, it is easy to see why Lewis considered paganism a far more desirable state for the cause of evangelism. The pagan, to begin with, is not separated from transcendent holiness. On the contrary, it is an integral part of his daily life. The gods that he worships exercise direct and ongoing control in the natural world. Earthquakes, volcanoes, good crops, bad crops, fat and lean cattle may all be signs of the good or ill favor of the gods. The pagan's ritual and pious acts are not means of controlling these gods, but of attempting to make peace with their holiness in the hope that any transcendent intervention will come in a positive form. Lewis writes of the ancient pagan that he approached his gods "as the accused person approaches his judge."[21] If the pagan's greatest wish is sometimes simply to be left alone, it is not because he does not believe in the power of the gods, but because he can never be sure of their beneficence. The idea of other and greater beings, of a realm "beyond nature," is never in doubt with the pagan, even if this realm and these beings do not take exactly the same form as in Christianity.

In addition to this basic congruence between the pagan and Christian cosmologies, the content of our religions is often similar as well. The cross-cultural nature of many myths (that of the Dying God, for example) is often used as evidence against the truth claims of Christianity. Some argue that if the same basic motifs found in Christianity appear in the sacred narratives of many other cultures (most of which predate Christianity), then the myth of Christ's incarnation, death, and resurrection can be no more valid than, say, the myths of Balder or Osiris. In answer to such claims, Lewis writes, "We must not be nervous about 'parallels' and 'Pagan Christs': they ought to be there—it would be a stumbling block if they weren't."[22] And:

> The truth is that the resemblances tell us nothing either for or against the truth of Christian Theology. If you start from the assumption that the Theology is false, the resemblances are quite consistent with that assumption. . . . But if you start with the assumption that the Theology is true, the resemblances fit equally well. Theology, while saying that special illumination

has been vouchsafed to Christians and (earlier) to Jews, also says that there is some divine illumination vouchsafed to all men.[23]

Lewis did not deny the mythic in Christianity, or even refuse to call the story of Christ a *myth*. Rather, he argued for an *additional* level of reality unique to the Christian Myth that gives it a qualitative superiority. "Now the story of Christ is simply a true myth: a myth working on us in the same way as the others, but with this tremendous difference that it *really happened*."[24] Elsewhere he writes, "It is the difference between a real event on the one hand and dim dreams or premonitions of that same event on the other."[25] It is precisely the union of the historical and the mythic that elevates Christianity above other world religions. "For this is the marriage of Heaven and Earth: Perfect Myth and Perfect Fact: claiming not only our love and obedience, but also our wonder and delight."[26]

From *within* Christianity these other mythologies then become not competitors of the Gospel, but precursors to it. They are *praeparatio evangelica*[27] in their own right, remembrances of "the first, faint whisper of the wind from beyond the world."[28] Lewis sums up this view of pagan mythology in a footnote to *Miracles*:

> My present view, which is tentative and liable to any amount of correction[29]—would be that just as, on the factual side, a long preparation culminates in God's becoming incarnate as Man, so, on the documentary side, the Truth first appears in mythical form and then by a long process of condensing or focusing finally becomes incarnate as history. This involves the belief that Myth in general is . . . at its best, a real though unfocused gleam of divine Truth falling on human imagination.[30]

We can see that what Lewis writes in "*De Descriptione Temporum*" is certainly true. "Christians and Pagans had much more in common with each other than either has with a post-Christian. The gap between those who worship different gods is not so wide as that between those who worship and those who do not."[31] But for all the *positive* characteristics of the pagan presented in this sketch, for all the points of congruence between the pagan and Christian worldviews, a gap does remain. The holiness of the pagan is a *dark holiness*—a shadow but not the substance of Truth. What goes on in the darkness of paganism, though in strict keeping with holiness, is often terrible in every sense of the word.

On the human level, the Gospel was so effectively preached to the pagan because it succeeded in convincing him of one historical fact: God (in whose holiness he was culturally conditioned to believe) so loved the world (a new concept to the pagan, at least in its scope) that He sent His Son (who was in very nature God) to settle once and for all the matter of substitutionary death (Hebrews 9:11-12). As Lewis puts it, "Something really new did happen at Bethlehem: not an interpretation, but an *event.*"[32] The story of Christ's birth, death, and resurrection is the fact missing from paganism. Though functioning with a similar conception of the universe, the pagan needs to be made aware of the universe's central event and have the reality and efficacy of that event impressed upon him. The pagan may be less outside of Christianity than the post-Christian, but he is no less in need of Christ.

Till We Have Faces: THE PAGAN AND THE POST-CHRISTIAN INCARNATE

Till We Have Faces could be called Lewis's fictional *summa*. When the book was first published, Chad Walsh had this to say about it: "It is rare that dust jackets make critical judgments which future critics affirm, but there is a sober chance that C. S. Lewis's *Till We Have Faces* is indeed 'the most significant and triumphant work he has yet produced.'"[33] Lewis himself called it his "best book,"[34] and it is not hard to see why. This retelling of the classic Cupid and Psyche myth is a profoundly rich and intricate novel of the human condition. Priests and sacrifice, veils and swords, blood and poetry, friendship and romance— *Till We Have Faces* has all of these and much more. The dust of which we are all made wafts up from its pages, and in this context Lewis fleshes out many of the central concepts of his nonfiction. (Orual's relationships in the novel, for example, all resound with the masterful insights of *The Four Loves*.[35]) And it is in *Till We Have Faces* that Lewis develops most intricately the differences (and similarities) between the pagan and the post-Christian by giving them life as characters.

The Fox: A Post-Christian in the King of Glome's Court

The clearest post-Christian representative in *Till We Have Faces* (and probably the most fully developed character with this worldview in all of Lewis's fiction) is the Fox. A Greek slave serving in the King of Glome's court, he is a thoroughgoing philosophical naturalist. His guiding principle is that all things are "according to nature." Arguing against the King's folly in preparing a sacred bed in which to conceive a male heir, he says to Orual, "These things come about by natural causes."[36] When Orual is upset about the jealousy of the gods and the danger Psyche has put herself in by allowing the common people to worship her, the Fox says, "Daughter, it doesn't matter a straw. . . . Those gods—the sort of gods you are always thinking about—are all folly and lies of poets. We have discussed this a hundred times."[37] When the rains return to Glome after Psyche has been left on the Grey Mountain as a sacrifice, he calls it "cursed chance" and explains, ". . . all these things had no more to do with that murder than anything else. They and it are all part of the same web, which is called Nature, or the Whole."[38] Even when Psyche is found on the Mountain alive, well-fed, and protected, he believes that the god under whose protection she claims to be living (and claims to have married) must be a criminal deceiving her for evil purposes.[39] Like Lewis's modern materialist sitting in the Lake of Fire and talking psychoanalysis, the Fox has decided against transcendent holiness and brings that presupposition with him into all his experiences and encounters.

By employing rhetorical techniques and well-reasoned arguments, the Fox eventually manages to turn Glome upside down. Taking Arnom, the *second* Priest of Ungit, under his wing, he even succeeds in uprooting the country's religion—the worship of the goddess Ungit. When Orual asks Arnom late in the novel, "Who is

Ungit?" he replies, "I think, Queen, . . . she signifies the earth, which is the womb and mother of all living things." And of the god of the Grey Mountain, Ungit's son, he says, "He is the air and the sky, for we see the clouds coming up from the earth in mists and exhalations." Orual tell us that this "was the new way of talking about the gods which Arnom, and others, had learned from the Fox."[40] These explanations are certainly telling of the Greek (and, in this context, post-Christian) influence.

Of our own faith, Lewis writes, "A naturalistic Christianity leaves out all that is distinctively Christian."[41] So too with the worship of Ungit. By the end of the novel, Arnom has completed the apostasy and is referring to himself as a priest not of Ungit, but of Aphrodite.[42]

However, the Fox is distinctively *not* the villain of *Till We Have Faces.* Though his influence in Glome is certainly evil in that it moves toward destroying the native awareness of holiness, he is no Miltonic Satan, deliberately out to lead a revolt against the gods. "To be greatly and effectively wicked," writes Lewis, "a man needs some virtue."[43] In accord with this, the Fox's "anti-holiness" philosophy takes hold in Glome only because of his *many* great virtues. Throughout the novel he remains generous, kind, patient, loyal, cultivated, sentimental, humble, poetic, a lover of life and beauty, and a surrogate father to our narrator. Orual writes of him: "I loved the Fox, as my father called him, better than anyone I had yet known."[44]

Along with all these personal qualities, the Fox brings the immeasurably valuable gift of education to Glome. His knowledge of medicine, agriculture, architecture, poetry, the arts, and philosophy all enhance the world of Glome. Psyche acknowledges, "It'd be as dark as a dungeon within me but for his teaching."[45] And even later when she has come to a knowledge of the truth about the gods, she tells Orual that in that knowledge "there was a lot of the Fox's philosophy . . . things he says about the gods or 'the divine nature.'"[46]

The Fox's role as a very "enlightening" influence and an extremely endearing figure cannot be denied; and it is vital in light of Lewis's other fictional representations of post-Christians, which tend to be very cold and steely (the N.I.C.E. group in *That Hideous Strength,*

Ginger the Cat in *The Last Battle*, and Weston in *Out of the Silent Planet* and *Perelandra*, to name a few of the most prominent). In *Till We Have Faces* Lewis brings home the fact that the post-Christian deception can be caught and spread by "good" people. Lewis himself experienced this through his tutor Kirkpatrick (a likely origin of the Fox himself). Though the man was an avowed atheist, Lewis acknowledges in *Surprised by Joy*: "My debt to him is very great, my reverence to this day undiminished."[47] A presupposition against holiness, as destructive as it is, may often exist side by side with a keen mind, great knowledge, an intriguing personality, and even a strong moral fabric— a reality the evangelist must be prepared to deal with.

The First Priest of Ungit: A Dark Servant of a Dark Goddess

The Fox's nemesis and counterpoint is the first Priest of Ungit—the representative of paganism in *Till We Have Faces*. In constructing his character, Lewis was faced with the difficult task of getting beyond twentieth-century misconceptions of the pagan. People in our age almost always make one of two errors when conceptualizing what the pagan must be like (or *must have been like*, to most). They either romanticize him as "the noble savage" or demean him as subhuman— a crouched and sniveling old man who digs grubs for supper and cowers in the shadows of deep forests. In his brief portrayal of the priest, Lewis manages to avoid both pitfalls.

He avoids the error of romanticizing the pagan by being honest with the Priest's less than pleasant side. There is no denying the dark and frightening shadow he casts in the novel. Orual writes of her childhood impression of him:

> I had a fear of the Priest that was quite different from my fear of my father. I think what frightened me (in those early days) was the holiness of the smell that hung about him—a temple-smell of blood (mostly pigeons' blood, but he had sacrificed men, too) and burnt fat and singed hair and wine and stale incense. It is the Ungit smell. Perhaps I was afraid of his clothes

too; all the skins they were made of, and the dried bladders, and the great mask shaped like a bird's head which hung on his chest. It looked as if there were a bird growing out of his body.[48]

So long as *this* Priest is overseeing the worship of Ungit, the "reek of holiness"[49] lingers in every shadowy corner of Glome. Human sacrifice, fear, ignorance, and temple prostitutes with "meaningless eyes looking always straight ahead"[50] are as much a part of paganism in its purest form as is the acceptance of holiness.

What philosophy or dogma the Priest of Ungit does possess is dark as well, in a different sense. It is the product of an intellectual framework that deliberately shies away from explanation. Lewis calls it "the surrender to the inextricable,"[51] and the Priest himself expresses it in these words:

> We are hearing much Greek wisdom this morning, King. . . . It is very subtle. But it brings no rain and grows no corn; sacrifice does both. . . . Much less does it give them understanding of holy things. They demand to see things clearly, as if the gods were no more than letters written in a book. I, King, have dealt with the gods for three generations of men, and I know that they dazzle our eyes and flow in and out of one another like eddies on a river, and nothing that is said clearly can be said truly about them. Holy places are dark places. It is life and strength, not knowledge and words, that we get in them. Holy wisdom is not clear and thin like water, but thick and dark like blood.[52]

Clarity is the enemy of the pagan. All things must be hidden, mysterious, and shrouded in darkness.

On the other hand, Lewis avoids the error of dehumanizing the pagan equally well by making the Priest of Ungit one of the most truly noble characters in *Till We Have Faces*. After watching his encounter with the Fox and the King, Orual comments, "The Fox had taught me to think—at any rate to speak—of the Priest as of a mere schemer and a politic man who put into the mouth of Ungit whatever might most increase his own power and lands or most harm his enemies. I saw it was not so."[53]

When the Priest comes to the palace in the dramatic fifth chapter of Book I, it is not (as the Fox and the King had suspected) with any intentions of treason in mind. He comes simply because he believes that Ungit is real and holy, that she has been offended by sacrifices offered to Psyche, and that the Great Offering, a human sacrifice, must be made at any cost. "I have served Ungit these fifty—no, sixty-three years—" he tells the King, "and I have learned one thing for certain. Her anger never comes upon us without cause, and it never ceases without expiation."[54]

The Priest believes strongly in the goddess whom he serves and in the service he does for her. When the King (fearing for his own life) holds a dagger to the Priest's ribs, the Priest calmly replies:

> Drive it in, King, swift or slow, if it pleases you. It will make no difference. Be sure the Great Offering will be made whether I am dead or living. I am here in the strength of Ungit. While I have breath I am Ungit's voice. Perhaps longer. A priest does not wholly die. I may visit your palace more often, both by day and by night, if you kill me. The others will not see me. I think you will.[55]

Remembering that moment, Orual writes, "I have never (to speak of things merely mortal) seen anything more wonderful than the Priest's stillness."[56] This is the power of holiness. His belief and devotion are marks of a man who truly knows there is more to life than himself or his race, a man who has the strength to act in accord with a greater cause. This is the high virtue of the pagan, the fearlessness imparted by a sure knowledge of the holy.

In the Fox and the Priest of Ungit we are given two men with two very different worldviews, and the differences are obvious. But Lewis also allows us to experience their common humanity, and that is the real genius of Till We Have Faces. It treats the generalities of the pagan and the post-Christian and yet gets beyond stereotypes. And how

Lewis's Understanding of Diversity Outside the Faith

much more there is to tell of Orual, Psyche, Bardia, Arnom, Ansit, and all the other characters "somewhere in between" the poles of the Priest and the Fox. Thankfully, *Till We Have Faces* is a novel that bears continual rereading—no, almost demands it. One of my hopes for this chapter is that it would be an invitation on behalf of the novel, an invitation to enter Glome and live among its characters again and again— not merely for enjoyment (though it is that) but to learn about different struggles on the road to the truth, different moments of crisis people experience, different blind spots to which we are all vulnerable. There is much that Lewis has yet to teach us through *Till We Have Faces*, not only about the pagan and the post-Christian, but about those people we encounter every day, non-Christians of many kinds desperately in need of Christ.

CONCLUSION

Consider the evangelist as an artist of encounters with God. Any artist must be intimately familiar with his medium. The poet must know his words, the watercolorist his paints and brushes. The sculptor must know how to be just forceful enough with his hammer and chisel for the stone to yield, but not so forceful as to crack it. The medium of the evangelist is the human person. Evangelism is an inherently *human* endeavor. Only to the degree that any evangelist understands the person before him, will he be able to do all he can to make the Gospel intelligible to that person.[57] Our Lord Himself understood this. His evangelistic approach with the woman at the well, an infant in spiritual matters (John 4:1-26), was very different from His approach with Nicodemus, a trained scribe and expert in the Law (John 3:1-21). The apostle Paul, the greatest human evangelist this world has ever known, writes, "I have become all things to all men so that by all possible means I might save some" (1 Corinthians 9:22).

Lewis took this same attitude. He did not want to adopt a method of delivering the truth that would be a hindrance to the Gospel rather than a help to it; therefore, he sought earnestly to know his medium and discovered that in England he was dealing with a different "sort" of non-Christian than those who had been effectively reached in the past with the plain facts of the Gospel (the pagan) or with a free-standing emotional appeal (the non-Christian in a "christened" Europe). Part of the reason Lewis was so effective for the cause of evangelism (and continues to be through his writings) was his awareness of the particular human medium he encountered. As Lewis's successors, we must share this awareness if we really wish to do all we can to reach *our* neighbors, *our* friends, and *our* fellow mortals with the good news of a holy, just, and loving God.

Bibliography

Dorsett, Lyle W., and Marjorie Lamp Mead, eds. *C. S. Lewis: Letters to Children*. New York: Simon & Schuster, 1985.

Dorsett, Lyle W., ed. *The Essential C. S. Lewis*. New York: Collier/Macmillan, 1988.

Hooper, Walter, ed. *They Stand Together: The Letters of C. S. Lewis to Arthur Greeves (1914-1963)*. New York: Collier/Macmillan, 1986.

Hopkins, Gerard Manley. "God's Grandeur." In *Gerard Manley Hopkins*, ed. Catherine Phillips. New York: Oxford University Press, 1986.

Lewis, C. S. "Christian Apologetics." In *God in the Dock*. Ed. Walter Hooper. Grand Rapids, MI: Eerdmans, 1970, 89-103.

_____. "The Decline of Religion." In *God in the Dock*. Ed. Walter Hooper. Grand Rapids, MI: Eerdmans, 1970, 218-223.

_____. "*De Descriptione Temporum*." In *Selected Literary Essays*. Ed. Walter Hooper. Cambridge: Cambridge University Press, 1967, 1-14.

_____. *The Four Loves*. New York: Harcourt Brace Jovanovich, 1960.

_____. "God in the Dock." In *God in the Dock*. Ed. Walter Hooper. Grand Rapids, MI: Eerdmans, 1970, 240-44.

_____. *The Great Divorce*. New York: Macmillan, 1946.

_____. "Is Theism Important?" In *God in the Dock*. Ed. Walter Hooper. Grand Rapids, MI: Eerdmans, 1970, 172-76.

_____. "Is Theology Poetry?" In *The Weight of Glory and Other Addresses*. Revised and Expanded Edition. New York: Macmillan, 1980, 75-92.

_____. *The Last Battle*. New York: Collier/Macmillan, 1970.

_____. *Miracles*. New York: Macmillan, 1960.

_____. "Miracles." In *God in the Dock*. Ed. Walter Hooper. Grand Rapids, MI: Eerdmans, 1970, 25-37.

Lewis's Understanding of Diversity Outside the Faith

_____. "Myth Became Fact." In *God in the Dock*. Ed. Walter Hooper. Grand Rapids, MI: Eerdmans, 1970, 63-67.

_____. *Out of the Silent Planet*. New York: Macmillan, 1965.

_____. *Perelandra*. New York: Macmillan, 1965.

_____. *The Pilgrim's Regress*. Grand Rapids, MI: Eerdmans, 1958.

_____. *The Screwtape Letters*. New York: Macmillan, 1982.

_____. *Surprised by Joy: The Shape of My Early Life*. New York: Harcourt Brace Jovanovich, 1955.

_____. *That Hideous Strength*. New York, Macmillan, 1965.

_____. *Till We Have Faces*. Harcourt Brace Jovanovich, 1980.

Manlove, C. N. *The Chronicles of Narnia*. New York: Twayne Publishers, 1993.

Moynihan, Martin, ed. and trans. *Letters: C. S. Lewis/Don Giovanni Calabria*. Ann Arbor, MI: Servant Books, 1988.

Walsh, Chad. Review of *Till We Have Faces* by C. S. Lewis. *New York Herald Times Book Review*, January 20, 1957, 3.

NOTES

1. Lewis, *The Great Divorce*, 72.
2. For the sake of simplicity I will use these two terms taken from "*De Descriptione Temporum*" throughout the essay, though Lewis himself used a variety of terms throughout his writings to refer to the same basic worldviews.
3. Lewis, "Is Theism Important?," 172.
4. Moynihan, *Letters: C. S. Lewis/Don Giovanni Calabria*, 89.
5. Lewis, *That Hideous Strength*, 293.
6. Manlove, *The Chronicles of Narnia*, 5.
7. Lewis, "*De Descriptione Temporum*," 7. Lewis is here referring to a series of novels written by Sir Walter Scott in the first half of the nineteenth century.
8. Ibid., 5.
9. Ibid.
10. Lewis, "Christian Apologetics," 94.
11. Lewis, *Miracles*, 3.
12. Ibid.
13. Ibid., 6.
14. Lewis, "Miracles," 25.

15. Hooper, *They Stand Together*, 427.

16. Lewis, "Christian Apologetics," 99.

17. Lewis, *Miracles*, 37.

18. Hopkins, "God's Grandeur," 128.

19. Lewis, *Miracles*, 8.

20. Lewis, "Is Theism Important?," 172.

21. Lewis, "God in the Dock," 244.

22. Lewis, "Myth Became Fact," 67.

23. Lewis, "Is Theology Poetry?," 83.

24. Hooper, *They Stand Together*, 427.

25. Lewis, "Is Theology Poetry?," 83-84.

26. Lewis, "Myth Became Fact," 67.

27. *Praeparatio evangelica* is the term Lewis uses to describe his efforts at communicating the Gospel as pre-evangelism. See Dorsett, *The Essential C. S. Lewis*, 11. The theme is pursued at greater length by Joel Heck in this volume.

28. Hooper, *They Stand Together*, 430.

29. Lewis's view of myth seems to have undergone no significant change after the publication of *Miracles*.

30. Lewis, *Miracles*, 133-34.

31. Lewis, "*De Descriptione Temporum*," 5.

32. Hooper, *They Stand Together*, 505.

33. Walsh, review of *Till We Have Faces*, 3.

34. Dorsett and Mead, *Letters to Children*, 88.

35. Compare, for instance, the Orual, Bardia, Ansit "love triangle" with the dynamic of friendship between men and women as opposed to the dynamic of romantic love in *The Four Loves*. Or note the ways in which Orual's genuine love for Psyche degenerates into destructive behavior. This is one of the central insights of *The Four Loves*. The relationship between these two works is vital to the life of the novel, but unfortunately too complicated to bring into this chapter with the full treatment it would deserve.

36. Lewis, *Till We Have Faces*, 10.

37. Ibid., 28.

38. Ibid., 85.

39. Ibid., 143-44.

40. Ibid., 270-71.

41. Lewis, *Miracles*, 68.

Lewis's Understanding of Diversity Outside the Faith

42. Lewis, *Till We Have Faces*, 308.

43. Lewis, *The Screwtape Letters*, 135-36.

44. Lewis, *Till We Have Faces*, 7.

45. Ibid., 70.

46. Ibid., 109.

47. Lewis, *Surprised by Joy*, 148.

48. Lewis, *Till We Have Faces*, 11.

49. Ibid., 62.

50. Ibid., 43.

51. Lewis, "Is Theology Poetry?," 76.

52. Lewis, *Till We Have Faces*, 50.

53. Ibid., 54.

54. Ibid., 45.

55. Ibid., 54.

56. Ibid., 53.

57. Of course, it is certainly true, as Lewis writes, that "Conversion requires an alteration of the will . . . which in the last resort, does not occur without the intervention of the supernatural" (Lewis, "The Decline of Religion," 221). It would be far beyond the scope of this chapter to try to work out exactly how God's role and the role of the individual (either the evangelist or the convert) coincide in the process of salvation. That this chapter keeps itself to the human side of evangelism, the *modus operandi* of God's sovereignty, should not, though, be taken as a denial of His ultimate role.

PART THREE

The Technique:
Making Christianity Plausible

9

EXORCISING THE *Zeitgeist*:
Lewis as Evangelist to the Modernists

GEORGE MUSACCHIO

In February 1941 the British Broadcasting Corporation invited C. S. Lewis to give the series of radio talks that would become the first part of *Mere Christianity*. In his reply to the Reverend J. W. Welch, director of the BBC's Religious Broadcasting Department, Lewis wrote:

> I think what I mainly want to talk about is the Law of Nature, or objective right and wrong. It seems to me that the N[ew] T[estament], by preaching repentance and forgiveness, always *assumes* an audience who already believe in the law of Nature and know they have disobeyed it. In modern England we cannot at present assume this, and therefore most apologetic begins a stage too far on. The first step is to create, or recover, the sense of guilt.[1]

Why did Lewis believe "modern England" needed *praeparatio evangelica*, as he calls his radio scripts elsewhere?[2] What was his audience like? What insulated them from natural moral law ("the Law of Nature") and a sense of guilt about having broken that law? Whatever it was, the insulation was keeping out the *evangelium*, the Good News.

A key term for this insulation appears in the first part of *Mere Christianity*, where Lewis contrasts "the religious view" of "the universe we live in" to "the materialist view."[3] To the materialist, matter is the only reality; everything in the world, including our thoughts, choices, and feelings, can be explained only in terms of material reality. Lewis believed his neighbors were infected with materialism, this disease that denies the reality of all metaphysical, supernatural concepts. *Mere Christianity* began as his attempt to clear up their materialist myopia.[4]

This chapter is an attempt to reconstruct the "spirit of the age" in Lewis's England around 1941, the materialist *Zeitgeist* that Lewis considered a stumbling block to his audience's acceptance of the Gospel of Jesus Christ. My focus is not so much on Lewis as on the world of ideas in which he lived. I want to explain why Lewis attempted the type of preparation for the Gospel that Joel Heck, in the next chapter, examines so ably.

We will examine five topics: 1) Enlightenment reason as it developed in contrast to the medieval concept of reasonable belief; 2) the scientific method, using empirical reason, as it was both used and abused in the course of the nineteenth century; 3) "scientism" as a worldview insulating the early twentieth century from anything supernatural; 4) logical positivism as the materialistic blight on language analysis in Lewis's Oxford; and, finally, 5) life-force philosophy as an unacceptable alternative to atheistic materialism. Throughout the five sections we shall see how our central term, *materialism*, links with scientism, logical positivism, and moral relativism, all in contrast to Lewis's Christian worldview, which was heavily dependent on the medieval worldview he expounded in *The Discarded Image* and other fruits of his professional career in medieval and Renaissance English literature.

FROM REASONABLE FAITH TO FAITH IN REASON:
THE MIDDLE AGES TO THE ENLIGHTENMENT

C. S. Lewis's own worldview was dependent on the medieval worldview that he encountered in his professional specialty—early English language and literature. Thus to understand his concept of England in 1941 we must first retreat to the Western world of the Middle Ages, so different from our own century in its attitude toward supernatural reality.[5]

Of course, it is tricky to generalize about historical eras and what "people" thought then. Not only do we know relatively little about

those persons, but like individuals of our own day, they varied greatly
in their knowledge, perspectives, and conclusions. Nevertheless, we
cannot say much about the past or present without generalizing. We
must keep in mind the limitations of our pronouncements even as we
pursue the truth that at best we shall see in a glass darkly. As I talk of
"the medieval mind" and "the modern mind," I am aware of the limitations but am convinced of the value of such terms.

The period known as the Middle Ages has been called the age of
faith or the age of belief. We can see why in the story of Caedmon,
recorded by an English priest in the eighth century. Caedmon was a shy
young man unlearned in poetry or music. If after a meal the diners
began in turn to entertain with a song, he would leave before the harp
reached him. On one such night he had retreated to the stable to care
for the animals. There he fell asleep and dreamed that an angel commanded him to sing, which he did. Upon awaking, he remembered his
lyrics, in praise of God as Creator, and henceforth he was able to com-
pose excellent verses. The Venerable Bede records this event as factual
history, with no hint of incredulity.[6] Nor would ninety-nine of a hundred medieval readers have doubted that Caedmon had suddenly
become a leading lyricist as the result of that dream-vision.

Similarly, if they heard that a virgin could catch a unicorn by sitting alone in the woods, they believed it (he would come and lie in her
lap).[7] If they read something in a book—those who could read—they
took it as fact; an author was by definition an authority.[8] It was an age
of belief.

Between the medieval and modern concept of reality there is a great
gulf fixed. Our worldview is not the medieval worldview (the term
translates German *Weltanschauung*, our way of looking at the universe
and our philosophy of life that results therefrom). Sometime between
Bede in the eighth century and Bertrand Russell in the twentieth, there
occurred a major change in the whole approach to what is real.

Jacob Burckhardt, the great nineteenth-century historian of the
Renaissance, would argue that the change came in the fifteenth cen-
tury, with the Italian rebirth of learning. Most modern scholars would,
I think, argue for the seventeenth century and the rise of modern sci-

Lewis as Evangelist to the Modernists

ence. And C. S. Lewis, while agreeing that the seventeenth-century rise of science caused the change, argued that the new *Weltanschauung* did not dominate western culture until after the era of Jane Austen and Sir Walter Scott in the early nineteenth century.[9]

But whatever the date at which the scales tipped the opposite way, all who study the subject must agree that the change has occurred. Lewis perceived this change as a barrier to Christian evangelism. In his expository apologetics and in much of his fiction, he attempted to show non-Christians their materialistic biases, biases that keep them from believing in a spiritual reality that is neither provable nor disproved by the scientific method.

Being brief, the following account of that complex historical shift in worldview is necessarily simplified, but it is not, I trust, distorted. Basically, the changeover involves epistemology—the theory of knowledge: its methods, its validity, its limits. Epistemology tries to answer such questions as "How can we know?" "How can we validate our knowledge?" and "What can we know?"

The epistemology of the Middle Ages was what we might call rational faith; medieval philosophers had reasons for the faith that was in them. They developed, and in general sustained, a complex system of rational faith built upon what Herschel Baker calls "the axiom of knowledge." This axiom—by definition a self-evident truth—comprised three links: 1) a "rational God created and sustains the universe for His own benevolent purposes"; 2) we can know this God through discursive reason (i.e., carefully argued, step-by-step reasoning), with divine revelation confirming that rational knowledge; 3) the pursuit of this knowledge is our proper task, its attainment our true happiness.[10] Thomas Aquinas, the influential thirteenth-century theologian, held that the proper goal of humanity is "to understand God."[11] In other words, for the Middle Ages the proper study of humankind was God, and humankind was equipped by the Creator for that study.

But after the Renaissance and the Enlightenment had come to Europe, we find Alexander Pope summing up a very different attitude toward the limits of human knowledge. In his *Essay on Man* (1733-1734), Pope versifies a widely accepted philosophy of human nature when he insists that "all our Knowledge is, OURSELVES TO KNOW" and concludes: "Know then thyself, presume not God to scan; / The proper study of Mankind is Man."[12]

To Pope it is presumptuous for us to try to understand God; our ability to know is limited to our own realm of existence, and we should realize and work within our limitations. Somewhere between Aquinas and Pope the axiom of knowledge had broken down. For Aquinas, "intellectual" and "spiritual" were compatible and complementary. For Pope, human intelligence could not reach beyond the physical world. An opaque curtain had been drawn between the world of matter and the world of spirit, leaving the human mind on the side of matter.

What caused this breakdown in the belief that we can know non-material reality? What crippled the medieval epistemology? What sent Western civilization down the road to modern materialism, the belief that there is no "nonmaterial reality" to be known?

There were multiple causes, surely, but the major one was the empirical approach to knowledge that developed between Aquinas's *Summa contra Gentiles* and Pope's *Essay on Man*.

Earlier I mentioned the role of seventeenth-century science in developing our modern approach to reality. Nothing is more important to true science than the empirical method—the investigation of phenomena by sensory observation and experiment; that is, learning about material reality by seeing, hearing, touching, tasting, and smelling. When in 1605 Francis Bacon argued for such an approach to nature so we could learn to harness nature for our own use, making this a more healthful and comfortable world to live in, it was a giant leap for humanity.[13]

But when in 1651 Thomas Hobbes's *Leviathan* treated the human mind as matter in motion and nothing else, that was a step toward spiritual darkness. In his first chapter Hobbes argues that "there is no conception in a man's mind, which hath not at first, totally, or by parts, been begotten upon the organs of sense. The rest are derived from that original."[14] In other words, our knowledge derives completely from sensory data; if we did not see, hear, touch, taste, or smell "it," then it is an abstraction from something we did see, hear, touch, taste, or smell. Otherwise it would not be in our minds at all. Since in Hobbes's view nothing but matter can be sensed, this concept of the mind does not allow for knowledge of the nonmaterial. The realm of the spirit, including God Himself, is either some form of matter or remains unknowable. Hobbes was a materialist.

Many readers rejected Hobbes's materialism, but then in 1690 came John Locke's *Essay Concerning Human Understanding* with its thesis that our mind at birth is a *tabula rasa*, a blank slate on which anything that is written is written by sensory experience. According to Locke, we have no innate ideas, no instinctive concept of God or of worship or of eternity. Only the material world, things that can be seen, heard, touched, tasted, or smelled, can write on the tablet of the mind. General ideas are abstractions from these specific impressions. Throughout our life all our knowledge derives from the material world. Locke's book was highly influential, its empirical epistemology becoming commonplace in the world of Alexander Pope.

To summarize, empiricism—the gaining of knowledge by sensory data, an invaluable tool of the new science in the 1600s—became, according to the British empirical philosophers, the only possible means of knowledge. A modern dictionary still defines the philosophical meaning of empiricism as "the theory that sense experience is the only source of knowledge."[15]

In the religion of Pope's era, the result of this epistemology was a rationalistic, non-supernatural Deism that affected such eighteenth-century American political leaders as George Washington, Benjamin Franklin, and Thomas Jefferson. Significantly, it was soon after this period that Unitarianism spread rapidly in America, a religious movement that denied the deity of Christ, the radical adherents rejecting supernaturalism altogether.

When we see the Enlightenment (late seventeenth through the eighteenth centuries) called the Age of Reason, we should remember that the reason referred to is based on empiricism, not on the medieval axiom of knowledge. Since the Enlightenment, more and more people are epistemologically from Missouri—they want to be shown.[16]

By the time of the Enlightenment, then, Western thought had undergone a major change in epistemology. By the middle of the eighteenth century, influential people were relying on purely empirical knowledge for their philosophy, religion, and (rapidly advancing) science. It was the eve of the Industrial Revolution.

SCIENCE USED AND ABUSED: THE NINETEENTH CENTURY

The Industrial Revolution of late eighteenth- and early nineteenth-century England proved the utility of the scientific method and its empiricism.[17] The first country to become industrialized, England became a leading world power within the nineteenth century. As England went, so went the values of Western civilization, for good and ill, in the course of the nineteenth century. Briefly put, the scientific method of knowing became the most valued way to truth.

The Industrial Revolution made life materially better for millions of England's people. If it was exploited by the rich to the detriment of the poor, that was not the fault of Francis Bacon or even of James Watt. Nor was the fault inherent in the material goods themselves. It was heady stuff, this material progress. We hear its praises sung throughout mid-nineteenth-century English letters, from the popular Whig historian Thomas Babington Macaulay[18] to poets and preachers.

One example of the euphoria of those times appears in Alfred, Lord Tennyson, the great poet whom the public considered a prophet in his own day. Though not always enthusiastic about the Industrial Revolution, he sometimes reflects its positive side. His young protagonist in "Locksley Hall," for example, though by no means uncritical of his society, envisions technological advances that will make the world safe for the British Empire:

> *. . . I dipt into the future, far as human eye could see,*
> *Saw the Vision of the world, and all the wonder that would be;*
>
> *Saw the heavens fill with commerce, argosies of magic sails,*
> *Pilots of the purple twilight, dropping down with costly bales; . . .*
>
> *There the common sense of most shall hold a fretful realm in awe,*
> *And the kindly earth shall slumber, lapt in universal law.[19]*

Lewis as Evangelist to the Modernists

Rejecting the temptation to withdraw from the greedy society that has cost him his beloved, the young man says, "Forward, forward let us range, / Let the great world spin for ever down the ringing grooves of change," the image of railroad tracks carrying the world's commerce.[20] The image of the tracks speeding "change" on its way, enabling the workaday world to "spin" on forever, is a brilliant metonymy for the Industrial Revolution. That is, the railroad itself was a part of the Revolution and in turn sped other products of technology on their way far and wide.[21]

"Locksley Hall" was written in 1837-38. In 1851 came the Great Exhibition in London, a kind of world's fair to show off the products of the Industrial Revolution. On May 1, Queen Victoria and Prince Albert opened the exhibition in Hyde Park, in the magnificent Crystal Palace built for the occasion. "The building itself, as well as the exhibits, symbolized the triumphant feats of Victorian technology."[22]

Meanwhile, other scientific developments were increasing the conflict between science and religion. To quote George Ford, "Although many English scientists were themselves individuals of strong religious convictions, the impact of their scientific discoveries seemed consistently damaging to established faiths."[23]

For instance, Victorian geologists declared that the earth's history goes back millions of years, thus contradicting the traditional interpretation of Old Testament chronology. In 1851, the very year of the Great Exhibition, John Ruskin complained that geology was undermining his fragile Christian faith: "If only the Geologists would let me alone, I could do very well, but those dreadful hammers! I hear the clink of them at the end of every cadence of the Bible verses."[24]

As geology undercut humanity's stature in time, so astronomy reduced our stature in space "by extending a knowledge of stellar distances to dizzying expanses."[25] In *The Discarded Image* Lewis describes a man of the Middle Ages looking not at outer space but into a vast starry world designed by God. Therein the medieval man discerned divine order, comfort, and love.[26] But in 1855 Tennyson's disturbed narrator of *Maud* calls the stars

> *. . . tyrants in your iron skies,*
> *Innumerable, pitiless, passionless eyes,*
> *Cold fires, yet with power to burn and brand*
> *His nothingness into man.*[27]

Then came biology. Charles Darwin's *The Origin of Species* (1859) "was interpreted by the nonscientific public in a variety of ways. Some chose to assume that evolution was synonymous with progress, but most readers recognized that Darwin's theory of natural selection conflicted not only with the concept of creation derived from the Bible but also with long-established assumptions of the values attached to humanity's special role in the world."[28]

So the Victorian Period in England was not as placid as our twentieth-century connotations often suggest. Historian David Thomson sums it up this way:

> The agrarian and industrial revolutions . . . transformed the face and life of the nation and brought immense prosperity and misery combined. . . . The whole meaning of Victorian England is lost if it is thought of as a country of stuffy complacency and black top-hatted moral priggery. [The Victorians'] failures, faults, and ludicrous shortcomings are all too apparent: but . . . we must ask ourselves the question whether we can laugh at our great-grandfathers' attempts to solve problems to which we have so far failed to find an answer.[29]

Some of the problems should sound familiar to us. In the same year of the Great Exhibition (1851), with its glorification of technological triumphs, the Rev. Charles Kingsley described the painful estrangements in Victorian households that had been brought about by the religious conflicts we've been observing: "The young men and women of our day are fast parting from their parents and each other; the more thoughtful are wandering either towards Rome [i.e., Roman Catholicism], towards sheer materialism [which says only matter is real], or towards an unchristian and unphilosophic spiritualism [as in my section "Unacceptable Alternative: Life-force Philosophy" below]."[30]

SCIENTISM

In other words, scientism, a misuse of science, had taken root, flowered, and was bearing bitter fruit. What worked wonders in science worked havoc when misapplied to religion and philosophy. Anyone with a religious orientation in our own day can see that the Victorian problem has not yet been solved. Kingsley's statement could have been written yesterday with equal applicability, in England or America.

C. S. Lewis's campaign against the scientism that developed in the nineteenth century is the subject of a fine book by Michael D. Aeschliman, *The Restitution of Man: C. S. Lewis and the Case against Scientism* (1983). So I turn to it for the next phase in the development of the modern materialist worldview.[31] Although the book is specifically about Lewis's *The Abolition of Man* (1943), its issues illuminate the situation that led Lewis to write defenses of Christianity such as *The Problem of Pain* (1940), *Miracles* (1947), and *Mere Christianity* in that same era. Aeschliman puts Lewis's case for humanity's needed restitution in the context of the scientism that won such victories in the Western world during the nineteenth century. By "scientism" Aeschliman means the extreme scientific materialism that denies the reality of the supernatural and sees humans as a part of nature, subject only to the laws of causality that scientific method discovers.

The difference between scientism and science is crucial here, as Lewis himself tried to make clear.[32] Scientism is a philosophical attitude toward science, sometimes even a worship of science, but empirical science itself does not generate scientism, nor are most scientists guilty of it.

Indeed, the great scientists are often those who can imagine beyond the paradigms of contemporary science, as Thomas Kuhn has persuasively argued.[33] It was Isaac Newton's Christian beliefs that led him to seek laws of motion applicable to the whole universe, and the result was a paradigm shift that wasn't superseded until Einstein came along. And Kepler's pythagoreanism led him to look for numerical relationships in the natural world that are aesthetically beautiful, a quality outside the scope of pure science. As the editor of this volume has said, "Scientism is actually bad for science, because great scientists have always been guided by non-scientific metaphysical 'prejudice' from Aristotle to Einstein."[34]

Scientism insists that the scientific method is the only way to truth, whatever the field of inquiry. In the social sciences, such scientism often appears as behaviorism or determinism.[35] Traditionally, we humans have considered ourselves free rational creatures; that is, in contrast to nonrational animals we think and choose in ways that make us morally responsible. Of course, we do not think ourselves totally free nor always rational, but we are free enough to make choices that count and rational enough to be distinguished from all other biological species of creation. The Protestant Reformers called our free will into question, but it was scientism that merged us with the other animals. No wonder there is current confusion about saving whales while aborting viable human fetuses.

Aeschliman clarifies this facet of scientism with a direct quotation from Jacob Bronowski: "Man is a part of nature, in the same sense that a stone is, or a cactus, or a camel."[36] Aeschliman sees dire implications in this concept of human nature:

> The distinction between . . . two senses of nature (i.e., nature as the essential character of a person, reality, or thing and nature as the vast mechanism of the physical universe) has served to generate much of the intellectual and moral history of Western culture during the past four hundred years. The chief fallacy of modern naturalism is its insistence upon a collapse of the two meanings of nature into one: for Bronowski and others like him, the essential character of man amounts to nothing more than his physical existence within the larger soulless ticking mechanism of the "natural" world, constituted by accident and impelled toward eventual entropic dissolution. Within the bounds of such a philosophy, free will, purpose, and rational thought itself are drained of any significant meaning and rendered absurd, for of

Lewis as Evangelist to the Modernists

what possible value are reason and action if they are merely the
necessary consequents of implacable natural laws?[37]

Aeschliman illuminates brilliantly the triumph of scientism in the late
nineteenth-century West.

Bronowski's naturalism is an example of "the materialist view"
we saw Lewis describe in *Mere Christianity*:

> People who take that view think that matter and space just hap-
> pen to exist, and always have existed, nobody knows why; and
> that the matter, behaving in certain fixed ways, has just hap-
> pened, by a sort of fluke, to produce creatures like ourselves who
> are able to think.[38]

As we have seen, in nineteenth-century England such scientism,
with its skepticism about the supernatural, created a growing conflict
between science and religion. It became increasingly difficult for educated people to maintain some traditional Christian beliefs. Thomas
Carlyle, for example, sarcastically complained that "in our age of
Down-pulling and Disbelief, the very Devil has been pulled down; you
cannot so much as believe in a Devil."[39] That was over a hundred years
before Lewis's *Screwtape Letters* came along to give us the demonic
perspective on this development.

In *The Screwtape Letters* (1942) the minor devil Screwtape explains
to his nephew Wormwood the pros and cons of disbelief in the existence
of demons: "When the humans disbelieve in our existence we lose all
the pleasing results of direct terrorism, and we make no magicians. On
the other hand, when they believe in us, we cannot make them materialists and sceptics."[40] Since Carlyle, materialists and skeptics have multiplied greatly. In Lewis's 1960 preface he makes explicit his own belief
in Satan and the other fallen angels,[41] thus going against the materialism
of the modern era. *The Screwtape Letters* was such a popular success in
England and America that *Time* magazine put Lewis and the Devil on
its cover for September 8, 1947. A scholarly defender of the Devil's existence was rare a century after Carlyle's witty lament.

Between Carlyle and *Screwtape* came Friedrich Nietzsche (1844-1900), who posted the obituary, not of Satan, but of God Himself. By the 1940s in Lewis's Oxford, atheism, or at best agnosticism, was more the rule than the exception, prompting the *Time* reporter to speak ironically of theism as a heresy; he called Lewis "one of a growing band of heretics among modern intellectuals: an intellectual who believes in God."[42]

James Patrick, in his close examination of the philosophical vistas in Lewis's Oxford, says succinctly, "Reason had led to skepticism throughout much of the nineteenth century."[43] No wonder then that in 1941, as Lewis assessed the worldview of his modernist neighbors, he saw the lamp of faith in nonmaterial reality flickering dimly, almost snuffed out by the bleak prospect of a world observed through the foggy lenses of materialism.

LOGICAL POSITIVISM

Lewis's "case against scientism" in *The Abolition of Man* attacks a linguistic facet of scientism that I must explain before summing up the materialist's worldview.[44] Logical positivism analyzes language in an attempt to eliminate nonsensical statements. One of its major popularizers, A. J. Ayer, was Lewis's contemporary at Oxford. We shall hear more of him presently. But first, some explanation of the term.[45]

Logical positivism was a philosophy developed in the 1920s by "the Vienna Circle" of philosophers. Moritz Schlick (1882-1936) and his followers declared metaphysics meaningless (*meta*physics is the study of whatever is beyond [Greek *meta*] the physical); they attempted to reduce all philosophy to propositions that are verifiable in a scientific (empirical) sense of the term. "Most logical positivists regarded religious and moral utterances as metaphysical and thus as meaningless."[46] Closely related to scientific empiricism, it looks back to such British philosophers as the skeptic David Hume (1711-1776) and the utilitarian John Stuart Mill (1806-1873), both of whose writings Lewis knew well, incidentally. The methodology of logical positivism mirrors the scientific methodology of the nineteenth century, with the addition of the logical analysis of language as developed by Bertrand Russell (1872-1970) and Ludwig Wittgenstein (1889-1951).

In *Surprised by Joy* Lewis says of his rigorous tutor W. T. Kirkpatrick (1848-1921), "Born a little later, he would have been a Logical Positivist."[47] In *That Hideous Strength* we meet John Wither, demon-possessed director of the evil N.I.C.E., which comes to be destroyed by heavenly powers. When Wither realizes that his cause is lost,

> It is incredible how little this knowledge moved him. It could not, because he had long ceased to believe in knowledge itself. . . . He had passed from Hegel into Hume, thence through Pragmatism, and thence through Logical Positivism, and out at last into the complete void. . . . He had willed with his whole heart that there should be no reality and no truth, and now even the imminence of his own ruin could not wake him.[48]

A. J. Ayer, a professor of logic at Oxford for many years, was a major voice of logical positivism (and thus of scientism) in the 1930s and following. His popular *Language, Truth and Logic* (1936 and often reprinted) denies the validity of traditional ethics. A radical empiricist, he argues that statements of normative ethical judgments cannot be either true or false, for they are not propositions at all. "Stealing money is wrong" is, he says, "a sentence which has no factual meaning—that is, expresses no proposition which can be either true or false."[49] To a logical positivist, "a sentence says nothing unless it is empirically verifiable."[50] All normative statements of ethical value, being empirically unverifiable, are to Ayer merely "emotive." They are "used to express feeling about certain objects, but not to make any assertion about them."[51]

Such is the skepticism expressed in "the Green Book," Lewis's name for the school textbook that prompted him to write *The Abolition of Man*. Indeed, Aeschliman believes Ayer's ideas to be the "chief targets in *The Abolition of Man*."[52] Although this book of Lewis's is too complex to discuss here, I'll mention that *The Abolition of Man* supplements the argument against the materialism that *Mere Christianity* seeks to overcome. Both books battle the modern view of value judgments as purely subjective. If we give up on all objectivity in the realm of value, of evaluation, in aesthetics or ethics, we end up like Bronowski's camel, cactus, and stone—just another part of nature, with no moral responsibilities.[53]

This elimination of objective values is a legacy of logical positivism, which says language is totally incapable of dealing with anything outside sensory experience. (It was left to Jacques Derrida and Deconstruction to question if language can even communicate sensory experience.)

This change to an empirical epistemology, then, seems to me the central aspect of the change from the medieval to the modern worldview. No one wants to return to the Middle Ages' naiveté about the workings of the natural world, but have we not thrown out too much with the bosh? Despite empiricism's invaluable benefits in the hands of science, its popular misuse—the scientism that Lewis fought—is alarming. Filtered down from philosophers such as Nietzsche and A. J. Ayer to us people on the pavement, this worldview, this way of looking at reality, has torn in two the spiritual and material, obscuring the former and spotlighting the latter. We have always liked things, but for centuries we believed that things did not exhaust reality. Then the Age of Reason and scientism took the empirical reason of the new science and made it seem the only kind.

UNACCEPTABLE ALTERNATIVE: LIFE-FORCE PHILOSOPHY

As mentioned earlier, in his radio broadcast of 1941 Lewis explained two contrasting views of "what this universe really is and how it came to be there: the Materialist view and the Religious view."[54] In his printed version of 1942, he added a third that constitutes my last topic: "the In-between view called Life-Force philosophy, or Creative Evolution, or Emergent Evolution." He credits Henri Bergson (1859-1941) with the most profound expositions of this philosophy.[55]

Bergson was dissatisfied with scientific materialism, seeing clearly that it gave only mechanistic explanations for the processes of life. In an attempt to counter such materialism, he developed the concept of the *élan vital* (French, "vital force"), by which he meant the creative principle behind evolution, the vital impulse necessary for animation and consciousness. This philosophy is sometimes called vitalism or creative evolution; its proponents contend "that the processes of life are not explicable by the laws of physics and chemistry alone and that life is in some part self-determining."[56] Bergson's was a misguided attempt to make room for some purpose behind the universe, now that science seemed to have eliminated God.

Lewis explains:

> When you are feeling fit and the sun is shining and you don't want to believe that the whole universe is a mere mechanical dance of atoms, it's nice to be able to think of this great mysterious Force rolling on through the centuries and carrying you on its crest.[57]

In England and the United States George Bernard Shaw popularized the idea of the life-force in plays such as *Man and Superman* (1905) and *Back to Methuselah* (1921, first produced in New York in 1922).[58]

For Lewis it was an unacceptable alternative to scientific materialism. He satirizes the idea of the life-force in Weston, his mad scientist in *Perelandra*. In *Out of the Silent Planet* Weston had been an immoral materialist, a brilliant scientist guilty of scientism. But when we hear him on the planet Perelandra (Venus), we perceive that in the interim he has become a Bergsonian. Weston tells how he "became a convinced believer in emergent evolution"; he now believes that an "unconsciously purposive dynamism" pervades organic and inorganic matter alike. In solemn tones he tells Ransom:

> "The majestic spectacle of this blind, inarticulate purposiveness thrusting its way upward and ever upward in an endless unity of differentiated achievements towards an ever-increasing complexity of organisation, towards spontaneity and spirituality, swept away all my old conception of a duty to Man as such. Man in himself is nothing. The forward movement of Life—the growing spirituality—is everything."[59]

This is the meaningless jargon of Bergson's creative evolution, the life-force philosophy of which George Bernard Shaw was enamored.

Lewis also satirizes creative evolution in his poem "Evolutionary Hymn" (1957). In the rhythms of Longfellow's once-popular "Psalm of Life," he ironically praises the "progress" of Life toward "nobody knows where" (line 6), led on by "Evolution" toward godhead itself.

> On then! Value means survival-
> Value. If our progeny
> Spreads and spawns and licks each rival,
> That will prove its deity. . . .
>
> (lines 31-34)[60]

If Weston had a hymnbook, "Evolutionary Hymn" would be in it, without verbal irony.

I could have explained life-force philosophy in a note, as Lewis did in *Mere Christianity*, for it is "history" now, as we say dismissively. But it warrants our attention for two reasons. First, it illustrates the human need for metaphysical explanations, whether in ancient Greece or modern America. Whatever the current explanations of how the universe works, we want to know *why*. What does it all mean? The *how* of science is never enough—thus the temptation of scientism. Second, the popularity of life-force philosophy, even though short-lived, illustrates the sort of thing that rushes into the vacuum in the modernist's soul, things like irrational philosophy, superstition, occultism, the New Age movement.

CONCLUSION

In 1941, as C. S. Lewis prepared his scripts for the British Broadcasting Corporation, with a world war escalating, the battle for human souls was already intense. Lewis saw that his neighbors' open-ness to the Gospel depended partly on their way of thinking about what is real, their mental and emotional conditioning concerning truth and value. That insight into his audience enabled him to begin at

Lewis as Evangelist to the Modernists

square one and produce a classic of Christian apologetics. In final form, *Mere Christianity* (1952) has been a tool of the Holy Spirit in the conversion of many.[61]

In many of his writings—fiction and nonfiction, articles and books—Lewis continued to battle this materialism, this scientism, this tunnel vision that sees no supernatural dimension to reality. Many of us are grateful that he did.

BIBLIOGRAPHY

Aeschliman, Michael D. *The Restitution of Man: C. S. Lewis and the Case Against Scientism*. Grand Rapids, MI: Eerdmans, 1983.

Ayer, Alfred Jules. *Language, Truth and Logic*. Second Edition. New York: Dover, 1952.

Bacon, Francis. *The Advancement of Learning* (1605). In *Selected Writings of Francis Bacon*. Ed. Hugh G. Dick. New York: Random House, Modern Library, 1955, 155-392.

Baker, Herschel. *The Wars of Truth*. Cambridge, MA: Harvard University Press, 1952.

Bede, The Venerable. *A History of the English Church and People*. Trans. Leo Sherley-Price. Harmondsworth, England: Penguin Books, 1955.

The Bestiary: A Book of Beasts, Being a Translation from a Latin Bestiary of the Twelfth Century. Trans., ed. T. H. White. New York: G. P. Putnam's Sons, Capricorn Books, 1960.

Bronowski, J. *The Identity of Man*. Revised Edition. Garden City, NJ: Doubleday, Natural History Press, 1971.

————. *Science and Human Values*. Revised Edition. New York: Harper, 1965.

Carlyle, Thomas. From *Sartor Resartus*. In *The Norton Anthology of English Literature*. Vol. 2, 933-58.

Colson, Charles W. *Born Again*. Old Tappan, NJ: Fleming H. Revell, Spire Books, 1977.

"Don v. Devil." *Time*, 8 September 1947, 65-74.

Ford, George H., and Carol T. Christ. "The Victorian Age: 1830-1901." In *The Norton Anthology of English Literature*. Vol. 2, 891-910.

Hobbes, Thomas. *Leviathan*. Ed. Michael Oakeshott. New York: Collier Books, 1962.

Hooper, Walter. Introduction. In C. S. Lewis, *Mere Christianity: An Anniversary Edition*. Ed. Walter Hooper. New York: Macmillan, 1981.

Kuhn, Thomas S. *The Structure of Scientific Revolutions*. Second Edition. Chicago: The University of Chicago Press, 1970.

Lewis, C. S. *The Abolition of Man*. London: Oxford University Press, 1943.

_____. *Broadcast Talks*. London: Geoffrey Bles, 1942.

_____. *The Collected Poems*. Ed. Walter Hooper. London: HarperCollins, Fount Paperbacks, 1994.

_____. "*De Descriptione Temporum*." In *They Asked for a Paper*. London: Geoffrey Bles, 1962, 9-25.

_____. *The Discarded Image: An Introduction to Medieval and Renaissance Literature*. Cambridge, England: Cambridge University Press, 1964.

_____. "The Funeral of a Great Myth." In *Christian Reflections*. Ed. Walter Hooper. Grand Rapids, MI: Eerdmans, 1967, 82-93.

_____. *Letters*. Edited, with a Memoir, by W. H. Lewis. Revised Edition. Ed. Walter Hooper. London: Collins, Fount Paperbacks, 1988.

_____. *Mere Christianity*. London: Geoffrey Bles, 1952.

_____. *Out of the Silent Planet*. London: John Lane, The Bodley Head, 1938.

_____. *Perelandra*. London: John Lane, The Bodley Head, 1943.

_____. "A Reply to Professor Haldane." In *Of Other Worlds: Essays and Stories*. Ed. Walter Hooper. London: Geoffrey Bles, 1966, 74-85.

_____. *The Screwtape Letters with Screwtape Proposes a Toast*. Revised Edition. New York: Macmillan, 1982.

_____. *Surprised by Joy: The Shape of My Early Life*. London: Geoffrey Bles, 1955.

_____. *That Hideous Strength*. London: John Lane, The Bodley Head, 1945.

Macaulay, Thomas Babington. "Lord Bacon" (July 1837). In *Critical and Historical Essays*. Vol. 1. London: Longman, 1856.

MacIntyre, Alasdair. *After Virtue: A Study in Moral Theory*. Second Edition. Notre Dame, IN: University of Notre Dame Press, 1984.

Musacchio, George. *C. S. Lewis, Man and Writer: Essays and Reviews*. Belton, TX: University of Mary Hardin-Baylor, 1994.

_____. "Materialism and the Problem of Belief." *The Southern Baptist Educator*, January-February 1974, 9-10.

Myers, Doris T. *C. S. Lewis in Context*. Kent, OH: Kent State University Press, 1994.

The Norton Anthology of English Literature. Ed. M. H. Abrams. Sixth Edition. Vol. 2. New York: Norton, 1993.

O'Hear, Anthony. *Introduction to the Philosophy of Science*. Oxford: Clarendon Press, 1989.

Patrick, James. *The Magdalen Metaphysicals: Idealism and Orthodoxy at Oxford, 1901-1945*. Macon, GA: Mercer University Press, 1985.

Lewis as Evangelist to the Modernists

Pope, Alexander. *The Poems*. Ed. John Butt. New Haven: Yale University Press, 1963.

Quinton, Anthony. "Logical Positivism." *The Harper Dictionary of Modern Thought*. Eds. Alan Bullock and Oliver Stallybrass. New York: Harper, 1977.

Stewart, J. I. M. *Eight Modern Writers*. Vol. 12 of *The Oxford History of English Literature*. Oxford: Clarendon Press, 1963.

Tennyson, Alfred. *Representative Poems*. Ed. Samuel C. Chew. New York, Odyssey Press, 1941.

Thomson, David. *England in the Nineteenth Century: 1815-1914*. Vol. 8 of *The Pelican History of England*. Harmondsworth, England: Penguin Books, 1950.

NOTES

1. Lewis, letter of 10 February 1941, quoted in Hooper, Introduction to *Mere Christianity: An Anniversary Edition*, xi.

2. Lewis, *Letters*, 193.

3. Lewis, *Mere Christianity*, 17.

4. The first of Lewis's *Screwtape Letters* discusses materialism as the Devil's tool.

5. This section of my chapter draws on my earlier article, "Materialism and the Problem of Belief."

6. Bede, *History of the English Church and People*, 245-46.

7. *The Bestiary*, 21.

8. See Lewis, *The Discarded Image*, 5, 17.

9. Lewis, "*De Descriptione Temporum*," 16-17.

10. Baker, *The Wars of Truth*, 4.

11. Aquinas, *Summa contra Gentiles*, III.xvii, quoted in Baker, 5.

12. Pope, *Essay on Man*, IV. 398, II.1-2.

13. Bacon, *The Advancement of Learning*, 193-94.

14. Hobbes, *Leviathan*, 21.

15. *Webster's New World Dictionary*, Third College Edition, s.v. "empiricism."

16. For readers outside the United States, I mention that Missouri is known as the "Show Me State."

17. This section owes a general debt to George Ford and Carol T. Christ, "The Victorian Age," which also directed me to some of the examples that follow. See Ford and Christ, 2:891-98.

18. See, e.g., his 1837 essay, "Lord Bacon."

19. Tennyson, "Locksley Hall," lines 119-22, 129-30.

20. Ibid., 181-82. Tennyson is notorious among students of English literature for

this misunderstanding of railroad tracks. It is of course the train's wheels that are made to fit over the tracks, not the tracks that are grooved for the wheels to fit into.

21. A metonymy is a figure of speech that uses something associated with the literal subject, as in "the White House issued a statement," meaning someone in the executive branch of our government issued a statement, or as in "he owns a hundred head of cattle," where the head represents the whole cow, one hopes. The latter example, the use of a part for the whole, is also called a synecdoche.

22. Ford and Christ, "The Victorian Age," 2:896. The reporter covering the opening for the London *Times* spoke of the Crystal Palace in religious terms. Above the thousands in attendance "rose a glittering arch far more lofty and spacious than the vaults of even our noblest cathedrals." Gathered there around the throne of Queen Victoria, "some were most reminded of that day when all ages and climes shall be gathered round the throne of their Maker." 2 May 1851, quoted in Thomson, *England in the Nineteenth Century*, 99. More than one cultural historian in our own day has noted that, whereas in earlier centuries the highest visible point in a city was a church spire, now it is usually an office building, a skyscraper that symbolizes a change in society's values.

23. Ford and Christ, "The Victorian Age," 2:897.

24. Ruskin, quoted in ibid., 2:897.

25. Ford and Christ, 2:897.

26. Lewis, *Discarded Image*, 119.

27. Tennyson, *Maud*, Part I, XVIII.iv.37-40. "His" refers to "man": the stars show man his nothingness. Lewis uses "Lucifer in Starlight" by George Meredith, a Victorian poet and novelist, to illustrate the same sort of contrast to the medieval view of the heavens. *Discarded Image*, 119. And Lewis's protagonist of the Ransom trilogy feels much the same way as these Victorians when he is first thrust into "space"; but then Ransom learns to see it as "the heavens," where real life teems. *Out of the Silent Planet*, 32, 44; see also *Perelandra*, 23, and my *C. S. Lewis, Man and Writer*, 53, 66-68.

28. Ford and Christ, "The Victorian Age," 2:897.

29. Thomson, *England in the Nineteenth Century*, 33-34.

30. Kingsley, quoted in Ford and Christ, "The Victorian Age," 2:898.

31. I review Aeschliman's book in my *C. S. Lewis, Man and Writer*, 154-56.

32. Lewis, "A Reply to Professor Haldane," 76-78.

33. *The Structure of Scientific Revolutions* (first published 1962). On the role of the imagination in scientific breakthroughs, see Anthony O'Hear, *Introduction to the Philosophy of Science*, 21-25.

34. Angus J. L. Menuge, letter to author, 10 September 1996. From this letter I also take the example of Kepler.

35. For example, in the work of B. F. Skinner and of course in Freud; on the latter see Myers, *C. S. Lewis in Context*, 17.

36. Bronowski, *The Identity of Man*, 2, quoted in Aeschliman, *The Restitution*

Lewis as Evangelist to the Modernists

of Man, 11. The quotation is on page 3 of the revised edition listed in my bibliography.

37. Aeschliman, *The Restitution of Man*, 11-12. Bronowski himself would not agree with these implications. See his *Science and Human Values*, 51-55, and *The Identity of Man*, Revised Edition, ix, 19-20.

38. Lewis, *Mere Christianity*, 17.

39. Carlyle, *Sartor Resartus*, II, ch. 7, in *The Norton Anthology of English Literature*, 2:936.

40. Lewis, *The Screwtape Letters*, 32.

41. Ibid., vii-viii.

42. "Don v. Devil," 65.

43. Patrick, *The Magdalen Metaphysicals*, 166-67.

44. For more of Lewis against scientism in addition to *The Abolition of Man*, see his "Funeral of a Great Myth" and "Reply to Professor Haldane."

45. On language analysis in Lewis's Oxford, see Myers's impressive book.

46. Quinton, "Logical Positivism."

47. Lewis, *Surprised by Joy*, 130.

48. Lewis, *That Hideous Strength*, 438.

49. Ayer, *Language, Truth and Logic*, 107.

50. Ibid., 73.

51. Ibid., 108; for more on Ayer in Lewis's Oxford see Patrick, 102-03, 135; and Myers, 183. On "emotivism" see MacIntyre, *After Virtue*, chap. 2.

52. Aeschliman, *The Restitution of Man*, 60. Myers, *C. S. Lewis in Context*, 72-84, discusses Lewis's annotated copy of *The Control of Language*, "the Green Book."

53. Again I stress that this is not Bronowski's view of values or ethics, but Lewis would argue, I think, that Bronowski's averred naturalism conflicts with the basis for ethics that the scientist asserts in *Science and Human Values*. See note 37 above.

54. Lewis, *Mere Christianity*, 17, 20-21.

55. Lewis, *Broadcast Talks*, 28; *Mere Christianity*, 21.

56. *Merriam-Webster's Collegiate Dictionary*, Tenth Edition, s.v. "vitalism."

57. Lewis, *Broadcast Talks*, 28.

58. Stewart, *Eight Modern Writers*, 143-52, 176.

59. Lewis, *Perelandra*, 102.

60. Lewis, *Collected Poems*, 69-70. See Screwtape on the "Life Force," *The Screwtape Letters*, 33; cf. 118-19.

61. One of the most notable examples is Charles Colson; see his *Born Again*, 112-14, and passim.

PRAEPARATIO
EVANGELICA

JOEL D. HECK

C. S. Lewis used the Latin term *praeparatio evangelica*, "evangelical preparation," or better, "preparation for the Evangel, the Gospel," to describe his role in the cause of evangelism. The term suggests that he did not see his role as that of an evangelist. His role was a preparatory role. He was a John the Baptist, a forerunner, a twentieth-century Elijah, preparing the way for those who would proclaim the Gospel–the priests and vicars and curates, in short, the evangelists.

Lewis was too modest about his contribution to evangelism to think of himself as an evangelist. In A. Clifford Morris's reminiscences of C. S. Lewis, Morris commented that it seemed to him a great pity that Lewis did not preach more often, until he learned the reason. Lewis told him one day after one of those sermons and the accolades he received, "I had to get to my knees pretty quickly, to kill the deadly sin of pride."[1]

As such, he downplayed his role in evangelism, stating, for example, about his BBC talks, "Mine are *praeparatio evangelica* rather than evangelism, an attempt to convince people that there is a moral law, that we disobey it, and that the existence of a Lawgiver is at least very probable and also (*unless* you add the Christian doctrine of the Atonement) that this imparts despair rather than comfort."[2] His role was to convince the atheists and skeptics that there was indeed a moral law and that the existence of the moral law testified to the existence of God.

At the same time, however, Lewis maintained, "Most of my

Praeparatio Evangelica

books are evangelistic, addressed to *tous exo*."[3] Does he here contradict himself, or does he merely indicate that his style is pre-evangelism? He goes on to explain himself in the same passage: "It would
have been inept to preach forgiveness and a Saviour to those who did
not know they were in need of either."[4] In short, then, his approach
was to prepare the person for the Evangel, the Gospel, rather than to
evangelize.

He saw his pre-evangelism, however, as only a shadow of God's
pre-evangelism. In his preface to *The Pilgrim's Regress*, Lewis spoke
of "the real *praeparatio evangelica*" in nature when he wrote, "The
one[5] exaggerates the distinctness between Grace and Nature in a sheer
opposition and by vilifying the higher levels of Nature (the real *praeparatio evangelica* inherent in certain immediately sub-Christian experiences) makes the way hard for those who are at the point of coming
in."[6] In other words, Lewis argues as Paul argues in Romans, chapters
1 and 2, that the non-Christian, "the natural man," knows certain
things about God by nature and sees those truths echoed in nature.
Theologians call this the natural knowledge of God.

Consequently, to understand Lewis as a pre-evangelist, we must
see the connection between his role and the role of nature. For Lewis,
nature, which he enjoyed greatly on his many, almost legendary walks,
will point people to God; his role is to make that connection more
explicit, to nudge the sleeping imagination, to point out the vague
longing for something greater than oneself. No doubt the natural
knowledge of God was a common topic for discussion on his trips
around Addison's Walk at Magdalen College, Oxford.

But there is more that Lewis does with this vague longing. Not
only does he point it out, he also sharpens that longing so that people might see the one thing that satisfies, Jesus Christ. He had found
in his own life that only Christ could satisfy his romantic longings,
and a Christian, biblical theology affirms the same thing. Writes
Lewis:

Has not every object which fancy and sense suggested for the
desire, proved a failure, confessed itself, after trial, not to be

what you wanted? Have you not found by elimination that this desire is the perilous siege in which only One can sit?[7]

This is where the Gospel must come in and point to that "only One" who can sit within that desire. In this sense, then, Lewis is doing *praeparatio evangelica* rather than evangelism. His role is not to proclaim the Gospel, but to prepare for it by pointing out the longing, sharpening the longing, but not satisfying the longing. That only Christ can do, and one must speak the Gospel in order for that evangelistic impact to be felt. Desire, on its own and at its best, can only know what it does not want, as Lewis states:

> . . . this endless desire which so easily confuses itself with other desires and, at best, remains pure only by knowing what it does not want—you see that it is a starting point from which one road leads home and a thousand roads lead into the wilderness.[8]

According to Lewis, this is how God works to prepare the way for the Gospel. Commenting on *The Pilgrim's Regress*, he wrote, "For as often as men become Pagans again, the Landlord again sends them pictures and stirs up sweet desire and so leads them back to Mother Kirk even as he led the actual Pagans long ago. There is, indeed, no other way."[9] Commenting on *Till We Have Faces*, he wrote, "Psyche is an instance of the *anima naturaliter Christiana* making the best of the Pagan religion she is brought up in and thus being guided (but always 'under the cloud,' always in terms of her own imagination or that of her people) towards the true God. She is in some ways like Christ because every good man or woman is like Christ. What else could they be like?"[10]

This chapter will especially address Lewis's role in pre-evangelism, but it will also make clear that he was truly an evangelist, although not in anything approaching the traditional sense of the term. Lewis probably understood the evangelist as the preacher of the Gospel, whether from the pulpit, the open air, or the revival tent (as did most people), and would not want to ascribe that role to himself. We will also see,

Praeparatio Evangelica

however, that Lewis was not only a pre-evangelist, but very much a lit-erary evangelist,[11] though he did not covet that title for himself.

He himself described some of his work as evangelism, not pre-evangelism. "Ever since I became a Christian I have thought that the best, perhaps the only, service I could do for my unbelieving neigh-bours was to explain and defend the belief that has been common to nearly all Christians at all times."[12] When his writing included the cen-tral message of the Christian faith, the sacrificial suffering, death, and resurrection of Jesus Christ, he was both apologist and evangelist.

He also stated the supreme importance of the evangelistic task. Lewis once wrote that "the salvation of a single soul is more impor-tant than the production or preservation of all the epics and tragedies in the world. . . ."[13] Again he wrote, "And woe to you if you do not evangelize."[14] Once more, "Yet the glory of God, and, as our only means to glorifying Him, the salvation of human souls, is the real busi-ness of life."[15] George Sayer wrote, "Almost from the year of his con-version, he wanted to become an evangelist for the Christian faith."[16] In *Mere Christianity* he wrote, "The church exists for nothing else but to draw men into Christ, to make them little Christs. If they are not doing that, all the cathedrals, clergy, missions, sermons, even the Bible itself, are simply a waste of time."[17] How much this conviction drove his writings will become clearer both in this chapter and throughout this book.

THE GOAL: THE UNWELCOME DIAGNOSIS

In a letter to the BBC prior to his first series of Broadcast Talks, Lewis talked further about his approach. "I think what I mainly want to talk about is the Law of Nature, or objective right and wrong. It seems to me that the New Testament, by preaching repentance and forgiveness, always assumes an audience who already believe in the Law of Nature and know they have disobeyed it. In modern England we cannot at present assume this, and therefore most apologetic begins a stage too far on. The first step is to create, or recover, the sense of guilt. Hence if I give a series of talks I should mention Christianity only at the end, and would prefer not to unmask my battery till then."[18]

This Law of Nature that the New Testament assumes, but which was absent in Lewis's England, is that natural knowledge of God and of God's Law spoken of in Romans 1: ". . . what may be known about God is plain to them, because God has made it plain to them. For since the creation of the world God's invisible qualities—his eternal power and divine nature—have been clearly seen, being understood from what has been made, so that men are without excuse" (Romans 1:19-20). This Law of Nature includes an awareness of a holy, supreme being to whom we are accountable and an awareness of the fact that we cannot stand before this supreme being; we are culpable.

People need to know they have sinned, since human nature wants to avoid facing that painful realization.[19] Until they know they have sinned, they will see no need for forgiveness. Writes Lewis, "The greatest barrier I have met is the almost total absence from the minds of my audience of any sense of sin."[20] Elsewhere he states, "We have to convince our hearers of the unwelcome diagnosis before we can expect them to welcome the news of the remedy."[21] That's why Mother Dimble did not approach Jane, in *That Hideous Strength*, with a testimony of her faith. But still, "Jane found Mother Dimble an embarrassing person to share a room with because she said prayers. One didn't know where to look."[22] Mother Dimble's prayers caused Jane to think about her own relationship to God. God was beginning to do "his strange work," "his alien task" (Isaiah 28:21).

Later in the same work we read of Jane's growing understanding of God. She was faced with the possibility of one of the realities of the Law of Nature—death. "Up to now she had not thought of Maleldil either. She did not doubt that the eldils existed; nor did she doubt the existence of this stronger and more obscure being whom they obeyed. . . . If it had ever occurred to her to question whether all these things might be the reality behind what she had been taught at school as 'religion,' she had put the thought aside. But this time, if it was really to be death, the thought would not be put aside. Because, really, it now appeared that almost anything might be true. One might be in for any-

Praeparatio Evangelica

thing. Maleldil might be, quite simply and crudely, God. There might be a life after death: a Heaven: a Hell."[23] Screwtape wrote to Wormwood that war has the same effect on people's minds—it focuses their minds on spiritual truth. "And how disastrous for us," says Screwtape, "is the continual remembrance of death which war enforces. One of our best weapons, contented worldliness, is rendered useless."[24]

We see echoes of this same understanding in other works of Lewis. For example, during the opening chapter of *The Pilgrim's Regress*, when John is learning about religion, we read, "Knowledge of broken law precedes all other religious experiences. . . ."[25]

Several examples from the Chronicles of Narnia will illustrate further. In *The Voyage of the "Dawn Treader,"* Eustace was very beastly toward his friends, not seeing his selfishness, his greed, and his loneliness, until he literally became a dragon.

> He could get even with Caspian and Edmund now. . . . But the moment he thought this he realised that he didn't want to. He wanted to be friends. He wanted to get back among humans and talk and laugh and share things. He realised that he was a monster cut off from the whole human race. An appalling loneliness came over him. He began to see the others had not really been fiends at all. He began to wonder if he himself had been such a nice person as he had always supposed.[26]

That Aslan must tear the dragon skin from him, after several unsuccessful attempts by Eustace to do it himself, clearly suggests the inability of human beings to change their nature and the power of God in Christ to change us as He forgives us of our sins.[27] In *The Horse and His Boy*, this recognition of the sinful self first occurred when Shasta met Aslan in the form of a cat and was delivered from jackals by Aslan.

> "I'll never do anything nasty to a cat again as long as I live," said Shasta, half to the cat and half to himself. "I did once, you know. I threw stones at a half-starved mangey old stray. Hey! Stop

that." For the cat had turned round and given him a scratch. "None of that," said Shasta. "It isn't as if you could understand what I'm saying." Then he dozed off.[28]

Later in the same book the talking horse Bree learned a similar lesson with the help of the boy, who now understood himself better. When Shasta jumped off Bree to make a run at a lion (actually Aslan, but he didn't know it at the time), Bree kept on running. The next day Bree made his confession:

> "How can I ever show my face among the free Horses of Narnia?—I, who left a mare and a girl and a boy to be eaten by lions while I galloped all I could to save my own wretched skin!"
> "We all ran as hard as we could," said Hwin.
> "Shasta didn't!" snorted Bree. "At least he ran in the right direction: ran *back*. And that is what shames me most of all. I, who called myself a war horse and boasted of a hundred fights, to be beaten by a little human boy–a child, a mere foal, who had never held a sword nor had any good nurture or example in his life!"[29]

Then came the lesson that Bree had to swallow. The Hermit of the Southern March needed to help Bree see himself in the proper perspective:

> "'My good Horse, you've lost nothing but your self-conceit. No, no, cousin. Don't put back your ears and shake your mane at me. If you are really so humbled as you sounded a minute ago, you must learn to listen to sense. You're not quite the great horse you had come to think, from living among poor dumb horses. Of course you were braver and cleverer than them. You could hardly help being that. It doesn't follow that you'll be anyone very special in Narnia. But as long as you know you're nobody very special, you'll be a very decent sort of Horse, on the whole, and taking one thing with another. . . .'"[30]

In *The Magician's Nephew*, Digory learned the importance of fac-

Praeparatio Evangelica

ing up to his sin, for only after that was Aslan able to use Digory in his service. Aslan asked him to explain how the Witch got into Narnia.

> "I brought her, Aslan," he answered in a low voice. . . .
>
> "How came she to be in your world, Son of Adam?"
>
> "By—by Magic."
>
> The Lion said nothing and Digory knew that he had not told enough.
>
> "It was my Uncle, Aslan," he said. "He sent us out of our own world by Magic Rings, at least I had to go because he sent Polly first, and then we met the Witch in a place called Charn and she just held on to us when—"
>
> "You met the Witch?" said Aslan in a low voice which had the threat of a growl in it.
>
> "She woke up," said Digory wretchedly. And then, turning very white, "I mean, I woke her. Because I wanted to know what would happen if I struck a bell. Polly didn't want to. It wasn't her fault. I—I fought her. I know I shouldn't have. I think I was a bit enchanted by the writing under the bell."
>
> "Do you?" asked Aslan, still speaking very low and deep.
>
> "No," said Digory. "I see now I wasn't. I was only pretending."[31]

A careful reading of the Chronicles of Narnia will uncover a similar confrontation of the individual with his or her own sin in each book.

We also see echoes of this in Lewis's own life. While discussing the time just shortly after Lewis's conversion, Roger Green and Walter Hooper write, "Lewis had by this time been going to confession for over a year and believed very firmly that people must be convinced of the unwelcome diagnosis of sin before they can welcome the news of the Remedy."[32]

In summary, Lewis wrote, "Christianity simply does not make sense until you have faced the sort of facts I have been describing. . . . It therefore has nothing (as far as I know) to say to people who do not know they have done anything to repent of and who do not feel that they need any forgiveness."[33] Earlier you read this quotation: "Mine are *praeparatio evangelica* rather than evangelism, an attempt to convince people that there is a moral law, that we disobey it, and that the existence of a Lawgiver is at least very probable and also (*unless* you add the Christian doctrine of the Atonement) that this imparts despair rather than comfort."[34] Some would express it this way: "If you wish to believe in Christ, you must become sick; for Christ is a physician only for those who are sick. He came to seek and to save the lost; therefore you must first become a lost and condemned sinner. He is the Good Shepherd who goes in search of the lost sheep; therefore you must first realize that you are a lost sheep."[35]

C. S. Lewis has performed a necessary and important task whenever he has written in recognition of the need of sinners to know they have sinned. In so doing, he has paved the way for the message of the Gospel, a message that he expects others, for the most part, to deliver. He has prepared "the way for the LORD," he has made "straight in the wilderness a highway for our God" (Isaiah 40:3), and in so doing, he has followed the biblical principle of not casting pearls before swine (Matthew 7:6).

The Strategy: Not Overt Evangelism

The preceding section suggests that Lewis avoided overt forms of evangelism. For example, Lewis didn't want non-Christians to notice the resemblance of Narnian theology to Christian theology. "His idea, as he once explained to me, was to make it easier for children to accept Christianity when they met it later in life. He hoped that they would be vaguely reminded of the somewhat similar stories that they had read and enjoyed years before. 'I am aiming at a sort of pre-baptism of the child's imagination.'"[36] These stories, he hoped, would awaken the Law of Nature in both children and adults.

Perhaps he was only thinking about his own experience and what would most likely have evangelized him effectively. Certainly C. N. Manlove thinks so. He writes of the Chronicles of Narnia, "Because he himself had been an atheist, he believed he understood the forces arrayed against his late-won faith, and felt particularly equipped to take them on."[37] He understood far more than the atheist's predicament, but this is one he actually lived through. A few examples will suffice.

In his book *A Severe Mercy*, Sheldon Vanauken credits Lewis's space trilogy as a factor in his conversion. Those books didn't actually convert him; they merely removed one of the major stumbling blocks to a serious consideration of the Christian faith. Lewis's method worked in Vanauken's case. Vanauken had said that the Christian God was too small. After reading *Out of the Silent Planet*, *Perelandra*, and *That Hideous Strength*, he thought "that the Christian God might, after all, be quite big enough for the whole galaxy."[38]

Indeed, that was Lewis's intent. Writing to a correspondent, Lewis wrote on 9 July 1939, "What set me about writing the book was the discovery that a pupil of mine took all that dream of interplanetary colonization quite seriously, and the realization that thousands of people in one way and another depend on some hope of perpetuating and improving the human race for the whole meaning of the universe—that a 'scientific' hope of defeating death is a real rival to Christianity. . . . You will be both grieved and amused to hear that out of about 60 reviews only 2 showed any knowledge that my idea of the fall of the Bent One was anything but an invention of my own. If there was only someone with a richer talent and more leisure I think that this great ignorance might be a help to the evangelisation of England; *any amount of theology can now be smuggled into people's minds under cover of romance without their knowing it*" (my emphasis).[39]

While that sounds manipulative, it is not. No one was ever manipulated into the kingdom of heaven. God doesn't work that way. People come to faith in Jesus Christ only by the power of the Holy Spirit, not through manipulation, smuggling, or any other method. Lewis was simply offering some of the teachings of the Bible through story, and story always has more than one level of meaning. His stories addressed the great themes of life, and any such story will always convey theology. To spell out the full meaning in theological terms is often to do an injustice to a story, for then the story loses its impact. But more will be said on story later.

Lyle Dorsett commented on the significance of the book (and, hence, the trilogy) that affected Vanauken so profoundly. "In 1938 the published poet and literary historian wrote his first novel, *Out of the Silent Planet*. Written for people who would never read the Bible or enter a church, this tale of fantasy was designed to draw unsuspecting materialists into a story that would tempt them to contemplate spiritual realities and the struggle between good and evil."[40]

This places the ten major works of Lewis's fantasy—the Chronicles of Narnia and the space trilogy—in the category of pre-evangelism. If that was a major function of those writings, exactly how did Lewis go about pre-baptizing people's imaginations? To that question we now turn.

The Style: Contemporary Parables

In order to communicate the Law of Nature and smuggle Christian theology undercover, Lewis had to write for the non-Christian community without using technical, theological jargon. His broadcasts over BBC radio were an attempt "to explain and defend Christianity in laymen's language to millions of people who had lost their moorings."[41] He was trying to reach people who had little or no knowledge of the Bible, many of them uneducated.

One cannot but admire the sincerity of a man whose life had been changed and who wanted others to have the same experience. In order for that to happen, he would have to learn to write with power, simplicity, and clarity. And he did. Lyle Dorsett puts it this way: "He likewise made a concerted effort to communicate the Christian story to a post-Christian culture by dropping the stained-glass language of a bygone era and using in its place earthy illustrations easily grasped by the public."[42] I know of a first-century preacher who did something very similar, teaching in parables and telling stories. Parables, and many stories, use images accessible to the modern secular mind, but they leave the spiritual meaning hidden. But that meaning often percolates under the surface until it bursts into life and meaning some time later. Because parable and story lend themselves to clarity of expression, Lewis, following the example of Jesus, had chosen the vehicle most likely to enable him to communicate well. But more on that later.

A letter to Arthur Greeves shortly after his conversion indicated his intention. "I aim," he wrote to Greeves on 4 December 1932, "chiefly at being idiomatic and racy, basing myself on Mallory, Bunyan, and Morris, tho' without archaisms: and would usually prefer to use ten words, provided they are honest native words and idiomatically ordered, than one 'literary word.' To put the thing in a nutshell you want 'The man of whom I told you' and I want 'The man I told you of'."[43]

In another place Lewis wrote of his writing style, "My task was therefore simply that of a translator—one turning Christian doctrine, or what he believed to be such, into the vernacular, into language that unscholarly people would attend to and could understand."[44] For example, when talking about using a mathematical comparison to speak of the Trinity, he wrote, "If it gets across to the unbeliever what the unbeliever desperately needs to know, the vulgarity must be endured."[45] To write clearly is to understand two languages—the language of the writer and the language of the people to whom he or she is writing.[46]

Lewis was consistent in his view of his own work of "Bible translating" and the technical work of Bible translating, for when discussing new Bible translations he wrote, "We ought therefore to welcome all new translations (when they are made by sound scholars) and most certainly those who are approaching the Bible for the first time will be wise not to begin with the Authorised Version."[47] In this view he was anticipating the modern era of communication theory.

"The man who wishes to speak to the uneducated in English must learn their language."[48] Another way of saying this is to say that Lewis took an incarnational approach to evangelism and pre-evangelism. Just as God did not expect the human race to achieve a certain level of spirituality or education before reaching out to us, so also Lewis did not expect the uneducated English to become educated, to study theology, or to learn a theological language before becoming worthy of the Gospel.

He would, in fact, wish those who are studying for the ministry of the church to share this same concern for the non-Christian. "The popular English language, then, simply has to be learned by him who would preach to the English: just as a missionary learns Bantu before preaching to the Bantus. . . . Every examination for ordinands ought to include a passage from some standard theological work for translation into the vernacular."[49]

Furthermore, Christians should not only be able to translate theological writings into everyday English—they must also understand everyday English in theological terms. As an example, Lewis writes, "When an uneducated Englishman says that he believes 'in God, but not in a personal God,' he may mean simply and solely that he is not an Anthropomorphist in the strict and original sense of that word. . . . The proposition 'So and so is not a Christian' would only be taken to be a criticism of his behaviour, never to be merely a statement of his beliefs."[50] We need to understand not only what people say, but also what they mean.

THE TECHNIQUE: STORYTELLING

The most important aspect of this subtle work of *praeparatio evangelica* was Lewis's use of story to reach people's imaginations. Lewis was "a master story-teller with an uncanny visual imagination."[51] Garrison Keillor, America's preeminent storyteller, has said, "I think people do want to hear the Gospel in the form of a story. There's a story at the heart of every sermon."[52] That, we might add, makes story a powerful tool for communicating biblical truth.

One of the most famous phrases in the writings of C. S. Lewis is his comment about the influence of George MacDonald's book *Phantastes* on his imagination. In the introduction to a later edition of *Phantastes*, Lewis wrote, "What it actually did to me was to convert, even to baptise . . . my imagination."[53] By that Lewis meant that his imagination had previously only been used to imagine, but now he could use his imagination for loftier purposes. Imagination does not merely daydream; it processes and composes truth. Lewis could see

Praeparatio Evangelica

that people arrive at truth not only through the intellect, but also through the imagination, the romantic side of the individual. It is similar to the revelation we receive when we first begin to appreciate poetry or when we first begin to appreciate theater.

The idea of baptizing children's imaginations so that they recognize Christian truths later in life was not original with Lewis. He first recognized it in himself and then saw it in others before putting it to work in his own writings. Of Rider Haggard's writings, for example, he states, ". . . people had first met in Haggard's romances elements which they would meet again in religious experience if they ever came to have any."[54]

Next, Lewis applied the idea to his own writings for children. He said, "I thought I saw how stories of this kind could steal past a certain inhibition which had paralysed much of my own religion in childhood. Why did one find it so hard to feel as one was told one ought to feel about God or about the sufferings of Christ? An obligation to feel can freeze feelings. And reverence itself did harm. The whole subject was associated with lowered voices; almost as if it were something medical. But supposing that by casting all these things into an imaginary world, stripping them of their stained-glass and Sunday school associations, one could make them for the first time appear in their real potency? Could one not thus steal past those watchful dragons? I thought one could."[55]

"One of the central threads of his 'Romantic theology' is a belief that certain images may act as temporary vessels of God, filling human beings with a longing, or *Sehnsucht*, for heaven."[56] Those images, Lewis felt, appear in the minds of other people and can be massaged by a good story with a deeper meaning, just as MacDonald had done for him. They can do the *praeparatio evangelica* at which Lewis aimed. This longing needs to be educated. In "The Weight of Glory," he stated that the problem was that we do not desire strongly enough what is heavenly. He said:

> We are half-hearted creatures, fooling about with drink and sex
> and ambition when infinite joy is offered us, like an ignorant

child who wants to go on making mud pies in a slum because he cannot imagine what is meant by the offer of a holiday at the sea. We are far too easily pleased.[57]

This Romantic theology, Lewis felt, can be conveyed especially well through the fairy tale. Since people think in images, we ought to write in images. Wrote Lewis, "It would be much truer to say that the fairy land arouses a longing for he knows not what. It stirs and troubles him (to his lifelong enrichment) with the dim sense of something beyond his reach and, far from dulling or emptying the actual world, gives it a new dimension of depth."[58] And here we are back to the concept of *Sehnsucht* once again.

The appeal of the fairy story, according to Tolkien, depends upon the reader exercising his function as a "subcreator." For Jung it lay in the "Archetypes which dwell in the collective unconscious, and when we read a good fairy tale, we are obeying the old precept 'Know thyself.'" For Lewis it lay in the other than human characters that behave as humans; they become "an admirable hieroglyphic which conveys psychology, types of character, more briefly than novelistic presentation and to readers whom novelistic presentation could not yet reach."[59] This "admirable hieroglyphic" to convey psychology and other concepts is exactly the technique used by MacDonald in *Phantastes*.

Stories, within which the fairy tale can be placed, call forth an imaginative response due to the giants or pirates or the moon or other people or objects in the story.[60] Writing about David Lindsay's *Voyage to Arcturus*, Lewis states:

Tormance, when we reach it, he forbodes, will be less interesting than Tormance from the Earth. But never will he have been more mistaken. Unaided by any special skill or even any sound taste in language, the author leads us up a stair of unpredictables. In each chapter we think we have found his final position; each time we are utterly mistaken. He builds whole worlds of imagery and passion, any one of which would have served another writer for a whole book, only to pull each of them to pieces and pour scorn on it. The physical dangers, which are plentiful, here count for nothing: it is we ourselves and the author who walk through a world of spiritual dangers which makes them seem trivial. . . . He is the first writer to discover what "other planets" are really good for in fiction. No merely physical strangeness or merely spatial distance will realize that idea of otherness which is what we are always trying to grasp in a story about voyaging through space: you must go into another dimension. To construct plausible and moving "other worlds" you must draw on the only real "other world" we know, that of the spirit.[61]

This, in fact, is what Narnia, Malacandra, and Perelandra do; they create other worlds within which Lewis can convey meaning. "Good stories often introduce the marvellous or supernatural. . . ."[62] Good stories provide ". . . a mythology [that] may serve as a guide, explaining conduct and regulating ethics on both material and spiritual planes."[63] Lewis's fantasy books fill this role. The structure of all of the mythical plots of these books is "the problem of human behavior."[64]

Lewis himself wrote, "Shall I be thought whimsical if, in conclusion, I suggest that this internal tension in the heart of every story between the theme and the plot constitutes, after all, its chief resemblance to life?"[65] Story gives us a plot, a direction, something that life does not always seem to have. People are drawn to story and imagine themselves in the story, stepping outside their world in a way not unlike the alcoholic who drinks to forget. They see themselves, their behavior, and the behavior of others.

Lewis wrote not so much about the story as about the need to view our experiences through the lens of the story.

As thinkers we are cut off from what we think about; as tasting, touching, willing, loving, hating, we do not clearly understand. The more lucidly we think, the more we are cut off: the more deeply we enter into reality, the less we can think. You cannot study Pleasure in the moment of the nuptial embrace, nor repentance while repenting, nor analyse the nature of humour while roaring with laughter. But when else can you really know these things? 'If only my toothache would stop, I could write another chapter about Pain.' But once it stops, what do I know about pain?[66]

The Chronicles of Narnia, then, perhaps best illustrate the value of story for evangelism. In *The Voyage of the "Dawn Treader,"* Lewis unveils one of the major reasons he wrote the Chronicles of Narnia. At the end of that book Aslan tells Lucy about another name that he has in our world. He further tells her that the reason she and the others were brought into Narnia was so they might later recognize him by his earthly name.[67] We are left to surmise that the name is Jesus, for just pages before, a white Lamb had morphed into the golden-maned Aslan after serving them a meal of fish (see John 21:12-13).

In commenting on that passage and others, Lewis wrote to eleven-year-old Hila, "As to Aslan's other name, well I want you to guess. Has there never been anyone in this world who (1.) Arrived at the same time as Father Christmas. (2.) Said he was the son of the Great Emperor. (3.) Gave himself up for someone else's fault to be jeered at and killed by wicked people. (4.) Came to life again. (5.) Is sometimes spoken of as a Lamb (see the end of the Dawn Treader). Don't you really know His name in this world? Think it over and let me know your answer!"[68]

In both the previous letter to Hila and a letter to thirteen-year-old Patricia, Lewis showed his gentle, pre-evangelistic style when he wrote, "Does not He say 'You have been allowed to know me in this world (Narnia) so that you may know me better when you get back to your own'?"[69] Obviously, his letters allowed him to do far more than baptize children's imaginations. He actually offered some of the instruction that ordinarily follows baptism, although without feeding the answers. He would much prefer the child (or any adult, for that matter) to discover the answer for herself.

When Lewis cited two reasons for writing an imaginative work, i.e., the author as author and the author as man, citizen, or Christian, he suggested that the Christian faith of the author may well be the rea-

Praeparatio Evangelica

son for writing imaginative stories. As this chapter has demonstrated, he has certainly said this was the case for himself.[70]

Lewis seemed to contradict himself, however, when he suggested that he had no explicitly Christian intent in his Narnia Chronicles. He wrote, "Some people seem to think that I began by asking myself how I could say something about Christianity to children; then fixed on the fairy tale as an instrument; then collected information about child-psychology and decided what age group I'd write for; then drew up a list of basic Christian truths and hammered out 'allegories' to embody them. This is all pure moonshine. I couldn't write in that way at all. Everything began with images; a faun carrying an umbrella, a queen on a sledge, a magnificent lion. At first there wasn't even anything Christian about them; that element pushed itself in of its own accord. It was part of the bubbling."[71]

Cannot both concepts exist side by side without contradiction? Could he not have written a story just for its own sake with the Christian element bubbling up of its own accord? Could he not then have thought, "Yes, that's good. That fits the purpose of my own writings. I won't force it, but I won't resist either"? Most likely, Lewis was so thoroughly Christian that the bubbling up was inevitable, whether conscious or not.

C. S. Lewis, the storyteller, especially aimed for children and for good reasons. "He simply regards children as more open to experience, and more open to being changed by experience."[72] "He simply believed that the evil could be more readily isolated, was less hidden beneath long-constructed trappings of adult rationality and evasion, and therefore might be more readily removed. He felt too that children's consciences were more acute. . . ."[73]

Though they might be more difficult to reach, Lewis had the same hope for adults, for he writes, "The inhibitions which I hoped my stories would overcome in a child's mind may exist in a grown-up's mind too, and may perhaps be overcome by the same means."[74]

C. N. Manlove writes, "Ransom in *Out of the Silent Planet* and *Perelandra* learns to undo his adult suspicions and inhibitions and open himself to full experience of strange new worlds; Mark and Jane

Studdock in *That Hideous Strength* must rediscover a childlike—not a childish—yielding of themselves to better directors than themselves of their confused lives."[75] Readers can see themselves in the Studdocks, and this identification by the reader with one or the other Studdock is the first step towards integrating the same solution to the problem that the Studdocks adopted.[76]

So how successful was Lewis in smuggling Christian theology through the story, awakening the innate longing for God that each person has (Ecclesiastes 3:11)? If the sales of his books are any indication, he has been wildly successful. He himself would admit, however, that "it is very difficult to tell in any given case whether a story is piercing to the unliterary reader's deeper imaginations or only exciting his emotions."[77] We could, I suppose, leave it to the angels in heaven, who rejoice over one sinner who repents (Luke 15:10), to determine what impact the fictional stories of C. S. Lewis have had on people. On the other hand, the testimonies of thousands answer that question for us on earth in the same way that it is undoubtedly answered in heaven.

Conclusion

Pre-evangelist and evangelist, proponent of the natural Law, smuggler of theology, author and apologist, storyteller and baptizer of imaginations, twentieth-century Elijah and preparer for the Gospel, Incarnationist. That was C. S. Lewis. If we learn anything from him about the evangelistic task, we learn the importance of preparation, patience, thinking the thoughts of the non-Christian, and clarity in our communication of God's truth. We learn also the necessity of the unwelcome diagnosis of sin and the wonderful vehicle of the story to convey both that unwelcome diagnosis and the cure—the Gospel of forgiveness through the suffering, death, and resurrection of Jesus Christ.

Bibliography

Dorsett, Lyle W., ed. *The Essential C. S. Lewis*. New York: Collier/Macmillan, 1988.

Praeparatio Evangelica

Dorsett, Lyle W., and Marjorie Lamp Mead, eds. *C. S. Lewis: Letters to Children*. New York: Simon & Schuster, 1985.

Ford, Paul F. *Companion to Narnia*. New York: HarperCollins Publishers, 1994.

Friad, Kimon and John Malcolm Brinnin. *Modern Poetry*. New York: Appleton-Century-Crofts, 1951.

Green, Roger Lancelyn and Walter Hooper. *C. S. Lewis: A Biography*. London: Collins, 1974.

Hooper, Walter. *Past Watchful Dragons*. New York: Collier Books/Macmillan, 1979.

Keillor, Garrison. "Caught Reading." *Christian Century*, April 10, 1996, 389.

Lindskoog, Kathryn. *The Lion of Judah in Never-Never Land*. Grand Rapids, MI: Eerdmans, 1973.

Lewis, C. S. "Christianity and Culture." In *Christian Reflections*. Ed. Walter Hooper. Grand Rapids, MI: Eerdmans, 1967, 12-36.

_____. "Fern-seed and Elephants." In *Fern-seed and Elephants*. Ed. Walter Hooper. Glasgow: Fount Paperbacks, 1975, 104-25.

_____. "God in the Dock." In *God in the Dock*. Ed. Walter Hooper. Grand Rapids, MI: Eerdmans, 1970, 240-44.

_____. *The Horse and His Boy*. New York: Macmillan, 1954.

_____. *Mere Christianity*. New York: Macmillan, 1952.

_____. "Modern Translations of the Bible." In *God in the Dock*. Ed. Walter Hooper. Grand Rapids, MI: Eerdmans, 1970, 229-33.

_____. "Myth Became Fact." In *God in the Dock*. Ed. Walter Hooper. Grand Rapids, MI: Eerdmans, 1970, 63-67.

_____. "On Stories," in *Of Other Worlds: Essays and Stories*. Ed. Walter Hooper. New York: Harcourt, Brace & Company, 1966, 3-21.

_____. "On Three Ways of Writing for Children." In *Of Other Worlds: Essays and Stories*. Ed. Walter Hooper. New York: Harcourt, Brace & Company, 1966, 22-34.

_____. *The Pilgrim's Regress*. London: Fount Paperbacks, 1977.

_____. "Rejoinder to Dr Pittenger." In *God in the Dock*. Ed. Walter Hooper. Grand Rapids, MI: Eerdmans, 1970, 177-83.

_____. *The Screwtape Letters & Screwtape Proposes a Toast*. New York: Macmillan, 1961.

_____. "Sometimes Fairy Stories May Say Best What's to Be Said." In *Of Other Worlds: Essays and Stories*. Ed. Walter Hooper. New York: Harcourt, Brace & Company, 1966, 35-38.

_____. *That Hideous Strength*. New York: Macmillan, 1946.

_____. *The Voyage of the "Dawn Treader."* New York: Macmillan, 1952.

Lewis, Warren. *Letters of C. S. Lewis*. London: Fount Paperbacks, 1966.

MacDonald, George. *Phantastes*. Grand Rapids, MI: Eerdmans, 1981.

Manlove, C. N. *The Chronicles of Narnia*. New York: Twayne Publishers, 1993.

_____. *C. S. Lewis: His Literary Achievement*. New York: St. Martin's Press, 1987.

Morris, A. Clifford. "C. S. Lewis Was My Friend," *His*, October 1978 (Vol. 39, No. 1), 7-12.

Sayer, George. *Jack: A Life of C. S. Lewis*. Wheaton, IL: Crossway Books, 1988.

Vanauken, Sheldon. *A Severe Mercy*. San Francisco: Harper & Row, 1980.

Walther, C. F. W. *God's No and God's Yes*. St. Louis: Concordia, 1973.

NOTES

1. Morris, "C. S. Lewis Was My Friend," 12.

2. Dorsett, *The Essential C. S. Lewis*, 11.

3. Greek for "those outside."

4. Lewis, "Rejoinder to Dr Pittenger," 181.

5. By "the one" Lewis means the North—narrow anti-Christian dogmatism.

6. Lewis, *The Pilgrim's Regress*, 18.

7. Ibid., 203.

8. Ibid., 196.

9. Ibid., 193.

10. Lewis, *Letters of C. S. Lewis*, 462-63.

11. Dorsett uses the term of Lewis, 8.

12. Lewis, *Mere Christianity*, 6.

13. Dorsett, *The Essential C. S. Lewis*, 8.

14. Lewis, "Fern-seed and Elephants," 105.

15. Lewis, "Christianity and Culture," 14.

16. Sayer, *Jack*, 231.

17. Lewis, *Mere Christianity*, 169-70.

18. Green and Hooper, *C. S. Lewis: A Biography*, 202. A penetrating analysis of the state of the non-Christian audience of Lewis's works is undertaken by George Musacchio in the previous chapter in this volume.

19. The theme of evading our evil natures is pursued at greater length by Jerry Root in this volume.

Praeparatio Evangelica

20. Lewis, "God in the Dock," 243.

21. Ibid., 244.

22. Lewis, *That Hideous Strength*, 50.

23. Ibid., 140.

24. Lewis, *The Screwtape Letters*, 27.

25. Lewis, *The Pilgrim's Regress*, 28.

26. Lewis, *The Voyage of the "Dawn Treader,"* 75-76.

27. Ibid., 90.

28. Lewis, *The Horse and His Boy*, 86.

29. Ibid., 145.

30. Ibid., 146.

31. Lewis, *The Magician's Nephew*, 135.

32. Green and Hooper, *C. S. Lewis: A Biography*, 203.

33. Lewis, *Mere Christianity*, I.5.

34. Dorsett, *The Essential C. S. Lewis*, 11.

35. Walther, *God's No and God's Yes*, 33.

36. Sayer, *Jack*, 318.

37. Manlove, *The Chronicles of Narnia*, 5.

38. Vanauken, *A Severe Mercy*, 83-84.

39. Lewis, *Letters of C. S. Lewis*, 166-67.

40. Dorsett, *The Essential C. S. Lewis*, 9.

41. Ibid., 10.

42. Ibid., 15.

43. Green and Hooper, *C. S. Lewis: A Biography*, 129.

44. Lewis, "Rejoinder to Dr Pittenger," 183.

45. Ibid., 182.

46. Both Mueller and Rossow in this volume explore at greater length the idea of Lewis's work as translating theology.

47. Lewis, "Modern Translations of the Bible," 231.

48. Lewis, "God in the Dock," 242.

49. Ibid., 243.

50. Ibid., 242-243.

51. Lindskoog, *The Lion of Judah in Never-Never Land*, 13.

52. Keillor, "Caught Reading," 389.

53. MacDonald, *Phantastes*, xi.

54. Lewis, "On Stories," 16.

55. Lewis, "Sometimes Fairy Stories May Say Best What's to Be Said," 37.

56. Manlove, *The Chronicles of Narnia*, 6.

57. Lewis, "The Weight of Glory," in Dorsett, *The Essential C. S. Lewis*, 362.

58. Lewis, "On Stories," 29.

59. Lewis, "On Three Ways of Writing for Children," 27.

60. Lewis, "On Stories," 8.

61. Ibid., 12.

62. Ibid., 13.

63. Friad and Brinnin, *Modern Poetry*, 421-22.

64. Lindskoog, *The Lion of Judah in Never-Never Land*, 87.

65. Lewis, "On Stories," 20.

66. Lewis, "Myth Became Fact," 65-66.

67. Ford, *Companion to Narnia*, 61.

68. Dorsett and Mead, *C. S. Lewis: Letters to Children*, 32.

69. Ibid., 93. And ". . . by knowing me here for a little, you may know me better there" (216, *The Voyage of the "Dawn Treader"*).

70. Lewis, "Sometimes Fairy Stories May Say Best What's to Be Said," 35.

71. Ibid., 36.

72. Manlove, *C. S. Lewis: His Literary Achievement*, 121.

73. Ibid.

74. Lewis, "Sometimes Fairy Stories May Say Best What's to Be Said," 38.

75. Manlove, *C. S. Lewis: His Literary Achievement*, 121.

76. For more on Lewis's engaging portrayal of conversion and on the conversion of the Studdocks in particular, see Michael Ward's chapter in this volume.

77. Lewis, "On Stories," 17.

OLD WINE IN
NEW WINESKINS[1]

FRANCIS C. ROSSOW

In the last chapter of *The Silver Chair* by C. S. Lewis, Jill Pole and Eustace Scrubb, having just witnessed the death of King Caspian in Narnia, are suddenly whisked off to Aslan's Country. When they arrive they see the body of King Caspian lying on the gravel bed of a clear stream (a common metaphor for death). Even Aslan weeps huge lion tears at the sight. Suddenly he commands Eustace to pluck a thorn from a nearby thicket and jab it into the lion's right front foot. Reluctantly, Eustace obeys. When he plunges the foot-long thorn into Aslan's paw, a huge drop of blood issues from the wound, splashing into the stream immediately above the corpse of the king. Not only is King Caspian resurrected, but all his youth and vigor are restored. In the ecstatic reunion scene that follows, Eustace suddenly checks his mirth with a worried question, "Hasn't he—er—died?" For which the resurrected king calls him an ass and to which Aslan replies, "He has died. Most people have, you know. Even I have."[2]

It occurs to me that this incident can serve as an inductive approach to the subject of this article: C. S. Lewis's capacity to give familiar Christian doctrine a new translation. Not only does the episode highlight that ability but also, as a bonus, exemplifies some of the multiple methods through which he exercises his skill. Even a Sunday school beginner will right away recognize echoes of some familiar Christian teachings: physical death and subsequent bodily resurrection to life in heaven (alias Aslan's Country) and the role of Christ's saving blood in effecting that miracle. But there is more in the scene—much more. The use of the thorn, for example, calls to mind not only the crown of thorns in our Savior's Passion but also the thorns (along with thistles and sweat, Genesis 3:18-19) symbolizing the consequences of the sin of Adam and Eve that necessitated the shedding of Christ's blood for human salvation.

Still more: the fact that Aslan's paw is wounded echoes the familiar assurance of the first biblical gospel promise that in His victorious struggle with Satan and sin, Christ's heel would be bruised—it would be a painful and costly victory for Him (Genesis 3:15). The lion's tears remind the reader of Jesus' weeping at Lazarus' tomb. The matter-of-fact, even humorous dismissal of Eustace's reservations about Caspian's prior death do more than volumes of sermons in portraying the delightful contrast between our shabby fears about death and the ecstatic joys attendant upon the bodily resurrection of loved ones.

Tucked into the middle of this humorous exchange is an ever-so-casual allusion to the death of Aslan (Christ) and the incarnation that made that death possible: "He [Caspian] has died. Most people have, you know. Even I have." That same remark, incidentally, hints at the familiar syllogistic premise, "All men are mortal." Perhaps even the fact that Eustace plunges the thorn into Aslan's paw is not only a reminder of our involvement in our Lord's death (we were indeed there when they crucified our Lord), but also an encouragement to us to tell and apply the saving Gospel to the human condition. Whether these latter inferences are legitimate or not, certainly the scene calls to mind an earlier incident in *The Silver Chair* where Puddleglum, the Marshwiggle, injures his foot in stamping out the Green Lady's magic fire, thereby saving his companions from her deadly enchantment—suggesting the scriptural parallel that we are to be little Christs and that vicariousness is to be a Christian way of life.

What can we infer about Lewis's methodology already from this initial example? To begin with, the economy of his metaphors. Look at all the Christian doctrines associated with a thorn-wounded lion's paw! So much from so little. Lewis's metaphors explode with possible meanings. To resort to metaphor myself, whenever Lewis throws a gospel rock into the water, the reader not only easily recognizes the point of impact but also experiences the thrill of seeing an ever-widening circle of doctrinal ripples. Where it will stop, who can say? Not to see these ripples at all is to be imperceptive; to see too many of them is to risk converting narrative into catechism (the risk this article—by the mere fact that it is undertaken—inevitably flirts with).

Even more evident in Lewis's methodology is his ability to suggest a truth rather than to state it explicitly—incidentally, a universally acknowledged literary virtue. In reply to a child in America who had written Lewis for some writing tips, Lewis had advised her not to use adjectives that merely tell the reader how the writer wants him to feel about the thing he is describing. "Instead of telling us a thing was 'terrible,'" Lewis continued, "describe it so that we'll be terrified. Don't say it was 'delightful,' make us say 'delightful' when we've read the description."[3] That Lewis practiced the precept he preached is evident from the incident cited above from *The Silver Chair*. Nowhere in that account does Lewis spoonfeed the reader by identifying Aslan as Christ or Aslan's Country as heaven. Thank goodness he did not cite Genesis 3:15 in depicting the wounding of Aslan's paw. He does not explain things (as I am doing in this article). Had he done so, he might have eliminated all possible disagreement in interpretation, but he would have eliminated all the fun of reading, too.

I will now turn to a few more examples from Lewis's novels, arranged in a doctrinally systematic manner, and then conclude with a brief response to the "*Cui bono*? / So what?" question: What difference does Lewis's approach to Christian doctrine make to our reception of and proclamation of the Christian Gospel?

THE FALL / ORIGINAL SIN

In *Out of the Silent Planet*, a space novel, Dr. Ransom, an inadvertent visitor to Mars, has a disconcerting moment when one of Mars's rational inhabitants, a sorn, shows him far-off in deep space the planet Earth from which Ransom had traveled. It was upside down—suggesting not merely a credible geographical possibility but also a probable theological truth. Earth is a fallen planet where everything is topsy-turvy, upside down. "It was the bleakest moment in all his travels," Ransom admits.[4]

In *Perelandra*, the sequel to *Out of the Silent Planet*, C. S. Lewis encounters for the first time an eldil (angel?) in the home of his friend, Dr. Ransom. It appears as a shaft of humming light, surprisingly, however, not striking the floor of the room vertically or at right angles. But Lewis immediately attaches an amendment to his description of the phenomenon: "What one actually felt at the moment was that the column of light was vertical but the floor was not horizontal."[5] Once again there is the faint suggestion that it is our world that is askew, our times that are out of joint—the result of some cataclysmic catastrophe.

It is in *The Pilgrim's Regress* that we encounter Lewis's most efficient metaphor for that cataclysmic catastrophe (the fall of humankind into sin): the metaphor of "The Grand Canyon." Not only does the word *canyon* suggest the unbridgeableness (by human effort) of the vast chasm between God and people that sin effected, but also the word *grand* captures the false appeal and lure of sin ("good for food," "pleasant to the eyes," Genesis 3:6).

The strategy Satan used in effecting the fall into sin is portrayed by Lewis the most completely and artistically in his account of Weston's temptation of the Green Lady in *Perelandra*. As her name suggests, the woman, like Eve initially, is innocent—"green" in respect to evil. Just as our first parents were forbidden to eat of a certain tree in their garden, so the Green Lady is forbidden to dwell on the Fixed Island on the planet Venus. But Dr. Weston, Satan's agent (perhaps Satan himself), tries to persuade her to dwell there anyhow in disobedience to Maleldil's clear directive. Weston's first ploy is merely to have the Green Lady *think* about living on the Fixed Island. Certainly no harm in that; after all, Weston adds, Maleldil hadn't forbidden the thought, just the act. Next Weston hints that Maleldil only *seemed* to forbid residence on the Fixed Island. (The Christian reader immediately calls to mind the "Yea, hath God said?" of Genesis. 3:1.)

Weston pursues the point: what Maleldil is really hoping for is that the woman will demonstrate courage by asserting herself and achieving independence. You will be a little Maleldil, he suggests more than once (echoing for the Christian reader the "Ye shall be as gods" of Genesis 3:5). Weston incessantly prods the lady toward the Great Deed, the Great Risk, the Upward Path, the Deeper Life. At one point he clothes her in a garment made of feathers (intriguingly called "leaves" on one occasion) and has her look into a mirror as steps toward vanity and pride. Weston's climactic thrust is to convince the Green Lady that as Eve's disobedience on Earth resulted in a glorious plan of salvation (called by theologians the *felix culpa*), so the Green Lady's disobedience might result in an even more glorious plan of salvation for Venus. Although the Green Lady (unlike Eve) does not succumb to the temptation, thanks to Maleldil's intervention through his instrument Dr. Ransom (note the name), the scene richly documents the Scriptures' claim that the serpent was more "subtle" than any beast of the field (Genesis 3:1).

Actual Sin: Its Belittling and Destructive Nature

It is in *The Great Divorce* that Lewis most fully and graphically portrays the capacity of sin to diminish and destroy us. Lewis pictures the damned as people whom sin has reduced to smudged, translucent ghosts; one can see through them, but only as through a dirty window. When a possessive mother (a visitor from hell) asks to see her child in heaven, snatched away from her by an early death, the request has to be denied because the petitioner isn't thick enough to be visible to the eyes of the saved child! In the same novel a grumbler becomes a grumble; that is, a person degenerates into a mere trait, the concrete becomes abstract. Robert's wife (on leave from hell), insisting too vociferously and loquaciously on controlling the formation of her husband (a resident of heaven), suddenly snaps and disintegrates; all that remains is a sour smell. A sort of "split personality" from hell is pictured as a dwarf leading a tragedian (or vice versa). As the tragedian takes over in his expression of falsely tragic and theatrical martyr-like views, the dwarf gets smaller and smaller and finally disappears; even the chain is swallowed up.

Old Wine in New Wineskins

The most vivid example of sin's capacity to destroy our humanity is that of Eustace Clarence Scrubb in *The Voyage of the "Dawn Treader."* Persisting in dragonish thoughts transforms this boy into a literal dragon, and the reader right away calls to mind the proverb that as a man thinks in his heart, so is he (Proverbs 23:7).

All these pictures are worth a thousand words in their ability to portray the belittling, destructive character of sin.

DEATH

Early in *The Pilgrim's Regress*, John, still a lad, is initiated into the flummery and hypocrisy so often accompanying the phenomenon of death—even in allegedly Christian circles. One day John finds "a great hubbub" in his house: his parents crying, the Steward (the pastor) present with a mask on. The explanation given is that the Landlord (God) has informed Uncle George that "his lease is up"; he has given Uncle George "notice to quit." Even though everyone, including Uncle George, had thought his lease would last for many more years, the Steward piously reminds the group that the Landlord always reserves "the right to turn anyone out whenever he chooses" and that it's really decent of him to let any of us remain on earth at all. To which John's parents agree with pious and time-worn clichés and to which Uncle George himself replies in classic self-contradiction, "I'm not complaining. . . . But it seems cruelly hard." Assured that he's being turned out here only to be made more comfortable somewhere else, Uncle George nods in agreement but can't find his voice.

To witness Uncle George's "journey," John is dressed in ugly, uncomfortable clothes that are tight under the arms and make him itch all over. After Uncle George has gone, the Steward uncorks a final cliché, "We've all got to go when our time comes," and both he and John's father immediately take up the more comfortable subject of how to dispose of Uncle George's pigs in the most profitable way possible (a scene reminiscent of Justice Shallow's memorable juxtaposition: "Death, as the Psalmist saith, is certain to all; all shall die. How a good yoke of bullocks at Stamford fair?").[6] In conversation with his mother, John learns that the Landlord frowns on human initiative in breaking the lease and that exercising that initiative risks being put into the black hole (hell). Even though the family officially acknowledges that all who break the Landlord's rules are in danger of the black hole and that all, in fact, have broken them, they deny to young John that Uncle George has broken the rules. "Uncle George was a very good man," John's mother affirms in an unguarded, works-righteous moment. To which John makes the devastating reply, "You never told me that before," a remark catching all of us at the discrepancy between our evaluations of people while they are alive and our evaluations of people after they are dead.[7]

A more positive portrait of death is provided in *The Last Battle*. There Lewis uses the metaphor of the stable door for death. In the battle that rages near the stable door between Aslan's followers and the followers of the false god Tash, the stable door is viewed as a place to avoid at all costs. Reportedly, it contains horrors (as indeed it does for the "unbelievers"). Losing the battle and eventually forced against their will through the dreaded stable door, the followers of Aslan experience a pleasant surprise: they are alive, cool, refreshed, fed, and reunited with all their friends who preceded them through the same door. Best of all, Aslan himself welcomes them. The explanation given is that the stable seen from within and the stable seen from without are two entirely different places—a simple way of capturing the discrepancy between appearance and reality in our own consideration of death. Even better, Lord Digory adds, the inside of the stable "is bigger than its outside," an observation reminding Lucy of a Stable in her own world that once contained "something inside it that was bigger than our whole world."[8] This allusion to the incarnation and birth of Jesus not only reminds us of the parallel discrepancy between appearance and reality in that earth-shaking event but also subtly suggests the truth conveyed in Hebrews 2:14—namely, that Christ partook of our human nature in order to experience death, so that through death He might destroy the devil, who had the power of death, and deliver us who, through fear of death, were all our lifetime subject to bondage.

Old Wine in New Wineskins

HELL

The picture of hell Lewis provides in the opening pages of *The Great Divorce* always reminds me of the desolation I view from the window of an Amtrak coach when I travel through the downtown section of some large city: windowless gray warehouses, tattered billboards, haphazardly stacked drums, weeds, and debris everywhere. The occupants of hell are forever quarreling and moving away from one another, some achieving separation distances of millions of miles. Yet capacious as hell is from the perspective of its denizens, it is, compared to the vast reaches of heaven, little more than a hard-to-see crack in the ground, a thing that if swallowed by one of heaven's butterflies would escape its notice.

As pointed out earlier, the damned themselves are mere vapors, translucent because they are too stained to be transparent. They don't cut heaven's grass—it cuts them! Too hard to walk on, the grass of heaven can be seen through their feet. They are unable to pluck the flowers of heaven or budge its golden apples. When one of them requests an interview with a relative in heaven, the request has to be denied because the petitioner isn't thick enough to be visible! The title of the novel *The Great Divorce* calls attention, of course, to the great gulf between heaven and hell alluded to in our Lord's parable of the rich man and Lazarus (Luke 16:26), unbridgeable, as Lewis portrays it, more for psychological than for geographical reasons. Even when "heretically" given a chance to span the chasm and visit heaven, the damned refuse to remain there. One of them (with delicious irony) insists that he'll "be damned" before he puts up with something so silly as salvation by grace. The doors of hell are, first of all, locked from the inside—only afterwards locked also from the outside. To people unable to say to God, "Thy will be done," God ultimately and reluctantly replies, "Thy will be done"—and, of course, that's the hell of it.

As Lewis himself cautions in the preface to *The Great Divorce*, all these images, suggestive as they are of the insubstantiality of hell and its occupants, are not to be taken too literally. Perhaps a more accurate portrait of the nature of hell (as utter, absolute, and final separation

from God) is provided in *Perelandra* by Dr. Weston. Weston himself is
an argument for the facticity and contemporaneity of demonic possession as he is so dedicated to the service of Satan that Satan has taken
over his personality. Weston is an It, a Thing, a Bogey, Un-Man, a mech-
anized corpse, the mere sight of whom constitutes a "Miserific Vision."
Is it Weston or Satan? So uncertain is the reader of the man's identity
that he may be tempted, in imitation of a popular television program
a few years back, to ask, "Will the true Weston please stand up?" At
any rate, this Weston (or Satan) in one place describes the universe as
a globe with a very thin crust on the outside, about "seventy years thick
in the best places." Born on the surface, a human being spends his life
sinking through that surface. When he's all the way through, he is what
people call "dead." God, meanwhile, is outside the globe "like a
moon." "As we pass into the interior," Weston continues, "we pass out
of His ken. He doesn't follow us in."[9] Nowhere, in my opinion, does
Lewis, through metaphor, more accurately—and more horrifyingly—
capture the ultimate character of hell as separation from God.

Always interested in theodicy, in "justifying the ways of God to
man," Lewis gives a novel twist to the doctrine of hell in *The Pilgrim's
Regress*. Without in any way denying the reality, permanence, or horrors of the self-chosen hell that the damned experience, Lewis
describes hell as a place of "fixed pains" and "eternal bounds" beyond
which even the damned in their search for misery and corruption cannot go. Elsewhere in the same book Lewis describes the fixed limits of
hell as "the tourniquet on the wound" without which the lost soul
"would bleed to a death she never reached." It is God's "last service
to those who will let him do nothing better for them."[10] Despite the
potential for false doctrine in Lewis's tourniquet metaphor, it strikes
me as a responsible effort on his part to accent the mercy of God without cooling the temperature of hell.

REPENTANCE

In *The Great Divorce*, the reader encounters a man with a red lizard
on his shoulder (a symbol of the sin of lust that the bearer had been

Old Wine in New Wineskins

luxuriating in all his life). Despite the pleasures the lizard had provided him, the man finds the creature to be an embarrassing nuisance. When an angel volunteers to help him get rid of his problem, the man consents—until he learns that killing the lizard is what the angel has in mind. The lust-ridden man had not expected so drastic a solution. He would prefer to have the lizard removed gradually, "some other day, perhaps."[11] The angel cautions the man that the gradual process will be of no use at all. Nor will he guarantee that the solution will be painless. After considerable dialogue, the man permits the angel to do what he likes with the lizard. The next moment there is a piercing scream of pain from the man, but he is free of the lizard—it lies broken-backed on the turf. Repentance, the episode suggests, is not easy. It is not a compromise with sin. It is not a cavalier promise to turn over a new leaf. It is not a sort of halfhearted New Year's Day resolution made in a moment of painful sobriety. Rather, repentance is radical, revolutionary, drastic. It is, as the Bible suggests with its own effective metaphor, like amputating a hand or a foot or like gouging out an eye (Mark 9:43, 45, 47).

But that isn't all. In *The Great Divorce*, the erstwhile fornicator suddenly becomes a sort of Prince Charming and the lizard is transformed into a noble stallion, designed for the ridership of the man whom the lizard before had ridden. How suggestive this is of the truth that repentance is not merely a negative experience, a painful loss of something, but also a positive experience, an ecstatic gain of something. "If any man be in Christ, he is a new creature: old things are passed away; behold, all things are become new"(2 Corinthians 5:17, KJV). Instead of being controlled, the man is now in control. Instead of finding pleasure eliminated, he finds pleasure transformed and multiplied.

The same is true of Eustace Clarence Scrubb, alluded to earlier, the lad whose dragonish thoughts had converted him into a dragon. Through the efforts of Aslan—and of Aslan alone—Eustace is dedragoned, not only negatively, getting rid of his dragon skin, but also positively, being restored to boyhood. Despite occasional relapses (*simul iustus et peccator?*), Eustace becomes a much better boy, fit for human companionship.

The Holy Scriptures

At one point in *The Voyage of the "Dawn Treader,"* Lucy is commissioned to find a spell in The Magician's Book that will restore the strange creatures called Dufflepuds to the visibleness they had once enjoyed. As she pages through the various spells in the beautiful book, Lucy is tempted to misuse the book, in one instance, by reading the spell that will make her so beautiful, she will be the envy of all other girls. In another instance she does succumb to a temptation, that of reading the spell that enables her to hear what her alleged friends are saying about her, an experience that causes her considerable grief. Ultimately, she finds the spell she was commissioned to find, the formula for making unseen things seen, and restores the Dufflepuds to visibility.

But there is a bonus: it renders Aslan visible too. Moments later the lion appears in the room, claiming to have been present all the time but made visible now through Lucy's use of The Magician's Book. In addition, Lucy, in the course of her search for the appropriate formula, had encountered a delightful story about a cup, a sword, a tree, and a hill. Although it is just as easy to find mythological equivalents to the items in this story,[12] it seems reasonable to see in these same ingredients parallels to aspects of our Lord's Passion: the cup being the cup of the upper chamber or of Gethsemane; the sword being Peter's weapon or the sword referred to in Luke 22:38; the tree and hill being references to the cross and to Calvary. Ever since her exposure to that portion of The Magician's Book, Lucy regards as a good story, Lewis tells us, any story that reminds her of the story of the cup, the sword, the tree, and the hill. "Shall I ever be able to read that story again?" Lucy asks Aslan. "I will tell it to you for years and years," Aslan assures her.[13]

Although the association of The Magician's Book with the Holy Scriptures, as well as the story of the cup, sword, tree, and hill with the gospel event in those Scriptures, is obviously more debatable than some of our prior associations, it seems at least mildly defensible. The Bible, like The Magician's Book, can all too easily be misused for superstitious, even unethical purposes. But used properly, the Bible not only accomplishes much good but, above all, renders Christ "visible." In short, the Scriptures reveal God. What's more, the Gospel is the most delightful, the most central, narrative in those Scriptures, a story that will be told for all time, "for years and years."

THE REALITY AND NATURE OF GOD

Despite Lewis's fondness for metaphor, God is never a metaphor in Lewis's theology. Rather, God is "Eternal Fact, the Father of all other facthood."[14] (One is tempted to quip, "very fact of very fact.") When an artist surveying the splendors of heaven exclaims, "God!" a resident of heaven replies, "God what? . . . In our grammar God is a noun."[15] The reply suggests that God, like a concrete noun, has definiteness, specificity; moreover, that God is a God who acts, even as a noun is usually followed by an action word called a verb ("God what?").

No one learns the lesson about the reality of God more dramatically than Bree, the proud and sophisticated talking horse in *The Horse and His Boy*. Asked one day by Aravis whether Aslan is really a lion, Bree condescendingly responds to the girl, "No, no, of course not."[16] He goes on to explain in his professorial style ("in rather a superior tone with his eyes half shut"[17]) that Aslan is merely represented as a lion to give us some idea of his strength, majesty, awesomeness, etc. Why, if he were a lion, Bree continues to lecture, he'd have to have paws, a tail, even whiskers. During Bree's lengthy and arrogant presentation, Aravis and her companions see Aslan, the lion, leap over a wall and, unseen by Bree, approach him from behind, eventually touching Bree's ear with his whiskers. Bree jumps the proverbial mile. It is the moment of truth. Bree discovers that God is for real and that His incarnation is no metaphor.

Although Aslan, the lion, is no metaphor in the world of Narnia, the lion becomes a metaphor for Christ when we turn to our world— for that Christ who became a man for our salvation (a transformation, again, that is no metaphor). To depict Christ in the metaphor of a lion not only has biblical warrant[18] but also is an effective way of capturing both the majesty and the tenderness of the Son of God. Throughout its history the Christian Church has had to guard against the extremes of picturing God either as too frightening or as too cuddly, and Lewis's lion metaphor for Christ helps us maintain a proper balance. On the one hand, the lion's appearance is majestic, his mien stern, his roar terrifying, his limbs awesome in their powerfulness. On the other hand, his breath is sweet, his fur soft, the tread of his feet gentle, and on occasion he romps with the Pevensie children.

Our age, of course, errs in the direction of trivializing and "informalizing" God, portraying Him as a sort of generous Santa Claus, Universal Dad, or "the Man Upstairs," a sort of avuncular deity who likes to see the young people enjoy themselves and who hopes that everyone has a good time. Lewis's depiction of the Son of God as a lion combats that distortion. "Aslan is not a tame lion" is a frequent refrain in the Chronicles of Narnia. "'Course he isn't safe," says Mr. Beaver. "But he's good. He's the King, I tell you."[19] There is nothing anemic or namby-pamby about Lewis's portrait of God. His lion metaphor helps us recapture the vision of God that Isaiah describes in the sixth chapter of his book.[20]

THE VICARIOUS ATONEMENT

No doctrine of the Scriptures receives more frequent "translation" in Lewis's novels than that of Christ's vicarious life, death, and resurrection. Since I have already briefly alluded to one such "translation" in the introductory paragraphs of this article, I shall limit myself here to just one more, the most famous one, namely that in *The Lion, the Witch and the Wardrobe*.

In that book Edmund proves to be a traitor to Aslan, the other Pevensie children, and all of Narnia. Stoked with Turkish Delight and promised a kingship, Edmund strikes up an alliance with the White Witch, who has cast a spell over Narnia, making it always winter there but never Christmas. After Aslan wins a major battle, thereby delivering Narnia from the immediate consequences of Edmund's treachery

Old Wine in New Wineskins

and breaking the Witch's spell, the White Witch reminds Aslan that Edmund still belongs to her. She cites the Deep Magic written on the Stone Table nearby that every traitor belongs to her as her lawful prey, that his life is forfeit to her and his blood is her property.[21] Much to the Pevensies' dismay, Aslan acknowledges the legitimacy of her claim and cautions them that they cannot ignore or work against the Deep Magic.

Aslan, however, takes Edmund's place. He voluntarily submits to the White Witch and her cronies and, in a scene echoing many aspects of our Lord's Passion, lets them bind him, mock him, and finally stab him to death on the very Stone Table where the Deep Magic is engraved.

Throughout that night Lucy and Susan sadly hold a wake over the lion's corpse. But at sunrise they witness an unexpected event. The Stone Table cracks in two, and the lion rises from death. A delightful romp with the children is the high spot in the ecstatic reunion scene that follows. By way of explanation Aslan calls to their attention an even "Deeper Magic from before the dawn of time," a magic unknown to the White Witch, that "when a willing victim who had committed no treachery was killed in a traitor's stead, the Table would crack and Death itself would start working backwards."[22] Aslan and his followers then go on to complete the rout of the Witch and the deliverance of Narnia.

Although some Christian readers have been disappointed that Aslan's substitute death is for just one individual rather than for all, most thrill to the numerous echoes in this event of Christ's saving life, death, and resurrection. And some have even seen in Lewis's portrayal not a denial of objective justification (a denial Lewis never intended) but rather an accent on subjective justification, that as Aslan died for one person, Edmund, so Christ died for the individual—specifically for me.

HEAVEN

As the sailors in *The Voyage of the "Dawn Treader"* approach the end of their world and Aslan's Country beyond it, the sun grows bigger and the light brighter. Everyone requires less sleep. The water they drink is sweeter and more satisfying; it literally brightens their features and makes them look younger. Only Reepicheep at the time is allowed to enter Aslan's Country, but for a brief moment the others get a beatific glimpse of the place: incredibly high but warm mountains teeming with vegetation and waterfalls, emanating a riot of colors and emitting exotic smells.

What Aslan's Country is really like is most evident in *The Last Battle*. When the Narnians arrive there through the stable door, they can run endlessly without fatigue and defy gravity as they climb mountains and swim up waterfalls. One of the most pleasurable sights is that of a unicorn scaling a waterfall and dividing the water with his solitary horn into two rainbow-colored cascades. There is a hilarious reunion with friends, loved ones, and acquaintances long gone. Even though gray hair and wrinkles disappear, everyone remains recognizable. The fruits they taste give pleasure that words cannot describe. Life there, as Lewis suggests elsewhere, is "trans-sensuous" rather than "non-sensuous."[23] The more the residents explore heaven, the wider and bigger it gets. It is—spatially, not only chronologically—"world without end." The Narnians discover that even if they try, they are incapable of being afraid or of wanting wrong things. All of them feel they are home at last. The book ends with a passage that gives many a reader goose bumps: "All their life in this world and all their adventures in Narnia had only been the cover and the title page; now at last they were beginning Chapter One of the Great Story, which no one on earth has read; which goes on for ever; in which every chapter is better than the one before."[24]

The caution with which Lewis prefaces his depiction of heaven in *The Great Divorce* no doubt applies as well to the descriptions provided above. They are not necessarily meant to be taken literally, nor "to arouse factual curiosity about the details of the after-world."[25] Nonetheless, they are richly suggestive of the quality of eternal life in heaven and of the delight we shall experience there.

It is *The Great Divorce*, of course, that provides the most stirring and the most complete portrait of that afterworld. In this fantasy the damned are "heretically" allowed to visit heaven for a look-see. There is, surprisingly, nothing ethereal, abstract, or "cloud-nineish" about what they see. The heavenly phenomena are consistently more concrete than the biblical/theological language (in their experience) describing those phenomena. The reality they examine is always more definite, more specific, more tangible (seeable, hearable, touchable, smellable) than the verbal descriptions they had previously encountered. As Lewis states elsewhere, "It is words that are vague. The reason why the thing can't be expressed is that it's too definite for language."[26] Thus, the rivers in heaven are like swiftly moving glass, waterfalls talk, the grass cuts, raindrops are like bullets, flowers are heavy as boulders, and apples can't be budged (at least by the damned). But all of these pose no problem for the saved—or the Solid People, as Lewis calls them. For them, truth tastes like honey and embraces them like a bridegroom.[27] You can't see through the Solid People; given the circumstances, they make a noise as they tramp across the floor and cast a shadow in the sunlight. Heat and light emanate from them; they are also called "Bright Spirits." Virtues like joy, courtesy, and honor are so tangible that they serve as clothing to the saved. Sarah Smith's love for others, for instance, is "liquid."

Cui Bono? / SO WHAT?

What difference does Lewis's "translation" of Christian doctrine make to our reception and proclamation of that doctrine?

It is my guess that for most readers of C. S. Lewis's works, a formal answer to this question is unnecessary. Exposed to the new translations Lewis has accorded Christian doctrine, these readers will be so enamored of and edified by what they read that what they read requires no defense. The proof has been in the pudding.

Nonetheless, even the Lewis enthusiast may appreciate a fleshing out in words of the good feelings he has about the value of what Lewis has done.

In the introduction to this article I described two techniques that Lewis has mastered: the snowballing metaphor and the art of suggestion. Both of these techniques invite reader participation. "Can the snowball receive still *another* layer? Is it possible that Lewis is suggesting *that* also in this passage?" Questions like these occurring to the reader demonstrate that he is involved not merely in the reading experience but, to a degree, in the writing activity as well. The reader fills in the blanks that Lewis provides. Lewis baits the hook, and we latch onto it—with this basic difference, that being caught and hauled in is a pleasurable experience. (Blessed are these fish!) We experience the thrill of discovery, the joy of seeing familiar truths in unexpected settings and in new arrangements, the excitement of seeing much-loved doctrines in a fresh perspective. The result is considerable "reader identification"— always the mark of successful communication, whatever the genre.

But there is even greater value in such reader involvement than being involved. To see Christian doctrine in a new perspective is sometimes to see it (really see it) for the first time—at the very least, to see it better than before. Of course, there is always the possibility of altering the doctrine itself in the process of according it a new translation. Content can never be totally divorced from form. To change form can, admittedly, change the substance—and sometimes for the worse instead of for the better. But I fear that the dangers of not according Christian doctrine a new translation are even greater. The customary language for doctrine becomes so familiar we don't hear it, or, if we do, it goes into one ear and out the other. Familiarity may not only invite indifference—it may even breed contempt. For that reason I feel it incumbent upon those readers who are communicators of Christian doctrine (such as teachers and preachers) to strive—continually and responsibly—to put the old wine of the Christian doctrine (especially the Gospel) into new wineskins. Lewis not only provides us specific ways to do this but also functions as a catalyst to come up with our own fresh and imaginative ways to communicate scriptural truth. Like Shakespeare's Falstaff, Lewis is not only "witty" himself but is the cause of "wit" in others.

Christ's incarnation and the Holy Scriptures, I believe, constitute the ultimate precedent for what Lewis has done (and for what we, too, are to do). To better communicate His plan of salvation, more specifically, His holiness and His love (His Law and Gospel), God sent His

Son to our world as a human being. By entering our history, in becoming flesh and blood, in living, dying, and rising again on our planet, Christ gave us a more concrete, a more tangible, a more complete revelation of God's saving plan. If you will, Christ gave the doctrine of God's holiness and love "a new translation." To be sure, Christ did more than reveal or translate the plan of salvation—He accomplished it! Still, Christ's incarnation is revelation too, revelation at its best, communication in its most effective mode—the abstract made concrete. As the evangelist puts it, "The Word was made flesh, and dwelt among us, (and we beheld his glory, the glory as of the only begotten of the Father,) full of grace and truth" (John 1:14, KJV).

In addition, God has inspired an account in human language of God's plan of salvation and its accomplishment through Jesus Christ. Ordinarily, we call it the Bible. First the Word becomes flesh; then the Word becomes words—the words of the Holy Scriptures. The same divine humility that prompted God to send His Son as "a baby at a peasant-woman's breast, and later an arrested field-preacher in the hands of the Roman police" is also the humility that prompted God to provide the Holy Scriptures.[28] In short, language is incarnational—not only the inerrant language of the Bible, but also our own language. Errant as our language can be, it nevertheless is an effective, God-chosen medium to communicate God's love. Language has magic in it. It packs a wallop. Hence communicators of Christian doctrine harness the power of language to the power of God's Word, not with the false assumption that by their efforts they are helping God do His job, but with the prayerful hope that through their efforts the Word of God "as becometh it, may not be bound, but have free course and be preached to the joy and edifying of Christ's holy people."

God's method, you see, is not exclusion (God without human language); nor is it cooperation (God plus human language); rather, it is transformation (God through human language). With that truth in mind, communicators of Christian doctrine tap the magic of language and exploit the medium in their continual efforts to tell "the greatest story ever told." C. S. Lewis, in my opinion, has done just that in a particularly admirable way.

Let Lewis take the stand in his own defense. In a surprisingly explicit passage at the end of *The Voyage of the "Dawn Treader,"* Aslan addresses the concern of Lucy, disappointed at being returned from Narnia to England and fearful that she will never see Aslan again, by assuring her that she will meet him back in England also. "But there," he continues, "I have another name. You must learn to know me by that name. This was the reason why you were brought to Narnia, *that by knowing me here for a little, you may know me better there"* (emphasis mine).[29]

The defense rests.

BIBLIOGRAPHY

Lewis, C. S. *The Great Divorce*. New York: Collier Books, 1946.

_____. *The Horse and His Boy*. New York: Collier Books, 1954.

_____. Introduction in J. B. Phillips, *Letters to Young Churches: A Translation of the New Testament Epistles*. New York: Macmillan, 1951.

_____. *The Last Battle*. New York: Collier Books, 1956.

_____. *The Lion, the Witch and the Wardrobe*. New York: Collier Books, 1950.

_____. *Out of the Silent Planet*. New York: Collier Books, 1965.

_____. *Perelandra*. New York: Collier Books, 1944.

_____. *The Pilgrim's Regress: An Allegorical Apology for Christianity, Reason and Romanticism*. Grand Rapids, MI: Eerdmans, 1943.

_____. *The Silver Chair*. New York: Collier Books, 1953.

_____. *The Voyage of the "Dawn Treader."* New York: Collier Books, 1952.

Lewis, W. H., ed. *Letters of C. S. Lewis*. New York: Harcourt, Brace & World, 1966.

Shakespeare, William. *Henry IV*, Part II. Eds. Louis B. Wright and Virginia A. LaMar. New York: Washington Square Press, 1961.

NOTES

1. This chapter originally appeared as "Giving Christian Doctrine a New Translation: Selected Examples from the Novels of C. S. Lewis," in *Concordia Journal*, July 1995, 281-97, and is reproduced here by kind permission of the author and the editors of *Concordia Journal*.

2. Lewis, *The Silver Chair*, 213.

Old Wine in New Wineskins

3. W. H. Lewis, *Letters of C. S. Lewis*, 271.

4. Lewis, *Out of the Silent Planet*, 96.

5. Lewis, *Perelandra*, 18.

6. Shakespeare, *Henry IV*, Part II, Act III, scene ii, 38-39.

7. Lewis, *The Pilgrim's Regress: An Allegorical Apology for Christianity, Reason, and Romanticism*, 9-11.

8. Lewis, *The Last Battle*, 140-41.

9. Lewis, *Perelandra*, 168.

10. Lewis, *The Pilgrim's Regress*, 180.

11. Lewis, *The Great Divorce*, 100.

12. The relationship between mythology and divine revelation in Lewis's works is a subject worthy of another full-blown paper. Briefly, however, I should point out here that Lewis never suggests that biblical truth is mythological. In fact, just the opposite is the case; according to Lewis, mythology, if anything, reflects (in varying degrees of accuracy) biblical truth. In short, Lewis doesn't find myth in the Bible, but he finds the Bible in myth. He does not "demythologize" the Scripture, but he "degospelizes" mythology. Lewis expands our horizons, giving us more to believe in, never less.

13. Lewis, *The Voyage of the "Dawn Treader,"* 136.

14. Lewis, *The Great Divorce*, 44.

15. Ibid., 79.

16. Lewis, *The Horse and His Boy*, 191.

17. Ibid., 192.

18. See Jeremiah 50:44, Lamentations 3:10, Hosea 11:10, and especially Revelation 5:5.

19. Lewis, *The Lion, the Witch and the Wardrobe*, 76.

20. See Isaiah 6:1-5.

21. Lewis, *The Lion, the Witch and the Wardrobe*, 139.

22. Ibid., 160.

23. Lewis, *Perelandra*, 32.

24. Lewis, *The Last Battle*, 184.

25. Lewis, *The Great Divorce*, 8.

26. Lewis, *Perelandra*, 33.

27. Lewis, *The Great Divorce*, 43.

28. Lewis, "Introduction," viii.

29. Lewis, *The Voyage of the "Dawn Treader,"* 216.

TRANSLATED THEOLOGY:

Christology in the Writings of C. S. Lewis[1]

STEVEN P. MUELLER

C. S. Lewis never claimed to be a professional evangelist or a professional theologian. His first nonfictional work of theology, *The Problem of Pain*, contains this disclaimer:

> If any real theologian reads these pages, he will very easily see that they are the work of a layman and an amateur. . . . If any parts of the book are "original" in the sense of being novel or unorthodox, they are so against my will and as a result of my ignorance.[2]

Even though he was not a professional theologian, he often engaged in the work of a theologian—work that properly belongs to all Christians. Likewise, though he was not a professional evangelist, his works are involved in evangelism. Through his writing and speaking, many have heard the Gospel articulated with clarity; and as the Spirit worked through these words, they believed.

Lewis would gladly consult those whom he called the "real theologians" when he considered it to be necessary or helpful. So, for example, before he published *Mere Christianity*, he sent a copy of the manuscript to clergy from four different Christian denominations for review. He wanted his writing to restate orthodox Christian doctrine, ignoring novelty and innovation. His works were designed to present the faith as it was confessed *ubique et ab omnibus*, always, by everyone, and therefore uniting all Christians.[3] At the same time, he strove to present the content of orthodoxy in a fresh, novel manner. This work he referred to as "translation," not necessarily in terms of language, but of ideas.

When an early critic, Dr. Norman Pittenger, accused Lewis of christological heresy and of being out of his depth, Lewis defended his work, saying:

> One thing at least is sure. If the real theologians had tackled this laborious work of translation about a hundred years ago, when they began to lose touch with the people (for whom Christ died), there would have been no place for me.[4]

But since theologians did not readily take to the task of popularizing Christianity, Lewis undertook this crucial work. This translation is seen throughout his Christian works. His overtly theological works (such as *Mere Christianity*, *Miracles*, and *The Problem of Pain*) demonstrate Lewis's effort to popularize orthodox theology. Christian theology is presented in an accessible manner.

Simultaneously, his fictional works demonstrate a deeper, richer, and more complex act of translation, not merely explaining, but creating new worlds and characters that reflect the Gospel. This does not imply that the works are allegories. With the exception of *The Pilgrim's Regress*, Lewis denied that his works were allegorical. Rather, his fictional works are mythical, revealing parallels to the Christian story, but not offering precise correlations or one-to-one correspondence to many elements of the biblical account. A reader who understands only the explicitly stated meanings of a story still has the benefit of reading the story. Another reader may discover a greater depth of its mythical meaning, but this does not negate the value of enjoying the story as it first appears. While different readers appropriate various degrees of understanding, both have benefited.

Lewis proclaimed this understanding about all of his fiction, but particularly in the case of the Chronicles of Narnia, which are often mistakenly described as allegories. In recounting the genesis of these stories, Lewis stated that they began with vivid mental pictures. The tales flowed quickly and easily, and he found Christian parallels becoming evident. His goal was to write a good story, and the books can be read on just such a level. But parallel to the narrative, the reader can see deeper meanings. Reflecting on this work, he said:

> I thought I saw how stories of this kind could steal past certain inhibitions which had paralysed much of my own religion in child-hood. Why did one feel it so hard to feel as one was told one ought to feel about God or about the sufferings of Christ? I thought the chief reason was that one was told one ought to. An obligation to feel can freeze feelings. And reverence itself did harm. The whole subject was associated with lowered voices; almost as if it were something medical. But supposing that by casting all these things into an imaginary world, stripping them of their stained-glass and Sunday School associations, one could make them for the first time appear in their real potency? Could one not thus steal past those watchful dragons? I thought one could.[5]

Indeed, he was correct. While seeing the Christian elements is not essential for enjoyment of these books, many readers have encountered Christian teaching through them, while others may encounter images and motifs that help prepare them to hear the Gospel at a later time.[6]

Lewis translates a wide variety of religious themes, many of which serve to present the Gospel itself or to prepare the reader for its presentation. Yet one theme is of paramount importance for evangelism: the identity of Jesus Christ. Who is Jesus Christ, and how may we understand Him and His work? Throughout Lewis's writings, he deliberately and thoroughly strives to answer these most foundational questions about Christianity.

THE CONTENT OF LEWIS'S CHRISTOLOGY

In presenting his ideas about Jesus Christ, Lewis is direct, preferring an honest and uncompromising Christianity to the liberalism of his day. The Christian doctrine that he presents is clearly consistent with that of the ecumenical creeds that he confessed. Comparison of his writings with the Second Articles of the Apostles' and Nicene Creeds demonstrates that Lewis presents a complete christology. Certain elements may not be fully developed within his writings; indeed, we would be surprised if an "amateur theologian" would fully develop each article of doctrine. However, every proposition of these Creeds is explicitly and implicitly noted with one exception. Lewis does not specifically state what he quite obviously implies: that following His death, Jesus was buried. One may see parallels to the burial of Christ in the Christlike character of Elwin Ransom in *Perelandra*, but there are no explicit references to Jesus' burial. However, since Lewis presents both the death of Christ and His resurrection from the dead, the fact of His burial is obvious. With this single exception, all the other christological teachings of the Creeds—from His Incarnation to His final return and reign—are directly presented in Lewis's writings.

At the same time, while he presents the content of the Creeds, he also feels free to speculate on particular points. So, for example, when he discusses the Virgin Conception of Christ, he clearly believes the facticity of this miracle. It was as shocking to Joseph and Mary as it is today, and we can believe as easily as they.

> If St. Joseph had lacked faith to trust God or humility to perceive the holiness of his spouse, he could have disbelieved in the miraculous origin of her Son as easily as any modern man; and any modern man who believes in God can accept the miracle as easily as St. Joseph did.[7]

Mary was a virgin when Jesus was conceived. Having stated the orthodox doctrine, Lewis proceeds to speculate, saying:

> The exact details of such a miracle—an exact point at which a supernatural [being] enters this world (whether by the creation of a new spermatozoon or the fertilisation of an ovum without a spermatozoon, or the development of a foetus without an ovum) are not part of the doctrine. These are matters in which no one is obliged and everyone is free, to speculate.[8]

Lewis feels free to speculate, even providing three possible explanations as to how this miracle occurred. Some readers would disagree with his explanations, but Lewis could always refer to his positive statement of the doctrines. He has stated his adherence to the credal doctrine before he speculates. His writing reveals his own efforts to understand complex and miraculous doctrines. Lewis wanted not only to confess the correct doctrine but to understand it. But while he grapples to understand, he continues to note that his guesses are just that. What has to be believed is the essential doctrine. Explanations may be useful, but if they fail to be helpful, they should be discarded.

The Presentation of Christology

Lewis's christological content clearly reveals an attempt to repristinate orthodox christology. Yet if that were his entire task, his work would be unremarkable. The key element in the effectiveness of Lewis's presentation of Christianity in general, and of christology in particular, is the diverse nature of his writing. Many of his readers frequently express an appreciation for a portion of his Christian work. Some prefer his apologetic or philosophical writings, citing their clear argumentation and uncompromising belief. Others gravitate toward his fictional and literary works, noting their rich use of imagination and the depth of writing. Still others express a preference for those writings that reveal more of the personal life of C. S. Lewis such as *Surprised by Joy* or *A Grief Observed*. While many readers express an appreciation for works within each category, most tend to prefer one particular grouping. It is this diverse writing that has enhanced his effectiveness. He has written in a variety of genres that appeal to different readers, thereby translating theology to a wider audience.

A rich image of Christ emerges throughout his writings. This depiction parallels the personal understanding of C. S. Lewis in his conversion and throughout his life. Lewis depicts the Christ in whom he believes. This provides a genuineness to which the reader responds. The questions asked and the answers seen are those of Lewis's own experience.

The image of Christ seen in Lewis's writings has four specific ele-

Christology in the Writings of C. S. Lewis

ments. First, Christ is seen as the fulfiller not only of Old Testament prophecy, but also of pagan mythology. Second, He is considered by means of very focused logical arguments. Third, He is presented in various imaginative and romantic images. Finally, in some of his later writings, Lewis appeals to the passion of Christ as a comfort and consolation to Christians in their own suffering. These four methods encompass Lewis's presentation of Christ.

The Fulfillment of Paganism

An essential step in Lewis's conversion was the realization that while Christianity makes exclusive claims and at times contradicts other religions, this does not negate true elements in other religions. While other religions may contradict Christianity at key points, they are not necessarily incorrect about all points. So Lewis is able to write:

> If you are a Christian, you are free to think that all these religions, even the queerest ones, contain at least some hint of the truth.... But of course, being a Christian does mean thinking that where Christianity differs from other religions, Christianity is right and they are wrong. As in arithmetic—there is only one right answer to a sum, and all other answers are wrong: but some of the wrong answers are much nearer being right than others.[9]

This understanding explained the similarities of various religions, and particularly their ethical similarities.

As he considered the great religions of the world, Lewis concluded that the ethical teachings of Christianity are quite similar to those of other religions. Among the world's great ethical teachers he includes Zarathustra, Jeremiah, Socrates, Gautama, Christ, and Marcus Aurelius. A footnote on Christ explains, "I mention the Incarnate God among human teachers to emphasize that the principal difference between Him and them lies not in ethical teaching (which here is my concern), but in Person and Office."[10] The ethics of Christianity are not what distinguish it from other religions, nor is the teaching of

Christ what sets Him apart. His teaching is good, but so was much of the teaching of others. The difference is that Christ claims to be more than a teacher. He claims to be God.

Being a Christian does not require the rejection of all the ethics or teachings of other religions. Only those teachings that contradict Christianity must be rejected. But where there is a difference, the Christian will reject the other religion and confess Christianity.

Similarly, and perhaps of greater consequence for Lewis, figures similar to Christ can be found in the world's mythologies. Lewis had a great love for mythology and saw clear prefigurement of Christ in a number of myths. This realization was an essential step in his own conversion. An early biography records Lewis's account of his conversion. Here he recalls a pivotal conversation with Hugo Dyson and J. R. R. Tolkien prior to his conversion to Christianity.

> Now what Dyson and Tolkien showed me was this: that if I met the idea of sacrifice in a Pagan story I didn't mind it at all: again if I met the idea of a god sacrificing himself to himself I liked it very much and was mysteriously moved by it: again, that the idea of the dying and reviving god (Balder, Adonis, Bacchus) similarly moved me provided I met it anywhere except in the Gospels. The reason was that in Pagan stories I was prepared to feel the myth as profound and suggestive of meanings beyond my grasp even tho' I could not say in cold prose "what it meant". Now the story of Christ is simply a true myth: a myth working on us in the same way as the others, but with this tremendous difference that it really happened: and one must be content to accept it in the same way, remembering that it is God's myth while the others are men's myths: i.e., the Pagan stories are God expressing Himself through the minds of poets, using such images as He found there, while Christianity is God expressing Himself through what we call "real things". Therefore it is true, not in the sense of being a description of God (that no finite mind would take in) but in the sense of being the way in which God chooses to (or can) appear to our faculties. The "doctrines" we get out of the true myth are of course

less true: they are translations into our concepts and ideas of that which God has already expressed in a language more adequate, namely the actual incarnation, crucifixion, and resurrection.[11]

Lewis found it easier to believe Christianity when it was viewed as the fulfillment and completion of pagan mythologies. In *Surprised by Joy*, he notes this growing understanding that was so crucial to his conversion, saying:

> Early in 1926 the hardest boiled of all the atheists I ever knew sat in my room on the other side of the fire and remarked that the evidence for the historicity of the Gospels was really surprisingly good. "Rum thing" he went on. "All that stuff of Frazer's about the Dying God. Rum thing. It almost looks as if it really happened once." . . . If he, the cynic of cynics, the toughest of the toughs, were not—as I would still have put it—"safe," where could I turn? Was there no escape?[12]

There was no escape. Lewis came to faith and continued to believe that the good elements in paganism—including their mythologies—are not to be regarded as evil or demonic. Indeed, they are a gift from God.[13] In *Mere Christianity*, Lewis writes that God responded to mankind's separation from Him by, first of all, giving a sense of conscience. Throughout history, people have tried to follow it, but "None of them ever quite succeeded."[14] This revealed to humanity the need for another solution. In the beginning of that solution,

> He [God] sent the human race what I call good dreams: I mean those queer stories scattered all through the heathen religions about a god who dies and comes to life again and by his death has somehow given new life to men.[15]

These "good dreams" are found throughout pagan mythologies. In *Miracles*, Lewis notes a number of specific myths, including Adonis, Balder, Bacchus, Osiris, and various "corn kings" or harvest deities.

Gods who die to rise again are seen throughout paganism. Lewis continued, "From a certain point of view Christ is 'the same sort of thing' as Adonis or Osiris. . . ." And yet Christ is ". . . the only dying God who might possibly be historical. . . ."[16] Myth becomes fact in Jesus Christ.

Lewis also saw traces of this in Plato who wrote in *The Republic* of a perfectly righteous man who, because of his goodness, was rejected, tortured, and impaled. While Plato surely was alluding to the death of Socrates (whose death was from hemlock, not from being impaled), Lewis sees it as a deeper point.

> Plato is talking, and knows he is talking, about the fate of goodness in a wicked and misunderstanding world. But that is not something simply other than the Passion of Christ. It is the very same thing of which the Passion is the supreme illustration. . . . Plato probably did not know that the ideally perfect instance of crucified goodness which he had depicted would ever become actual and historical.[17]

In fact, Lewis maintained that we have a greater knowledge of this than the original writers.

> There is a real connection between what Plato and the myth-makers most deeply were and meant and what I believe to be the truth. I know that connection and they do not. But it is really there. It is not an arbitrary fancy of my own thrust upon the old words. One can, without any absurdity, imagine Plato or the myth-makers if they learned the truth, saying, "I see . . . so that is what I was really talking about!"[18]

Lewis again discusses mythology in *The Discarded Image*. As he discusses the medieval view of beasts, he comes upon two descriptions that clearly have christological implications but are not noted by the author, Isidore.

> One of the most remarkable things about Isidore is that he draws no morals from his beasts and gives them no allegorical

interpretations. He says the Pelican revives its young by its own blood (XII, vii, 26) but draws no such parallel between this and the life-giving death of Christ as was later to produce the tremendous *Pie Pelicane*. He tells us from unnamed "writers on the nature of animals" (XII, ii, 13) that the unicorn is a beast too strong for any hunter to take; but if you set a virgin before him he loses all his ferocity, lays down his head in her lap, and sleeps. Then we can kill him. It is hard to believe that any Christian can think for long about this exquisite myth without seeing in it an allegory of the Incarnation and Crucifixion. Yet Isidore makes no such suggestion.[19]

The richness and depth of pagan mythology helped Lewis believe in Christ, for in Christianity he saw the same sorts of things as he saw in other religions. But in Christianity, he saw myth becoming fact.

This theme of Christianity fulfilling and exceeding other religions and other mythologies finds regular expression in Lewis's writings. Not only does he explicitly discuss these fulfillments, he also develops mythological themes and crafts new myths that continue to point to Christ. His prose affirms the usefulness of these genres while his fiction develops them. Christianity is the highest and clearest expression of the truth, but not its only expression. It does not exist in a vacuum. Rather, echoes of its truth are heard in other religions and philosophies.

LOGICAL EXPLANATION OF CHRIST

A second major factor in Lewis's conversion and writing is logic. His education with W. T. Kirkpatrick strongly emphasized logic and critical thinking, and his acceptance of Christianity included an evaluation of its claims on logical terms. Lewis could not have believed the Christian faith if he was unable to make sense of it. This does not preclude the possibility of the miraculous or mysterious in Christianity, but a logical coherence was vital. As he writes, Lewis applies a very focused, deliberate logic to Christian doctrine. In a letter Lewis wrote:

The first real work of the Gospels on a fresh reader is, and ought to be, to raise very acutely the question, "Who or What is this?" For there is a good deal in the character which, unless he really is what he says he is, is not loveable or even tolerable. . . .[20]

Who or what is Jesus? That is the question of paramount importance for Lewis. He could not provide an answer until he fully considered Christ's claims about Himself.

One popular conception of Jesus Christ presents Him not as divine, but merely a good teacher. Lewis responds to this idea, saying:

I am trying here to prevent anyone saying the really foolish thing that people often say about Him: "I'm ready to accept Jesus as a great moral teacher, but I don't accept His claim to be God." That is the one thing we may not say. A man who was merely a man and said the sort of things Jesus said would not be a great moral teacher. He would either be a lunatic—on a level with the man who says he is a poached egg—or else he would be the Devil of Hell. You must make your choice. Either this man was, and is, the Son of God: or else a madman or something worse. You can shut Him up for a fool, you can spit at Him and kill Him as a demon; or you may fall at His feet and call Him Lord and God. But let us not come with any patronising nonsense about His being a great human teacher. He has not left that open to us. He did not intend to.[21]

The same idea is repeated in *Miracles*.

The discrepancy between the depth and sanity and (let me add) *shrewdness* of His moral teaching and the rampant megalomania which must lie behind His theological teaching unless He is indeed God, has never been satisfactorily got over.[22]

A notable characteristic of Lewis's writing is that he often reduces an issue to a narrow and sharply defined set of alternatives. Proper understanding of the argument necessitates understanding of its focus.

Christology in the Writings of C. S. Lewis

Is it logical to say that Christ was a good moral teacher but not the Son of God? Lewis denied such a claim. Since Jesus claimed to be God, He could not have been merely a "good teacher." If He was not divine, He might have been a liar, or a lunatic, or a devil from Hell, but He was not just a "good teacher." Good teachers and sane people do not falsely claim divinity. For an ordinary human to claim deity in the way that Christ did is a horrendous lie, insanity, or demonic act. It is not a mark of a good teacher. The success of this argument is its simplicity and focus. What are we to make of Christ? We may not call Him merely a good teacher, for this fails to account for all of Jesus' claims. Either we believe what He says about Himself, that He is God, or we reject Him. There is no middle ground.

Lewis is often lauded for his lucidity and focus. Indeed, many have noted that what is most notable in his writings is common sense. Lewis was not a biblical literalist and was willing to look at the transmission of Christianity with a critical eye; yet he would typically hold to the simplest reading of the biblical text. Questions might arise regarding particular readings, but the essential points are straightforward. What the text says is ordinarily what it means. Application may be difficult, but the need to apply the Bible is obvious. In an era when Christians may be confused by the work of many theologians, such a simple acceptance and defense of Christianity appeals to many readers. Such teaching may be challenging but may also have greater integrity. This is the application of his logic. Logical argument was vital to his understanding, but he understood that logical arguments had their limits. Part of Christianity's appeal is that it is something that could not be figured out. At times it transcends expectations. Lewis's presentation of Christianity is logical yet believing, conservative yet intellectual. This combination enhances his impact on many readers.

An Imaginative Presentation

A third element in Lewis's presentation of Christ is seen in the nature of his writings. While some of his work is very focused and logical, a great deal of his writing does not directly present logical arguments.

Much of Lewis's writing is richly imaginative, and imagination also was important both in Lewis's conversion and in his continued understanding of Christ. Lewis's personal and professional background was literary. He was a literary critic and professor, a voracious reader with a great love for a variety of writing, particularly imaginative, mythopoeic writings. His fiction reflects the tremendous breadth of his reading as well as his own fertile imagination. It also strongly reflects the faith that was so important to him. Throughout his fiction, clear Christ figures are seen.

Many readers, even critics, have noted that one of Lewis's chief virtues was his ability as a storyteller and myth-maker. This is largely due to his method of crafting a story. Lewis was simultaneously unoriginal and very original. He made extensive use of the writings of other authors. Basic story lines and literary tools and motifs are freely borrowed from others. *Till We Have Faces*, for example, is a retelling of the myth of Psyche and Cupid. The Space Trilogy was significantly impacted by David Lindsay's *Voyage to Arcturus*, H. G. Wells's *The First Men on the Moon*, Spenser's *The Faerie Queene*, Milton's *Paradise Lost*, and many other books. Lewis freely drew from his deep literary background and incorporated diverse elements into his own writings.

At the same time, Lewis did not simply retell the story; he recast it. The general direction of the narrative may be heavily reliant on past literary patterns, but Lewis's retelling transforms the stories. Often readers do not even notice the literary dependencies. Lewis wrote with deliberate complexity and richness. Because they are mythical, his stories often contain multiple levels of understanding.[23] Lewis has crafted his fiction in a manner that provides different levels of reading. This depth rewards the reader.

The Chronicles of Narnia

The best-known Christ image in Lewis's fiction is undoubtedly Aslan. That the central figure of the Chronicles of Narnia is analogous to Christ is undeniable. He is the Son of the Emperor-beyond-the-Sea whose coming is prophesied in Messianic terms.

Wrong will come right when Aslan's in sight,
   At the sound of his roar there'll be sorrows no more,
When he bares his teeth winter will meet its death,
   And when he shakes his mane there'll be spring again.[24]

His coming coincides with the coming of Father Christmas, and, true to the prophecy, spring follows. When he comes, he gathers a group of followers around him, teaching, guiding, and strengthening. But the clearest parallel to Christ is in his death. Aslan dies in the place of Edmund who has been a traitor and has been condemned to die by the White Witch. When Aslan trades places with Edmund, he is mocked, beaten, bound, and killed on an altar-like stone table.[25] Shortly after his death, Aslan returns to life, explaining that this is the Emperor's "deep magic." Since Aslan was an innocent victim, he was raised to life again.[26]

At first glance, it appears that Aslan's death was for the sake of Edmund alone. However, as the narrative continues, the benefits of his death and resurrection are extended to others. Those who had been turned to stone statues by the White Witch are brought back to life. Narnia is freed from the Witch's tyranny, and peace comes to the land. Later, in *The Voyage of the "Dawn Treader,"* that salvation extends to Eustace, who by his selfish greed was transformed into a dragon. Aslan peels off his dragon's skin and throws him into a pool of water. Following this "baptism," Eustace is a boy again. As Eustace tells Edmund about these events, Edmund tells him who Aslan is, including the critical words, "He is the great Lion, the son of the Emperor over the Sea who saved me and saved Narnia."[27] Aslan's death and resurrection was occasioned by Edmund's sin, but it was for all of Narnia.

The identity of Aslan is made quite clear at the end of *The Voyage of the "Dawn Treader."* There, after traveling to the edge of Narnia (which is a flat world), the children travel through a sea of white lilies. On the shore they meet a Lamb who invites them to a breakfast of fish, just as Christ invited His disciples to a breakfast of fish following His resurrection (John 21:1-14). As the Lamb spoke to them, he was transformed into Aslan himself, who tells the children that they are returning to their own world. When Edmund asks if Aslan is in their world, he replies,

> "I am," said Aslan, "but I have another name. You must learn to know me by that name. This was the very reason why you were brought to Narnia, that by knowing me here for a little, you may know me there better."[28]

The thought that this great Lion might be in our world did not go unnoticed. In 1953 a child wrote to Lewis, asking about Aslan's other name. Lewis responded:

> As to Aslan's other name, well, I want you to guess. Has there never been anyone in this world who (1) Arrived at the same time as Father Christmas. (2) Said he was the son of the Great Emperor. (3) Gave himself up for someone else's fault to be jeered at and killed by wicked people. (4) Came to life again. (5) Is sometimes spoken of as a Lamb (see the end of the Dawn Treader). Don't you really know His name in this world?[29]

Even more revealing is a letter Lewis wrote to a worried parent, saying, "Lawrence can't really love Aslan more than Jesus. . . . For the things he loves Aslan for doing or saying are simply the things Jesus really did and said."[30]

Clearly, Lewis was writing of Christ. He explained in another letter, "The reason why the Passion of Aslan sometimes moves people more than the real story in the Gospels is, I think, that it takes them off their guard."[31] Lewis has effectively translated Christ, preparing both children and adults for an encounter with Jesus Christ[32] or helping them to consider His salvific work in a new light.

The Space Trilogy

But Aslan is not the only Christ figure in Lewis's fiction. His space trilogy contains two figures that may translate Christ to the reader. The first is Maleldil-the-Young. Maleldil is consistently spoken of as God, though he is never seen directly. Maleldil creates and sustains the worlds. He became a man at Bethlehem, ". . . dared terrible things, wrestling with the Bent One [Satan] in Thulcandra [earth]," was crucified as a ransom and is still alive. With his blood, ". . . Maleldil remade the worlds before any world was made."[33] Though He never appears directly in the narrative, Maleldil is clearly evocative of Christ.

Simultaneously, the character of Elwin Ransom is evocative of Christ. Ransom is not identified as divine. Rather, he is a Christian with an active faith. Yet in this role he exemplifies Christ. Ransom is transported to Perelandra by the eldila, angelic beings who serve Maleldil. There he meets "the Green Lady," who is the first woman on Perelandra. She is being tempted by Weston, a demon-possessed man from earth. She resists the temptation, but Weston does not relent. Eventually Ransom begins to realize that he is present as Maleldil's representative and that Maleldil was calling him to physically stop the temptation. "Here in Perelandra the temptation would be stopped by Ransom, or it would not be stopped at all."[34]

When Ransom begins to fight, Weston, "the Un-Man," drags him beneath the sea. They arise in the darkness of a subterranean cave where Ransom kills him by crushing his head with a stone. Eventually, Ransom finds his way out of the cave and is restored to health. As he recovers, he discovers a wound to his heel. It was a human bite that was bleeding and would not stop. This wound remained, even when Ransom returned to earth.

Note the implicit christological parallels. Ransom fought and destroyed the demonic Weston vicariously on behalf of the first woman. In so doing, he was dragged down into the dark pit of the earth, only to later emerge, just as Christ was buried and rose again. He has crushed the head of the enemy who wounded his heel. Afterwards he emerges alive from a cave. His life and actions are parallel to Christ.

But Ransom is not Christ. Indeed, in realizing his own role, he knew he was only a representative.

. . . if he left it undone, Maleldil Himself would do some greater thing instead. In that sense, he stood for Maleldil: but no more than Eve would have stood for Him by not eating the apple, or than any man stands for Him in doing any good actions.[35]

That is Lewis's precise intent. Ransom is like Christ just as all Christians can be "little Christs" by carrying out God's will in their lives.

Till We Have Faces

Another Christ parallel is seen in *Till We Have Faces*. The character of Psyche, like Ransom, is not meant to be Christ but nonetheless parallels and exemplifies Him. In a letter to Clyde Kilby Lewis wrote:

Psyche is an instance of the *anima naturaliter Christiana* making the best of the Pagan religion she is brought up in and thus being guided (but always "under the cloud," always in terms of her own imaginations or that of her people) to the true God. She is in some ways like Christ because every good man or woman is like Christ. What else could they be like?[36]

Consider the many parallels between Psyche and Christ. As a beautiful child, she aids the people. "You healed them, and blessed them, and took their filthy disease upon yourself,"[37] her sister says, and yet the people reject her. When the land falls under a drought, Psyche is chosen by lot to be sacrificed. She becomes the accursed, dying on a tree. After her death, Psyche is called the blessed and is later seen alive, living in a great house across a river, a symbol of death. The house, however, cannot ordinarily be seen by mortal eyes.

Many commentators have expressed the similarities of Psyche to Christ, perhaps none better than Gibson:

Psyche forgives Redival with the comment, "She also does what she doesn't know." Like the High Priest's remark at the judgment of Christ . . . the King says, "It's only sensible that one should die for many." And when Orual tells her, "You healed

them, and blessed them, and took their filthy disease upon yourself," this not only suggests the ministry of Christ but also
echoes the messianic statement of Isaiah, "Surely he hath borne
our griefs. . . ." And the statement of the Fox that at the Holy
Tree she did not cry out even when they left her, reminds us
again of Isaiah, "As a sheep before her shearers is dumb, so he
opened not his mouth." So Psyche, who is to become a goddess,
reflects the image of Christ.[38]

Lewis stated that Psyche is like Christ because of her goodness, but the
similarities are far deeper. Her entire life is parallel to His. Psyche is
richly evocative of Christ and further translates Christ to the reader.

Other Imaginative Images

These imaginative examples are all found within extended narratives.
There also are, in Lewis's writing, a number of shorter passages that provide imaginative presentations of Christ. One of the more significant is
in *The Great Divorce*. One of the souls from hell, who has come to the
edge of heaven, is met by one of the blessed souls who had been a murderer on earth. The ghost immediately objects to the presence of the
murderer and asks about his victim. He is told that both are in heaven
(though the victim is "deeper" in heaven). At this, the ghost grows bel-
ligerent. He cannot understand why he has been in hell while a murderer
is in heaven. Finally the ghost begins protesting about his own rights.

> "I'm asking for nothing but my rights" . . .
> "Oh no. It's not so bad as that. I haven't got my rights or I
> should not be here. You will not get yours either. You'll get
> something far better. Never fear" . . .
> "I only want my rights. I'm not asking for anybody's bleed-
> ing charity."
> "Then do. At once. Ask for the Bleeding Charity. Everything
> is here for the asking and nothing can be bought. . . . You
> weren't a decent man and you didn't do your best. We none of
> us were and we none of us did."[39]

Lewis is at his best as he here illustrates grace. Reliance on rights is a hopeless matter when eternal salvation is at issue. While pride may make one hesitant to accept charity, that charity is the only hope. The charity that is offered is the Bleeding Charity. Christ Himself is the Charity, the Love that gives Himself to save us. This short image helps translate Christ to the reader.

Lewis's storytelling and myth-making are regarded by many as the high point of his work. The characters of Aslan, Maleldil, Ransom, or Psyche all convey cognitive data about Christianity, but their impact transcends the mere transmission of information. Indeed, what they present is a consistent representation of the Christ of Scripture. But in recasting elements of Christianity, Lewis enables the reader to consider its claims in a new manner. Indeed, it is not only in his fiction that Lewis uses stories. Other writings contain shorter illustrations that are likewise products of his literary skills. His images in *Miracles* that describe the incarnation and work of Christ in terms of a strongman lifting an enormous burden or of a diver who plunges to the depths to recover a precious object[40] both demonstrate his use of literary illustrations to better explain Christianity. Lewis's use of imaginative writing appeals to readers at many levels.

The Comforting Passion

There is one further facet of christological expression in the writings of C. S. Lewis. In his later years, especially after the tragic death of his wife, Joy, Lewis found understanding and consolation in the midst of his own suffering by remembering the Passion of Christ. Remembering Christ's struggles does not eliminate our own, but it does show us that we are not unique in facing them. Seeing how Christ reacted, particularly in Gethsemane, was a comfort to Lewis. In *Letters to Malcolm* Lewis writes:

> We all try to accept with some sort of submission our afflictions when they actually arrive. But the prayer in Gethsemane shows that the preceding anxiety is equally God's will and equally part

of our human destiny. The perfect Man experienced it. And the servant is not greater than the master. We are Christians, not Stoics.[41]

Christ's anguish is typical of human experience. Expanding this idea, he continues:

> Does not every movement in the Passion write large some common element in the sufferings of our race? First, the prayer of anguish; not granted. Then He turns to His friends. They are asleep—as ours, or we, are so often, or busy, or away, or preoccupied. Then He faces the Church; the very Church that He brought into existence. It condemns Him. This also is characteristic. . . . There is, then, nothing left but God. And to God, God's last words are "Why hast thou forsaken me?" You see how characteristic, how representative it all is. The human situation writ large. These are among the things it means to be a man. Every rope breaks when you seize it. Every door is slammed shut as you reach it.[42]

Christ was the perfect Man, fully human, and therefore He experienced all these things. He has undergone all that we have to face, and more, for He was forsaken by God. Christ faced not only the human situation, which is bad, but even "the human situation writ large," suffering intensified. While this may appear bleak, it was a great comfort to Lewis, who believed in the resurrected Christ.

Lewis knew that life was often difficult, but he did not avoid the challenges, nor would he ignore them. Having undergone suffering, Lewis comforted others.

> Some people feel guilty about their anxieties and regard them as a defeat of faith. I don't agree at all. They are afflictions, not sins. Like all afflictions, they are, if we can so take them, our share in the Passion of Christ.[43]

Afflictions can be transformed in the life of the Christian. The suffering of Christians is directly related to the suffering of Christ; it is our share in His Passion. The relationship between the suffering of Christians and of the Savior is a frequent component of Lewis's letters. To a lady, he wrote:

> You needn't worry about not feeling brave. Our Lord didn't— see the scene in Gethsemane. How thankful I am that when God became man He did not choose to become a man of iron nerves; that would not have helped weaklings like you and me nearly so much.[44]

The struggles of Christ were encouraging to Lewis in his personal struggles. Similarly he wrote, "Fear is horrid, but there's no reason to be ashamed of it. Our Lord was afraid (dreadfully so) in Gethsemane. I always cling to that as a very comforting fact."[45] A focus on Christ's suffering doesn't explain suffering, pain, or evil, but it does provide the ultimate solution and helps one cope with personal suffering.

CONCLUSION

The image of Christ that Lewis presents throughout his writings is the Christ of historic Christianity. Fully divine, incarnate as a human being, the God-man was crucified, resurrected, and ascended in both natures. He is the Savior of the world. Lewis consistently presents the person and work of Jesus Christ in various genres, thereby making his message accessible to a broad readership. He claimed that he was not a theologian, but C. S. Lewis knew and presented orthodox christology.

Through an emphasis on the fulfillment of paganism, logical arguments, application of the Passion of Christ, and most of all, through imaginative, fictional presentations, the Gospel is translated to a wide variety of readers. Though he did not claim to be an evangelist, he proclaimed the Gospel, and his works continue to do so. "What are we to make of Christ?" Lewis asks, and then shows the answer. He is the Savior of the world. Having seen this truth, Lewis also responds, "The real question is not what are we to make of Christ, but what is He to make of us?"[46]

BIBLIOGRAPHY

Gibson, Evan K. *C. S. Lewis, Spinner of Tales: A Guide to His Fiction.* Washington D. C.: Christian College Press, 1980.

Green, Roger Lancelyn and Hooper, Walter. *C. S. Lewis: A Biography.* New York: Harcourt Brace Jovanovich, 1974.

Kilby, Clyde S. *The Christian World of C. S. Lewis.* Grand Rapids, MI: Eerdmans, 1964.

Lewis, C. S. *The Discarded Image: An Introduction to Medieval and Renaissance Literature.* Cambridge: Cambridge University Press, 1964.

_____. *God in the Dock: Essays on Theology and Ethics.* Edited and with a preface by Walter Hooper. Grand Rapids, MI: Eerdmans, 1970.

_____. *The Great Divorce.* New York: Macmillan, 1946.

_____. *Letters of C. S. Lewis.* Ed. W. H. Lewis. New York: Harvest/Harcourt Brace Jovanovich, 1966.

_____. *Letters to an American Lady.* Ed. Clyde S. Kilby. Grand Rapids, MI: Eerdmans, 1967; London: Hodder and Stoughton, 1969.

_____. *Letters to Children.* Eds. Lyle W. Dorsett and Marjorie Lamp Mead. Foreword by Douglas H. Gresham. New York: Macmillan 1985.

_____. *Letters to Malcolm, Chiefly on Prayer.* New York: Macmillan, 1964.

_____. *The Lion, the Witch and the Wardrobe.* New York: Macmillan, 1950.

_____. *Mere Christianity.* New York: Macmillan, 1952.

_____. *Miracles.* New York: Macmillan, 1947.

_____. *On Stories and Other Essays in Literature.* New York: Harcourt Brace Jovanovich, 1982.

_____. *Out of the Silent Planet.* New York: Macmillan, 1965.

_____. *Perelandra: A Novel.* New York: Macmillan, 1944.

_____. *The Pilgrim's Regress: An Allegorical Apology for Christianity, Reason, and Romanticism.* New York: Bantam Books, 1933.

_____. *The Problem of Pain.* New York: Macmillan, 1962.

_____. *Reflections on the Psalms.* New York: Harcourt Brace Jovanovich, 1958.

_____. *Surprised by Joy: The Shape of My Early Life.* New York: Harcourt Brace Jovanovich, 1955.

_____. *That Hideous Strength: A Modern Fairy-Tale for Grown-ups.* New York: Macmillan, 1946.

_____. *Till We Have Faces.* New York: Harcourt Brace Jovanovich, 1956.

_____. *The Voyage of the "Dawn Treader."* New York: Macmillan, 1952.

Notes

1. This chapter is drawn from my forthcoming Ph.D. dissertation, *Christology in the Writings of C. S. Lewis* in the Department of Theology at the University of Durham.

2. Lewis, *The Problem of Pain*, 10.

3. Lewis, "What Are We to Make of Christ?," in *God in the Dock*, 336.

4. Lewis, "Rejoinder to Dr Pittenger," in *God in the Dock*, 183.

5. Lewis, *On Stories and Other Essays in Literature*, 47.

6. Cf. Joel Heck, "*Praeparatio Evangelica*," in this volume.

7. Lewis, *Miracles*, 48.

8. Letter to Mary Willis Shelburne, 13 June 1951, in Lewis, *Letters to an American Lady*, 233.

9. Lewis, *Mere Christianity*, 43.

10. Lewis, *The Problem of Pain*, 63.

11. Green and Hooper, *C. S. Lewis: A Biography*, 117-18.

12. Lewis, *Surprised by Joy*, 223-24.

13. This theme is also developed in *The Pilgrim's Regress*, 154-59 where Lewis writes of the contrast between the rules (God's Law) and the pictures (mythology), both of which are gifts of the Landlord (God).

14. Lewis, *Mere Christianity*, 54.

15. Ibid.

16. Lewis, *Miracles*, 113-14.

17. Lewis, *Reflections on the Psalms*, 104-05.

18. Ibid., 108.

19. Lewis, *The Discarded Image*, 149-50

20. Letter to a lady, 26 March 1940, in *Letters of C. S. Lewis*, 180-81.

21. Lewis, *Mere Christianity*, 55-56.

22. Lewis, *Miracles*, 109.

23. Cf. Francis C. Rossow, "Old Wine in New Wineskins," the previous chapter in this volume.

24. Lewis, *The Lion, the Witch and the Wardrobe*, 74-75.

25. Ibid., 152.

26. Ibid., 160.

27. Lewis, *The Voyage of the "Dawn Treader,"* 92.

28. Ibid., 216.

29. Lewis, *Letters to Children*, 32.

Christology in the Writings of C. S. Lewis

30. *Letters to Children*, 52.

31. Letter to Thomas Howard, cited in Kilby, *The Christian World of C. S. Lewis*, 136.

32. Cf. Joel Heck, "*Praeparatio Evangelica*," in this volume.

33. Lewis, *Perelandra*, 121; *That Hideous Strength*, 262; *Out of the Silent Planet*, 121; *Perelandra*, 148, 220.

34. *Perelandra*, 142, 143, 146.

35. Ibid., 150.

36. *Letters of C. S. Lewis*, 274.

37. Lewis, *Till We Have Faces*, 39.

38. Evan K. Gibson, *C. S. Lewis, Spinner of Tales: A Guide to His Fiction*, 242-43.

39. Lewis, *The Great Divorce*, 33-35.

40. Lewis, *Miracles*, 111-12.

41. Lewis, *Letters to Malcolm*, 42-43.

42. Ibid., 43.

43. Ibid., 41.

44. Letter to a lady, 17 July 1953, in *Letters of C. S. Lewis*, 250.

45. Letter to Mary Willis Shelburne, 2 April 1955, in *Letters to an American Lady*, 41.

46. *God in the Dock*, 156.

PART FOUR

The Argument:
Defending the Faith

JOY, THE CALL OF GOD IN MAN:
A Critical Appraisal of Lewis's Argument from Desire

DOUGLAS T. HYATT

LEWIS'S CONCEPT OF "JOY" OR "DESIRE"

The concept of "joy" or "desire" played a pivotal role in the life of C. S. Lewis. He wrote two books that dealt rather extensively with this theme (*The Pilgrim's Regress* and *Surprised by Joy*), included a chapter on the concept in his book on suffering (*The Problem of Pain*), and delivered what was surely his most famous sermon on the topic ("The Weight of Glory"). In addition to these works where he focuses his attention on the concept, the theme appears directly or is just beneath the surface in a number of his works of creative fiction.[1] There can be no doubt that Lewis attached a great deal of significance to the argument from desire for belief in God, especially because it played such a critical role in his own conversion to Christianity.

Lewis by his own confession became a Christian in September of 1931. Less than a year and a half later he completed the manuscript of *The Pilgrim's Regress* and sent it to the publisher. It must be remembered, however, that he had experienced a rather dramatic conversion to theism two years earlier. Being a reflective sort and a keeper of a journal, he had assiduously recorded his thoughts during the entire process. *The Pilgrim's Regress* and *Surprised by Joy* (published twenty-two years later) are the fruits of those efforts. The first book is an allegorical account of his intellectual sojourn to faith. The second

A Critical Appraisal of Lewis's Argument from Desire

book is more nearly an autobiography of the conventional sort but is also organized around the most important event in his life, namely his conversion to faith. Both works make it clear that joy or desire were of pivotal importance in this conversion. In the first he emphasized the persistence of his desire to find the object of his longing despite all the contrary streams of thought he encountered that explained the desire away. Taken together with *Surprised by Joy*, a good understanding of how Lewis perceived this phenomenon and its significance as a pointer or guide to the living God can be gained.

Though Lewis uses the term "joy" to describe the experience in question, it is not the only term he employs. "Desire," "*Sehnsucht*," and "longing" are also used to describe certain workings of the phenomenon. Joy, as Lewis conceives of it, is not merely a feeling, nor is it simply a concept or an idea. It is first of all an experience. The experience, however, is not easy to identify. As is typical for experience, it must be interpreted. It cannot be placed in the category of other emotions such as anger or sadness. Though different people are made angry or sad by different causes, we all know immediately what is meant by the terms "anger" or "sadness." Joy, on the other hand, is not just a reaction of the emotions to some happy circumstance. In Lewis's view, it is not even an emotional phenomenon at all, even though it may be accompanied by emotions.

Joy, or desire, is not, then, to be equated with a physical sensation but with longing for something "other and outer." This is not to deny that the "thrill" or bittersweet longing associated with joy is pleasurable. Indeed, it is a highly desirable experience in itself. The error is to think that is the end, the *telos*, itself. It comes about because of the intense longing for something else, something other than a mere feeling. But what is the object of this desire of which he speaks? What is this longing that is also experienced as joy?

Lewis reasons that a desire for something that cannot be satisfied by any earthly object is an indication, indeed, almost a proof, that we are born with the desire for something over or beyond what this world can give. As John, the Pilgrim, learned from old Wisdom:

What does not satisfy when we find it, was not the thing we were desiring. If water will not set a man at ease, then be sure it was not thirst, or not thirst only, that tormented him: . . . How, indeed, do we know our desires save by their satisfaction?[2]

In other words, he begins with the premise that nature makes nothing in vain. If we have natural desires for food, it is because something exists that can be eaten. It can, of course, be argued that the mere existence of hunger does not mean that one will get something to eat. To this Lewis readily agrees but then replies:

But surely a man's hunger does prove that he comes of a race which repairs its body by eating and inhabits a world where eatable substances exist.[3]

If, however, an innate or natural desire exists that is not satisfied by any earthly object, then no earthy object was really the source of that desire. The point is that the sheer existence of natural desires is explicable only on the hypothesis that a corresponding object exists that will or would satisfy the desire. The validity of Lewis's reasoning depends, of course, on the correctness of his premises—i.e., is it true that nature makes nothing in vain? A closer look at this question follows later.

As Lewis sees it, then, joy had to be a desire for something other than itself and something other than a physical or emotional state, a desire for something "other and outer." This pointing in a direction, this signifying of something other than itself, is at the heart of what Lewis claims for joy. If listened to, he insists that it proclaims something—indeed, *someone*—else:

Inexorably Joy proclaimed, "You want—I myself am your want of—something other, outside, not you nor any state of you." I did not yet ask, Who is the desired? only What is it? But this brought me already into the region of awe, for I thus understood that in deepest solitude there is a road right out of the self, a commerce with something which, by refusing to identify itself with any object of the senses, or anything whereof we have bio-

A Critical Appraisal of Lewis's Argument from Desire

logical or social need, or anything imagined, or any state of our own minds, proclaims itself sheerly objective.[4]

Such conclusions bring one very close to identifying the object of desire with God. Lewis was slow to make this connection in his own life (and hence in *The Pilgrim's Regress*). The Pilgrim wonders where desire comes from, that is, why men have it. The answer he is given is that some image or picture is given that "sets men longing for something East or West of the world."[5] For Lewis, this means origin or eschaton. In *The Pilgrim's Regress* the utter East is the Landlord's castle, where one goes after death. The utter West was the place of the vision of the island. Lewis refers to it as "a place very ancient, . . . a place, in some sort, lying rather at the world's beginning, as though men were born travelling away from it."[6] Desire, then, is rooted somewhere in the primordial memory of paradise or in the hope of perfect fulfillment in the consummation of all things.

This answer clearly points to God. It is, nevertheless, difficult for the Pilgrim at first to see desire as coming from God for two reasons: 1) God seems the opposite to him of what his desire was—at least what he thought his desire was. He wished to escape the Landlord's demands on his life and do what he wanted to. 2) As he followed his desire, it led him in all kinds of directions that clearly led away from the Landlord. When the Pilgrim asks History whether desire can have anything to do with the Landlord, he gets this reply:

> It comes from the Landlord. We know this by its results. It has brought you to where you now are: and nothing leads back to him which did not at first proceed from him.[7]

This, of course, is an assertion of central significance. Conscience, the awareness of moral law, is commonly recognized as a means whereby God speaks to man. God can easily be conceived of as demanding right behavior; hence, rules and laws on morality seem to fit what might be expected of Him. Lewis portrays John as fleeing exactly this burden. His first memories of the Landlord are connected with rules of behavior and the fear that comes upon him when he fails to keep the rules. Hence, to flee the rules by disbelieving in the Landlord initially brings great relief to him. He spends much of his life pursuing his vision of the island (his desire) and not concerning himself much with the rules. He is not aware until very late in his sojourn that his desire is leading him to the Landlord. In fact, even when he discovers it, he remains unsure that he wants to get near the Landlord. It is his desire that draws him. Lewis, it seems clear, is saying that desire is a means God uses to draw people to Himself that they may not consciously recognize as having anything to do with God. Desire, as Lewis envisions it, is a positive force for attracting men to God as opposed to the negative force contained in a bad conscience and the need for forgiveness in order to stand before a righteous judge.

It is important to note that Lewis does not say, indeed does not believe, that some innate sense (the longing of the heart) is capable of leading a person to God entirely by itself. One has the impression at times that he is implying that. But in the end he presents the picture of desire, if the dialectic is faithfully followed, bringing the Pilgrim to the point of recognizing there is no ultimate satisfaction for him in this world. But where the ultimate satisfaction is to be found—whether ultimate satisfaction for his longing is even possible—requires that he gain knowledge from other sources. During the process of pursuing his "island" (the object of his desire), the Pilgrim was increasingly applying reason to the various philosophies and worldviews that he encountered. Here, too, he was working through a dialectic. As Lewis remarks in the preface of *The Pilgrim's Regress*: "This lived dialectic, and the merely argued dialectic of my philosophical progress, seemed to have converged on one goal. . . ."[8]

In other words, his experience and intellectual interaction with Freudianism, materialism, and finally idealism led him to the point that he saw God as the most reasonable explanation of reality at the same time that his experience with joy led him to conclude that the object of his desire was not to be had in this world. He was, therefore, prepared for making the connection between what the dialectic of desire had shown him and what his reason had shown him.

A Critical Appraisal of Lewis's Argument from Desire

A Philosophical Evaluation of Lewis's Concept of Joy

The Reality of Desire

Lewis is, of course, not alone in attaching a metaphysical meaning to desire. Even Nietzsche said: "*Alle Lust will Ewigkeit, will tiefe, tiefe Ewigkeit.*"[9] This is a startling admission. It certainly affirms what Lewis, along with many other Christian thinkers, assert about desire or longing. Perhaps the most familiar pronouncement on this is Augustine's famous remark at the beginning of his *Confessions*: "You have made us for Yourself, and our hearts are restless until they find their rest in You."[10] Whether Augustine meant the same thing by "restlessness" that Lewis means by "desire" is, of course, debatable. Blaise Pascal wrote in his *Pensées* in a similar vein:

> All men seek happiness. This is without exception. Whatever different means they employ, they all tend to this end. The cause of some going to war, and of others avoiding it, is the same desire in both, attended with different views. The will never takes the least step but to this object. This is the motive of every action of every man, even of those who hang themselves. And yet after such a great number of years, no one without faith has reached the point to which all continually look. . . . What is it then that this desire and this inability proclaim to us, but that there was once in man a true happiness of which there now remain to him only the mark and empty trace, which he in vain tries to fill from all his surroundings, seeking from things absent the help he does not obtain in things present? But these are all inadequate, because the infinite abyss can only be filled by an infinite and immutable object, that is to say, only by God Himself.[11]

Both Augustine and Pascal clearly envision man as an unsatisfied being, one who is driven to seek after something that is missing in his life. Both also see his search as a hopeless search until he finds God (or is found by Him). That is to say, all other objects that are sought in order to satisfy the longing are inadequate to the desire, for it can be satisfied only by "an infinite and immutable object, that is to say, only by God Himself." Diogenes Allen of Princeton Theological Seminary analyzes man's condition in a similar fashion but emphasizes that the beginning of man's search is not for God but for other things, things that man can imagine.

> We spend our lives seeking to satisfy our never-ending desires. . . . But we never seek God. In fact, we cannot at first seek God; initially, we have no idea of what it is that we are seeking. God is unlike anything of this world, unlike anything that we can imagine. Not only do we lack an idea of him so that we could seek him if we wished, we have at first no desire for him. Our desires are for things we can imagine, and they push us on and on relentlessly from one thing to another, seeking in one place after another to satisfy that hunger for fullness.[12]

Allen's analysis is very similar to Lewis's in that he sees man restlessly driven to seek in the wrong places for the satisfaction of his desires. In fact, the search as he describes it is for "fullness" or satisfaction from things that can be imagined or perceived on a human plane. Only when the discovery is made that none of the things tried provides the desired fullness does one begin to desire something beyond the world—that is, God. According to Allen, this place of "renouncing" the world—i.e., the supposed satisfaction offered by things in the world—is painful and comes only after suffering the pain of emptiness. It is at this time that God can be heard.

> To be hungry for life, and to admit that there is no proper food, is to suffer and know that there is no proper food. . . . That is why we let all sorts of things rush in to fill that painful emptiness, and will do almost anything except let ourselves feel, know, and live with the fact that we are creatures who crave and crave, and there is nothing of this world to fill us. It is at this time that God comes.[13]

A Critical Appraisal of Lewis's Argument from Desire

Peter Kreeft, a philosophy professor at Boston College, attaches great significance to the longing he sees in man's heart. In his view, the longing is innate, an intrinsic aspect of man's nature. Like Pascal, he emphasizes the vacuum, the hole that is present within the heart of man that cannot be filled by any earthly thing: "What you will find in your heart is not heaven but a heavenly hole, a womblike emptiness crying out to be filled, impregnated by your divine lover."[14]

All these thinkers insist that man's basic condition, his existential position, is one of lack. Despite all his efforts to find satisfaction in what the world offers, he fails. This is not to say that man never feels happy or contented or that he is constantly discouraged or depressed. As Lewis described the process in *The Pilgrim's Regress*, there may be many things that will offer temporary satisfaction, but they eventually fail to satisfy. This cycle of desire—activity aimed at satisfying the desire followed by momentary or partial satisfaction followed by renewed dissatisfaction and the desire to search further—is the basic pattern that all these writers maintain characterizes human existence. Man is neither a self-sufficient being nor one who can attain satisfaction through the objects present in the world.

This viewpoint is, of course, essentially different from hedonistic viewpoints that assert that man is happy when he experiences pleasure and avoids pain. It is also different from existentialist interpretations of reality that view man as able to choose and define his meaning individually and hence attain a certain self-satisfaction in life by means of the will. It naturally differs widely from a positivistic viewpoint that denies that any metaphysical statements can be made about man. It is, however, not strictly a revelational viewpoint. There is an empirical aspect to the view. Those who hold it maintain that the longing described is there in themselves and in people they observe everywhere. Nevertheless, it is not of the same order with other psychological phenomena that can be quantified and statistically analyzed. The existence of those who insist that they are entirely happy and content does nothing, however, to overturn the viewpoint contained in the argument from desire. Such claims of felicity are simply believed to be the consequence of the temporary situation or the suppression of deeper desires that one chooses to ignore or reinterpret. Ultimately, it is a philosophical position that starts with experience and empirical observation and places a metaphysical interpretation on what has been observed. Other interpretations are, of course, possible. This is an interpretation, however, that makes sense of the data of our lives. Peter Kreeft goes so far as to say:

> . . . it is far more moving, arresting, and apologetically effective than any other argument for God or for Heaven . . . it is more than an argument. Like Anselm's argument, it is also a meditation, an illumination, an experience, an invitation to an experiment with yourself, a pilgrimage.[15]

Whether or not the argument is as strong as Kreeft thinks it is, the question must still be addressed as to whether Lewis's version of the argument is essentially the same as Augustine's and Pascal's. On closer examination it appears there are significant differences. It is true that Lewis, like Augustine and Pascal, apprehends the need of man, his ontological incompleteness in the world. For Augustine this condition drives him to seek peace. Lewis, however, sees more than the deficiency in man. He regards the flashes of joy, which he sees as the positive side of desire, as signposts to God. Both saw man as valuable but unable to realize his potential apart from his Maker. Both saw God alone as able to satisfy or bring fulfillment to man. But Augustine saw man as broken and in need of repair, whereas Lewis, at least in his treatment of the argument from desire, saw man as *incomplete* and in search of the One who could complete him.

It would be unfair to imply that Lewis did not see man's sin and need for forgiveness. Nevertheless, his development of the argument from desire presents a picture of something positive driving man—namely, joy. Desire can be seen to drive man to experiment with any number of different things. These things may or may not be sinful, but the desire itself, at bottom, is seen as the magnetic pull of the heart for God. The glimpses of joy are then like flashes of light giving assurance that the desire is for something real, something that is not an illusion. Lewis,

A Critical Appraisal of Lewis's Argument from Desire

then, has a more positive conception of man and the working of desire than Augustine, whose concept of the restless heart is more like a negative push that results from the frustrations and disappointments one experiences in life. There are, indeed, many parallels, but their perspectives are not identical. Lewis's writings give evidence of a broad familiarity with Augustine, quoting him numerous times. Nevertheless, he does not lay claim to Augustine as corroborating his own view of desire.

Pascal's view seems, at first, closer to Lewis's than Augustine's. It is "happiness" that motivates man's every decision, according to Pascal. But happiness in Pascal's view is not the same as joy in Lewis's view. Pascal, indeed, sees the longing in man and the restless striving to find happiness. Man is "incomplete." In fact, there is an "abyss" within, and only the eternal God can fill it. But man's search for "happiness" (also called his "good"), as envisioned by Pascal, is self-centered, not other-directed. That is to say, the striving after happiness is not seen as positive, driving man toward that one object that can fill the void in his life. On the contrary, Pascal says:

> A trial so long, so continuous, and so uniform, should certainly convince us of our inability to reach the good by our own efforts. But example teaches us little. No resemblance is ever so perfect that there is not some slight difference; and hence we expect that our hope will not be deceived on this occasion as before. And thus, while the present never satisfies us, experience dupes us, and from misfortune to misfortune leads us to death, their eternal crown.[16]

Lewis speaks confidently of the "dialectic of experience" and says "experience is . . . such an honest thing. You may have deceived yourself, but experience is not trying to deceive you. The universe rings true wherever you fairly test it."[17] Pascal, in contrast, speaks of experience "duping" us. Whereas Lewis sees desire operating in such a way as to draw man—however gradually—toward God, Pascal would seem to say that it works in just the opposite way. In speaking of man's chief problems, Pascal says:

Your chief maladies are pride, which takes you away from God, and lust, which binds you to earth; and they have done nothing else but cherish one or other of these diseases.[18]

So, according to Pascal, our desires (our lusts) "bind us to earth" or, as he says in another passage, "our lusts turn us away from Him, we are full of unrighteousness."[19] In the end, then, it seems that Pascal and Augustine are closer to each other than either is to Lewis. Pascal's view that man is driven by his desire for happiness is only roughly parallel to Lewis's view. He would agree with Lewis that the very presence of his desires points back to his origin, to a time when he possessed a true happiness. He also affirms that the dialectic of experience should lead him to recognize that he is unable to attain happiness on his own efforts. But he is skeptical of man's ability to perceive these things. His desires have become "lusts," and he is "filled with unrighteousness."

In summary, it can be said there are good reasons to affirm Lewis's view that desire for an object beyond this world is innate in man. Both Augustine and Pascal, as well as contemporary Christian philosophers, argue forcefully in various terms that man is characterized by an onto-logical deficiency. By this it is not meant that man was deficient in his original design, but that he is now deficient in his being. The conse-quence of this deficiency and the effectiveness of man's restless desires in leading him to God are, however, points on which significant dif-ferences exist. Nevertheless, it should be added that Kreeft is entirely in agreement with Lewis, and Allen, though not to the same degree, is in substantial harmony with him also.

The Meaning of Desire/Joy

Even if the reality of desire is accepted, it remains to be considered what its existence signifies. John Beversluis categorically rejects any signifying meaning for joy: "Joy leads nowhere, and *Surprised by Joy* is wholly unconvincing as an attempt to demonstrate that there is a 'road right out of the self!' that points straight to God."[20]

To do justice to Lewis, it is necessary to remind ourselves that joy and desire are not two separate and distinct experiences, but more like two sides of one coin. To see "Joy" as the "thrill" or the bittersweet stab of longing apart from the more diffuse desire that drove him in his search for fulfillment would be a faulty understanding of his concept. It is, therefore, necessary to see the restless dissatisfaction that Lewis speaks of in *Surprised by Joy* and *The Pilgrim's Regress* as part of what he meant by joy—despite the fact that we do not easily associate "restless dissatisfaction" with our usual understanding of the word *joy*. The restless heart was for him the sign that he did not yet have real satisfaction; the brief sensation of joy was the sign that kept hope alive that real satisfaction was somewhere, somehow to be gained.

The reality of the "restless heart" makes man what modern-day sociologists refer to as "alienated." Certainly there are senses in which alienation is the consequence of social, economic, and political change or upheaval. Beyond that, however, the restless heart of man can be seen to point to a type of alienation from the temporal and spatial parameters of his existence. He longs for freedom from the limits that time and space and death place upon him. In Kreeft's words, "We long for the infinitely old and the infinitely new because we long for eternity."[21] This longing is, according to Malcolm Muggeridge, man's protection against "the only ultimate disaster that can befall us"—that is, "to feel ourselves to be at home here on earth. As long as we are aliens, we cannot forget our true homeland."[22] Kreeft analyzes this feeling of alienation and concludes that it points to a fundamental condition in our existence—namely, that we are not at home in this world.

> Alienation is the opposite of being at home. If the Bible is not wrong when it calls us "strangers and pilgrims," then that's why we feel alienation: We feel what is. When any organism is at home, there is an ecological fit with its environment, a harmony, a rightness. If the environment does not supply this, that environment is not its home.[23]

This alienation, this restless heart, is not just the consequence of scarcity, i.e., the lack of desirable things. "Things" are, as Kreeft points out, merely bridges, means, to something else. Having gotten to the "other side" of a bridge, that is, having acquired the "thing," be it a material thing or a position or a relationship or something else, the question reasserts itself: "Is this what I wanted? Is this all there is? Is there more?" These questions press themselves upon those who have attained what they thought they wanted. It is the person who has apparently arrived at the place where he wanted to be who feels these questions most acutely because that person is freed from what Kreeft calls the "'if only' syndrome: If only I had this or that, I would be happy."[24] As Pascal pointed out, "All complain, princes and subjects, noblemen and commoners, old and young, strong and weak, learned and ignorant, healthy and sick. . . ."[25] The attainment only accentuates the fact that the deeper desire was not for what was or even could be attained in this life but for something more. This is Lewis's dialectic of desire. The absence of something points to the existence of something. Contrary to what Beversluis thinks, the lack of satisfaction for innate desires signals that those desires require satisfaction from another source, a source beyond this world.

The danger, of course, is that one will cease applying the dialectic of desire. If one rigorously applies this dialectic and does not acquiesce in the partial satisfactions available in aesthetics, material prosperity, power, sex, or whatever else seems to promise fulfillment, the persistent desire does point beyond itself to an infinite object. It must be admitted, however, that very few people are so rigorous in thinking about their lives. They do not, in Lewis's words "fairly test" their experience. The "thousand false trails" of which he spoke in *The Pilgrim's Regress* seem to have ample appeal to people "bound to earth by lust" (to use Pascal's terminology). This lamentable result does not, however, controvert the sign function of desire. It only underscores the complication that sin inserts into the equation.

The Validity of the Major Premise of Lewis's Argument from Desire

The major premise in Lewis's argument from desire is that nature makes nothing in vain. Theoretically, it is possible that the existence

A Critical Appraisal of Lewis's Argument from Desire

of desire for an infinite object can be established and a reasonable interpretation of what is signified by such a desire defended; but if the major premise is erroneous, then obviously the whole argument collapses. Beversluis asserts that Lewis makes a grave error in logic in deducing from the existence of desire that a corresponding object must also exist. In part, his reason for this judgment is the rejection of the major premise of Lewis's argument.

> Just as we cannot prove that we inhabit a world in which food exists simply on the ground that we get hungry, so we cannot prove that an infinite Object of desire exists simply on the ground that we desire it. The desire in and of itself proves nothing, points to nothing. For all we know, perhaps some desires *are* in vain. Inferences from our own psychological makeup to what actually exists, much less to what *must* exist, are fallacious.[26]

Though Beversluis does not deny the existence of desire (how could he?) in many people, he does deny that it is universal or innate in man. The sheer fact of a widespread desire among people that cannot be satisfied by any earthly object cannot, according to Beversluis, be used as evidence that an infinite object for that desire exists. Strictly speaking, it must be granted that he is at least partially right. The widespread existence of desire for an infinite object cannot be said to *prove* that object exists. Lewis, however, does not claim that it does. He specifically says that "it is a pretty good indication that such a thing exists."[27] Beversluis, however, rejects even this conclusion. As an empiricist he points out that hunger as a phenomenon not only does not prove that a person will get something to eat, it does not even prove that anything such as eatable substances exist. For him, the only thing that proves that food exists "is the discovery that certain things are in fact 'eatable' and that they nourish and repair our bodies."[28]

Philosophically speaking, his case is difficult to refute. It is, perhaps, hypothetically possible that hunger could exist but that food does not, but the possibility is so remote as to be absurd. Beversluis's epistemology appears to be so circumscribed by his empiricism that he has slipped into the ludicrous. With such a limited epistemology, it would appear there would be very little indeed that would qualify as "knowledge." Let it, then, for the sake of argument, be granted that desire *proves* nothing; but the assertion that the widespread existence of desire *points* to nothing is an assertion that only appears reasonable in the eyes of a hard-boiled empiricist.

It is clear that neither Lewis, nor the other thinkers considered above, are philosophical empiricists. In order to make sense out of the world, one must assume that some things do point to others, that they are a sign of something else. In a pointed illustration of this principle Peter Kreeft offers some biting criticism of Beversluis's rejection of the significance of desire:

> This is simply to presuppose empiricism and to blind oneself to the sign-nature, the significance, of desire, as empiricists tend to do to everything. . . . My finger points to my dog's food. My dog, a true empiricist, comes and sniffs my finger. Dr. Beversluis is a dogged empiricist. To this mentality nothing has a built-in, real, metaphysical significance. Only words are signs, things are not, to the empiricist.[29]

The point is that there is in nature a correspondence between desire and the object that is desired. It can be argued that this applies only to some desires and not to all of them. No one claims that it applies to *all* desires. Imaginary desires, desires that come from the environment rather than from within, are not natural, innate desires. Such desires commonly have no real objects. They are not part of the common fund of desires that people everywhere generally have. The lack of real objects for such desires indicates nothing about nature other than the imaginative capacity of people. In contrast, *natural* desires for nonexistent objects imply an irrational universe—a universe in which nature misleads its members. If we find this notion unacceptable, i.e., that the universe is irrational and that nature routinely deals out desires for which there is no object, then the implication is that people's desire for an object that is not found in this world

A Critical Appraisal of Lewis's Argument from Desire

must be a desire for something beyond or outside of this material world. The question could be formulated in yet other terms: is there a sound basis for concluding that man's nature is in fundamental harmony with the reality within which he finds himself, or might he be what the Germans call a "Fehlkonstruktion" ("failed design")?

There is, of course, much—indeed, an overwhelming amount of—evidence that nature is purposeful. Lewis's major premise in his version of the argument from desire was that nature does nothing in vain. This is not to say that nothing happens in nature that is not rationally explicable. The point is, that which exists in nature can generally be seen to have a purpose.

Philosophically, it seems fair to conclude that Lewis's argument from desire, though not above criticism, is basically sound on its major points. His arguments are cogent if one is prepared to accept his premises. They are not compelling in the sense of forcing assent, but they are quite plausible interpretations of the phenomena of our experience. A positivist, or a rigid empiricist, such as Beversluis apparently is, will not accept the cogency of Lewis's arguments, but this is a result of his rejection of Lewis's premises as well as his epistemology.

A Theological Evaluation of Lewis's Argument from Desire

Lewis, as is characteristic of his writing, is rather restrained in his use of Scripture to support his views. Nevertheless, as is also typical, there are biblical motifs and principles that can be marshaled in support of the position he has taken. In this case, there are biblical and theological considerations that reveal both strengths and weaknesses in his argument.

Weaknesses of the Argument

The basic weakness of Lewis's argument from desire, as has already become evident in the discussion of Pascal's and Augustine's viewpoints, is the insufficient attention to the effects of sin. This is ironic in that Lewis held orthodox views on the Fall and the propensity to sin that resulted from it. He devoted two chapters in *The Problem of Pain* to sin ("Human Wickedness" and "The Fall"). He compares the downward drag of sin to the gravitational pull one feels on a smooth slope.

> Thus all day long, and all the days of our life, we are sliding, slipping, falling away—as if God were, to our present consciousness, a smooth inclined plane on which there is no resting. And indeed we are now of such a nature that we must slip off. . . . The gravitation away from God, 'the journey homeward to habitual self,' must, we think, be a product of the Fall.[30]

It seems somewhat incongruous that he could write so bluntly about sin in a book written in 1940 but reflect that thinking so little in books published in 1933 and 1955. This is not to say that he should have repeated much of what he had already said in *The Problem of Pain* and *Surprised by Joy*. The problem, however, amounts to a hamartiological weakness in his argument per se. When he speaks of joy as being a "road right out of the self . . . that proclaims itself sheerly objective,"[31] does he mean that man can perceive God apart from revelation and in spite of the effects of sin on his mind? When he speaks of desire being at bottom the desire for God, even though man is not aware that God is the object of his desire, has he not overlooked the effects of sin on the human heart? It is true that he speaks of the errors into which his desire led him and that he looks penitently on his errors, but he speaks with great optimism that the dialectic of desire will work, that desire listened to will inexorably attract one toward God. It is here that he fails to reflect the hamartiology of *The Problem of Pain*.

It is, of course, an old debate as to just how much unregenerate man is able to apprehend God. It is a difficult question to answer in a precise way.[32] Ephesians 2:3 and Romans 1 both seem to have a critical contribution to make to the discussion of the effect of desire. In the Ephesians passage we find a description of the condition of man before coming to faith. The apostle writes: "Among them we too all formerly lived in the lusts of our flesh, indulging the desires of the flesh and of the mind, and were by nature children of wrath, even as the rest"

A Critical Appraisal of Lewis's Argument from Desire

(NASB). Especially significant in this passage is the fact that *epithumia* ("lusts") and *thelema* ("desires") are both used. Both words are capable of having either positive or negative meanings, though *epithumia* is more commonly used for strong desires of a negative sort. Secondly, "desires of the flesh and of the mind" are mentioned. It seems clear that not only sins of the flesh are in view, but sins of the mind, i.e., a mind set in opposition to God. This condition by nature leads away from God rather than toward Him. Clearly, the picture that emerges from these passages is one of natural desires, either physical or intellectual, reinforcing man's separation from God rather than serving to attract him toward God. This, of course, is the marvel of Ephesians 2:5 where we read that "even while we were dead in our transgressions, [He] made us alive together with Christ (by grace you have been saved)" (NASB).

Romans 1:24-32 adds further details to this picture. In verse 24 (NASB) Paul says that "God gave them over in the lusts (*epithumia*) of their hearts to impurity." The situation described in this section is not one of ascent from wrong desires to increasingly better ones, but from bad to worse, to the practice of every kind of impurity with greediness. In these passages we see the principle of desire not leading to God but working against Him. The case is well summarized by Paul in Galatians 5:17 (NASB): "the flesh sets its desire against the Spirit, and the Spirit against the flesh; for these are in opposition to one another, so that you may not do the things that you please (*thelete*)."

All of these passages and many others in the New Testament point to a basic fact of our existence that Lewis failed adequately to take into account. The desire of man, like man himself, can be and is corrupted. His false paths are not just a matter of insufficient knowledge as to which path he should choose. His desire for wrong things leads him to culpably choose wrong paths; those choices are not merely the result of honest error. The New Testament picture is of desires becoming lusts—i.e., the desire for earthly objects becoming so strong that they control the individual rather than the individual controlling them. Though Lewis is surely right in saying that the earthly objects on which desire fixes itself do not truly satisfy, it is wrong to imply that most people draw this conclusion and therefore leave off pursuing things that do not satisfy. A more realistic and biblical picture is that the more freely one gives oneself to the objects of one's desires, the more enslaved one is likely to become to them. Unfortunately, Pascal's assessment of experience is often much nearer the truth, i.e., that "the present never satisfies us, experience dupes us, and from misfortune to misfortune leads us to death."[33]

It must be said yet again that Lewis did not claim to have sought God. He openly admits that he was pursuing his desire. Yet, he does claim that his experience of joy drew him on to the point that he eventually recognized that his desire was for something beyond this world. At that point he was fortunate enough to have been confronted with Christianity from various sources, including his friends (especially Dyson and Tolkien) and his reading (especially Chesterton and MacDonald). This fortunate convergence of two movements in his life resulted in Lewis coming to faith in Jesus Christ. Nevertheless, the point of his argument from desire is that he was being led toward God by his experiences of joy, even though he was long unaware of it. This is not easy to accept in light of the biblical data just looked at.

Perhaps a better way of conceiving of the process is to distinguish between desires and "joy"—joy being a particular desire, the desire for the infinite, for something beyond this world. Desires can be seen as regularly leading him astray, down one of the "false paths" that he mentions. But "joy" per se can be viewed as the call from beyond, that which causes the restless heart (*Sehnsucht*), the longing for something not of this world. Lewis, of course, comes close to this in the end when he speaks of joy pointing to something "other" and "outer," but he fails to make it clear or perhaps even to see that there is a disjunction between his (sinful) desires, which were not leading him toward God (biblically speaking), and "joy" (in the sense just defined). Biblically speaking, he arrived where he did, not because his desires led him there, but because he was given the wisdom to recognize his mistakes. Repentance is not a continuation in the same direction, just going further and deeper, but rather a turning from a wrong direction.

A Critical Appraisal of Lewis's Argument from Desire

Strengths of the Argument

Despite the legitimate criticisms that must be lodged against Lewis's version of the argument from desire, it must be admitted that it is an argument that has had a powerful effect. The power of the appeal is a consequence of the genuine realities that are imbedded in man's metaphysical situation. Pascal said:

> The greatness and the wretchedness of man are so evident that the true religion must necessarily teach us both that there is in man some great source of greatness, and a great source of wretchedness.[34]

One of the strengths of Lewis's argument from desire is that it focuses our attention on that "great source of greatness." Despite the realism and the necessity of what has just been said about sin, it must be insisted that is not the whole story. Man, indeed, has a "great source of wretchedness" within, but he is not only wretchedness. The implications of the argument from desire are that the greatness is a sign there is something eternal—something not reducible to pleasures or physical satisfactions—that corresponds to something outside of us that is greater than the wretchedness, and that the great can overcome the wretched.

Much of *The Pilgrim's Regress* is devoted to demonstrating that man is not just matter or biology or inherited complexes. Lewis vehemently rejects all reductionist notions of man. His argument from desire is especially impressive in presenting a vision of man as having a link with eternity. Our existence is never entirely explicable by what we see before us or by what we do. There is more to our being than our temporal existence. To this vision the Bible gives strong support. The very structure of the Canon as it has come down to us substantiates man's value and spiritual identity. According to the Scriptures, we stem from the garden, and our destiny, according to God's plan, is heaven. The first chapters and the last chapters of the Bible proclaim a vision of man that makes him only a little less than a god. Caught in the misery of suffering and death, it is easy to forget this—or not to believe it at all. Yet the memory of Eden and the hope for the New Jerusalem are kept alive by faith in the Word of God.

As preposterous as such faith might appear at times, particularly when under the dominance of the *Zeitgeist*,[35] there is something within man that answers to the call of eternity. Though the wisdom of Ecclesiastes must be applied with caution, Ecclesiastes 3:11 (NASB) can well be said to provide the explanation of why this answer to the call of eternity is in man: "He [God] has also set eternity in their heart, yet so that man will not find out the work which God has done from the beginning even to the end." This eternity in our hearts is the source of the longing for that which is greater than our earthly existence and without which all that we attain is, as the preacher proclaims, "vanity."

Despite the corruption of desire that is so clearly spoken of in the Scriptures, it would be a distortion of the biblical message to fail to see how strongly desire that is *properly directed* is encouraged. In the light of our ontology and our destiny, a longing for our home, for unity with God, is not only reasonable, it fits perfectly with our identity and our need. It is especially striking that Jesus came proclaiming the advent of the kingdom and inviting those who wanted it, those who desired it, who thirsted after it to come.[36] In the opening words of the Sermon on the Mount, He pronounces those "who hunger and thirst for righteousness" to be "blessed, for they shall be satisfied" (Matthew 5:6, NASB). In John's Gospel, it is reported that Jesus stood up during the feast of the tabernacles and cried out, "If any man is thirsty, let him come to Me and drink" (7:37, NASB). God's provision of water in the desert for His people serves to powerfully underscore Jesus' invitation to come to Him for the satisfaction of spiritual thirst in the desert of our existence. Those who respond to this invitation are promised a deep and inner satisfaction that is effected by the Holy Spirit. In the very last chapter of the Apocalypse, in the closing verses of the New Testament, the invitation is repeated to all who thirst after eternal life to come and satisfy that thirst, that desiring (*thelon*) by taking from "the water of life without cost" (Revelation 22:17, NASB).

A final point deserves to be made with respect to Lewis's develop-

A Critical Appraisal of Lewis's Argument from Desire

ment of the theme of desire or joy. Though Lewis failed, in my view, to adequately portray the corruption of desire in fallen man, his overall treatment does make a salutary contribution to our understanding of God. Our moral failures and the fear of judgment can quite easily create a rather, or even highly, negative image of God. We dare not lose sight of the fact that He is a God of righteousness, but at the same time it is also absolutely crucial that we not lose sight of the fact that He is desirable, not only because He is good, but because He is love and is the giver of joy. Any picture of God that is presented that lacks that aspect of His character is, to that degree, unbiblical. The clearer the vision becomes of who, not what, is the object of our desire for eternity, the better we shall understand and join in with the words of the psalmist:

> O God, Thou art my God; I shall seek Thee earnestly;
>   My soul thirsts for Thee, my flesh yearns for Thee,
> In a dry and weary land where there is no water. . . .
> Because Thy lovingkindness is better than life,
>   My lips will praise Thee. . . .
> My soul is satisfied as with marrow and fatness,
>   And my mouth offers praises with joyful lips.
>   —Psalm 63:1, 3, 5, NASB

BIBLIOGRAPHY

Allen, Diogenes. *The Traces of God.* Boston: Cowley Publications, 1981.

Beversluis, John. *C. S. Lewis and the Search for Rational Religion.* Grand Rapids, MI: Eerdmans, 1985.

Kreeft, Peter. *Heaven: The Heart's Deepest Longing.* San Francisco: Ignatius Press, 1989.

_____. "C. S. Lewis's Argument from Desire." In *G. K. Chesterton and C. S. Lewis: The Riddle of Joy.* Eds. Michael H. Macdonald and Andrew A. Tadie. Grand Rapids, MI: Eerdmans, 1989.

Lewis, C. S. *The Pilgrim's Regress.* Grand Rapids, MI: Eerdmans, 1943.

_____. *The Problem of Pain.* London: Geoffrey Bles, Centenary Press, 1940.

_____. *Surprised by Joy: The Shape of My Early Life.* New York: Harcourt Brace Jovanovich, 1955.

_____. "The Weight of Glory," in *The Weight of Glory and Other Addresses*. New York: Macmillan, 1975.

Pascal, Blaise. *Pensées*. Trans. W. F. Trotter. New York: The Modern Library/Random House, 1941.

Notes

1. This is especially so in his novels *Till We Have Faces*, *Perelandra*, and *The Voyage of the "Dawn Treader."*

2. Lewis, *The Pilgrim's Regress*, 128.

3. Lewis, "The Weight of Glory," 8.

4. Lewis, *The Pilgrim's Regress*, 176-77.

5. Ibid., 156.

6. Ibid., 171.

7. Ibid., 152.

8. Ibid., 10.

9. Author's translation: "All desire wants eternity, wants deep, deep eternity."

10. Augustine, *Confessions*, I.1.

11. Pascal, *Pensées*, #425, 134-35. Note: there are several editions of Pascal's *Pensées* in English. Unfortunately the paragraph numbering is not uniform in the various editions. Trotter's translation and paragraph numbering are used here along with the page numbers in the Modern Library edition of the work.

12. Allen, *The Traces of God*, 14.

13. Ibid., 16.

14. Kreeft, *Heaven: The Heart's Deepest Longing*, 35.

15. Kreeft, "C. S. Lewis's Argument from Desire," 249.

16. Pascal, *Pensées*, #425 (p. 134 in the Modern Library Edition).

17. Lewis, *Surprised by Joy*, 143.

18. Pascal, *Pensées*, #430 (p. 136 in the Modern Library Edition).

19. Ibid.

20. Beversluis, *C. S. Lewis and the Search for Rational Religion*, 16. Beversluis's work is a thoroughgoing rejection of C. S. Lewis's apologetic. In this author's view, his work is unbalanced and is frequently characterized by the very failures of which he so often scathingly accuses Lewis.

21. Kreeft, *Heaven: The Heart's Deepest Longing*, 80.

22. Malcolm Muggeridge, *Jesus Rediscovered* (London: Fontana Books, 1969), 16-17.

A Critical Appraisal of Lewis's Argument from Desire

23. Kreeft, *Heaven, The Heart's Deepest Longing*, 66.

24. Ibid., 58.

25. Pascal, *Pensées*, #425 (p. 134 in Modern Library Edition).

26. Beversluis, *C. S. Lewis and the Search for Rational Religion*, 19.

27. Lewis, "The Weight of Glory," 9.

28. Beversluis, *C. S. Lewis and the Search for Rational Religion*, 18.

29. Kreeft, "C. S. Lewis's Argument from Desire," 270.

30. Lewis, *The Problem of Pain*, 64.

31. Lewis, *Surprised by Joy*, 176.

32. Nevertheless, such passages as 1 Corinthians 2:14, Galatians 5:16-21, Ephesians 2:1-5 and 4:17-19, and Romans 1:24-32 and 3:10-18 are an essential part of finding a biblical answer to the question.

33. Pascal, *Pensées*, #425 (p. 134 in the Modern Library Edition).

34. Ibid., #430 (p. 136 in Modern Library Edition).

35. Lewis describes slavery to the giant, whom he calls *Zeitgeist*, in book three of *The Pilgrim's Regress*.

36. This is not to suggest that the Old Testament did not make similar calls. See especially Psalm 37:4, Isaiah 55:1-3, and Jeremiah 2:13 among other passages.

14

UNIVERSITY BATTLES:
C. S. Lewis and the Oxford University Socratic Club

CHRISTOPHER W. MITCHELL

When assessing C. S. Lewis's role as a defender of the faith, one area stands out for the lack of attention it has received. With the exception of Walter Hooper's fine essay "Oxford's Bonny Fighter,"[1] one is hard pressed to find anything else of article length written on the subject of the Oxford University Socratic Club. This is difficult to account for, because with the exception of his published work, no other activity that Lewis engaged in has proven more beneficial and far-reaching in its influence on Christianity than his participation in the Socratic Club. More often than not, when the subject of C. S. Lewis and the Socratic Club is raised, the conversation turns to Lewis's encounter with Catholic philosopher G. E. M. Anscombe. On the one hand, this is not surprising, given that many believed Lewis was so thoroughly trounced that February 2 evening in 1948 that he never fully recovered, either from the personal humiliation he is thought to have suffered or from the loss of confidence in his abilities as a defender of the Christian faith. Yet the inordinate amount of attention given to this one meeting has tended to distort not only Lewis's encounter with Miss Anscombe, but also his presence and role in the Socratic Club.

For thirteen years running, from 1942 to 1954, C. S. Lewis served as the Club's president. Meetings were held every Monday evening during each of the three academic terms, and unless he was ill or had some other engagement that he was unable to get out of, he was there.

C. S. Lewis and the Oxford University Socratic Club

As a University Club, the Socratic was a phenomenon. Meetings routinely had standing room only. During the years Lewis was president, the Socratic entertained some of the most influential atheists of the day, along with the weighty arguments they brought against Christianity. As the Socratic's point man, Lewis was relied upon to represent the Christian position and to argue its case against the opposition. Lewis accepted this role willingly. His one aim was to create and maintain an atmosphere in which faith could thrive. To do this he used the Socratic arena as a means of challenging the prevailing intellectual prejudices against the Christian faith.

In view of the more than 200 meetings of the Socratic Club that took place during Lewis's presidency, no more than a limited reassessment of its purpose and influence is aimed at here. In what follows, therefore, I intend, first, to demonstrate the inadequacy of evaluating Lewis and the Socratic enterprise through exclusive consideration of any single meeting by looking at the Club's overall purpose and impact, and second, to reassess within this larger context Lewis's importance as a defender of the faith in the Socratic arena. In order to do this we must begin by looking at the Club's founding and original vision.

THE FOUNDING OF THE SOCRATIC CLUB

One afternoon toward the end of 1941 during a tea party for newly matriculated freshmen at Oxford University, Monica Shorten, a student at Somerville College (one of the five women's colleges in Oxford), complained to Miss Stella Aldwinckle, a staff member of the Oxford pastorates, that no one seemed ready to seriously discuss the deeper questions raised by agnostics and atheists. "The sermons and the religious clubs just take the real difficulties as solved—things like the existence of God, the divinity of Christ and so on." Miss Aldwinckle asked the young woman whether there were others who felt like her. "Yes, plenty!" she replied. "Plenty of agnostics and atheists."[2]

Miss Aldwinckle had just joined the Oxford pastoral staff, a position that was designed to provide students with spiritual guidance. Having struggled herself with similar questions, she suggested they set up a meeting in the college and that Miss Shorten bring these agnostics and atheists along to ask questions. A notice, described by Miss Aldwinckle as "lurid" and full of "blobs of ink," went out on Somerville notice-boards, inviting "all atheists, agnostics, and those disillusioned about religion or think they are" to meet at the East Junior Commons Room to discuss the matter. In spite of the ghastly notice, the meeting was well attended. "I went a few days later as a Daniel to a den of lions," Miss Aldwinckle recalled, "expecting to be torn limb from limb." But the entire affair proved quite civil. Many good and thoughtful questions were raised. Everyone was interested and wanted to know if they could meet again and bring their boyfriends. It was agreed that they would, and at the next meeting it was standing room only. People squeezed together, and floods of good questions again poured forth. It was decided that what was needed was an open forum for the discussion of the intellectual difficulties connected with religion in general and with Christianity in particular. This was the Socratic Club in embryo.[3]

The next order of business was to decide on a president. Obviously not just anyone would do. Miss Aldwinckle recognized that the success of the entire enterprise hung on this decision. She entertained the idea of Dorothy L. Sayers but decided against it because Sayers lived in London. However, Miss Aldwinckle had recently heard of a don at the University who was an outspoken Christian but had been an atheist for many years. He taught English Language and Literature at Magdalen College. This was our man, she thought, and immediately wrote Mr. C. S. Lewis to ask him whether he would honor them by becoming president.[4] Lewis promptly responded, "Dear Miss Aldwinckle, This club is long overdue. Come to coffee on Tuesday evening in my rooms to discuss plans."[5] By the beginning of the next term, January of 1942, the University Socratic Club had been granted official approval and was up and running.

THE MAKING OF A SOCRATIC PRESIDENT

Now I must digress a moment to look a bit more closely at Miss Aldwinckle's choice of a president. At first glance, it may not at all be obvious why she should have chosen a teacher of English Language and Literature to lead such an undertaking. But C. S. Lewis was not your typical English don.

Lewis was born into a Protestant home in Belfast, Ireland, in 1898. His exposure to Christianity during his childhood had little influence upon him intellectually. By the time he entered Oxford University in 1917 he was a confirmed rational atheist. After finishing a degree in "Greats" (i.e., classics and philosophy), Lewis continued on for a second degree in English Language and Literature. During this period of time, his atheistic assumptions increasingly came under attack by much of what he read. Especially alarming was Lewis's realization that writers like George MacDonald, George Herbert, and G. K. Chesterton, who were avowedly Christian in their orientation, proved far more interesting and sensible than their "enlightened" counterparts. But a more important and sustained challenge to Lewis's atheist assumptions came from a fellow student and friend, Owen Barfield. Barfield's success became evident when in 1929 Lewis renounced his atheism and confessed a belief in God. Two years later he would take the final step and express faith in Jesus Christ as the Son of God.[6]

But Lewis's pilgrimage through intellectual atheism to Christianity was not the only asset he brought to the presidency. His training, temper, and conviction were a natural fit for the kind of intellectual rigor and butting of heads the Socratic model assumed. Lewis's preparation for this role began at Malvern College, the school he attended in 1913. Harry Wakelyn Smith, or "Smewgy" as the students called him, was Malvern's Classics Master, and it was under his tutelage that Lewis said his first real training in thinking as a method of intellectual endeavor really began. "He could enchant but he could also analyze," recalled Lewis. "An idiom or a textual crux, once expounded by Smewgy, became clear as day. He made us feel that the scholar's demand for accuracy was not merely pedantic, still less an arbitrary moral discipline, but rather a niceness, a delicacy, to lack which argued 'a gross and swainish disposition.'"[7]

In September of the next year, Lewis found himself in Bookham, Surrey, under the instruction of yet another formative influence,

William T. Kirkpatrick. For the following two and a half years Lewis was tutored by the "Great Knock," as he affectionately called Kirkpatrick. "If ever a man came near to being a purely logical entity, that man was Kirk," said Lewis. Kirkpatrick was an Ulster Scot who had turned atheist. As a teacher, he was a born Socratic, querying his pupils with probing questions until he had elicited a clear expression of the truth or facts under discussion. His "ruthless dialectic" came as naturally to him as did walking, and he applied it across the board. Under his mentoring, Lewis mastered the art of refutation and developed a passion for precise terms.[8] All the time he was at Bookham,

> [t]he most casual remark was taken as a summons to disputa-
> tion. The loud cry of 'Stop!' was flung in to arrest a torrent of
> verbiage which could not be endured a moment longer; . . . The
> hastier and quieter 'Excuse!' ushered in a correction or distinc-
> tion merely parenthetical and betokened that, thus set right,
> your remark might still, without absurdity, be allowed to reach
> completion. The most encouraging of all was, 'I hear you.' This
> meant that your remark was significant and only required refu-
> tation; it had risen to the dignity of error.[9]

In the school of the Great Knock, Lewis the pupil began to put on "intellectual muscle," eventually becoming a skilled dialectician who could hold his own before his master. It was a great day, Lewis recalled, "when the man who had so long been engaged in exposing my vagueness at last cautioned me against the dangers of excessive subtlety."[10]

The next stage in Lewis's training as an apologist and disputant came during his days as a student at Oxford University. The trainer on this occasion was friend and fellow classmate Owen Barfield. With Barfield, Lewis entered what might be called a boot camp for *civil* disputation. Lewis said Barfield was both his *alter ego* in that he shared all his most secret delights, but also his antiself. "He shared [my] interests, . . . but he . . . approached them all at a different angle. . . . It is as if he spoke your language but mispronounced it. . . . When you set out to correct his heresies, you [found] that he foresooth [had] decided to correct yours! And then you go at it, at it hammer and tongs, far into the night, night after night."[11]

Barfield's conversion to Anthroposophy (theistic in its orientation but not Christian) marked the beginning of what Lewis referred to as the "Great War." Lewis's atheism now came under skilled assault, and his comment about their disagreements is telling: "It was never, thank God, a quarrel, though it could have become one in a moment if he had used to me anything like the violence I allowed myself to him . . . it was an almost incessant disputation, sometimes by letter and sometimes face to face, which lasted for years."[12] Barfield modeled the virtue of argumentation that is ruled by civility and in the process further honed and refined Lewis's dialectical skills.

Out of the Great War with Barfield came one of the great turning points in Lewis's intellectual life, one that would shape him as an apologist. Lewis speaks of a prevailing assumption that he later was to dub "chronological snobbery," that is, the "uncritical acceptance of the intellectual climate common to our own age and the assumption that whatever has gone out of date is on that account discredited." Chronological snobbery, which by this time had become one of the central tenets of Lewis's intellectual makeup, was used to make Christianity irrelevant. As the result of one of Barfield's counterattacks, this supposition was destroyed forever. Neither the uncritical dismissal of premises nor the complacent acceptance of contemporary assumptions was any longer admissible. Concerning the former, Lewis realized, "you must find why it went out of date. Was it ever refuted (and if so by whom, where, and how conclusively) or did it merely die away as fashions do? If the latter, this tells us nothing about its truth or falsehood." Regarding the latter, Lewis passed on to the realization that our own age was also a period, like all periods before it, and that it had its own characteristic illusions. Such illusions, he began to perceive, are often to be found "in those widespread assumptions which are so ingrained in the age that no one dares to attack or feels it necessary to defend them."[13]

A most startling and unforgettable encounter Lewis had about this time reinforced the lesson. During the early part of the twentieth century, it had become routine within the academy to reject the historicity, that is to say the historical reliability, of the Gospel accounts. This was an assumption that for many had become an indubitable fact. Early in 1926, Lewis recounted, "the hardest boiled of all the atheists I ever knew sat in my room on the other side of the fire and remarked that the evidence for the historicity of the Gospels was really surprisingly good. 'Rum thing,' he went on. 'All that stuff of Frazer's about the Dying God. Rum thing. It almost looks as if it had really happened once.'" Here was a rather interesting anomaly, both because of who the person was and because he defied protocol and actually investigated a matter that among his circle of colleagues was a dead issue. Lewis was stunned. "If he, the cynic of cynics, the toughest of the toughs, were not—as I would still have put it—'safe,' where could I turn? Was there then no escape?"[14] What Lewis had bumped up against was an important bit of chronological snobbery put to the test, and it hadn't fared too well.

Upon renouncing his historical snobbishness, Lewis found his defenses against Christianity alarmingly depleted. Intellectual prejudices that had securely insulated him from the momentous claims of the Christian faith now failed him. It was a moment he was never to forget. Having learned the lesson well, it was to become one of his most formidable weapons in defense of the Christian faith.

Furthermore, by the end of 1941, when Lewis was asked to become the first president of the newly formed University Club, he had already published several books and articles in defense of Christianity and others written from a Christian point of view. Among these were *The Pilgrim's Regress*, *Out of the Silent Planet*, *The Problem of Pain* and *The Screwtape Letters*. By this time Lewis had also completed a series of highly successful radio talks on Christianity, which later became part of his book *Mere Christianity*.

Lewis was then, by nature and training, a naturally Socratic soul. The inspiration of Smewgy and the rigorous intellectual fencing experienced with Kirkpatrick and Barfield prepared Lewis for the role he would be called upon to fill in the Socratic. Consequently, when Miss Aldwinckle scanned the intellectual terrain of Oxford, she found no Christian quite so outspoken or experienced in the defense of the Christian faith as the English don from Magdalen.

C. S. Lewis and the Oxford University Socratic Club

THE INTELLECTUAL CHALLENGE AND THE SOCRATIC AGENDA

The Socratic Club was established for the express purpose of answering the intellectual challenge to belief in the tenets of the Christian faith. The atmosphere of Oxford before the war years was marked by skepticism and disillusionment. Many of the University's faculty taught that there was no such thing as truth in the ultimate sense. The advent of war only contributed to the already growing sense of intellectual despair that was gripping much of the University. Yet there were those who did not want to give in to the prevailing skepticism. And as Monica Shorten and her friends had shown, it was not only seeking and questioning Christians who wanted honest answers to their questions; unbelieving agnostics were equally interested to see if Christianity could successfully challenge the prevailing anti-Christian ideas.[15] These were students, Miss Aldwinckle said, who believed that existence had some significance and were prepared to contend with it till it yielded its secret. They persisted in asking ultimate questions because they were convinced skepticism was inadequate. But the Christian faith they had experienced in conventional settings—hypocritical Christians, bad sermons and ineffective Scripture lessons—had proved less relevant. It was primarily for such "ruthless realists" as these that the Socratic existed.[16]

The challenge, as Lewis and Miss Aldwinckle saw it, was to help these young realists find their way spiritually. In order to do this, they would have to challenge the various intellectual prejudices arrayed against Christianity by demonstrating the integrity of the Christian's belief system. And to do this effectively they would need highly qualified participants. So they turned to the *Who's Who* and scoured it to find Christian and non-Christian speakers who were specialists in their respective fields of study. As Lewis put it, they sought out "intelligent atheists who had the leisure or zeal to come and propagate their creed."[17] Both Lewis and Aldwinckle were convinced of the truth of Christianity, and they were ready and willing to test its mettle in the Socratic arena before all comers.

The reason for Lewis's own willingness to accept the position of president is stated in his preface to the first *Socratic Digest*. Socrates,

Lewis comments, had exhorted men to "follow the argument wherever it led them." As he envisioned it, the Socratic Club was created to apply this principle to one particular subject—the pros and cons of the Christian religion. In the process, he hoped it would be shown that Christianity was far more rational and sensible than many had been led to believe. Lewis's observations at this point are critical for a proper understanding of the purpose and vision of the Socratic Club and for Lewis's role as its president.

> It is a little remarkable that, to the best of my knowledge, no society had ever before been formed for such a purpose. There had been plenty of organisations that were explicitly Christian . . . and there had been plenty of others, scientific or political, which were if not explicitly, yet profoundly anti-Christian in outlook . . . but an arena specially devoted to the conflict between Christian and unbeliever was a novelty. Its value from a merely cultural point of view is very great. In any fairly large and talkative community such as a university, there is always the danger that those who think alike should gravitate together into *coteries* where they will henceforth encounter opposition only in the emasculated form of rumour that the outsiders say thus and thus. The absent are easily refuted, complacent dogmatism thrives, and differences of opinion are embittered by group hostility. Each group hears not the best, but the worst, that the other groups can say.[18]

One of the things Lewis had in mind that went unchallenged under the cultural conditions he described was that prevailing premise of modern intellectual inquiry, "chronological snobbery." The Socratic arena was a place where this assumption could be properly challenged. In the Socratic, he continued, "a man could get the case for Christianity without all the paraphernalia of pietism and the case against it without the irrelevant *sansculottisme* of our common anti-God weeklies."[19]

Having said this, however, Lewis went on to emphasize two further critical points: first, the partisan nature of the enterprise, and second, the intellectual honesty of the Socratic arena.

C. S. Lewis and the Oxford University Socratic Club

> Those who founded it do not for one moment pretend to be neu-
> tral. It was the Christians who constructed the arena and issued
> the challenge. It will therefore always be possible for the lower
> (the less Athenian) type of unbeliever to regard the whole thing
> as a cunningly—or not even so very cunningly—disguised form
> of propaganda. . . . But when all is said and done, the answer to
> any such suspicion lies deeper. It is not here that the honesty of
> the Socratic comes in. We never claimed to be impartial. But
> argument is. It has a life of its own. No man can tell where it
> will go. We expose ourselves, and the weakest of our party, to
> your fire no less than you are exposed to ours. . . . The arena is
> common to both parties and cannot finally be cheated.[20]

The Socratic Club was deliberately designed to be an arena where
Christian and non-Christian could intellectually lock horns in an
atmosphere that was fearless and unyielding in argumentation, yet
ruled by civility.

THE SOCRATIC ARENA

The tendency has been to portray the Socratic Club as simply a platform
for Lewis, one from which he could bully his opponents into submis-
sion while a host of devotees cheered him on to victory. One of the more
extreme depictions of Lewis's Socratic persona illustrates this well.

> [I]t was not always easy to find a tame atheist who was prepared
> to come along and be mauled in public debate; for on these occa-
> sions he reverted to type and became again the P'daytabird
> prosecuting an unlikely prisoner in the Belfast police courts. No
> one who witnessed these debates has ever suggested that Lewis
> played fair. He argued with tremendous vigour, and when he
> demolished his victims it was with evident relish.[21]

Such a portrayal of Lewis and the Socratic Club is, however, mis-
leading. He was not the tormenting bully that is here portrayed. The
spirit of triumphalism was never part of Lewis's or Miss Aldwinckle's

agenda, although admittedly there was a great tendency among many of the students who attended to view it in such terms. According to John Wain, one of Lewis's pupils during the war years, Lewis had a permanent audience who "passionately wanted him to win."[22] In contrast with the perspective of the students, it is interesting to hear what Lewis wrote to his friend Dom Bede Griffiths in April of 1954, his last year as president. "At the Socratic the enemy often wipe the floor with us. *Quous que domine?*"[23] Although Lewis believed the Christian faith was superior to all rival faiths and ideologies, he never assumed that the Christian's particular defense and representation of it would necessarily always come out on top. In August 1946 he confessed to Dorothy L. Sayers, "My own frequent uneasiness comes from another source—the fact that apologetic work is so dangerous to one's own faith. A doctrine never seems dimmer to me than when I have just successfully defended it."[24] Austin Farrer, the distinguished theologian and a close personal friend of Lewis who attended and participated in the Socratic meetings, has, I believe, captured both the spirit of the Socratic Club and Lewis's leadership in his description of him as an apologist.

> Lewis was an apologist from temper, from conviction, and from modesty. From temper, for he loved an argument. From conviction, being traditionally orthodox. From modesty, because he laid no claim either to the learning which would have made him a theologian or the grace which would have made him a spiritual guide. His writings certainly express a solid confidence; but it is the confidence that he can detect the fallacy of current objections to belief, and appreciate the superiority of orthodox tenets over rival positions; that he has some ability, besides, to make others see what he so clearly sees himself. These are modest claims, when compared with the pretension to look deeply into the things of God: a pretension he never advanced, even by implication, either on intellectual or spiritual grounds.[25]

But Lewis did love a good fight and was well known for his combative spirit. In relation to apologetics, he explained his passionate and

C. S. Lewis and the Oxford University Socratic Club

forceful defense of the Christian faith in terms of Donne's maxim, "'The heresies that men leave are hated most.' The things I assert most vigorously," he stated, "are those that I resisted long and accepted late."[26] In the intellectual arena of the weekly Socratic meeting, Lewis was both protagonist and antagonist. Students and colleagues alike looked almost exclusively to him to uphold the Christian position against those who came to challenge it.

Rachel Trickett, who later became principal of St. Hugh's College, was an undergraduate at the University during the years 1942 to 1945. She remembers Lewis as extremely lucid and forceful in lectures, though not particularly inspiring. However, she indicates that in the Socratic, all was changed. There he was the great gladiator whom "we'd all flock to hear every week for his brilliant and dazzling encounters with atheists, psychical researchers, [and] people of different denominations." She recalls that Lewis seemed always to have just the right analogy for every situation, often leaving his opponents stunned.[27] In the early years of the club's existence, Austin Farrer was occasionally called upon to be ready to fill in for Lewis in case he didn't show up. Farrer remembers going in fear and trembling, "certain to be caught out in debate and to let down the side." But then Lewis would show up, "snuffing the imminent battle and saying 'Aha!' and all Farrer's anxieties would roll away."[28]

Visiting opponents typically viewed Lewis as a fearless and formidable opponent, yet equally "generous" in argument. He was admired for the intellectual rigor he brought to each topic and discussion and was known both for his "courage" and "open-mindedness."[29] Often it was the chance to cross intellectual swords with him more than anything else that attracted some of Britain's best non-Christian thinkers. One such opponent was the Irish writer and playwright Shaw Desmond. Desmond was a brilliant speaker. He lectured throughout Britain, Scandinavia, and the United States and founded the International Institute for Psychical Research. Hearing of the Socratic Club, he wrote to Lewis in September 1945 to ask if he might himself have the privilege of entering the arena with him. "I have heard that you are fearless and generous to those with whom you have the happiness to differ, and possibly you might be disposed to entertain angels unawares (as an Irishman I may be permitted to throw bouquets at myself and brickbats at the Other Fellow!)."[30] An invitation was indeed forthcoming.[31]

The meetings were typically held in college common-rooms and were always well attended.[32] One of the most notable encounters pitted Lewis against Professor C. E. M. Joad. Joad was then head of the department of philosophy at Birkbeck College, University of London and a popular radio broadcaster on the BBC's Brain Trust. Miss Aldwinckle described the meeting as the most memorable and amusing in the history of the Socratic. It took place on the evening of January 24, 1944. It was scheduled to be held in the Senior Commons Room of St. Hilda's College, but due to the size of the crowd, a second commons room was added. Soon, however, it became apparent that even this arrangement would not be adequate to accommodate everyone; so through the kindness of the bursar, they were allowed to move into the dining room, and even then there was standing room only. Joad was an agnostic who had struggled with the problem of suffering and evil for some years and had recently found Lewis's treatment of the issue in *The Problem of Pain* convincing. He was already moving in the direction of Christianity when he met Lewis that January evening, and his paper "On Being Reviewed by Christians" was only moderately critical of the Christian faith. Even so, the atmosphere was combative and the interchange electrifying.[33] Not long after, Professor Joad embraced Christianity. In his autobiographical work *The Recovery of Belief*, Joad carefully traced the stages in the development of his beliefs from agnosticism to Christianity, noting along the way how important Lewis was in his pilgrimage to faith.[34]

Another celebrated meeting, and the one that has figured large in assessments of Lewis, came during the Hilary term of 1948. The guest speaker on this occasion was fellow Christian and Catholic philosopher G. E. M. Anscombe. The previous year Lewis had published a work of apologetics entitled *Miracles*. In chapter 3, "The Self-Contradiction of the Naturalist," he argued that naturalism was self-refuting.[35] Miss Anscombe, who was at the time a philosophy tutor at

C. S. Lewis and the Oxford University Socratic Club

Somerville College, came prepared to refute Lewis's position.[36] Lewis's central premise was that the naturalist's belief in the validity of reason is contradicted by one of the fundamental tenets of naturalism, which is that all human thought is a product of irrational causes. If this is true, Lewis pointed out, then human thought itself is irrational and so too naturalism.

Although Anscombe stated she did not think there was sufficient reason for believing the naturalist "hypothesis about human behaviour and thought," she also maintained that someone who did could not be refuted by Lewis's argument because he mistakenly equated irrational causes with non-rational causes and confused the concepts of cause, reason, and explanation.[37] Although the audience that evening was divided in their opinion as to who got the better of whom, it is often stated (as noted above) that the spirited philosophy tutor thoroughly demolished Lewis's entire premise. Such a portrayal, however, is a distortion not only of Lewis's encounter with Miss Anscombe, but also his own reaction to the outcome. While a full analysis of the debate cannot be undertaken here, a modest reappraisal of these two aspects of the meeting will shed some additional light on Lewis's role as a defender of the faith.

A couple of days after the Socratic meeting, Lewis dined with his friend and colleague Hugo Dyson and four of their pupils. Derek Brewer, one of the students, distinctly remembers that Lewis was greatly troubled by the outcome of the encounter, and his sense of defeat cast a shadow over the entire dinner conversation.[38] George Sayer, a friend and biographer of Lewis, has given a similar account of Lewis's response to the outcome of his meeting with Anscombe. He recalls that not long after the debate, Lewis told him that Anscombe had destroyed his argument for the existence of God and that he considered it a most serious matter.[39] However, Miss Anscombe, who also dined with Lewis not long after the meeting, gives a conflicting account of Lewis's feelings. "The meeting of the Socratic Club at which I read my paper has been described by several of his friends as a horrible and shocking experience which upset him very much. Neither Dr. Havard (who had Lewis and me to dinner a few weeks later) nor Professor Jack

Bennett remembered any such feelings on Lewis's part. . . . I am inclined
to construe the odd accounts of the matter by some of his friends . . .
as an interesting example of the phenomenon called 'projection'."[40]

Anscombe's experience notwithstanding, it does not seem possible
to reduce the perceptions of Brewer and Sayer to mere "projection."
Lewis was clearly troubled. But the question is, over what? Sayer's recollection of Lewis's struggle strikes to the heart of the matter. When
Lewis told Sayer that his defeat was a serious matter, he said it was
because in the minds of many people, "the disproof of an argument for
the existence of God tended to be regarded as a disproof of the existence of God."[41] At the center of Lewis's struggle was a concern for the
faith of the Christians he represented. He could live with the fact that
he had been bested; but he continued to struggle with the implications
his defeat may have had for the faith of others. In his essay on Lewis
as apologist, Austin Farrer brings this point into sharper focus.

> It is commonly said that if rational argument is so seldom the
> cause of conviction, philosophical apologists must largely be
> wasting their shot. The premise is true, but the conclusion does
> not follow. For though argument does not create conviction, the
> lack of it destroys belief. What seems to be proved may not be
> embraced; but what no one shows the ability to defend is
> quickly abandoned. Rational argument does not create belief,
> but it maintains a climate in which belief may flourish. So the
> apologist who does nothing but defend may play a useful,
> though preparatory, part.[42]

Lewis was well aware of the truth of Farrer's observation. More than
two years after the debate with Anscombe, he was still wrestling with
the issue. Writing to Miss Aldwinckle in June 1950, he proposed a list
of potential speakers for the next term's Socratic Club. Number four
on the list was Miss Anscombe. "I shd. press hard for no. 4," he said,
"The lady is quite right to refute what she thinks bad theistic arguments, but does this not almost oblige her as a Christian to find good
ones in their place: having obliterated me as an Apologist, ought she

C. S. Lewis and the Oxford University Socratic Club

not to succeed me?"[43] I do not mean to imply that Lewis did not struggle with the reality that his argument had been found wanting in his encounter with Anscombe, for it is only reasonable to assume that he did. But the more profound and long-lasting concern was for others.

Looking at the Anscombe encounter from this angle, it is evident that in the Socratic arena Lewis self-consciously worked as an apologist for educated laypersons. On their behalf he labored to clear away the intellectual obstacles that unnecessarily impeded either the unbeliever's acceptance of Christianity or the Christian's growth in the faith. It was a labor he was committed to and one that continued to occupy him until his death in 1963.

The second aspect of the debate that concerns us here is its long-term impact on Lewis's work as an apologist. Was Lewis's confidence to defend the faith completely shaken by his encounter with Miss Anscombe, and did he believe that his entire premise (naturalism is self-refuting) had been shown to be invalid? There are at least four good reasons to think he did not. First, Lewis took the time to revise his argument in light of Anscombe's criticisms. The revised chapter, published in 1960 with the new title "The Cardinal Difficulty of the Naturalist," replaced the last five pages of the original chapter with ten new pages.[44] Such an exercise would make little sense if Lewis thought his entire argument was fundamentally flawed.

Second, many observers did not come away from the meeting with the impression that Lewis's basic position was shown to be wrong. Among them was Miss Anscombe herself. In the introduction to the second volume of her collected works, she states that she believed her criticisms of Lewis's first edition were still just and that there remained elements within the second edition to which she took exception. However, she acknowledged a marked improvement in the overall argument of the revised chapter. Nowhere does she suggest that Lewis's entire premise was misguided.[45] Moreover, Professor Basil Mitchell, the distinguished University of Oxford philosopher who was present at the debate and succeeded Lewis as president of the Socratic Club in 1954, insists there was no reason to believe Lewis was shown to be "hopelessly wrong."[46]

Third, it is not true that Lewis ceased writing and lecturing in the field of apologetics after the debate. Two obvious examples are his ongoing involvement in the Socratic Club and his revision of chapter 3 of *Miracles*. However, the meeting was a turning point in his career as an apologist. For one thing, he never again attempted to take on the professional philosophers of the day. He told George Sayer, "I can never write another book of that sort," referring to *Miracles*.[47] I believe Professor Mitchell has judged the impact of Lewis's meeting with Anscombe on this point correctly.

> [T]here was no warrant for supposing that in the original debate Lewis had been shown to be just hopelessly wrong. It was rather that he was not equipped with the kind of philosophical techniques which were needed at that stage to cope with a highly professional performer like Elizabeth Anscombe. And so Lewis probably drew the correct inference and decided that he couldn't take on the professional philosophers at their own game . . . if he was . . . he would have to do a lot of homework. He had no particular aptitude for—and no particular interest in—the dominant philosophy of his day, and he could better spend his time doing other things that he was supremely good at.[48]

Lewis continued to present the Christian faith as something worth believing in, but he engaged less in the overtly apologetic work that relied exclusively on the well-reasoned argument. Ten years after his encounter with Miss Anscombe, Lewis wrote, "Christians and their opponents again and again expect that some new discovery will either turn matters of faith into matters of knowledge or else reduce them to patent absurdities. But it has never happened."[49]

Lastly, a little known sequel to the debate suggests that Lewis had no reason to think his position was completely erroneous. Sometime in the 1960s John Lucas, a philosophical colleague of Professor Mitchell's, conceived the idea of having a rerun of the Anscombe-Lewis encounter with himself taking up Lewis's side of the argument. Anscombe agreed, and on that occasion the general consensus, accord-

C. S. Lewis and the Oxford University Socratic Club

ing to Professor Mitchell, seemed to be that Lucas successfully upheld Lewis's position.[50]

What remains to be emphasized is that Lewis's weekly presence in the Socratic arena was not dependent upon a triumphal outcome. As he remarked to his friend Dom Bede Griffiths, those who opposed the Christian faith often came out on top.[51] Nor was he there solely because of his love for disputation, though he certainly enjoyed the opportunity the Socratic arena afforded him to indulge this side of his temperament. Rather, the overriding reason he came week after week was his deep conviction of the truth and reasonableness of Christianity and his desire to help others come to the same conviction.

THE SOCRATIC LEGACY

At a time when many had begun to believe Christianity was dying, if not already dead, as a plausible system of belief, the Socratic Club reasserted the intellectual vitality and integrity of the Christian faith. From its inception the Socratic Club demonstrated to those who attended that in spite of the intellectual hostility arrayed against Christianity, there were many who found the positions of atheists and agnostics inadequate and were willing to put the case against Christianity to the test. Week in and week out, Lewis and others showed that the Christian faith had not been rendered intellectually inferior by the "enlightened" thinking of the age.

Those who benefited the most were those who had been brought up Christian and were hoping for a reason to believe Christianity was true.[52] Although Rachel Trickett could remember little about the Socialists Club she attended as an Oxford undergraduate, she has retained vivid memories of the Socratic Club, and especially of Lewis. Nobody could escape his influence, she recalls. The effect he had on the young people was enormous. More than anything, it was the "kind of direct sincerity and immediacy in his approach to ethical, moral, as well as theological problems," she stated, that made the greatest impact. At the Socratic one was certain to get an up-to-date and relevant case for Christianity.[53] His lucid and clear presentation of both sides of the argument helped them see and understand what he understood and to incorporate it into their thinking.

This particular aspect of Lewis's influence is nicely illustrated by the experience of Lady Elizabeth Catherwood (daughter of renowned minister Martyn Lloyd-Jones). Although she never attended a Socratic meeting (she attended the Christian Union that met at the same time as the Socratic Club), all her friends did. When they would return, they would sit up, often until 2 in the morning, going through all the discussions. What she remembers most from those late-night discussions was Lewis's "way of thinking through a thing."[54] By retracing the points of Lewis's argument, they began to detect the fallacies of current objections to belief. They also gained a new appreciation and understanding of Christianity's ability to answer the moral and theological problems that had before filled them with doubts.

By breaking down the intellectual prejudices to Christianity, Lewis freed many to reaffirm a faith they had lost confidence in, and for some he made faith in Christianity plausible for the first time. The importance of the Socratic enterprise was not in its ability to create faith, but to maintain an atmosphere where faith was possible, and where it could be rekindled, grow, even thrive. This is the Socratic legacy, and its benefits extended to Lewis's writing enterprise as well. Often the apologetics that go out under the cover of a book do so without having been tested and sometimes go unchallenged once in print. This was seldom the case with Lewis's works. Most of what he published in the way of apologetics found its way into the Socratic arena at some point, either after the fact or before. In the case of his argument against naturalism, he was found wanting, but Lewis used what he learned to revise and strengthen his position. The point is that although Lewis worked on a nonprofessional level in the field of apologetics, his arguments were frequently tested in ways that many of his professional colleagues never faced. For those who knew of Lewis's weekly encounter, his published work took on an added dimension of authenticity.[55]

It is worth noting that the idea that Lewis only surrounded himself with inferiors, as the recent motion picture *Shadowlands* has conveyed, simply does not stand up to the facts. During his years as president of

C. S. Lewis and the Oxford University Socratic Club

the Socratic Club, Lewis faced some of Christianity's most potent foes and was able to consistently demonstrate the plausibility of the Christian position. The legacy of the Socratic Club is ultimately the legacy of the apologetic enterprise—namely, the continuing existence of Christianity as a viable system of belief. As Austin Farrer reminds us, "what no one shows the ability to defend is quickly abandoned." Christianity continues to endure, in part, because of individuals like C. S. Lewis who have willingly entered into the wider intellectual arena and with courage followed the Christian argument wherever it led.

BIBLIOGRAPHY

Aldwinckle, Stella. "Socrates Was a Realist," *Socratic Digest* (No. 1), June 1943.

_____. Oral History Interview, conducted by Lyle W. Dorsett, Oxford, England, July 26, 1985, for the Marion E. Wade Center, Wheaton College, Wheaton, IL.

Anscombe, G. E. M. "A Reply to Mr. C. S. Lewis's Argument that 'Naturalism' is Self-Refuting," *Socratic Digest* (No. 4).

_____. *The Collected Philosophical Papers of G. E. M. Anscombe*, Vol. 2, *Metaphysics and the Philosophy of Mind*. Minneapolis: University of Minnesota Press, 1981.

Blamires, Harry. Oral History Interview, conducted by Lyle W. Dorsett, Wheaton, IL, October 23, 1983, for the Marion E. Wade Center, Wheaton College, Wheaton, IL.

Catherwood, Lady Elizabeth. Oral History Interview, conducted by Stephanie L. Feecke, Wheaton, IL, August 3, 1991, for the Marion E. Wade Center, Wheaton College, Wheaton, IL.

Carpenter, Humphrey. *The Inklings*. Boston: Houghton Mifflin, 1979.

Como, James, ed. *C. S. Lewis at the Breakfast Table and Other Reminiscences*. New York: Macmillan, 1979.

Desmond, Shaw. Unpublished letter to Lewis, September 24, 1945, Marion E. Wade Center, Wheaton College, Wheaton, IL.

Farrer, Austin, "The Christian Apologist." In *Light on C. S. Lewis*. London: Geoffrey Bles, 1965.

Griffiths, Dom Bede. Oral History Interview, conducted by Lyle W. Dorsett, Wheaton, IL, August 26, 1983, for the Marion E. Wade Center, Wheaton College, Wheaton, IL.

Lewis, C. S. *Letters of C. S. Lewis*. Revised Edition. Ed. Walter Hooper. New York: Harcourt, Brace, 1993.

_____. *Miracles*. London: Geoffrey Bles, 1952, and Glasgow: William Collins Sons, 1976.

_____. Preface, *Socratic Digest* (No. 1), June 1943.

_____. "Religion and Rocketry." In *The World's Last Night and Other Essays*. New York: Harcourt, Brace, 1960.

_____. *Surprised by Joy: The Shape of My Early Life*. New York: Harcourt, Brace & Company, 1984.

_____. Unpublished letter to Dom Bede Griffiths, April 24, 1954, Marion E. Wade Center, Wheaton College, Wheaton, IL.

_____. Unpublished letter to Stella Aldwinckle, June 6, 1950, Marion E. Wade Center, Wheaton College, Wheaton, IL.

Mitchell, Basil. "Reflections on C. S. Lewis, Apologetics, and the Moral Tradition, Basil Mitchell in Conversation with Andrew Walker." *A Christian for All Christians: Essays in Honour of C. S. Lewis*. Eds. Andrew Walker and James Patrick. London: Hodder & Stoughton, 1990.

Moynihan, Martin and Monica. Oral History Interview, conducted by Lyle W. Dorsett, Wimbledon, England, July 24, 1984, for the Marion E. Wade Center, Wheaton College, Wheaton, IL.

Olford, Stephen F. Oral History Interview, conducted by Lyle W. Dorsett, Wheaton, IL, November 7, 1983, for the Marion E. Wade Center, Wheaton College, Wheaton, IL.

Sayer, George. *Jack: A Life of C. S. Lewis*. Wheaton, IL: Crossway Books, 1994.

Trickett, Rachel. Oral History Interview, conducted by David Dodds, St. Hugh's College, Oxford, July 18, 1989, for the Marion E. Wade Center, Wheaton College, Wheaton, IL.

Wain, John. *Sprightly Running*. London: Macmillan, 1962.

Wilson, A. N. *C. S. Lewis, A Biography*. New York: W. W. Norton & Company, 1990.

NOTES

1. Como, *At the Breakfast Table*, 137-85.

2. Audio Interview with Stella Aldwinckle, 8. When speaking of agnostics, both Monica Shorten and Miss Aldwinckle have in mind Christians who in their confusion no longer know what to make of their faith and non-Christians who do not know what to make of Christianity but are not opposed to trying.

3. Ibid., 8-9. An abbreviated version of this story appeared in the *Socratic Digest*, No. 1, 6.

4. Ibid., 9.

C. S. Lewis and the Oxford University Socratic Club

5. Ibid.

6. Lewis, *Surprised by Joy*.

7. Ibid., 110-12.

8. Ibid., 135, 137-39.

9. Ibid., 136.

10. Ibid., 137.

11. Ibid., 199-200.

12. Ibid., 207.

13. Ibid., 207-208.

14. Ibid., 223-224.

15. The view of Oxford presented here was gathered from the following audio interviews: Harry Blamires, Lady Elizabeth Catherwood, Dom Bede Griffiths, Martin Moynihan, and Rachel Trickett, all of whom were students during this period. Additional insight was gathered from Wain, *Sprightly Running*, 98-157.

16. Aldwinckle, "Socrates Was a Realist," 6-7.

17. *Socratic Digest*, No. 1, 4.

18. Ibid., 2-4.

19. Ibid., 4. "*Sansculottisme*" means militant extremism.

20. Ibid.

21. Wilson, *C. S. Lewis*, 182. "P'daytabird" was a nickname used by Jack and Warnie for their father who was a police court solicitor in Belfast.

22. Wain, *Sprightly Running*, 141.

23. Unpublished letter.

24. Lewis, *Letters of C. S. Lewis*, 382.

25. Farrer, "The Christian Apologist," 24.

26. Lewis, *Surprised by Joy*, 213.

27. Oral History Interview with Rachel Trickett, 6.

28. Farrer, "The Christian Apologist," 25.

29. The picture of Lewis presented here was gathered from various testimonies and oral histories from both participants and members. See, for example, the Oral History Interviews at the Marion E. Wade Center with Stella Aldwinckle, Harry Blamires, Lady Elizabeth Catherwood, Dom Bede Griffiths, Martin Moynihan, Stephen Olford, and Rachel Trickett.

30. Unpublished letter.

31. Desmond spoke on two different occasions. On the first, January 28, 1946, his topic was "Religion in the Post-War World."

32. Oral History Interview with Aldwinckle, 10.

33. Ibid., 25.

34. Cf. Oral History Interview with Stephen Olford, 4-5.

35. By *naturalism* is meant the doctrine that only nature exists, that nothing that exists has supernatural significance, and that scientific laws are adequate to account for all phenomena.

36. Miss Anscombe went on to become professor of philosophy at Cambridge University.

37. *Socratic Digest*, No. 4, 7-11. Professor Anscombe's original paper is also included in her *Collected Papers*, Vol. 2, 224-32.

38. Carpenter, *The Inklings*, 217.

39. Sayer, *Jack*, 186.

40. Anscombe, *Collected Papers*, Vol. 2, x.

41. Sayer, *Jack*, 186.

42. Farrer, *Light on C. S. Lewis*, 26.

43. Unpublished letter, June 12, 1950.

44. The 1960 revised edition was published by William Collins Sons and issued as a Fontana Book. Macmillan (New York) published the revised chapter in their 1978 edition of *Miracles*.

45. Anscombe, *Collected Papers*, Vol. 2, ix-x.

46. Mitchell, *A Christian for All Christians*, 10.

47. Sayer, *Jack*, 187.

48. Ibid., 10-11.

49. Lewis, *The World's Last Night*, 92.

50. Mitchell, *A Christian for All Christians*, 98.

51. Unpublished letter, April 22, 1954.

52. See Mitchell, *A Christian for All Christians*, 7f.

53. Oral History Interview with Rachel Trickett, 6-8.

54. Oral History Interview with Lady Catherwood, unnumbered. One of the students that Lady Catherwood mentions as benefiting from these discussions was James I. Packer.

55. Specific examples of this can be found in: Oral History Interviews with Lady Catherwood; Harry Blamires, 18-19; Martin Moynihan, 23; Stephen Olford, 4-7; Rachel Trickett, 9. Basil Mitchell and Andrew Walker touch on this point as well in *A Christian for All Christians*, 14-18; and Anscombe displays this attitude as noted above.

15

C. S. Lewis and the Problem of Evil

Jerry Root

If someone's only encounter with C. S. Lewis was the portrayal of him in the film *Shadowlands*, they might get a false impression of the man. The film presents him as a man who lived an ivory-tower existence, untouched by pain or sorrow. The portrayal is inaccurate. Out of fairness to Hollywood, when a story is told on film in a limited time frame, the peaks will be higher, the valleys lower, the blacks blacker and the whites whiter. The genre of film demands that story (whether it be biography or fiction) be truncated to fit the medium. The real Lewis was not a man who escaped suffering until the woman he loved was diagnosed with cancer. He knew pain throughout his life.

Lewis's Early Personal Struggles with Pain and Suffering

It is not difficult to highlight many personal tragedies in Lewis's life. His mother died when he was not quite ten years old. Within months his father, struggling with his own grief, sent Lewis and his brother off to a boarding school managed by a headmaster who was eventually declared insane. Imagine the trauma for two small boys having lost their mother, having been separated from their father, and being placed in that environment. Also, Lewis was born with a deformity in his thumbs. Consequently he was always awkward. When the day came for him to enter public school, he was not able to keep up in

C. S. Lewis and the Problem of Evil

games with the other boys. This forced him to hide in order to avoid the bullying of the older boys. Later during World War I, he trained as an army officer at Oxford University. He anticipated that when he reached the front, he, like so many of England's young men, might lose his life. Being unable to secure long enough leave to visit his family in Ireland, he wrote asking his father to meet him, perhaps for the last time, in Oxford. Three times Lewis made his appeal, practically begging his father to visit. His father never came.

Lewis arrived in the trenches in France on the day of his nineteenth birthday, an officer responsible for troops under his care. During the battle of Arras, two of his close friends were killed, and Lewis himself was seriously wounded by friendly fire. In time he was evacuated to a hospital in England. Again he wrote to his father requesting a visit, and still his father never came. It does not appear that his father was a malicious man in any way, just a man who did not understand the common graces of fatherhood. Perhaps these failures of his father's left wounds deeper than those the young Lewis had experienced in war.

In the early days of his teaching at Oxford University, Lewis became a Christian. He took his faith seriously and engaged in evangelistic efforts that included popular radio broadcast talks, a student outreach known as the Oxford University Socratic Club, itinerant preaching, and the writing of books for the masses on Christianity (often the kiss of death for an academic). Consequently, he suffered the criticism of many of his contemporaries at the University. This led in part to his being passed over for promotion at Oxford. He was never awarded a professorial chair there. His was not the life of a man unacquainted with disappointments and suffering.

It is significant that in his autobiography, Lewis writes that what drove him to atheism in his early days was his sense that the universe was unfair. As a young man of fourteen, he thought that the strongest argument for atheism was the problem of evil. When Lewis converted to Christianity, the second book of Christian apologetics that he wrote was *The Problem of Pain*. The issue of suffering, pain, and evil in the universe was a matter that occupied a great deal of his thinking throughout his life. Due to his evangelistic concerns and because the problem of evil had been a stumbling block to himself and many others, Lewis brought the wide range of his reading and the clarity of his pen to bear on this subject.

The Problem of Evil Defined

The problem of evil, simply stated, is: If God is good and all-powerful, why does He allow evil to exist in the universe?[1] The existence of evil is a given that has led many to question whether God is truly good or all-powerful, if He exists at all. Rabbi Harold Kushner, in his book *When Bad Things Happen to Good People*,[2] does not doubt the goodness of God. He does, however, question God's power. He suggests that though God appears to have the best of intentions, the universe has gotten out of hand. In the Old Testament book of Job, Job has no doubt of God's power; he simply doubts His character and wonders if God is truly good. Lewis, by contrast, invites his readers to ask if we have properly understood what the goodness and power of God actually mean.

Preliminary Considerations

Before looking at the way Lewis dissects the problem, it is necessary to familiarize ourselves with some important preliminary considerations. First, any human approach to this problem is a finite approach. We must always beware of the pretense of making judgments about how God should have governed His world. Such a stance assumes too much on our part. At the end of Canto XIV of *The Purgatorio*, Dante is reminded that "He who discerns all things, scourges you."[3] God's governance of the universe may be informed by a wisdom that in our finitude eludes us.

Second, no human investigation of the problem of evil can be attempted without consideration of the fact that we are a part of the problem. In "The Triumph of Easter," Dorothy Sayers reminds her readers of this not insignificant point.

> "Why doesn't God smite this dictator dead?" is a question a little remote from us. Why, madam, did He not strike you dumb

C. S. Lewis and the Problem of Evil

and imbecile before you uttered that baseless and unkind slander the day before yesterday? Or me, before I behaved with such cruel lack of consideration to that well-meaning friend? And why, sir, did He not cause your hand to rot off at the wrist before you signed your name to that dirty little bit of financial trickery?

You did not quite mean that? But why not? Your misdeeds and mine are none the less repellent because our opportunities for doing damage are less spectacular than those of some other people. Do you suggest that your doings and mine are too trivial for God to bother about? That cuts both ways; for, in that case, it would make precious little difference to His creation if He wiped us both out tomorrow.[4]

Lewis also often reminds his readers that they cannot divorce themselves from the problem of evil. As a race, all humans are infected. It is not good enough to acknowledge the deficiencies and failure of others, all the while ignorant of the shortcomings within ourselves. In *The Great Divorce* Lewis finds himself on a bus from hell to heaven. He describes the hideous appearance of others making the trip with him. Condescendingly, he comments on their every flaw, their twisted character, and their heinous behavior. Just as he becomes smug in his own self-righteousness, he catches a glimpse of his own visage reflected in the window of the bus.[5] He recognizes to his horror that he too is part of the problem. In such backhanded ways he reminds his readers that they have also failed to escape corruption. He takes the lead in remembering and allows his readers to follow.

Similarly, in the introduction to the second edition of *The Screwtape Letters* Lewis writes:

Some have paid me an undeserved compliment by supposing that my *Letters* were the ripe fruit of many years' study in moral and ascetic theology. They forgot that there is an equally reliable, though less creditable, way of learning how temptation works. "My heart"—I need no other's—"showeth me the wickedness of the ungodly."[6]

His self-effacing style will not permit his readers to forget that when considering the matter of evil, they are also included as part of the problem. This is not an issue that any of us can think about disinterestedly.

Not long ago I was asked to preach at an evening chapel service in one of the Oxford University colleges. After the service was over, the chaplain invited me to join him at high table where we ate with the fellows of the college. After introductions, a fellow sitting across from me, a history teacher, asked, "So why are you a Christian?"

I answered, "I am aware of deficiencies and failures in my life—mind you, not all of them, but enough of them to be devastated. I am a Christian because I believe that Christ died and rose again to forgive me of my sins. I believe He loves me and forgives me, not because I have done anything to merit His kindness, but rather because He delights to love us and forgive us. I believe that forgiveness is necessary if I am to look at my life honestly and not be devastated."

This fellow responded, "I can appreciate that, but it's just not my issue."

To which I replied, "I think I understand what you mean. I didn't become a Christian until I was in my first year at college, and I didn't become perfect overnight. That took two or three weeks to happen."

She burst into laughter and was joined by the other fellows at the table.

I responded to the laughter by noting, "Your laughter has betrayed you. Since we just met, I am aware that you do not know the specific issues of my life that made that statement about perfection utter nonsense. But still you laughed, which tells me you were aware my comments were preposterous. You gained this awareness by some means. Perhaps it was as an astute observer of human history, or perhaps it was due to familiarity with the themes of your own heart."

She smiled and said, "You got me."

Then I asked, "Knowing what you know about yourself, how can you live with yourself? How do you look yourself in the mirror each night before you go to bed, aware of your own deficiencies?"

She responded, "I have faith in humanity." Moments before she

C. S. Lewis and the Problem of Evil

did not sense a need for help in coping with shortcomings in her own life, and now she claimed to find help by believing in humanity.

I asked her, "How does this faith in humanity work pragmatically? Have you ever been wounded by another human being?"

She answered abruptly, "Of course!"

I asked, "Have you ever wounded another human being?"

She answered, "I suppose so." She was softer on herself.

I asked, "How does it work pragmatically, this faith in humanity, when you live in a world where you have been both wounded by others and have wounded others?"

She asked, "How does it work pragmatically for Christianity?" For the rest of the meal the discussion centered on the forgiveness of sins and themes of grace.

That conversation progressed in a manner respectful of these preliminary considerations found in Lewis's approach to the problem of evil. None of us have escaped being affected by the problem. Reading Lewis will not allow us to forget. His self-effacing style permits his readers to be honest about the issue of evil as it exists not only in the world, but in their own thoughts, choices, and actions.

Reconsidering the Meaning of Omnipotence

As Lewis approaches the problem of evil, he draws on a broad survey of literature on the subject, derived from a variety of times and places. The sheer volume of his reading and his fertile memory, as well as his capacity to reason carefully and critically, provided him with the resources to distill the issues for a popular audience. When he came to a re-investigation of the omnipotence of God, he used a statement from Thomas Aquinas's *Summa Theologica* as a North Star to guide him. Aquinas had written, "Nothing which implies contradiction falls under the Omnipotence of God."[7] There are some things God cannot do. If He is love, He cannot be unloving. If He is good, He cannot do that which is not good. If He is just, He cannot do that which is unjust. In essence, God cannot do nonsense. He can do nothing that violates the integrity of His own nature. Lewis wrote:

The inexorable "laws of Nature" which operate in defiance of human suffering or desert, which are not turned aside by prayer, seem, at first sight, to furnish a strong argument against the goodness and power of God. I am going to submit that not even Omnipotence could create a society of free souls without at that same time creating a relatively independent and "inexorable" Nature.[8]

For Lewis, the self can only exist "in contrast with an 'other,' a something which is not the self."[9] God has created a world of material objects and sociological beings that function independently from our selves. We may "bump up" against such a world at times in ways most uncomfortable. Years ago I was working in my garage. When I opened a cupboard, a wrench fell to the floor. As I bent over to pick it up, I forgot about the open cupboard door. When I stood up, I banged my head against the door. In my pain I communicated to God quite clearly what I thought about His world. I cried out, "God, why did You make the world like this?" As soon as the pain started to subside, I thought more deeply about what I was asking God to do. Did I really want a world where things did not stay where you put them? Did I want a world where cupboard doors did not stay put? Did I want to park my car in a parking lot only to return and eventually find it on top of a building six blocks away? Did I want to leave my house for work in the morning and return in the evening to a vacant lot? Of course not. If God's character is consistent, when He creates a world, it will not be capricious. The stability of that world may cause us pain when, in our misjudgments, we "bump up" against it.

Of course, we must remember that Lewis was a supernaturalist. His view of order in the universe did not discount the possibility of miracles. For Lewis, miracles can happen. But they are rare. And the existence of miracles does not necessarily violate the ordered character or purposes of God. Lewis's Christ-figure in his children's stories, a lion named Aslan, reminds the children there is a deeper magic from before the dawn of time.[10] This is not equivocation on Lewis's part. He simply recognizes a general order in the universe and a possibility for miracles that do not necessarily violate that order.[11] This general order, when resisted by an individual (whether accidentally or intentionally), can have painful consequences.

Lewis addresses the issue of omnipotence as it relates to the creation of human will. Lewis, being a Christian, believed in a God who is essentially relational. He believed in a God of Trinity. Consequently, when God creates man in His own image, He creates him as a relational being. For relationships to exist among humans, it is necessary that they have volition, wills to choose, in order for them to love. When God commands His creatures to love, response to this command would be impossible without the power to choose. Many years ago a toy company in America produced a doll named Chatty Cathy. This doll had a tape recorder inside her. Pull the ring on her neck, and she would say, "I love you." God could have created us in a similar manner. However, such expressions of love, being programmed and without volition, would not be genuine. God in His omnipotence, made creatures capable of relationship and gave them wills. Then He provided them with the capacity to love. Such a gift has its risks. A God who cannot contradict Himself must allow the consequences of the ill use of that gift.

Perhaps I have prayed for God to remove the consequences of the inappropriate exercise of my will. For Him to respond to this according to my desire would be for Him to function in a manner that is nonsense. If I, in anger, went to hit somebody over the head with a club and God prevented it by turning the club into a feather at the moment of contact, that would have checked my bad act. Frustrated by this divine intervention, I further exhibit my anger by shooting this individual, only to have God again intervene by turning the bullets to marshmallows. I throw the gun, intending to hit my victim with it; this action too is rendered ineffectual. When I curse, God dissipates the sound waves before their offense reaches the ears of others. God would thus have checked my evil acts but would have done so by violating His own nature. In essence, He would have put a ring in my neck and a programmed response within me. By checking the consequences of the ill use of my free will, He would have removed any morally significant free will. It is nonsense to believe that God could grant such free will and, by removing the consequences of its evil exercise, not grant it at the same time. God cannot do nonsense. Even God cannot both grant and not grant free will at the same time. Again, Aquinas reminds us that "nothing which implies contradiction falls under the omnipotence of God."

The ill use of free will accounts for pain and suffering that are the consequence of human error and violence. It does not, however, account for the things insurance policies call "acts of God." What are we to make of natural disasters? It is possible to attribute these to the divine judgments of an all-wise and holy God whose actions are proper in light of our sins. There may be another source for these natural disasters. Lewis suggests they might also be the ill use of another supernatural being's will, whose power is less than God's but greater than man's. Lewis's idea is that Satan might be the source behind these tragic natural occurrences.[12] Judgments of these events from the perspective of time can run the risk of error. To make sense of these events, it is necessary to have a transcendent perspective. This perspective is best supplied by revelation.

The cross on which the Son of God died, from one point of view, may be considered the most heinous human act ever. In it, the fallen creatures' rebellion against their Creator has its zenith. From another point of view, it may also be seen as God's greatest demonstration of love and grace. He takes man's worst and produces from it His best. Here is a historic event that is seen differently when interpreted from either a temporal or a revealed perspective. This may be true of all tragedies experienced in this life.

Lewis anticipates objections. Someone may complain that if the universe is like this, if pain is a real possibility, perhaps it would have been better to have never existed. Lewis says that no human scale can make possible such a judgment. While things that exist can be compared with one another, it is impossible to compare something with nothing. Lewis, stressing the difficulty, asks, "How should I, if I did not exist, profit by not existing?"[13]

C. S. Lewis and the Problem of Evil

Reconsidering the Meaning of Goodness

Some would have us believe that pain and suffering are incompatible with goodness. Lewis directs his attention to a reexamination of this idea. Are there times when goodness might allow pain as an expression of its benevolence? Lewis gives four examples that he takes from Scripture. The first of these comes from texts where God's relationship with His creation is compared to that of an artist for his art.[14] He is seen as a potter in relationship to the clay. It may be necessary for the potter to knead the clay aggressively as he fashions it into the form he desires. The illustration expresses its point but must not be pressed too far. It is valid in shedding light on the sovereignty of the potter over the clay. In this regard it expresses truth. But the clay, having no feelings, will not experience discomfort and will certainly not complain.

The second example used by Lewis to show that goodness may not be incompatible with pain is that of the animal husbandman and the animal.[15] The Scriptures compare the Creator-creature relationship to that of the shepherd for the sheep. The sheep may not understand the temporary discomforts administered to them by the shepherd, but those discomforts are means to a greater good. Recently my cat had a problem with ear mites. This necessitated the application of ear drops, a procedure my cat did not take a fancy to. The application of these drops required that my wife and I use all the muscle and gymnastic ability within our power to constrain the cat and apply the medicine. For hours after the procedure, we could not convince the cat that it was safe to come to us. If the cat was a writer, I'm sure it would have written deplorable things about us, questioning completely our good intention for her health.

The third example is that of a father for his son.[16] It may be necessary for the father to apply discipline as the son matures. At the moment this discipline may be misunderstood and resisted. But in the best of cases, the father's will and intention would always be expressions of love and genuine concern.

The fourth and final example, taken from Scripture to explain a love that is not necessarily incompatible with pain, is the love of a man for a woman. Lewis recognizes this as an illustration fraught with difficulties but explains it simply. He asks:

> Does any woman regard it as a sign of love in a man that he neither knows nor cares how she is looking? Love may, indeed, love the beloved when her beauty is lost: but not because it is lost. Love may forgive all infirmities and love still in spite of them: but Love cannot cease to will their removal. Love is more sensitive than hatred itself to every blemish in the beloved.[17]

These illustrations form a composite picture of divine love. As with any composite, no single portion provides a complete picture, but the combined result is quite compelling. And here Lewis stands in a great tradition.[18]

CONCLUSION

The issue of evil is complex, and its dimensions exceed what can be explored in a short chapter of a book. Throughout the corpus of his work, Lewis continues to be intrigued by the complexities of the problem. What are the consequences of evil as it impacts our ability to think and reason? Have the tentacles of the Fall affected our ability to know and appreciate beauty? Are our loves and friendships susceptible to misunderstanding, misjudgments, and disappointments? Is our understanding of the divine purposes clouded because we have pursued our wills over His? These are questions that Lewis explores throughout his books. In fact, this issue of evil may be the predominant, unifying theme running through his work. But it is not evil without a solution. In Lewis we are constantly reminded of God's triumph in Christ. God is the forgiver of sin. He is the great lover of His creatures. Our failures are the canvas on which He paints his masterpiece.

With Lewis the problem of evil is real. It is not an issue of mere speculation. Nor is it a matter that concerns others only. Lewis is vitally aware that he is infected. He is a man passionately conscious

C. S. Lewis and the Problem of Evil

of the antidote. He has tasted and seen that the Lord is good. He has accepted God's provision for the problem of evil in the Atonement. He is familiar with the humility that recognizes that the cross of Christ was necessary for him. The problem of evil and its solution in the Gospel was at the very core of Lewis's evangelistic zeal.

BIBLIOGRAPHY

Augustine. "Enchiridion." *A Select Library of the Nicene and Post-Nicene Fathers of the Christian Church*, Vol. 3. Ed. Phillip Schaff. Grand Rapids, MI: Eerdmans, n.d.

Dante. *The Divine Comedy of Dante Alighieri*. Trans. Charles Eliot Norton. *Great Books of the Western World*, Vol. 21. Chicago: Encyclopedia Britannica, 1952.

Hick, John. *Evil and the God of Love*. London: Macmillan, 1966.

Kushner, Harold S. *When Bad Things Happen to Good People*. New York: Schocken, 1981.

Lewis, C. S. *The Great Divorce*. London: Fount, 1977.

_____. *Letters: C. S. Lewis—Don Giovanni Calabria, A Study in Friendship*. Trans., ed. Martin Moynihan. Ann Arbor, MI: Servant, 1988.

_____. *The Lion, the Witch and the Wardrobe*. New York: Macmillan, 1950.

_____. *Miracles: A Preliminary Study*. London: Macmillan, 1947.

_____. *The Problem of Pain*. London: Fount, 1977.

_____. *The Screwtape Letters*. New York: Macmillan, 1971.

MacDonald, George. *Phantastes and Lilith*. Grand Rapids, MI: Eerdmans, 1971.

Milton, John. *Paradise Lost*, Book I. *Great Books of the Western World*, Vol. 32. Chicago: Encyclopedia Britannica, 1952.

Ridler, Anne. Introduction in *The Image of the City*. London: Oxford, 1958.

Sayers, Dorothy L. "The Triumph of Easter." In *Creed or Chaos?* Manchester, NH: Sophia Institute, 1974.

NOTES

1. Hick, *Evil and the God of Love*. Though written with a particular slant, Hick's book provides important references as well as a broad survey of those who have contributed to the discussion of the problem of evil.

2. Kushner, *When Bad Things Happen to Good People*.

3. Dante, *The Divine Comedy of Dante Alighieri*, 75.

4. Sayers, "The Triumph of Easter," 12-13.

5. Lewis, *The Great Divorce*, 25.

6. Lewis, *The Screwtape Letters*, 5.

7. Lewis, *The Problem of Pain*, 21.

8. Ibid., 23.

9. Ibid.

10. Lewis, *The Lion, the Witch and the Wardrobe*, 132-33.

11. The reader interested in discovering more of Lewis's concept of miracles may want to consult his book, *Miracles: A Preliminary Study*.

12. Lewis, *The Problem of Pain*, 71.

13. Ibid., 29.

14. Ibid., 34.

15. Ibid., 35.

16. Ibid., 36.

17. Ibid., 37.

18. Examples of this tradition would include 1) Augustine (*Enchiridion XCVI*): "Nor can we doubt that God does well even in the permission of what is evil. For He permits it only in the justice of His judgment. And surely all that is just is good. Although, therefore, evil, in so far as it is evil, is not good; yet the fact that evil as well as good exists, is a good. For if it were not a good that evil should exist, its existence would not be permitted by the omnipotent Good, who without doubt can as easily refuse to permit what He does not wish, as bring about what He does wish. And if we do not believe this, the very first sentence of our creed is endangered, wherein we profess to believe in God the Father Almighty. For He is not truly called Almighty if He cannot do whatsoever He pleases, or if the power of His almighty will is hindered by the will of any creature whatsoever." Phillip Schaff, ed., *A Select Library of the Nicene and Post-Nicene Fathers of the Christian Church*, Vol. III, 267. 2) William Shakespeare: "God Almighty! There is some soul of goodness in things evil, would men observingly distill it out . . . thus may we gather honey from the weed, and make a moral of the devil himself." Shakespeare, *King Henry V*, Act IV, Scene I, ll. 3-5, 11-12. 3) John Milton: "And high permission of all ruling heaven left him [Satan] at large to do his own dark designs, that with reiterated crimes he might heap on himself damnation, while he sought evil to others, and enraged might see how all his malice served but to bring forth infinite goodness, grace and mercy shewn on Man by him seduced, but on himself treble confusion, wrath, and vengeance poured." John Milton, *Paradise Lost*, 105. 4) George MacDonald: "Yet I know that good is coming to me—that good is always coming; though few have at all times the simplicity and courage to believe it. What we call evil, is the only and best shape, which for the person and his condition at the time, could be assumed by the best good." George MacDonald, *Phantastes and Lilith*, 182. 5) Charles Williams. Referring to Satan as "The Son of Mystery," Charles Williams wrote,

C. S. Lewis and the Problem of Evil

> The son of mystery;
> And since God suffers him to be,
> He, too, is God's minister,
> And labors for some good
> By us not understood!

Quoted from Ridler, Introduction in *The Image of the City*, xiii-xiv. 6) Lewis himself: "Satan is without doubt nothing else than a hammer in the hand of a benevolent and severe God. For all, either willingly or unwillingly, do the will of God: Judas and Satan as tools or instruments, John and Peter as sons." *Letters: C. S. Lewis—Don Giovanni Calabria, A Study in Friendship*, 33-35.

16

A Vision, Within a Dream, Within the Truth:

C. S. Lewis as Evangelist to the Postmodernists

Gene Edward Veith

I have long had the custom of lending a copy of *Mere Christianity* to non-Christian friends and acquaintances who seem to have little clue about what orthodox Christianity is all about. Among Lewis's many virtues as a writer is his clarity in explaining, in his words, "what Christians believe," and his way of showing that Christianity is no subjective fantasy but a series of truth claims with a measure of plausibility. The book, if I can get my unbelieving friends to read it, has always provoked some interesting reactions and conversations and has functioned as serious evangelistic proclamation.

The last two times I tried this, however, the responses were far different from what I had encountered earlier. One young man, one of my students, liked the book very much and was greatly impressed with Lewis and his faith. And yet he seemed unable to conceive of the possibility that what Lewis was saying might have some relevance to his own life, that what Lewis found to be true would also be true for him. He stated no disagreements and had nothing to say against any of Lewis's arguments. The gist of my student's response was that Lewis had developed a strong belief system, but that he, the student, had to develop his own. Lewis's whole argument—that Christianity is objectively *true*, that Jesus is either the Son of God or He is something worse—rolled off my student's mind like water on vinyl. But I got much further with him than with the last person to whom I lent my

C. S. Lewis as Evangelist to the Postmodernists

well-worn Macmillan paperback. She handed it back soon after, complaining about Lewis's sexist language. She could not get past Lewis's jovial men's club tone and his use of masculine pronouns. She could not even hear his ideas.

Lewis wrote mostly in the first half of the twentieth century, the age of modernism. The trust in scientific truth and the demand for rational certainty characterized the modernists, most of whom assumed Christianity was an outdated superstition that would soon give way to the irresistible tide of intellectual and social progress. And yet Lewis cast his apologetic for Christianity in the very teeth of the modernists, employing their very rationalism in proclaiming the Gospel. No wonder he was such an effective "apostle to the skeptics," to use Chad Walsh's term; he spoke their language, thought in their terms, and boldly confronted the modern mind.

November 22, 1963, could well be the day modernism died. President Kennedy, with his social and technological optimism, was assassinated, and soon afterwards America and much of the West slipped into cynicism, self-doubt, and generational rebellion. C. S. Lewis, of course, died on the very same day. Since then, we have been in postmodern times. In this new climate, evident everywhere—from the sophisticated scholarship of the universities to the banality of pop culture—truth is believed to be relative; there are no absolutes; we construct our own reality; culture determines everything; belief systems are masks for oppressive power.

Postmodernists, rejecting modernists' rationalism and their progressive assumptions, are willing to accept religion as long as it remains a private construction to give a sort of virtual meaning to one's life. But there can be no warrant for trying to win someone over to one's own faith. Since no one can claim possession of absolute truth and since all religions are equally valid, each person is entitled to his or her beliefs. Evangelism, therefore, like all other attempts at persuasion, is construed as an act of oppressive power, of trying to "impose your beliefs on someone else." In this climate, rational apologetics are obsolete, and Lewis, with his lucid chains of reasoning, can never communicate with the postmodern mind.

And yet, he can. Though my friends were oblivious to Lewis's apologetic, his writings still manage to connect to the postmodern mind. Lewis was almost prescient in anticipating Postmodernism. He not only envisioned the current state of thought, but he dealt with its implications and offered a telling response. He also found ways to proclaim the Gospel to what would become the postmodernist sensibility. Far from offering merely a rationalistic proof of Christianity, Lewis addressed his audience's imagination, using self-conscious story, artistic defamiliarization, and fantasy—all of which are now employed in postmodernist fiction—to communicate the truth of Christianity even to relativists.

The Apologetic for the Existence of Truth

A continual motif in Lewis's philosophical and theological writings is the meaningfulness of reason. "All possible knowledge," he insists in *Miracles*, "depends on the validity of reasoning."

> No account of the universe can be true unless that account leaves it possible for our thinking to be a real insight. A theory which explained everything else in the universe but which made it impossible to believe that our thinking was valid, would be utterly out of court. For that theory would itself have been reached by thinking, and if thinking is not valid that theory would, of course, be itself demolished. It would have destroyed its own credentials. It would be an argument which proved that no argument was sound—a proof that there are no such things as proofs—which is nonsense.[1]

This is also a summary of postmodernist ideology. Much contemporary scholarship revels in these contradictions—chains of reasoning that conclude that chains of reasoning have no meaning; façades of objectivity that maintain that objectivity is impossible; the elaborate paraphernalia of academic scholarship arguing that all scholarship is merely an ideological construct (including, presumably, itself).

C. S. Lewis as Evangelist to the Postmodernists

What for Lewis was a *reductio ad absurdum* has become a methodological principle. A major strain of Postmodernism busies itself with deconstruction, uncovering the hidden contradictions in all texts, showing how all assertions of meaning "destroy their own credentials."

Such thinking, of course, is exceedingly weak, as Lewis persuasively demonstrates. "Reason is our starting point," he shows. "There can be no question either of attacking or defending it."[2] He goes on to develop the validity of reasoning, the necessary assumption that our thoughts can correspond to realities outside our minds, into an argument for the necessity of God. A transcendent mind and an overarching reasonableness built into creation must exist in order for the conclusions of our own minds to have any meaning. As Lewis says in *Mere Christianity*:

> There is a difficulty about disagreeing with God. He is the source from which all your reasoning power comes: you could not be right and He wrong any more than a stream can rise higher than its source. When you are arguing against Him you are arguing against the very power that makes you able to argue at all: it is like cutting off the branch you are sitting on.[3]

Contemporary thought has sawn off the branch. Having rejected God, it no longer has a basis for rationality—just as Lewis said would happen.

Lewis surveys the line of thinking that has culminated in Postmodernism in his essay "The Poison of Subjectivism":

> After studying his environment man has begun to study himself. Up to that point, he had assumed his own reason and through it seen all other things. Now, his own reason has become the object: it is as if we took out our eyes to look at them. Thus studied, his own reason appears to him as the epiphenomenon which accompanies chemical or electrical events in a cortex which is itself the by-product of a blind evolutionary process. His own logic, hitherto the king whom events in all possible

worlds must obey, becomes merely subjective. There is no reason for supposing that it yields truth.[4]

Today, as Lewis suggests, the dominance of the natural sciences
through the modern era has been replaced by the dominance of the
social sciences. Sociology and anthropology attempt to reduce everything to "culture," while psychology measures external reality by the
yardstick of the self. In postmodernist scholarship today, "logocen-
tric" reasoning and the methodology and findings of empirical science
are interrogated for their allegedly political crimes, as constituting
power structures for the white male ruling class. In universities today,
reasoned discourse attempts to prove there can be no such thing as reasoned discourse. To repeat Lewis's rather Oedipal metaphor, postmodernists are gouging out their eyes in order to look at them.

Postmodernism, though only now dominant, had its origins in
nineteenth-century Romanticism and twentieth-century Existentialism, in philosophies that Lewis both knew and had been tempted
by. Nietzsche, the German idealists, Wagnerian aestheticism, and the
solipsistic Romantics were the forerunners of Postmodernism, which
continued to develop through Fascism (with its cultural reductionism
and its apotheosis of power) and Existentialism (with its rejection of
absolutes, the sense in which meaning is created by the will, and the
technical vocabulary and methodology of Heidegger).[5]

Postmodernism, in short, is prefigured in the subjectivist swamps
of *The Pilgrim's Regress*, through which Lewis himself had to traverse
in his own intellectual pilgrimage. It is the possibility offered by the
witch in *The Silver Chair*, who, like a contemporary critic, decon-
structs language by showing its metaphorical complexities, then concludes that "there is no Narnia, no Overworld, no sky, no sun, no
Aslan." They are all "made-up"; that is to say, in postmodernist terms,
they are constructions.[6]

If intellectual relativism was a live option throughout the modernist period, moral relativism had already established itself, both
among intellectuals and in the popular mind. Lewis discusses the dif-

C. S. Lewis as Evangelist to the Postmodernists

ference between evangelizing in past ages and in the twentieth century. In our day, he writes:

> A sense of sin is almost totally lacking. Our situation is thus very different from that of the Apostles. The Pagans . . . to whom they preached were haunted by a sense of guilt and to them the Gospel was, therefore, "good news."[7]

> The early Christian preachers could assume in their hearers, whether Jews, Metuentes [the "God-fearing" Gentiles], or Pagans, a sense of guilt. (That this was common among Pagans is shown by the fact that both Epicureanism and the Mystery Religions both claimed, though in different ways, to assuage it.) Thus the Christian message was in those days unmistakably the *Evangelium*, the Good News. It promised healing to those who knew they were sick. We have to convince our hearers of the unwelcome diagnosis before we can expect them to welcome the news of the remedy.[8]

And yet people continue to make moral judgments, though they do not necessarily recognize that they are doing so—as Lewis memorably demonstrates at the very beginning of *Mere Christianity* by analyzing the phenomenon of quarreling.[9]

Lewis goes on to anticipate what has blossomed into the "culture of victimization" and the blasphemously inverted moral *hubris* by which individuals presume to find fault with God.

> We address people who have been trained to believe that whatever goes wrong in the world is someone else's fault—the Capitalists', the Government's, the Nazis', the Generals' etc. They approach God Himself as His judges. They want to know, not whether they can be acquitted for sin, but whether He can be acquitted for creating such a world.[10]

> The ancient man approached God (or even the gods) as the accused person approaches his judge. For the modern man the

roles are reversed. He is the judge: God is in the dock. He is quite a kindly judge: if God should have a reasonable defence for being the god who permits war, poverty and disease, he is ready to listen to it. The trial may even end in God's acquittal. But the important thing is that Man is on the Bench and God in the Dock.[11]

Lewis shows himself to be not merely an academic apologist but an *evangelist* in his almost Lutheran awareness that the proclamation of the Gospel must be preceded by the proclamation of the Law, that only those who know themselves as having failed to keep the moral law, as being lost and condemned sinners, can cling in faith to the Good News of forgiveness in Christ.

In *Mere Christianity* Lewis spends the first five chapters showing there is, in fact, a moral law, that however people today might deny the objective reality of moral principles in theory, they nevertheless assume them in practice. He is not arguing the point in abstract, rationalistic ways; rather, he is appealing to ordinary human experience, to how we react, for example, when someone takes our seat on the bus. He uncovers the guilt that lies beneath the surface of the relativistic evasions. Lewis does not assume there is a transcendent moral law, as he might in addressing a pagan Roman; rather, as in dealing with a postmodernist, he begins by establishing the first principles.

These first principles have to do not only with morality but with truth. Continually, as an apologist, he comes back to the concept of truth—its either/or quality, its independence of subjective perception, its intractable "otherness"—to an audience that is not at all used to thinking in such terms.

One of the great difficulties is to keep before the audience's mind the question of Truth. They always think you are recommending Christianity not because it is true but because it is good. And in the discussion they will at every moment try to escape from the issue "True—or False" into stuff about a good society, or morals, or the incomes of Bishops, or the Spanish Inquisition, or France, or Poland—or anything whatever. You have to keep forcing them back, and again back, to the real point. . . . One must keep on pointing out that Christianity is a statement which, if false, is of no importance, and if true, of infinite importance.[12]

Lewis, as a twentieth-century apologist, must continually argue not only that God exists, but that truth exists. As a twentieth-century evangelist, whether of modernists or postmodernists, he must then convict his audience of sin by showing how they have violated the objectively true Law of God, and then confront them with the objectively true Gospel, that Jesus is God in the flesh and our sacrifice.

MULTICULTURALISM

In *The Abolition of Man*, published in 1947, Lewis directly addresses—and answers—a set of assumptions that would soon blossom in postmodernist thought. The catalyst for his book was a seemingly offhand remark in a textbook for a high school English class. Discussing Coleridge at the waterfall and overhearing one tourist say it was "sublime" and the other say it was "pretty," the authors of the textbook make the by-now familiar distinction between facts and values:

> When the man said *That is sublime*, he appeared to be making a remark about the waterfall. . . . Actually . . . he was not making a remark about the waterfall, but a remark about his own feelings. What he was saying was really I have feelings associated in my mind with the word "Sublime," or shortly, I have sublime feelings. . . . This confusion is continually present in language as we use it. We appear to be saying something very important about something: and actually we are only saying something about our own feelings.[13]

This might seem like a rather mild assertion to provoke such a diatribe from Lewis, but this is because today the notion has become so commonplace. This same distinction between facts and values appears now not in one textbook but throughout the curriculum, even, as I have noted with my own children, in Christian schools.

The assumption is that aesthetic assertions (such as whether or not a waterfall is "sublime") and, more seriously, moral judgments belong in the subjective realm, that they are a matter of feelings, personal taste, individual choices, or private opinion. "Facts" have to do with what is tangible and observable. The waterfall was a fact; both tourists were entitled to their opinion, and Coleridge had no right to impose his own beliefs by saying that one was right and the other was wrong. Such thinking has a double effect: it removes aesthetics and morality from the category of truth; it also drains significance away from the material world of facticity. Sublimity is only a feeling, and the water-fall is only water.

This distinction between facts and values is a methodological prin-ciple of the social sciences that attempts to rigorously exclude the pos-sibility of "value judgments" intruding upon their research.[14] This split between meaning and truth is fundamental to Existentialism, which labels the objective universe, with its scientific laws and orderly pre-dictability, as "absurd," as being in the most literal sense without meaning. Since meaning for human beings is intrinsically subjective, it becomes a function of experience and the will, whether this mean-ing is passively and inauthentically accepted from one's culture or con-structed in good faith from one's own choices.

In its postmodernist permutations, even the pretense of objectiv-ity on the part of natural and social scientists is only a mask for their private and self-interested values; even the word "facts" is now rou-tinely qualified by quotation marks. The very language with which we discuss such matters takes for granted the subjectivity of meaning. We refer to moral principles as "values," as if morality were a matter of what a person values rather than what is true.

In *The Abolition of Man*, Lewis refutes this line of thinking, which—extending the notion that "this confusion is continually pre-sent in language as we use it"—has become axiomatic in postmod-ernist thought. He does so by arguing that "value-judgments" must be connected to transcendent—and thus objective—ideals. Ethical thought, which is inescapable even in those who ostensibly reject it, depends by its very nature on appealing to extra-subjective principles, which must have the status of truth. These principles he defines as the *Tao*, the universal good that is built into the fabric of existence as surely as the laws of physics.

One of the major axioms of Postmodernism is cultural relativism. Since both morality and truth are held to be cultural constructions, every culture has its own truth and its own morality. What is bad (or false) for us may be good (or true) for someone from another culture. Who are we to judge? Cultural relativism, of course, casts all intellectual and ethical assertions in doubt, since "our own" societal "values" thus lose all ontological grounding.

Lewis answers cultural relativism—now endemic in contemporary thinking both among intellectuals and among the general public—in an elegantly simple way: by examining the moral teachings of various cultures and seeing whether they do, in fact, differ or not. In an appendix, he quotes texts from ancient Egypt, China, India, and other civilizations on such topics as beneficence, duties to family, justice, honesty, mercy, maganimity. These moral precepts do not, of course, differ at all. No culture preaches the virtues of injustice, dishonesty, or cowardice. All cultures, for all of their different nuances and customs and despite the fact that sometimes societies violate their own best principles, are in fundamental agreement in testifying to a universal moral law.

Lewis illustrates the point in *Mere Christianity*, where he asks "the reader to think what a totally different morality would mean":

> Think of a country where people were admired for running away in battle, or where a man felt proud of doublecrossing all the people who had been kindest to him. You might just as well try to imagine a country where two and two made five.[15]

To be sure, he continues, opinions have differed on the scope of unselfishness—whether it extends to everyone or only one's tribe; but no culture admires always putting oneself first. Some cultures practice monogamy, and others practice polygamy, but all of them believe in marriage. Customs, practices, and the consistency of application may differ (and, one might add, some cultures have institutionalized evil, such as infanticide and the abuse of women), but the moral *principles* seem to be transcultural and thus objective.

Refuting the tenets of Postmodernism is, of course, not the same as evangelizing postmodernists. Rational dismemberment of relativism will not be convincing to those who reject rational arguments, much less to those who will not even grant a hearing to those who use masculinist language (as in *The Abolition of Man*, *man* being a naughty word with postmodernists).

And yet, as apologists specializing in reaching the postmodern mind are saying, it is often necessary to first show that there is a truth as a prelude to showing that Christ is the truth. The postmodernist can be made to realize that relativism is philosophically indefensible and that, on a personal level, it is impossible to live with such unstable beliefs; this may usher in a new openness to the concept of religious truth. At this stage, rational apologetics again come into play, answering objections to the faith, explaining what doctrines mean, and offering reasons to believe.[16]

If Lewis were merely a modernist, he would not have had to establish the validity of reason or the necessity of truth. He could have taken that for granted. Instead, he begins on an even more basic level, addressing the intellectual crisis that had already started in his time. But what about my friends who failed to respond to the rational progressions, however relevant, of *Mere Christianity*?

The fact is, many contemporary, postmodern readers *do* find the arguments of *Mere Christianity* compelling. Others respond best to the apologetic and evangelistic impact of Lewis's fiction.

THE TRUTH OF STORY

As a writer and as a thinker, Lewis was critical of modernism, both philosophically and imaginatively. He rejected the scientific materialism of his day, and he disliked immensely the dreary realism of mod-

C. S. *Lewis as Evangelist to the Postmodernists*

ernist literature. Lewis loathed T. S. Eliot's poetry, and perhaps more importantly its influence on twentieth-century literature—even after Eliot became a Christian and Lewis's friend.[17] In his rejection of literary modernism, Lewis, perhaps ironically, anticipated much of the theory and practice of literary Postmodernism.

Postmodern writers are reacting against the modernist literary styles, particularly the modernist canons of realism. The very notion of "realism," of course, as if there is one static reality that writers have only to copy, is rendered utterly problematic by postmodern relativism. More than that, fiction, by its very nature, is "made up." Faulkner's Yoknapatawpha county, for all of its verisimilitude and sense of social and psychological accuracy, is just as much an imaginative creation as Spenser's Faerie Land. Faulkner's fictional world creates an illusion of being true-to-life because it skillfully orchestrates various "realistic" literary conventions (social stereotypes, stream-of-consciousness narration, local color description, and the like).

Postmodern novelists stress that literary conventions are, in fact, the very building blocks of fiction. There are only so many plots and character types, and they are arranged, as the structuralists have shown, according to time-honored patterns, mythological motifs, and recurring variations. There can be no fully original story, since every story has an intertextual relationship to other stories and to the culture as a whole.

What this means in practice is that postmodern novelists prefer fantasy to realism. Since even a realistic novel is an imaginative construction, why not let the imagination construct whatever it finds pleasing, free from the positivist bias of modernist literature? Postmodernists, recognizing the conventions of both fantasy and realism, play with those conventions. The popular style of "magical realism," pioneered by Latin American authors such as Gabriel García Márquez, combines the genres, setting up a grittily realistic village in which scraps of paper turn into butterflies and women are assumed into heaven while hanging up the laundry. Italo Calvino spins out premise fiction—such as a story imagining what it would be like if the whole world were compressed into one point—and writes new fables and fairy tales.

Postmodern fiction writers also have a new respect for the so-called "formula fiction" beloved by the masses but scorned by high-brow modernists. Science fiction, mysteries, adventure tales, romances, and other popular genres tend to follow predictable conventions (a murder is committed; a detective assembles clues; the murderer is discovered). Modernists could not consider such writing as serious art, but postmodern critics argue that all fiction, including serious art, consists of conventions (so that even a classic tragedy such as *Oedipus* follows the conventions of the murder mystery). The very popularity of these genres, to postmodernists, means they have a deep cultural resonance that makes them particularly significant.

As a result, serious postmodern novelists are experimenting with popular genres. The postmodernist scholar Umberto Eco writes a combination murder mystery and historical novel in *The Name of the Rose*. The respected American novelist Larry McMurtry writes westerns such as *Lonesome Dove* that embody the conventions so well and so entertainingly that the novel is turned into a hit TV mini-series. William Gibson and other contemporary writers are exploring postmodernist themes such as virtual reality and the fracturing of identity by writing science fiction.

Since, according to Postmodernism, reality itself is an imaginative construct, all ideologies, laws, cultural institutions, and epistemological paradigms are essentially "texts," with the same status as fiction. This is why postmodernist scholarship emerged largely out of literary criticism, and why interpretive and deconstructive methodologies once used to dissect literature are now being applied to culture as a whole. In literature, postmodern authors now enjoy testing the boundaries between the fictional and the real. They do this by constructing elaborate levels of fictionality, spinning stories within stories within stories, and by purposefully confusing fiction and truth, as in movies that purport to be historical while incorporating the director's fantasies, such as Oliver Stone's *JFK* and Richard Attenborough's *Shadowlands*, a shamelessly inaccurate rendition of Lewis's life.

Lewis does some of the same things as postmodern writers, although for completely different reasons. In his reactions against the claustrophobic materialism of modernists, he champions fantasy.

C. S. Lewis as Evangelist to the Postmodernists

Modern realistic stories, he argues—not fairy tales—are what can give a child a false impression of the world. "Fairy land arouses a longing for he knows not what. It stirs and troubles him (to his lifelong enrichment) with the dim sense of something beyond his reach and, far from dulling or emptying the actual world, gives it a new dimension of depth. He does not despise real woods because he has read of enchanted woods: the reading makes all real woods a little enchanted."[18] In *The Voyage of the "Dawn Treader,"* Eustace is morally and spiritually disabled because he "had read only the wrong books. They had a lot to say about exports and imports and governments and drains, but they were weak on dragons."[19]

Lewis defended—and wrote—fairy tales, fantasies, and science fiction. In *An Experiment in Criticism* he demolishes the false distinction between "high brow" and "low brow" books, in a way reminiscent of postmodern defenses of popular culture, championing adventure writers such as H. Rider Haggard and popular genres such as mysteries and thrillers. The whole literary circle to which he belonged was working in the same vein. His friend and mentor J. R. R. Tolkien turned the "sub-creation" of fantasy into a monumental work of twentieth-century fiction; Dorothy L. Sayers showed what good writing could do for the mystery genre; Charles Williams's "supernatural thrillers" anticipated and in many ways went beyond magical realism.

The Chronicles of Narnia even employ the postmodern device of levels of fictionality. The tales are framed by the children's ordinary existence of World War II precautions and brutal boarding schools. Within this frame, the children enter into the magical realm of Narnia, which, however, for all of its wonders, is no escapist utopia. In fact, it intensifies moral conflicts and spiritual problems, externalizing them through symbols but making them matters of life and death. The two levels of the novels—the realistic and the magical—are related to each other. This relationship is thematic (for example, Eustace's obnoxious materialism in this world is transformed when Aslan in Narnia changes his dragon-self). It is also narrative, as when the children go from one realm to the other. In *The Last Battle*, the levels suddenly collapse in a way characteristic of postmodern fiction when the children have a reunion in Narnia as we learn they have been killed in a train wreck.

As a fiction writer, Lewis is thus in synch with the postmodern imagination. Of course, Lewis has an entirely different basis for his art than the postmodernists do. He can agree that reality is an imaginative construction, but it is a construction not of individuals, cultures, or even authors; rather, it is an imaginative construction of God. Beyond Narnia, beyond the children's England, beyond the reader's world, is yet another level, the absolute reality of spiritual truth.

A common motif in postmodern fiction is the analogy between the author and God. In postmodern plays, from Pirandello to Sondheim, the characters sometimes overthrow their narrator/authors. John Barth interrupts the self-reflexive narrative of "Life-Story" to make the connection between the absence of God and the characteristics of contemporary literature:

> Inasmuch as the old analogy between Author and God, novel and world, can no longer be employed unless deliberately as a false analogy, certain things follow: 1) fiction must acknowledge its fictitiousness and metaphoric invalidity or 2) choose to ignore the question or deny its relevance or 3) establish some other, acceptable relation between itself, its author, its reader.[20]

For Lewis, though, the analogy between God and the author holds, so that fiction retains its metaphoric validity. He explains how God transcends time with the illustration of a writer being outside the time of the characters in the novel he is writing.[21] He describes the universe as a cosmic drama that will end in an apocalyptic finale: "When the author walks onto the stage the play is over."[22] Lewis's protégé Sheldon Vanauken develops the analogy in perhaps the most detail, describing the Incarnation—in a postmodernist collapse of levels—as the Author becoming a character in His own story.[23]

Lewis's own journey to faith, as he describes it in *Surprised by Joy*, had to do not merely with a rational, philosophical search for truth, though that played an important role. A more important impetus was an ineffable longing, stimulated by imaginative literature, that he later understood as a sign of spiritual reality. The joy, the *Sehnsucht*, he writes about in the autobiography is essentially the "longing for he knows not what" that he cited as one of the virtues of the fairy tale. Lewis's Narnia books, his science fiction, and his symbolic fantasies at their best evoke the same sense of "enchantment," opening the reader's mind to supernatural possibilities.

And yet, Lewis knows that evangelism can never be grounded in subjective experience, however mystical. His fantasies go on to present, in propositional though imaginatively realized terms, the extrafictional truth of God's Word (the sacrificial death and resurrection of Aslan; the evocations of the Fall in *Perelandra*; the anatomy of God's love in *Till We Have Faces*).

Scholars of Postmodernism, recognizing the eclipse of abstract, rational discourse, have been stressing the role of *story* as a way to embody thought. Contemporary apologetics is emphasizing the use of narrative as a way to communicate with the postmodern mind. Lewis's fiction often has a powerful resonance for contemporary readers. Though some are likely to dismiss his tales as merely imaginative constructions, their gospel-bearing symbolism has an efficacy of its own.

Theologically, of course, what converts sinners from unbelief to faith is never either a rational argument nor an imaginative experience, but the Word of God, which in Law and Gospel is "living and active" (Hebrews 4:12). This efficacious Word can be conveyed in human language, whether in a sermon, a rational discourse, or a story. The trick is to command the hearer's attention, to navigate through the barriers, and to gain a hearing for this Word, which can be used by the Holy Spirit to kindle faith.

Thus, for example, when *Mere Christianity* does not seem to connect with my unbelieving friends, I have been recommending *The Great Divorce*. Moral relativists naturally have a hard time believing in hell or how anyone could deserve eternal punishment. Lewis's book, by means of symbol and story, shows how damnation is not only eternal punishment but a spiritual condition. Its symptoms—pride, disdain, self-righteousness, existential self-pity, boredom, the rejection of love—are imminently recognizable as familiar, contemporary states of mind, which the novel presents convincingly as damning sin. Also salutary is its lampoon of theological liberalism (the Bishop who congratulates himself for rejecting Christ's resurrection and who refuses to acknowledge a literal life after death, even as he languishes in hell, where theologians continue to give papers on modernist theology).

But the best effect of *The Great Divorce* on postmodernists is its exposition of reality, its evocation of hard, intractable truth to those who have been taught that it is all in their minds. In the novel, hell is the city of vagueness, and earthly existence is ghostly. Thus far, perhaps, a postmodernist convinced of the evanescence of human truthclaims might agree. Heaven, however, is what is solid. Inverting the convention by which matter is tangible and spirit is ethereal, *The Great Divorce* portrays our world as transient and insubstantial; the spiritual realm, on the other hand, is concrete, unyielding, objective, and absolutely true. Becoming a solid person, in turn, depends on acknowledging that truth, repenting of one's condition, and being transformed by grace.

This motif, that we are living in "shadowlands" and that genuinely substantial reality can be found only in God, occurs throughout Lewis's writings, but *The Great Divorce* helps readers imagine what this means. The novel is also thoroughly postmodern in its very structure. The author, Lewis himself, is a character in his novel; his spiritual tour guide is George MacDonald, whose writings were instrumental in Lewis's conversion. The model, of course, is *The Divine Comedy*, in which Dante puts himself into his poem, along with his literary mentor Virgil, for a symbolic tour of the afterlife. Dante addressed the medieval imagination by means of allegory, imagining the horrors of hell as a way to symbolize the nature of sin on earth. Lewis addresses the postmodern imagination in much the same way.

In the last chapter, the narrative collapses—three times—in a very postmodern way. "And suddenly," the chapter begins, "all was changed." The Solid World and its inhabitants disappear. In their place the author/character sees gigantic forms surrounding a chessboard. The chessmen being moved on the board, he realizes, are men and women as they appear in the world. The gigantic forms determining their actions are their immortal souls. The author/character realizes that the whole narrative up to this point has not been a literal rendition of heaven and hell, as if it really were possible for the damned to take a tour bus to heaven and decide whether they want to stay; rather, what he has seen has been "the mimicry of choices that had really been made long ago."[24]

His teacher assures him that what he has been seeing is "a vision within a dream" and solemnly warns him against taking it literally (as theologically conservative critics of this book need to realize). Then the narrative collapses again, and the setting is once again the Solid World as the sun is rising. This time the author/character is experiencing the crisis that his characters had been going through.

> "The morning! The morning!" I cried, "I am caught by the morning and I am a ghost." But it was too late. The light, like solid blocks, intolerable of edge and weight, came thundering upon my head.[25]

The detached, omniscient narrator that so puts off postmodern readers in Lewis's nonfiction is in this novel a fellow sinner, a ghost like the readers he is attempting to evangelize. "There have been some," warned his mentor, "who were so occupied in spreading Christianity that they never gave a thought to Christ!"—a comment that makes the author want to change the subject.[26] The implication is that Lewis finds himself in hell because he was so busy writing Christian apologetics that he neglected the whole point of the Christian life. Throughout this novel the author presents himself as being on the same level as those in need of conversion, making his insights, for a postmodern reader, much easier to take.

In a final collapse of narrative and ontological levels, his Teacher's robe to which he was clinging becomes a tablecloth, and the blocks of light become books that he had pulled off with it when he fell out of his chair. "I awoke in a cold room, hunched on the floor beside a black and empty grate, the clock striking three, and the siren howling overhead."[27] The vision gives way to a dream, and the dream gives way to ordinary waking life, the "real world" that, with its bleakness and air raids, bears a disturbing similarity to hell.

Postmodernists, who despair of finding solid truth in this bleak world of violence and power, can easily agree that this world is a shadowland. Lewis has a way, in both his nonfiction and his fiction, of showing them their own complicity in these shadows, the reality of their sin. But he also has a way of evoking another realm, one in which truth is both absolute and compelling, a realm of mystery that nevertheless can be known; a realm of grace as intractable as heavy blocks of light; a realm whose King became incarnate in the shadowland to become our sacrifice and our Savior.

BIBLIOGRAPHY

Barth, John. "Life-Story." In *The Norton Anthology of American Literature*. Third Edition. Ed. Nina Baym et al. New York: W. W. Norton, 1989.

Hooper, Walter. *C. S. Lewis: A Companion and Guide*. San Francisco: Harper, 1996, 332.

Lewis, C. S. *The Abolition of Man*. New York: Macmillan, 1947.

————. "De Futilitate." In *Christian Reflections*. Ed. Walter Hooper. London: Fount, 1991.

————. *The Great Divorce*. New York: Macmillan, 1946.

————. *Mere Christianity*. New York: Macmillan, 1960.

————. *Miracles*. New York: Macmillan, 1960.

————. "On Three Ways of Writing for Children." In *Of Other Worlds*. Ed. Walter Hooper. San Diego: Harcourt Brace, 1966.

————. "The Poison of Subjectivism." In *Christian Reflections*. Ed. Walter Hooper. London: Fount, 1991.

————. "Religion without Dogma?" In *God in the Dock*. Ed. Walter Hooper. Grand Rapids, MI: Eerdmans, 1970.

————. *The Silver Chair*. New York: Collier Books, 1970.

————. *The Voyage of the "Dawn Treader."* New York: Collier Books, 1970.

McCallum, Dennis, ed. *The Death of Truth*. Minneapolis: Bethany House, 1996.

Vanauken, Sheldon. "Christmas Eve: That Difficult Birth." In Sheldon Vanauken, *Under the Mercy* (San Francisco: Ignatius Press), 1985.

C. S. Lewis as Evangelist to the Postmodernists

_____. *A Severe Mercy*. San Francisco: Harper & Row, 1977.

Veith, Gene Edward. *Modern Fascism*. St. Louis: Concordia, 1993.

_____. *Postmodern Times: A Christian Guide to Contemporary Thought and Culture*. Wheaton, IL: Crossway Books, 1994.

NOTES

1. Lewis, *Miracles*, 14-15. This was the subject of a celebrated debate between Lewis and Miss G. E. M. Anscombe. See "Religion without Dogma?" in *God in the Dock*, 145-46, in which Lewis qualifies his use of the term "valid" and addresses the philosophical issues in more detail.

2. Ibid., 21.

3. Lewis, *Mere Christianity*, 52-53.

4. Lewis, "The Poison of Subjectivism," 98. See also the essay "*De Futilitate*" in the same collection, 80-97.

5. For the historical and philosophical connections between Fascism and Postmodernism, see my book *Modern Fascism*.

6. See Lewis, *The Silver Chair*, 151-59.

7. Lewis, "Christian Apologetics," in *God in the Dock*, 95.

8. Lewis, "God in the Dock," in *God in the Dock*, 244.

9. Lewis, *Mere Christianity*, 17-18.

10. Lewis, "Christian Apologetics," 95.

11. Lewis, "God in the Dock," 244.

12. Lewis, "Christian Apologetics," 101.

13. Quoted in Lewis, *The Abolition of Man*, 14. Hooper, *C. S. Lewis: A Companion and Guide*, 332, identifies the textbook and its authors, whom Lewis grants anonymity, as *The Control of Language* (1940) by Alex King and Martin Ketley. Edmund Burke and the classical critics maintained that sublimity, like other aesthetic qualities, was an objective property, and in the anecdote Coleridge, for all of his romanticism, agreed.

14. The major promoter of the "facts/values" distinction was the influential sociologist Max Weber. That social scientists fail in their attempt to exclude their "value-judgments" and to be pristinely objective is obvious. Postmodernist scholars have since been arguing that such impersonal objectivity is epistemologically impossible. In that light, many contemporary social scientists go to the other extreme and make no attempt to be unbiased, since in the absence of objective truth scholarship itself is a construction of reality.

15. Lewis, *Mere Christianity*, 19.

16. See, for example, Dennis McCallum, "Practical Communication Ideas" and the other essays in *The Death of Truth*, edited by McCallum. This book was put together by an organization specializing in Christian apologetics and

evangelism that address the postmodern mind—the Crossroads Project, a ministry of Xenos Christian Fellowship, 611 E. Weber Road, Columbus, OH 43211. Their web site, which is a forum for ongoing discussions and ideas, is http://www.crossrds.org/index.htm.

17. See Hooper, C. S. Lewis: A Companion and Guide, 653.

18. Lewis, "On Three Ways of Writing for Children," 29-30.

19. Lewis, The Voyage of the "Dawn Treader," 71.

20. Barth, "Life-Story," 2152.

21. Lewis, Mere Christianity, 146-47.

22. Ibid., 66.

23. Sheldon Vanauken, "Christmas Eve: That Difficult Birth," 132-36. He also wrote a postmodernesque play carrying out the idea, "The Playwright Incarnate." See also Vanauken's A Severe Mercy, 116-17.

24. Lewis, The Great Divorce, 127.

25. Ibid., 128.

26. Ibid., 72.

27. Ibid.

NAME INDEX

Name Index

Name Index

SUBJECT INDEX

Subject Index

Subject Index